The 1920's

Problems and Paradoxes

selected readings

The 1920's
Problems and Paradoxes

selected readings

EDITED BY *Milton Plesur*
State University of New York at Buffalo

Allyn and Bacon, Inc.
Boston, Mass.

Library of Congress Catalog Number: 69–14513

Printed in the United States of America

Preface

This collection of readings, designed for use in the American history survey course or in advanced courses dealing with the twentieth century, focuses on political, diplomatic, economic, and social-cultural aspects of the 1920's. The selections present various interpretations and provocative and challenging points of view. They not only illustrate the nature of historical writing and research, but, it is hoped, will stimulate the students' examination and study of historical problems.

The importance of utilizing source material in addition to a standard textbook has long been recognized. A textbook alone never can furnish the complete story. The primary source documents—or in the case of the present volume—the monographic interpretations, afford an exposure to historical data, sources, and criticism. In the articles that follow, it is possible for the reader to broaden his understanding of recent American history by becoming aware of challenging problems and interpretations. It is desirable for the student to then relate what is read to a larger context by careful application of textbook or classroom instruction. Our aim is, therefore, the achievement of thoughtful analysis rather than a meaningless memorization of facts.

The selections which follow, culled from monographs and journals, are not generally accessible or are relatively unknown to the average student. The selections were made with a view to their significance, interest, appropriateness, literary merit, and provocativeness. Thus, the selections are not so much descriptive and narrative as analytic and interpretative.

The selections are grouped under specific questions or problems, each relating to a particular facet of the twenties. For example, as one of our problems we ask whether the rural-urban conflict in the 1920's resulted in a crisis in values, and seven selections are included which shed light on such tensions as intolerance, prohibition, and fundamentalism. On the other hand, in the case of other problems, such as isolationism, there are listed two selections representing different points of view. Each writer has been allowed to present his material as fully as possible and hence there has been a minimum of editing.* Preceding each selection is a short introductory statement describing the theme and scope of the material and placing it in its historical context.

While it is the intention of these readings to provide as complete a review of the period as possible, it is obvious that in dealing with historical phenomena, there are no definitive answers. While controversies about historical issues are often sophisticated matter for the general reader, it is assumed that a textbook can provide the necessary background. The 1920's have something significant to say to students of American history. They have been fascinating as the "Roaring" or "Golden" Twenties. But, in analyzing their importance in the weaving of the total fabric of twentieth century America, can be discovered a degree of historical sophistication and the true excitement the study of history affords.

Thanks are due the authors and publishers who granted permission to reproduce their work. Specific acknowledgment appears in footnotes. My chief debt is to my assistant, Ross Runfola, who searched for material, helped in the preparation of text material, and assisted in reading proof. Graduate Assistants at the State University of New York at Buffalo, Douglas Frank and James J. Horn, provided valuable suggestions and were always eager to render assistance. I also wish to acknowledge the generous advice and helpful comments of my teacher and colleague, Selig Adler, Samuel Paul Capen Professor of American history at the State University of New York at Buffalo, not only on this project but in all phases of my professional career. The cooperation of the staffs of the Lockwood Memorial Library and the Department of History of the State University of New York at Buffalo was extremely helpful. Lastly, I acknowledge the faith, interest and cooperation of my parents, Mathew and Sophie Plesur.

MILTON PLESUR

* In any edited collection, there may be terms, persons, and events that are not identified. It is suggested that the student consult the original work or possibly a textbook in the field.

Contents

Introduction

To attempt a description of any historical period is almost a futile enterprise. The 1920's have been variously described as the "Era of Wonderful Nonsense," the "New Business Epoch," the "Jazz Age," the "Great Spree," the "Dry Decade," the "Age of the Flapper," the "Lawless Times," or most often, the "Roaring Twenties." At the same time, they have been recognized as years of excessive materialism, wild speculation, disorder of all types, and indulgence in strange fads and fashions.

One cannot even be positive where to date the real "beginning" or "end" of the spirit that marked these years. Did whatever was "special" about the decade originate with the defeat of the Treaty of Versailles in the Senate in 1919, or with the election of Warren Gamaliel Harding the next year? Should a study of the 1920's conclude with the stock market crash of October, 1929, or with the accession of the second Roosevelt four years later? Not only are descriptions of the period illusive, but to depict, as so many historians have done, the 1920's as a conservative period sandwiched in between two eras of reform, is to deny the cultural creativity and still potent progressive impulses which lingered on after Versailles. This approach also fails to take into account some of the recent research which has found essentially conservative forces dominant even in the Progressive and New Deal Eras.

The 1920's (for our purposes in the present volume, 1920–1929) seems to be the rejection of all those 19th-century values that culminated in the smoke of World War I. Idealism, progressivism and communal concerns appear to have given way to materialistic cynicism, reaction, rugged individualism, xenophobia and iconoclasm. A new *Zeitgeist* was ushered in as old and tried moral issues were corroded by "the acids of modernity." Life was undoubtedly gay and frivolous, but there was the bitter as well as the sweet; crop failures, strikes, and organized bigotry provided a more sobering substance. Spanning the years that elapsed from the accession of Harding to that of Hoover, a new business supremacy evolved bolstered by political "stand-pattism," a frenetic emphasis on youthful abandon, a crass materialism, and the penultimate conflict between rural and modernist values. It was "normalcy" (as Harding erroneously and crudely put it), a world marked by complacency, isolationism, and selfish nationalism. Perhaps the supreme paradox of the 1920's is that while traditionalism and conservatism dominated governmental circles, society itself underwent a rapid and radical change.

It is undeniable that the 1920's was an age of ballyhoo with a "Hellzapoppin" attitude toward life, as well as a prolonged spree of bizarre behavior. At times this restless spirit was channelled into positive efforts; more often it meandered into negative or senseless happenings. All the old rules became subject to a new scrutiny. With bootleg gin lubricating the thoughts and throats and weakening the inhibitions of Charleston-dancing flappers and their sheiks, the era seemed one of wonderful nonsense. Such behavioral patterns developed a hunger for heroes both real and superficial, and this search represented not only a social revolt, but also a strange nostalgia for old-fashioned and virtuous ideals. Thus, that unreconstructed Yankee, President Calvin Coolidge, became an authentic hero. The nation venerated this Chief Executive of modest talents at the same time that his dour visage led one wit to remark that he seemed to have been weaned on a dill pickle. William Allen White dubbed Coolidge "a Puritan from Babylon," explaining that the President's popularity derived from the fact that he was the antithesis of the materialism, luxury, and flexible moral standards then in vogue with his electorate. The decade's paramount hero was Charles A. Lindbergh, who, despite his daring flight, possessed a modesty that swelled every mother's pride, titillated girls looking for a "he-man" to love, and aroused envy in men of all ages. "Lucky Lindy," young, boyishly handsome, and still unspoiled by the marketplace, typified an older America of the pre-"city-slicker" age. Here was an Horatio Alger, Tom Swift, and Frank Merriwell rolled into one.

On another level, the golden age of sports made possible by increased leisure time led to million dollar gates promoted by such public relations wizards as Tex Rickard. Here the worship of great individual accomplishments stood out in sharp contrast to an otherwise herd-like, conforming world. The star home-run slugger Babe Ruth, the manly pugilist Jack Dempsey, the English Channel swimmer Gertrude Ederle, and the amazing Four Horsemen from Notre Dame serve as a few examples. The veneration of Lindbergh and those who performed great athletic feats can best be understood in terms of significant accomplishment and the need of society to fill an emotional void. This also explains the vogues of championship marathon winners of all sorts, flagpole sitters, and goldfish swallowers. Hollywood stars such as the "overloved one," Rudolph Valentino, provided in H. L. Mencken's language, a "catnip to women." He was milady's sheik furtively stealing into boudoirs at night promising excitement and escape, just as he did on the silver screen. And for the men there was "The Vamp," Theda Bara, or Clara Bow, possessor of "It," that mystical essence most men knew about and most women secretly envied.

All this nonsense aside, what were these exciting years really like? Did they form a period of sterile reaction, political mischievousness, economic excess, and cultural sterility, or were they years of substantial developments and positive achievements? The traditional interpretation of the 1920's depicts these years as differentiating sharply from the ferment of domestic progressive reform and foreign crusading zeal which preceded their advent. The quest for social justice of the Progressive Era followed by America's bold but futile attempt to "make the world safe for democracy" makes it difficult to explain the 1920's in terms of positive achievements. Certainly the period just before Sarajevo was one of idealism, optimism for the success of reform, muckraking, business regulation, and attempted purification of political practices. It is also clear that the Republican leadership after 1921 was "regular" or "stand-pat" in contrast to the progressive insurgents whose hey-day coincided with the early years of the century.

Warren Harding was a weak, limited, unintellectual but good-hearted man whose administration was tainted by scandals that strongly resembled the age of Grant. In the first reading, Andrew Sinclair captures the tragedy of this "time of troubles." This "Second Era of Good Stealing" was followed by the honest, taciturn, and frugal Coolidge, who, despite his popularity, was as unimaginative a chief of state as ever occupied the White House. He was the symbol of the Puritan ethos—thrift, work, and respect for business, and the traditional interpretation holds that his administration marked time rather than made progress. On the other hand, Donald R. McCoy, argues that Coolidge deserves a better reputation and that his administration made some positive accomplishments. Hoover's four-year ordeal goes beyond our scope, but essentially the Quaker President failed to meet the unprecedented problems posed by the Depression.

Politically, then, the G.O.P. return-to-power precipitated a new mood; one that can hardly be described as creative or imaginative. But to maintain that this era was completely devoid of positive accomplishment is to assert that progressivism vanished entirely as the doughboys embarked for France.

In his survey of current opinion on the decline of the Progressive Movement, Herbert F. Margulies isolates a strain of historical thought that looks to internal weaknesses rather than the war as the principal cause for the waning of progressivism. The traditional interpretation also overlooks the significant accomplishments and the real contributions of the Farm Bloc protestors, budget reform enthusiasts, idealistic social workers, and public power protagonists—all lively offshoots of pre-1914 progressivism. The mythology of American history fosters the belief that remaining liberal tendencies were destroyed by the bigotry emanating from the "Rum, Romanism and Prosperity" election of 1928. In a provocative manner, Paul A. Carter examines this contention in the light of John F. Kennedy's 1960 victory.

It is erroneous to label America's foreign policy after 1921 purely isolationist. To be sure, the League of Nations was rejected and an aggressive Senate throughout the 1920's delineated America's world role in narrow and parochial terms. Yet Selig Adler contends that a plethora of internationalist groups searched earnestly for peace and world security, albeit they operated outside of the political establishment. Moreover, our refusal to join the League did not preclude our participation in many non-political conferences and associations which originated in Geneva. If the leadership of the United States under the restored Republicans did not prove distinguished or ultimately successful, it had its ephemeral triumphs which shone brightly in contrast to the sorry failures of the United Nations in a later day. William Appleman Williams also revises the traditional interpretation, finding that the promotion of overseas trade and investments was carried on with renewed vigor by a business-oriented government. Williams views the United States as anything but isolationist under the post-war Republicans.

Amazing material advances, a relatively low rate of unemployment, increased wage levels, the introduction of installment and credit purchases, large—scale high corporate profits, and a lively market speculation combined to make the 1920's seemingly as golden a time of prosperity as this nation ever enjoyed. Hence, Herbert Hoover was not entirely unrealistic when he boasted in 1928 that Americans were closer to a "final triumph over poverty than ever before." Spurred on by the example of the planned economy of World War I and the organizational methods dating back to the latter 19th Century, men like Frederick W. Taylor (scientific management) and Henry Ford (the assembly line and development of interchangeable parts) became symbols of ever-increasing progress. Business became the religion of the country; its promoters were its kings and they wore their crowns with a swagger. The Garden of Eden was here and it was America, not some promised land at the end of a distant, unreachable rainbow. This illusion was fostered in part by welfare capitalism, profit sharing, the "American Plan," and Kiwanis-type service clubs. Bruce Barton rose to fame by portraying Jesus Christ as an organizational genius and explaining his success in terms of the high-pressure salesmanship and public relations policies developed by Barton's own advertising firm. The achievements of the producers were impressive. For example, the radio introduced the world, near and far, to Everyman whether he lived in a dilapidated city ghetto or on an isolated farm. That chief symbol of the boom—the automobile—meant increased mobility; it revolutionized education, extended suburbia, and changed the whole pattern of conventional courtship and sexual mores once geared to a rural culture. At the same time, the growth of the cinema as middle class entertainment made that fantasy and escape unattainable in the real world possible in the "reel" world.

Advertising exaggerated people's needs, coaxed along their dreams, exploited their fears, threatened the values of both producers and consumers, and introduced planned obsolescence into the economy. Building upon the new freedom and changes in morality, the accent was on youth and the artificial creation of needs. Get more, be smart, for there was a balm or salve for every ill or anxiety to be purchased. The new advertising also put to use Freudian and behavioristic psychology and seldom stressed the intrinsic merit of the product to be sold. That perennial evil, halitosis, became the object of the "Listerine war" and the vulgar admonition of a deodorant company to young ladies "to make their arm pits charm pits" signified the depth to which the ad writers were willing to descend.

"Normalcy," meant to the Republican leadership an aggressively pro-business governmental policy. Laissez faire became the watchword, except for the indirect subsidies in the form of high protective tariffs. In addition, regulatory commissions were allowed to atrophy, trade associations with monopolistic inclinations were encouraged, and the program of Secretary of the Treasury Andrew W. Mellon provided for reduced corporate and inheritance taxes at the expense of the small taxpayer. The country was business-oriented and government was conducted in a way that allowed for maximum freedom for producers with a minimum of government intervention. Nevertheless, such policies were not necessarily entirely reactionary. Morrell Heald argues that if the government did not possess a strong feeling of social responsibility, capitalist thought was becoming increasingly socially oriented. At the same time welfare capitalism was actively promoted by the government and the Social Darwinian "dog-eat-dog" mentality became as outmoded as walking to work in the automobile age, or engaging chaperones for the "smart set's" fraternity dances. Hoover, as Secretary of Commerce, in 1922 set down the rules. American individualism, he proclaimed, was based upon equality of opportunity, efficiency, individual liberty, and personal service. He praised the positive benefits of business, big or small, extolled industrial research and scientific management, and spoke of the federal government as the partner rather than the policeman of free enterprise. Business was a temple and President Coolidge admonished Americans to worship therein. "Silent Cal" summed it all up in his usual pithy way when he proclaimed that "the business of America is business."

But, on the other hand, there were irksome weeds in an otherwise well-cultivated garden. Pockets of depression and such sick industries as coal mining and textiles, were ominous signs foolishly ignored. The growth in wealth was real enough but these riches were not equally shared. Farmers and laborers naturally wanted the wartime prosperity which had raised their standard of living to continue. But too often, these pressure groups could not counteract the forces of Big Business. Agricultural malaise, caused by unmarketable surpluses, began early in the decade. A rash of violent labor strikes in 1919 revealed that the workers' needs and desires were being ignored. These strikes were caused by labor's dissaffection with the government over substantial issues but Robert K. Murray explains how the public was led to associate labor with radicalism. Eventually the stock market crash of 1929 pricked the bubble of prosperity and the resultant depression brought with it a decade-long debate over its causes and what role Washington must play in regulating the economy. With the lengthening of historical perspective, John Kenneth Galbraith has been able to isolate the cardinal factors that caused the business slump which brought more suffering to the United States than any event save the Civil War.

Many of the intellectuals of the 1920's were distressed by the political and economic scene and by the philistinism of "booboisie" America. The alienation of the intellectual was so complete that a vast chasm separated the intellectual community from the masses. A coterie of the *literati,* such as Ernest Hemingway, F. Scott Fitzgerald, and John Dos Passos, expatriated and formed the "Lost Generation" on Gertrude Stein's Left Bank paradise in Paris. Some, like H. L. Mencken and Sinclair Lewis, remained behind but they were just as critical, joining in the general indictment of naive materialism, the Babbitt-like existence, cultural conformity, and political sterility of the Coolidge Era. T. S. Eliot's poem, "The Waste Land," and Sinclair Lewis' novels described the scene in bleak terms. And yet, despite these sharp barbs, the 1920's witnessed a literary productivity seldom equalled in any other decade of our history. As the present century wore on, many writers came to regard their earlier colleagues critically, even referring to them as mordant and irresponsible. Fiction characteristically expresses moods in vivid coloring and the authors of this era were never quite as much "lost" as they were disenchanted and disillusioned. The question might well be posed: which generation of writers were ever genuinely pleased with the society they described? Moreover, the literary artists of the post-war decade were fresh and sharp in their insights and their technical creative contributions to English prose are impressive indeed. Experimentation was in the air and it was reflected in literary achievements. Despite the fact that Lewis and Mencken, for example, enjoyed popularity among their contemporaries, these and other gifted artists were not writing for the masses. Public tastes gloried in the more banal, the fluff, the escapist, and sugary substance of life. The small town experiences of a Penrod as sketched by Booth Tarkington or the homey and uncomplicated verses of Edgar A. Guest were more suitable to the popular mood.

Antagonisms and confusions there were in abundance, and Paul Murphy's study explores the causes for this disturbance. Hence, critics who picture this decade as one of moral disintegration and withdrawal from the realities of life can find considerable corroboration for their thesis. Following the 1918 armistice, still-aggressive Americans found others besides "Huns" with whom to do battle. Minorities were shamefully treated. At the same time, a new type of reformer came to the fore in the aftermath of war. The selection from H. L. Mencken offers a vivid example of a vitriolic critic of the time who was more concerned with fighting a stifling conformity than with fostering economic and political progressivism. (The proof positive of this is the fact that in the following decade he aimed his barbs against the New Deal reforms.)

Negro migrations northward precipitated race riots, laborers fought capitalists while conservatives developed a pathological fear of radicalism. Meanwhile, native-born Americans pressured successfully for the severely-restrictive immigration law that John Higham examines in detail. The irrational cult of the eugenists was never more active. Jews were always fair game whether as scapegoats in the pages of Henry Ford's *Dearborn*

Independent or as victims of the outrages perpetrated by the Ku Klux Klan. The Fundamentalists—so often the antagonized and wretched farmers trying to eke out a livelihood—attacked the new modernism with its unorthodox views of the origin of man, religion, and education. In their eyes, modernism was the city with all of its sin. The decade was a pathetic last-ditch stand of a rural, traditional orthodoxy doing battle against the new wave of the future—the mores of the megalopolis. Norman Furniss argues that the rural-urban conflict was not precipitated by World War I. Instead he sees a rapidly-declining William Jennings Bryan winning an empty victory by convicting a high school biology teacher named Scopes for teaching evolution contrary to Tennessee law. The whole episode arose by chance, and chance made it the focal point in the *Kulturkamp* of the 1920's.

The small-town forces, however, did score an ephemeral victory with the passage of the Eighteenth Amendment and the Volstead Act. But, unexpectedly, Prohibition precipitated a national dialogue that lasted until the New Deal era. Was Prohibition an essential offshoot of the progressive impulse? James H. Timberlake finds that it was and reasons that the dry crusade was nourished on the same moral idealism as the more sensible reforms of the day. The passage of the Eighteenth Amendment poses other questions, as well. Was Prohibition an invasion of personal liberty? Was it enforceable, and how could the sordid forces that accompanied bootlegging and the speakeasies be contained? Hoover—before the Depression destroyed his optimism—viewed Prohibition as a nobly motivated and fruitful experiment. But undoubtedly there was another side to the coin. Enforcement involved the usual struggle between the new, urban groups and the small-town, agrarian middle-class. The story of the dry years is the colorful stuff which television and movie scenarists have exploited, but if the original idea had a noble purpose, in practice the experiment proved sad and disillusioning.

The fear of the immigrant radical—real or imagined—amounted at times to a phobia. Some bomb outrages by small, isolated groups of radicals brought into being the "Red Scare" of 1919–1920. The government's subsequent suppression, repression, and even exportation of undesirable aliens raised the question of how far a democracy should go to protect its form of life. Amid an atmosphere of hysteria and dread, World War I and bolshevism were blamed for attacks on cherished American values. All that the country had so long held sacred seemed in jeopardy. Sacco and Vanzetti became a *cause célèbre* which divided the land and aroused heated passions from their arrest in 1920 to their execution seven years later.

Those who sought to curb the coalition of urban "wets," Bible-denouncing "sinners," and immigrant radicals, found secretive Ku Klux Klan meetings a natural outlet for their emotions. The organization's popularity was enhanced by colorful ritual and fraternal rites so dear to the heart of small-town America. Not only did the Triple K speak out against non-"Wasps" (non-white, non-Anglo-Saxon Protestants), but it also held inflexible ideas on the absolute authenticity of the Testaments, the sin of teaching evolution, the horror of movie licentiousness, and the necessity of "blue laws." Added to this was a general suspicion of all things foreign. Undoubtedly, the KKK was the most pronounced expression of reaction to afflict the land in the present century, but Emma Lou Thornbrough's examination of Klan activities in Indiana casts doubt on the contention that segregationist measures there can be blamed on the Klan. By 1928 our political parties clearly reflected the growing divide in American thought. Alfred E. Smith was the spokesman for the newer groups—the city dwellers, the "wets," the immigrants, and the Catholics, while Herbert Hoover epitomized the dry, old-stock, small-town Protestants. Yet Smith's inroads into northern and eastern city voting blocs presaged, despite his defeat, new promises for the Democrats.

Closely related to the tensions and ballyhoo of the 1920's was the growing challenge to conventional nineteenth-century morality. Beyond all doubt this cultural revolt existed but some argue that its roots are to be found in the period preceeding 1914 rather than in the war that followed. Selections by Frederick Lewis Allen and Henry F. May reflect this division of opinion. Regardless of when the upheaval really got started, by the 1920's it was clearly evident that moral standards were rapidly relaxing. Women, flushed with victory in the battle over the saloon, and newly-invested with suffrage, tried to ameliorate their lot in life by promoting the single standard. The flapper—as the younger woman was called—now frequented speakeasies, her dress hiked up to the knee daringly revealing rolled hose; the protective corset was shed, her hair was bobbed, and she "painted" her face. Companionate marriage schemes were contemplated, the "kitchen revolution" freed housewives from many chores, and women invaded the man's world of business. The feminine market was actively sought by producers, while whole new industries such as cosmetics altered to her whims. The flapper's male companion was not dressed in style unless he sported bell-bottom trousers or plus-fours, a hip flask, and a raccoon coat. Youth became syncopated, they swilled forbidden strong waters, they worshipped movie stars and athletes, and they read the scarlet pages of trash contained in "true confession" and movie magazines. Repressions and inhibitions were dropped as the roomy sedan or open touring car with a rumble seat, the roadhouse, and a misreading of Sigmund Freud combined to destroy the emphasis on pre-marital virginity. The neck, once a noun connoting a part of the anatomy, was now used as a verb. Petting had once implied a simple act of affection toward little children or animals, but it, too, now joined the lexicon of verbs. The candle seemed to be burning at both ends and as Edna St. Vincent Millay expressed it, "It will not last the night; But, ah my foes, and oh, my friends—it gives a lovely light." Emancipation from hide-bound moral values seemed to be the key to zest in life. "Makin' Whoopee" and "Show Me The Way To Go Home" were but two songs which mirrored the age. And yet, while parents and others bemoaned then as now, the new freedom of youth, fundamentally the "revolt" was more a fad than a true revolution. Most American youth were not members of that period's "jet set." Most of them were not, in Francis Scott Fitzgerald's language, angry young men (or women), whose God was dead, whose wars were fought, and whose faiths had been shaken. In truth, only a minority, although an identifiable one, had even seen the inside of a speakeasy.

Problems

The 1920's, then, as with any time-span in history, presents problems to the historical guild who are all too prone to compartmentalize the past. Contrasted with the New Deal Era which succeeded it and the Progressive Age which preceded it, the 1920's appear as a roadblock to the flow of American liberalism. With the apparent rejection of a world role suitable to a prime power, the 1920's can be likened to a detour in foreign policy between the activist policies pursued during the two world wars. But the *interregnum* idea is a denial of the consensus approach which emphasizes history as a continuum. To contend that all liberal reform in the political, economic, and cultural areas of life disappeared after 1921 is, of course, to oversimplify and distort reality. On the other hand, to argue that there was little difference between the 1920's and the decades that came before and after, is to fall into the reverse fallacy. Historians, it is suspected, like the lay public, find "watersheds" convenient separations upon which to peg their pet ideas or order their lives. Yet, it cannot be denied that the return of the G.O.P. in 1921 and the Depression at the end of the decade do provide convenient divides. From one angle of vision, the years between these two milestones appear as the one last fling of a carefree America, so soon to be burdened with the usual problems of a prime power. The older view of the 1920's emphasizes reaction, business control of the government, a low grade of political morality, and a general downgrading of reform. On the other hand, the revisionists now view the period as one of genuine vitality and cultural creativity. The work of these trail-blazers is summarized in the final article by Burl Noggle, who regards the decade as a new historiographical frontier.

A review of a recent motion picture ("Thoroughly Modern Millie," *Time,* April 7, 1967), stated that it would take a miracle of invention to revamp so well-traversed a territory as the Jazz Age. The period was, as we have seen, often viewed as a nostalgic idyll—flamboyant, false, but fascinating, especially as viewed in contrast to the grim world of the later 1960's. In an age of never-ending crises and unprecedented domestic racial tensions, the "Good Old Days" of Coolidge are hyper-nostalgic to the present generation. In the contemporary idiom, the 1920's can be summarized as "camp." The work of historians and writers who fill in the following pages take individual points of view on given questions or issues which loomed large forty years ago. Viewed in total, they refute the impression that the period was a superficial one marked only by a haunting romantic flavor. These authorities present the paradoxes and incongruities of the decade and develop differing attitudes toward the same perplexing questions, or else provide provocative, contrasting interpretations. By spotlighting the murky problems of the age they further illuminate a gay and heady era which will always attract historians and laymen alike. Perhaps the decade can be best viewed in Dickens' classic words, "the best of times, the worst of times."

I ~ *Two Republican Leaders: Wooden Kings?*

1 ~ Preface*

[Author's Note] *Around no other President have rumors so screened historical fact from fiction than Warren G. Harding. The facts of his birth and death are beclouded, his private life is still gossiped about, and the effluvia of Teapot Dome has made his administration synonymous with scandal. Although writers have looked through a glass darkly when portraying Harding, the indictment presented by William Allen White in* Masks in a Pageant (1930) *set the stage for future assessments of his career. The great muckraking journalist, Samuel Hopkins Adams, painted a more favorable picture, using more delicate hues and subtle tones, but it was left for Andrew Sinclair to put the Ohioan in proper historical perspective. Using the recently opened Harding Papers, Sinclair, a British journalist and commentator, finds that Harding, although a poorly-educated man of mediocre talents, did possess keen political acumen. To Sinclair the essential tragedy is that as a man Harding symbolized the "Babbittry" of the whole nation to a greater degree than the facts would actually warrant.*

"Let me urge you again to write the Harding story," Brand Whitlock wrote to William Allen White, as one progressive Republican to another. "It has all the elements of an old Greek tragedy, with the angry and disgusted gods at the end wiping out all of the personages in a kind of Olympian Fury."[1] White did not write the Harding story. For the Kansas editor was as fervent a believer in the small-town myths of America as was his proposed subject. When the disgusted gods had wiped out Warren Gamaliel Harding and his friends, they had also begun to wipe out the myths that had made him President of the United States. Main Street was rarely to enter the White House so easily again.

Warren Harding became the most notorious President in American

* Reprinted with permission of The Macmillan Company from *The Available Man: The Life Behind the Masks of Warren Gamaliel Harding* by Andrew Sinclair. Pages vi–viii. Copyright by Andrew Sinclair 1965.

history because the myths that had formed him were not adequate to meet with the power and responsibility of the Presidency after the First World War. As Will Hays commented when he was a member of Harding's Cabinet, "The government is like a corner grocery which a few years ago could be run by one man, and now we try to use the same system in running Marshall Fields."[2] Harding could have run admirably a corner grocery, as he ran his small-town newspaper, the Marion (Ohio) *Star*. Unfortunately, social and political myths washed him into the Presidency and left him stranded there. He could not cope with the international and industrial complexity of postwar America with the beliefs of small-town Ohio. It was too late to muddle through.

As a man, Harding was uninteresting. He was not important in himself. But the reasons for his political success were all-important. As a representative of the power of folklore and past morality, he revealed how much politics was and is ruled by dead men. The concepts of the nineteenth century made him President in the twentieth. For his life and vocabulary nourished the Victorian and moral myths so dear to most American people that they could benefit from the machine without losing the values of the farm.

These myths, which formed Harding and in which he mostly believed, made him the Available Man in the Republican Party in 1920. There were the myths of the Country Boy, of the Self-made Man, of the Presidential State, of the Political Innocent, of the Guardian Senate, of America First, of the Reluctant Candidate, of the Dark Horse, of the Smoke-filled Room, of the Solemn Referendum, and of the Best Minds. With the help of these and other fictions, a most ordinary man reached the White House.

Harry Daugherty, the political manager of Harding, shrewdly pointed out how well Harding fitted the nostalgic folklore of American party politics when he pushed his candidate into the Presidential race in December, 1919. His eulogy of Harding was an admirable synthesis of the facts and fictions that made Harding both available and inadequate, the candidate who had not dared to be himself. Daugherty's statement was also something new in American politics. It was the first case of a manager selling his candidate as a winning image rather than as a great man:

> Senator Harding has practically been forced into every contest for high honors he has ever received. He has been generous in supporting others. He is a thorough-going Republican partisan who always supports his own party but never offends those who belong to other parties. In many

> respects that make men great and attractive, no man was ever as much like McKinley as is Harding. He is patient, he does not rush in with a positive opinion until he has taken all the time necessary to consider a subject and receive all the good advice he can find or is offered. He is a charming man to meet and people like him immediately upon meeting him. The liking lasts. As a clear, convincing, pleasing orator he has no superior in the United States. When he takes a stand he stands there until he advances. He was born a poor boy and knows all the hardships that accompany a man who makes his own way in the world. He is kindly, considerate, sympathetic and good-natured. He is a great American and for everything that is American. There is no man so humble that he would not stop and stoop to do a favor and help lift up in the world. He is well posted and sound on all the great questions of interest to the welfare of our country. He is sound in his ideas about finances. He is of the McKinley type in his ideas on the protective tariff. He is a good judge of human nature. He has lived a pure life. He has the very appearance of a president of the United States. Harding is one man sure to carry Ohio if the great Republican Party were to nominate him.[3]

Such was the image of the unknown politician who was nominated by his party and who reached the White House with the greatest majority of votes given to a President in a century. But once in the White House, Harding was faced with the reality of power. The myths faded or turned upon him. Main Street morality could not cope with Wall Street complexity. The "best minds" often disagreed. In an effort to prove yet another myth of democracy, that the office makes the man, Harding tried to free himself from the corruption and entanglements brought about by his small-town loyalties. He did too little too late, and he died too soon. After his death, this creature of myth became its victim, for the theories of conspiracy at the grass roots of democracy fed on new myths of the Poisoned President and the Ohio Gang. Harding, in his coming and his going, was the apotheosis of the American rural dream.

In this way, the Harding story is like "an old Greek tragedy." The old gods struck down a folk hero. For in his time Harding did seem to be hero enough. He seemed to represent the truth of many legends: that Presidents did come from the backwoods, that opportunities were equal, that small towns were the homes of goodness and democracy. On his death, he was mourned more than any President since Lincoln. But his example proved that Washington had become a world city and could no longer be ruled by the man from Marion. Harding was a small man in a great place, which was daily becoming greater.

NOTES

1. Brand Whitlock to William Allen White, October 8, 1926, in *The Letters of Brand Whitlock,* A. Nevins, ed. (New York: 1936), p. 389.
2. Quoted in Merriman Smith, *A President Is Many Men* (New York: Harper, 1948), p. 2.
3. Press release of Harry Daugherty on December 17, 1919, *HP* [Harding Papers].

2 ∽ The Evil That Men Do*

The legacy of Harding's death was chiefly the myths about his life. He left little permanent trace. The Supreme Court, to which he had appointed four conservatives, including William Howard Taft as Chief Justice, did interpret the Constitution in a most conservative way for two decades; but eventually it was to become one of the most progressive forces in American life. Harding's Cabinet did remain much unchanged by the cautious Coolidge, who was reluctant to shed even the liability of Daugherty. Harding had set a fortunate precedent in inviting Coolidge to attend Cabinet meetings in order to prepare him for stepping into the White House, and he had also set a model in the treatment of the press by the White House. Some credit must be given him for the Washington Conference, although his acceptance of political and economic isolationism proved disastrous in the long run—if any President can be blamed for the continuing of his bad policies after his death.

For one appropriate act, Harding deserves to be remembered. He had always stood on the platform of the Constitution and had declared his intention to preserve it. The latter he did, in literal fact. Three previous Presidents from Ohio, Hayes and McKinley and Taft, had tried to get Congress to appropriate enough money to construct a fireproof hall for the government archives. They had failed. By the time Harding came to office, both the Declaration of Independence and the Constitution were in danger of falling to pieces through exposure to light and bad handling. By executive order, Harding had these documents transferred from the files of the Secretary of State to the Library of Congress. And under his prodding, Congress at last appropriated enough money to build "a special marble

* Reprinted with permission of The Macmillan Company from *The Available Man: The Life Behind the Masks of Warren Gamaliel Harding* by Andrew Sinclair. Pages 291–299. Copyright by Andrew Sinclair 1965.

and bronze shrine" for the two documents. This was done, according to Harding, "to satisfy the laudable wish of patriotic Americans to have an opportunity to see the original fundamental documents upon which rest their independence and their Government." [1] In truth, Harding was the preserver of the Constitution; and today, those who visit its glass-and-bronze shrine in the National Archives might think of him.

Harding's wife was accused of destroying his papers by those who believed in a conspiracy. She did take all her husband's correspondence with her from Washington; and for the remaining eighteen months of her life, she did work at destroying some of his papers. But 325,000 documents still remain. They are now available for the research of qualified scholars at the Ohio Historical Society, where they were deposited after being held for forty years by Harding Memorial Association—a group of Harding's friends in Ohio. In collecting and sorting out Presidential papers, Mrs. Harding was only following the personal or family custom of many Presidents. The precedent was set by George Washington himself, who took his Presidential papers with him into retirement. All Presidents followed his example until Franklin Delano Roosevelt. The papers of Van Buren and Fillmore and Pierce and Grant and Arthur were all carefully edited and partially destroyed, while those of the Adams family and Garfield and McKinley and Taft and Wilson were kept for restricted eyes. [2] Mrs. Harding and the Harding Memorial Association only did what was *usual* with the Presidential papers of Warren Harding, although they were later blamed for destroying and restricting the use of these papers.

The interring of the bones of a public figure means the birth of gossip. Harding's memory suffered from this more than that of any other President. He suffered at the hands of both his friends and his enemies. It was convenient for Republican politicians to bury all the scandals of his Administration with his body. It was Daugherty's purpose to prove that his dead master had been a political figurehead, an impractical politician of no willpower, the creature of Daugherty. This, Harding had never been, however much it soothed the vanity of Daugherty and the President's other friends to think so. Nor was Harding the lecherous and lazy fool that gossip made him out to be.

Like many other Presidents, Harding had had extramarital affairs. His bad luck was that one of his ladies, Nan Britton from Marion, provided the material for a book after his death called *The President's Daughter*. In this work, Miss Britton proved to all except the most charitable that she was the mother of Harding's daughter. [3] Although an Ohio jury found against her claim on Harding's estate, most of Harding's friends and some of his family believed her story. The wonder was that the affair was held so much against the dead man. Grover Cleveland had been elected to the Presidency *after* admitting to siring a bastard son. Yet Warren Harding was not allowed to lie quiet in his grave once he had been accused of siring a bastard daughter. Victorian times were more forgiving than the emancipated 1920's. The recent discovery of a collection of Harding's love letters to another mistress, Mrs. Carrie Phillips, has shown that the people of the permissive 1960's still seem as interested as those of past ages in the lechery of the great. [4]

The gossip about the Hardings was not diminished when President Hoover finally agreed in 1931 to dedicate the large and noble and hollow-centered memorial put up at Marion in memory of its dead President. Hoover was advised that in his speech in front of the worthies of Ohio politics, he should "aim at under, rather than over-statement." [5] His dislike of the furious Daugherty, who was sitting in the audience in front of him, conquered his discretion. After praising the dead Harding as a man of peace and a man of the people, Hoover talked of Harding's "great disillusionment" on his Western trip. The dying President had weakened "not only from physical exhaustion but from mental anxiety." Warren Harding, in the words of his old Secretary of Commerce, "had a dim realization that he had been betrayed by a few of the men whom he had trusted, by men whom he had believed were his devoted friends. It was later proved in the courts of the land that these men had betrayed not alone the friendship and trust of their staunch and loyal friend but they had betrayed their country. That was the tragedy of the life of Warren Harding. . . . There is no disloyalty and no crime in all the category of human weaknesses which compares with the failure of probity in the conduct of public trust. [6]

In fact, Daugherty had not been *proved* guilty of crime in the courts of the land. After Harding's death, he had refused to resign. He had preferred to stay where he was and to use the weapons of the Department of Justice against his enemies. The whole Cabinet quaked at the thought of the revelations he would make if he were dismissed from office. Yet Coolidge, in the end, had grasped the nettle and asked for Daugherty's resignation on the technical ground that a Cabinet officer should not testify before a Senate committee that was investigating him. Later, Daugherty had survived two trials for graft because of hung juries. He had done so only by putting the blame on the dead Jess Smith and by refusing to testify on the grounds that he might incriminate the dead President. "The Ohio Gang never surrenders," Bruce Bliven wrote; "and neither does it die. It piles its corpses on the breastworks, and holds the fort." [7]

After his dismissal, Daugherty survived for more than two decades, getting along "on the principle that the Lord tempers the wind etc., and the devil takes care of his own." [8] His pride lay in the fact that he had been *technically* cleared by the courts of law.

As a lobbyist, he had never drawn the distinction between politics and the law. He thought that one trade should merely whitewash the other. He would have agreed with Mr. Dooley that the Supreme Court follows the election returns. "Law and politics, you know," he was quoted as saying, "go hand in hand."[9] In his own case, the master politician from Ohio had administered the law of the land in Washington, and nothing was ever proved against him, despite all the thunderings of prosecutors and the liberal press and Congress. "Getting a man's goat is a great game," declared the unrepentant operator. "I never had a goat farm and they could not get a goat where there was none."[10]

The rest of the profiteers under Harding's regime fared less well. Sinclair and Doheny went to jail over the question of the oil leases; Denby resigned; and Doheny's son, who had carried the bribe to Fall, committed suicide. Of those connected with the scandal in the Veterans' Bureau, two committed suicide and two went to jail. Of the Ohio Gang, two were jailed and one committed suicide and one died awaiting trial. Daugherty's brother's bank crashed in the Great Depression, with debts of $2,600,000; the owner was convicted of operating it in a disreputable way. A fortunate pardon freed him from jail. "Ohio immunity," as Samuel Hopkins Adams observed, "was still potent in 1930."[11]

With the trials of Daugherty and Fall and Forbes and their associates continuing during the years after his death, Harding was not allowed to rest in peace. Once these scandals were brought to court and forgotten, new gossip arose in the memoirs of the various members of the White House staff. A mail clerk wrote of destroying Nan Britton's letters to Harding in the White House. A White House maid told of Harding and his wife's drifting apart and of Mrs. Harding's icy calm at her husband's funeral. A White House secretary told of Mrs. Harding's choosing which of the "political" prisoners should be pardoned; she quoted Mrs. Harding as saying, "Well, Warren Harding, I have got you the Presidency; what are you going to do with it?" The White House housekeeper testified to Mrs. Harding's domineering over her husband. And a medium, Madame Maria,

Stearns to Paris thought that they were fleeing from the incompetent and the stupid in American government. To them, the memory of the early twenties was a memory of a materialistic America that was held by the crass and the venal. In their shame at this memory, the American intellectuals chose Harding as the gullible scapegoat of his time.

Nothing shows more the swing in American opinion on the subject of Harding than the second change in attitude of William Allen White, whose running commentary on Harding's career reflected the malleable nature of intelligent small-town feeling. When White was still a progressive, he thought Harding a vile reactionary. Once Harding was President, White thought him the decent representative of small-town life, an average man doing a better-than-average job. But as the effluvia of the scandals rose to drown the dead President's good name, White wrote in 1926 to the old Ohio progressive Brand Whitlock, "God, what a story! The story of Babylon in a Sunday School story compared with the story of Washington from June 1919 until July 1923, and so far as that goes, considerably later. We haven't even yet got back to our Father's house. He can't see us even from afar off. It's invisible. And the whole thing is epitomized by the rise of Harding. If ever there was a man who was a he-harlot, it was the same Warren G. Harding. But I suppose it ought not to be written now. It would hurt too many hearts. I don't know. I could write it and I dare to write it, but it would be a bitter and awful thing."[15]

White made his attitude clear enough in his later history books of the period and in his autobiography. He never gave Harding after his death the credit that he had given the President during his life. In this, he set or shaped the fashion of nearly all historians and journalists. Harding's name has become a byword as the worst American President, the prime example of incompetence and sloth and feeble good nature.

The verdict of Harding's own time was different. And it cannot be the verdict of any historian who has looked at the evidence of the papers preserved at the Ohio Historical Society. Harding was a hardworking and shrewd Ohio politician. He was always his own master. He used compromise and humility as political tactics. He listened to the opinions of others in order to flatter their vanity and educate himself. He was a man of mediocre intellect, but of great presence, ambition, and political talent. He was exceedingly fortunate in rising so high, but he was helped by his own persistence and strategy of harmony. He was a good friend, and he was a formidable opponent in an election. He resembled in his abilities President Hayes, whom he thought had been misjudged because of partisanship and prejudice.

even declared that she was once "the hub round which the nat ment revolved" through her power over the superstitious M to whom she had declared that her husband would meet poisoning at the hands of an enemy near to him.[12]

Harding and his wife could not reply to these innuenc false or true. They—the representatives of decency in M subjected to the gossip of that overblown small town, Washi of the stories about the Hardings were absurd, but they claime tion of fact. Yet, curiously enough, Harding's reputation politician and as a President at least as competent as Hayes more by writers of fiction than of fact. When Sinclair Lewis *Street* and *Babbitt,* the comments were that Main Street and come to the White House. Because Harding had many of t of the small-town booster, people tended to confuse him w whom, after all, Lewis had created from the mere sum of h characteristics.

Scott Fitzgerald began a Broadway fashion by modelin on Harding's presumed incompetence. In this play, *The V* supremely average Jerry Frost becomes President, appoints h office, declares Idaho independent to be rid of its Senator, and i His defense is, "I don't want to be President. I never asked to l Why—why, I don't even know how in hell I ever *got* to be Pres The play flopped, although other versions of the same theme h runs on Broadway twice in the next forty years. Samuel Hop also set a profitable fashion for best-selling novels on supp Washington. In his inferior and notorious novel *Revelry,* he p dead Harding in the character of the easygoing and incompete Willis Markham, with his "streaky cut of bacon, the Cabin real center of government, the little house of his poker-pl "The Crow's Nest." In the novel, the President is betrayed by and dies, accidentally taking poison by his own hand. The mor out by a wise Senator: "Friendship in politics undermines mor than fraud, and gratitude is a worse poison than graft."[14]

It so happened that Harding's term of office coincided w full-scale onslaught by the American intellectuals on the values town, which the President represented so perfectly in all its inc and grandiloquence. With such a splendid specimen of the "bo assault, Mencken did not spare his darts, nor did Sherwood spare his bitter memories of Ohio. The expatriates who fled w

Harding's defects lay in his lack of education. He had a fuzzy mentality, what Woodrow Wilson termed a "bungalow mind." He never questioned the easy assumptions of right and wrong of the shoddy Ohio towns in which he grew up. He knew nothing of the science of government, only of the gutter politics of Ohio and the Senate. It was no training for the White House. As an economist, Harding was limited to the kind of observation that he made on Social Justice Day in Marion: "It is our duty as a whole people to see if we cannot make every job in the country a small business of its own."[16] As a statesman, he was limited to the principle of America First. As a philosopher, he was limited to the concepts that friends should come before principles and that loyalty to party should come before loyalty to an abstract ideal. Harding believed in the nineteenth-century system of corrupt politics and unrestricted business opportunity, because this was the university of his youth and middle age. Although, in the White House, he began to learn painfully the duties and the role of a modern President, his education came too late. The office can make the man, but only when the man is ready to shed his old friends as well as his old misconceptions.

Harding clung foolishly to the Daughertys of the world because he was too weak to give up the nostalgic joys of his life, the parties of cronies, and the stories of the small-town smoking room. He was not ruthless enough to be President—perhaps he feared the example of the ruthless Wilson. "He was a mother's boy," observed Hudson Maxim, "—that was the trouble with him. Not enough of a brute—too much of a gentleman."[17] Unfortunately, Harding viewed his own tolerance of his old friends in office as an amiable weakness, not as a national disaster. *The New York Times* noticed that Harding seemed to take comfort when he spoke before the Lincoln Memorial and described the great Republican as "a very natural human being, with the frailties mixed with the virtues of humanity."[18]

Harding was the representative of normalcy in abnormal times. In office, he had to discard this nostalgic program of returning to a time that never was. He came to realize that the President in the White House was no more the harmonizer between farm and city, between labor and capital, between West and East, between poor and rich than was the rural businessman in the small towns of the Midwest. The President might seem to symbolize the whole nation, and the rural businessman to represent the individual flowering of the American dream; but both had to fight daily for a successful living. Both might cry for harmony and the good old days, but both had to grapple with the pressure groups of the new. Both might boost American industry while praising the American farmer, but both knew that one was growing rich at the expense of the other. Harding was the frock-coated businessman with mud on his boots whom most Americans thought that they wanted in the White House. Only after his death did they see that he was out of his place and out of his time and fortunately in his grave.

Because a man is available, he should not necessarily choose to be chosen.

NOTES

1. See Robert Connor, "Shall the Constitution Be Preserved?" *Ohio State Archaeological and Historical Quarterly,* XLIV, July, 1935.
2. See Buford Roland's illuminating "The Papers of the Presidents," *American Archivist,* XIII, July, 1950.
3. Nan Britton, *The President's Daughter* (New York: 1927). The book seems authentic in its wealth of haphazard detail. Miss Britton is still alive, and she visited Harding's home in Marion only a few years ago. No one noticed her until her name was discovered in the visitor's book.
4. For extracts from Harding's 250 letters to Mrs. Phillips, see *The New York Times,* July 10, 1964. It is to be hoped that these letters will soon be made available to qualified scholars, as have the rest of the Harding papers in the Ohio Historical Society, without restriction on their use. They are said to contain material of historical and psychological importance to biographers of Harding. The extracts from the letters which have been printed show little more than Harding's adolescence in matters of the heart. The heirs of Warren Harding have instituted a lawsuit for $1,000,000 against those responsible for the publication of part of the letters, and they are also attempting to recover the letters, which were bought by American Heritage from the estate of the deceased Mrs. Phillips. Until the fate of the letters is decided, they cannot be published by historians, for the copyright belongs to the family.
5. This was the advice of Harlan Fiske Stone, quoted in A. T. Mason, *Harlan Fiske Stone: Pillar of the Law* (New York: Viking, 1956), p. 270.
6. *Address of President Hoover on the Occasion of the Dedication of the Harding Memorial,* Marion, Ohio, June 16, 1931.
7. Bruce Bliven, "Not Proven Guilty: The Ohio Gang in Court," *New Republic,* October 27, 1926.
8. Harry Daugherty to N. H. Fairbanks, April 3, 1924, Fairbanks papers, *OHS* [Ohio Historical Society].
9. "How Daugherty Helped Harding into the White House," *Literary Digest,* April 9, 1921.
10. Harry Daugherty to Ray Harris, November 18, 1932, Harris papers, *OHS.* Clinton W. Gilbert correctly appraised Daugherty as early as 1922 in *Behind*

the Mirrors. "Your professional politician," he wrote, "for that is what Daugherty was, always is an object of doubt. And for this reason he always seeks what is technically known as a 'vindication.' Conscious of his own rectitude, as he measures it, he may come out of office cleared in the world's eyes, and with a fine title, to boot, ready for life upon a new level."

11. Samuel Hopkins Adams, *Incredible Era: The Life and Times of Warren Gamaliel Harding* (Boston: Houghton Mifflin, 1939), p. 421.
12. See Ira Smith and Joe Morris, *Dear Mr. President: The Story of 50 Years in the White House Mail Room* (New York: Messner, 1949), pp. 110–114; Lillian Parks and Frances Leighton, *My Thirty Years Backstairs at the White House* (New York: Fleet, 1961), pp. 170–171; Mary Randolph, *Presidents and First Ladies* (New York: 1936), p. 229; Elizabeth Jaffray, *Secrets of the White House* (New York: 1927), pp. 87–88; and Madame Marcia, "When an Astrologer Ruled the White House," *Liberty,* April 9, 1938. Such exposés played the part of the old courtiers' memoirs of Europe, which they matched in inaccuracy and fell behind in style.
13. Scott Fitzgerald, *The Vegetable* (New York: 1922).
14. Samuel Hopkins Adams, *Revelry* (New York: 1926), pp. 41–42, 318.
15. William Allen White, *Selected Letters of William Allen White,* W. Johnson, ed. (New York: Holt, 1947), p. 260.
16. See "Harding the Sentimentalist," *New Republic,* October 20, 1920.
17. Quoted by Clifton Johnson in *Hudson Maxim* (New York: 1924), p. 250.
18. Quoted in Dixon Wecter, *The Hero in America* (New York: Scribner, 1941), p. 269.

3 ~ A President Restrained*

[Author's Note] *In this recent biography of Calvin Coolidge, Donald R. McCoy of the University of Kansas dispels the familiar notion of Coolidge as a thrifty, unsophisticated Yankee provincial. Above all, McCoy credits Coolidge for the retrieval of public confidence in the Presidency, which had sunk so low after the Harding debacle. Coolidge proved to be a shrewd administrator, McCoy contends, for he demanded able and economical performance from public servants. He helped to lay the foundation of the "Good Neighbor policy" of the 1930's by his determination to improve relations with Latin American nations (albeit his interference in the Nicaraguan revolution was somewhat unfortunate). McCoy tempers his well-balanced study by pointing out that Coolidge was the spokesman for the materialistic values of a business civilization and was therefore a product of his age.*

At the beginning of the 1924 election campaign, George Harvey said that Calvin Coolidge would be elected or rejected by the people "not for what he has said nor what he has done, but for what he is."[1] Harvey was largely right, for the new President had done and said little, but as a public figure he contrasted sharply with his competitors and, equally important, with his two immediate predecessors, Woodrow Wilson and Warren G. Harding. Coolidge's character was not as well known as it would become, but it was remarkably like the general portrayal of it in 1924. It was already clear that he was a man of honesty and integrity and a believer in representative and constitutional government. He was thrifty, cautious, and shy. He believed in fattening the golden goose of big business, so that it might produce bountifully for all society.

Coolidge's ordinariness inspired confidence. Physically, he was of average height and of facial features that, however delicately chiseled, were not commanding of attention. He exuded an appealing balance of modesty and self-confidence and left no doubt that he had good reason to be both modest and confident. If he was no Harding, neither was he a Wilson. He exalted stability, unity, and harmony, and after the ups and downs of the Wilson and Harding Administrations, most Americans were ready to settle for the genius of the average. Reliability, not brilliance or good fellowship, was what Calvin Coolidge held up as the prime virtue before the nation, and he personified it. If he was slow to judge, he was also unlikely to prejudge. Certainly, he appeared to have enough strength, intelligence, knowledge, and tough-mindedness to run the government. He was also intent upon discussing the promise of the future instead of the troubles of the past. For a nation that was tired of having the ship of state rocked, he was a reassuring skipper.

Of course, Coolidge was other things, about which the public either did not care or was not informed. Although his ideas of God and religion were mystically vague, it was clear he believed that man had a duty under God's laws to give service. Yet there was no reason why service could not be both pleasant and profitable. Because of that Coolidge could be a happy Christian since he prospered from politics and usually enjoyed the attention which public life brought him. Not that anyone at the time much cared, but the President narrowly focused his intellect on the work that came before him day by day. In dealing with large, long-range issues he substituted his broad idealism for intellect: And make no mistake, Coolidge was an idealist. He wanted to do right by all men and see others do likewise. He believed in man's perfectibility, in terms of honesty, dependability, industry, service, fairness, kindliness, tolerance, and harmoniousness. The problem was that he did not know how wide the gap was between belief and achievement.

Yet Coolidge cannot be considered just on the basis of his character and beliefs. What he did, or did not do, obviously is more important in its effects on people. Although he is seldom remembered for his accomplishments, a number of them must be credited to his Presidency. Most outstanding, after the Harding days, was his retrieval of public confidence in the office he held. As the Democratic senator from Arizona, Henry F. Ashurst, wrote in his diary when Coolidge left office, "Time's perspective will appraise Calvin Coolidge, but with certainty it may *today* be said that he restored the White House to a symbol of dignified an moderate living."

Ashurst also praised the departing Chief Executive because he had "defied politicians who advocated nostrums."[2] Such praise, one can suggest, Coolidge most deserved for his resistance to the McNary-Haugen bill, which, by adding to inflation at home and by dumping surplus farm products abroad, would have created problems at least as bad as those it might have solved.

Another accomplishment of note was administration, an aspect of the Presidency often underappreciated by the public and even scholars. Coolidge made his mark as an administrator by demanding able and economical performance from public servants, by making maximum use of the Bureau of the Budget, and by extending the civil service merit system. In related functions he deserves credit for the release of the remaining political prisoners and for helping to raise the level of competence among career Foreign Service officers and federal judges. Government under Calvin Coolidge did not undertake all that it might have, but what it did it accomplished with considerable efficiency.

Relations with Congress were another matter, for Coolidge, however able as an administrator, was clumsy in dealing with the House and Senate. The President and the lawmakers got out of step during the Teapot Dome conflict of early 1924 and only occasionally got together again. Nevertheless he got Congress to give him the program closest to his heart and the one he most esteemed among his accomplishments. That was his fiscal policy of holding down appropriations, with the surplus to be applied to reducing taxes and paring the national debt. The rising levels of income and of stock prices, which were labeled the Coolidge Prosperity, proved to him that his fiscal policy was a success. Yet his pride was mocked as the prosperity was shattered in the Great Crash of 1929 and as government expenditures and debt mounted quickly to meet the exigencies of the consequent depression.

The Administration's other accomplishments were achievements that the President either encouraged or allowed. His interest in them ran all the way from his determination to improve relations with Latin American nations to his unhappy support of naval development after his international arms limitation program had failed. The result of the former was the dawning of the Good Neighbor policy of the 1930s and in the latter lay the germ of America's preparation for World War II. Other accomplishments of the Coolidge Administration include harmonizing the relations between the United States and the Philippine Islands, development of waterways, orderly growth of civil and even military aviation, regulation of radio broadcasting, expansion of the technical and information services of the Departments of Agriculture and Commerce, straightening out of some of the fierce disputes over use of Colorado River waters, encouragement of cooperative solutions to farmers' problems, and negotiation of the Kellogg-Briand Pact, which still stands as a statement in international law of the goal that men of good will hope to achieve. All together the record of his Administration was substantial in terms of the number and variety of works, even if the President was less tied up in its making than most American Chief Executives have been in making the records of their administrations. The flaws in the Coolidge Administration's accomplishments were that, in most cases, they were too puny and too tardy to be effective in dealing with the problems that were to lead to economic calamity and eventually to another world war.

Equally important were the Administration's failures. On some things the deck was stacked against Coolidge. The League of Nations had not a wisp of a chance in the United States and genuine arms limitation enjoyed only little more favor abroad. It is true that he fumbled America's adherence to the World Court, although it is farfetched to believe that the nation's membership on the Court would have stopped the rise of aggressor powers during the 1930s. Other failures represented the Administration's lack of vision. Its inflexibility toward Communist Russia and unquestioning acceptance of Fascist Italy dissipated whatever moderating influence the United States might have had over those totalitarian powers. Regarding international economics, the American government's policies were imaginative, but to the point of foolishness. To try to insure repayment of war debts by financing the effort with Yankee dollars only worked the United States deeper into the mire of European politics and economics from which the nation hoped to extricate itself. And that went on while America was engaged in the absurdity of trying to boost sales abroad while fortifying barriers to international trade.

If the idea of a world economic conference ever entered President Coolidge's head, he probably expelled it. He certainly turned aside ideas of federal control of American investments abroad or of speculation at home and of reorganization and regulation of banking and public power. In other areas, he failed to make more than gestures in support of a federal antilynching law, he ignored pressure for desegregation in the civil service, and decided to let the Ku Klux Klan burn itself out instead of providing the moral leadership which his code of service sanctioned. He even refused to push for adoption of one of his favorite ideas, the reorganization of railway transportation.

Coolidge's share of responsibility for the inadequacies of his administration derived largely from his restraint in both thought and action. He was like the naval officer who runs his ship according to the letter of the book, on the premise that nothing can go wrong that way. Coolidge's book was the Constitution and he interpreted it almost literally as far as the Chief Executive's powers were concerned. He addressed himself only to those problems *clearly* provided for in the Constitution and by judicial interpretation of it. As Coolidge saw it, the Constitution did not authorize the President to fuss over problems that belonged to other jurisdictions or to posterity.

He stated his view well in his comments, "Do the day's work" and "If you see ten troubles coming down the road, you can be sure that nine will run into the ditch before they reach you." Although there is much to be said for letting evil forces spend themselves, there is great danger that those that do not run into the ditch will gather so much momentum that they will become overwhelming. Coolidge had neither the conception of duty nor energy to enable him to deal effectively with all of the many problems that kept coming down the road.

In short, Calvin Coolidge was a statesman of the later nineteenth-century kind. He had modeled his career on what he had found there. By training and by feeling he was unable either to look forward or to comprehend satisfactorily the tendencies of his time. He thought he was presiding over the renovation of society, when, in fact, he was floating on top of a nation that was drifting into a new era. A man of his time, Coolidge was not a man for his time. As such he did not seek problems. That was, however, what most people wanted. In the 1920s the prime concern was to make money, and the rising tide of prosperity seemed to confirm that that was the thing to do. The result was that most Americans felt secure with Coolidge in Washington. As Henry Stoddard happily wrote in 1927, "They have faith in him beyond any they have shown in any other President of my time. . . . He inspires a deep, nation-wide confidence that all will go well with the country while he is in the White House."[3]

Yet the consequences of Coolidge's popularity in the 1920s went further in terms of his reputation. During the middle of the Great Depression of the 1930s, mining magnate John Hays Hammond said that "part of the resentment which even today is directed towards him is due to the fact that thousands of his former constituents believe that, had he chosen to run again, he would somehow miraculously have saved their personal fortunes and the country from depression."[4] Coolidge was doubly blamed for his failures. He was reproached for pursuing the domestic policies he did and for not pursuing them for four more years. That was also true in foreign affairs where he was to receive blame, on the one hand, for not bringing enduring world peace and, on the other hand, for not sufficiently preparing the nation for the collapse of peace.

Coolidge's signal fault was his pursuit of the policies approved by most Americans. When such policies fail, the people blame the President. They do not expect him to be representative unless his policies succeed. They do expect him to have special insight. That Coolidge lacked, as did the people. As Hammond remarked, with a hint of confession: "While many people attribute the financial collapse of 1929 in part to some of his policies, I consider the justice of this debatable. I would ask them if these same policies had not been their own."[5]

Even if Calvin Coolidge were representative of the majority when a leader was needed, he was also responsible for looking only to the day's work when vision was required. It is probable, of course, that had he been a leader and man of some vision, he would have failed to prevent depression and another great war because of the monumental disorder created by World War I and of the popular craving for political simplicity. But there was a good chance that had he been a less restrained Chief Executive the civil rights movement would not have been so long impeded, a chance that depression and aggression might not have reached such devastating proportions, and even a miniscule chance that they might have been averted.

As Walter Lippmann wrote in 1927, Coolidge had stopped the "nationalizing tendency" of the Republican party. "He has just stopped it, mind you. He has not replaced it with anything."[6] Like his time, Coolidge had the opportunity for greatness, a greatness born of his actual accomplishments and of his possible accomplishments. But he refused to seek the power to achieve more. He might not have achieved more for the seeking, but even noble failure would have saved him from Peter Levin's apt assessment that "Coolidge, the success of his times, is a failure in history."[7] A struggle to accomplish more might have saved his party, for which he cared, from disintegration and have reduced the loss of confidence during the early 1930s in the nation's leaders.

The lesson of Calvin Coolidge is that of a man bred and trained to avoid the daring. From that background he never freed himself. Consequently the story of Coolidge's life is more of what he became than of what he did. As a representative of the people, he rose to eminence; as the same, he failed to use his position to any great end. Yet in fairness it must be recalled that in Coolidge's days of national prominence, Harding was also President, Friedrich Ebert and Paul von Hindenburg were presidents of Germany, Stanley Baldwin and Ramsey MacDonald were prime ministers of Great Britain, and failure after failure trooped in and out of office as premiers of France. Italy's Benito Mussolini and Soviet Russia's Nicolai Lenin towered over all other chiefs of state, but it must be said of Coolidge that if he did not have their flair for leadership, neither did he possess their megalomania or their instinct for terror.

What Coolidge was and did are not too difficult to comprehend. Why at bedrock he was what he was, however, is a question that can at best be only plausibly answered. Yet the question should be asked for no other reason than that Coolidge was a most untypical man. His attributes of honesty, reliability, unpretentiousness, thriftiness, and caution, his ideals, his interest in public service, and his sketchy political and economic philosophies clearly derive from his family training and his school and college experiences.

His was a heavily idealistic upbringing, one that was fortified by what he learned at school, academy, and college. His religious vagueness came from his mother and the unstructured nature of church in Plymouth Notch. His mother also contributed to the development of his sentimentality and apparently transferred to him her desire for life beyond the Notch. Both contributions were complemented by his father, who increasingly during Calvin's adolescence relied on the boy for sentimental comfort as John Coolidge's father, wife, and only other child were taken from him by death. His mother, Calvin's grandmother, was too flinty a person to be an emotional anchor. Yet, because the boy and the father were taciturn, their affection was more understood than expressed, which must have been a frustrating business for them both. As for leaving the Notch, that might have been young Coolidge's way of proving himself to both his father and mother and of intentionally seeking to beat his father at his own game of public leader. One can guess that Calvin's mild hypochondria also derived from his mother, whose illnesses were an integral part of his first dozen years. His lack of expressiveness came in part from the model set by his father and from his grandmother's disapproval of much expression by the boy. This may permanently have fettered his imagination or at least have internalized it in the form of elaborate daydreams.

Calvin Coolidge also was influenced by the community of Plymouth Notch. It was a democratic society, one not much bothered by intrigue or chicanery and one without serious social distinctions. Coolidge carried that spirit of easygoing democracy with him the rest of his life, not only politically, but also in terms of being personally rather free from bigotry, snobbishness, and prejudice. As a lawyer he had to serve a widespread clientele which fortified his open-mindedness about people, as did his need as a politician to appeal for the votes of a wide range of individuals and groups. The fact that until he became President he had not become a member of a social elite helped keep him favorably disposed towards various minorities. Yet his was not a crusading tolerance, for he also gained from the Notch, and from law and politics, the belief that man had to claim his rights and rewards.

Amherst largely bolstered Coolidge's tendencies. What Professors Garman and Morse taught him about idealism, service, and stability augmented and clarified what he had already acquired in the Notch and from his family. The college allowed him to bud, if only as an occasionally droll fellow. By making him something of a scholar and a gentleman, Amherst also made it difficult for him to go home. Indeed, by mixing him with young men from other stations in life the college gave him career goals that could not be satisfied in Plymouth Notch. Northampton became his proving ground, and there he found he could become professionally and politically accepted without the shelter of home or college.

The first twenty-five years of Coolidge's life were important, not only in setting him on the path to the Massachusetts governorship and the White House, but in shaping how he would act when he got there. His hypochondria kept him from being too active, for it was a good excuse to do just the day's work and not to worry about the future. Of course, he was restrained by other things. He probably did possess less stamina than most men. His shyness and taciturnity also kept him in check, and his daydreams siphoned off most of his imaginativeness. These factors fitted in well with his tame 1890s philosophy, and in the absence of any great pressure to reconstruct his thought, he was able to believe that his philosophy and action met the requirements of American life in the 1920s. In fact, not only was there no compelling force to pull Coolidge out of his lassitude, but instead the flattery of his supporters, his ability to disregard his critics (who were far from being astute), and the superficial evidence that everyday in every way things were growing better made it easy for him to hold a narrow view of his responsibilities as President.

In reputation as well as in fact Coolidge has been a victim of his reserve and of his popularity, for together they restrained him from serious involvement in most of the great problems of the 1920s. He has further suffered from his lack of charm, boldness, and brilliance, qualities for which ambition, dignity, and kind feelings are inadequate substitutes. As it turned out, there was no great achievement with which posterity could identify Coolidge alone. His most vaunted accomplishments, debt and tax-cutting, went for naught with the coming of depression, and the Kellogg-Briand Pact soon became a mockery. The President was also the victim of the suppositions that what he fought against, measures like the McNary-Haugen bill, would have been more beneficial than his policies and that what he ignored, such as adherence to the League of Nations, could have been achieved.

With what, then, is one left in assessing Calvin Coolidge as President? He restored public confidence in the White House, but that drained away during the term of his successor. He was a skillful administrator, but he had little to administer that met the pressing needs of the time. He was a man of considerable courage in not yielding to congressional petulance, but his courage was outweighed by his reluctance to recognize the problems underlying dissidence. When Coolidge acted, he did so forcefully, but his restraint led him to act too seldom. His avoidance of theatrics is a virtue one wishes for in all Presidents and has found in few, but dignity and simplicity of expression are not prime qualities for successful Chief Executives. Coolidge's failure was the failure of a President who does not look ahead and does not fight to head off the problems of the future. Of course, there is little to indicate that he could have succeeded in such a struggle or that there was anyone else available in national politics in the 1920s who could have done substantially better, but the nation would have been morally and intellectually better for the attempt.

NOTES

1. Washington *Post,* June 8, 1924.
2. George F. Sparks, ed., *A Many-Colored Toga, The Diary of Henry Fountain Ashurst* (Tuscon, 1962), 267.
3. Henry L. Stoddard, *As I Knew Them* (New York, 1927), 532.
4. John Hays Hammond, *The Autobiography of John Hays Hammond* (New York, 1935), II, 693.
5. *Ibid.*
6. Walter Lippmann, *Men of Destiny* (New York, 1927), 15.
7. Peter R. Levin, *Seven by Chance: The Accidental Presidents* (New York, 1948), 262.

II ∽ Politics: Progressivism and the Election of 1928

4 ⁓ Recent Opinion on the Decline of the Progressive Movement*

[Author's Note] *In his survey of current historical opinion on the reasons for the decline of the Progressive movement, Herbert F. Margulies of the University of Hawaii finds that while there is some difference among historians as to whether progressivism remained vibrant during the 1920's, they agree that the movement had declined significantly by the end of the decade. The most recent historical opinion traced in this article, while by no means disparaging the importance of World War I, emphasizes internal weakness of the Progressive movement itself as the crucial factor in the decline of political liberalism. In conclusion, the author suggests that additional studies are needed to round out our assessment of this problem.*

Many historians have commented on the reasons for the decline of the Progressive movement, but as yet no full scale study has emerged. A preliminary step in that direction is a survey of current historical opinion on the subject. What factors have been emphasized, what measure of agreement has been achieved, what remains to be done? These are some of the questions with which this article is concerned.

The scope of this survey is limited in several ways. Though attention is focused on the opinion of historians, this is not an exercise in historiography. The writer is interested in the decline of the Progressive movement, not in how historical opinion on the subject has developed or why interpretations have changed as they have. Thus, attention is directed with

* Reprinted with permission of *Mid-America* and Herbert F. Margulies from *Mid-America,* XL (October, 1963), pages 250–268.

but few exceptions to the views of our contemporaries, on the assumption that in most instances earlier works have contributed to the making of more recent accounts. Also, this is a preliminary survey of conclusions about the decline of the movement, not an original exploration in depth of any of the alleged factors. A great body of literature that would take us deep into the subject is therefore reluctantly but deliberately ignored.

Since the literature directed specifically and exclusively to the decline of the Progressive movement is severely limited in quantity, most of the relevant conclusions and arguments appear as parts of studies centered on other topics. In many instances, I must impute to historians views which in fact are only implied, or, are but a part of a more complete set of opinions. Seeming contrasts in view, then, often are due merely to the perspective of the viewer or to differences in subject matter or approach. The makings of a good dispute may be present, but few of the heavier intellectual blows have yet been struck. Indeed, it may even prove possible to effect a synthesis of the views of many historians without doing violence to the positions on particular aspects of the subject taken by any of them.

Few historians would deny the adverse effect of external events like World War One or the Bolshevik Revolution on the Progressive movement. The variation in emphasis on such factors is considerable, however. While some comments seem to ascribe to the war full blame, greater stress has been placed on the erosion of the movement from internal causes. From this perspective, the war was at most only an accelerating agent in the process of dying, but the death of progressivism was nevertheless natural, not inflicted from outside. An extreme form of this view has progressivism dead before the war began.

Emphasis on internal factors occurs in many ways, one of which is the cyclical theory. Thus, George Mowry, noting that the progressive spirit was flagging before the war, explains that "The political pendulum with its almost rhythmic movement in American history was already swinging to the right."[1] Charles Forcey also endorses the cyclical view.[2]

The fullest statement of the cyclical approach to the decline of the Progressive movement remains that of Arthur M. Schlesinger, Sr., who in 1922 outlined the general theory as well as its specific application.[3] "Every movement of radical tendency has developed through certain clearly defined stages, as if in obedience to some immutable law of social dynamics," Schlesinger wrote "Epochs of radicalism and conservatism have followed each other in alternating order." Reform movements have three stages.

> The third and final stage of the reform is reached when the new doctrines, having lost their air of strangeness and demonstrated either their utility or harmlessness, become imbedded in the conscience and philosophy of the people at large. . . . The cycle of reform has about completed itself; for public opinion hardens into a new conservatism and forms a crust that toughly resists any further efforts for change. . . .

Applying the general view to the Progressive movement, Schlesinger wrote:

> When the United States entered the World War in 1917 the signs of the times indicated that the generation had about run its course. Its program of domestic reform had been enacted; Roosevelt passed away in 1919, Wilson, La Follette and other vigorous reformers of an earlier day were beginning to show signs of physical decline. . . .[4]

Various opinions stressing specific internal factors involved in the pre-war decline of the movement seem entirely compatible with the cyclical view. One major body of historical opinion of this sort probes the decline of the movement with reference to the progressives' own thought.

A number of historians stress the limitations implicit in the Wilsonian ideology. John Blum writes of Wilson that after the Clayton Anti-trust Act had been passed, "so far as domestic legislation is concerned, he had exhausted the stock of ideas he had brought to his office."[5] And Wilson, Blum feels, reflected the mainstream of progressive thought. The progressives had accomplished their purpose, "the purpose of their generation," before the entry of the United States into the war.[6] Arthur Mann expresses much the same idea: ". . . A humanitarian generation ran out of ideas by the second Wilson administration."[7] Richard Hofstadter notes that progressives had little appeal for immigrants and concludes that this "reduced the social range and the radical drive of his program and kept him genteel, proper, and safe." In the same vein, Hofstadter points out, as have other historians, that progressivism took place in a context of prosperity. The movement sprang from "mass sentiments of responsibility, indignation, and guilt." But in such an economic climate, "Hardly anyone intended that these sentiments should result in action drastic enough to transform American society."[8] Discussing the California progressives, Mowry writes: "Like many of their fellow ideologues elsewhere, California progressives had no more issues by 1914 and could not bring themselves to take that long, and to them radical, jump onto the new ground of socio-economic legislation and direct cooperation with labor."[9]

If the Jeffersonian promise of the New Freedom had been fulfilled by 1916, the same cannot be said for the New Nationalism of Theodore Roosevelt and Herbert Croly. Yet some historians have focused attention on the ideology most fully expressed by progressives of this persuasion in explaining the decline of the Progressive movement. William Leuchtenburg, writing about the Insurgent Republicans and the Bull Moosers, points to nationalism as the Achilles heel. Using Senator Beveridge as an example of the imperialistic-minded progressive, Leuchtenburg writes that "Beveridge's imperialism ultimately proved his undoing as a Progressive."[10] Despite the fact that Wilson pushed through reforms dear to him, differences on Mexican policy and the Panama Canal tolls questions caused Beveridge, by 1914, to be "bitterly opposed to him." Nationalistic feelings so eroded Beveridge's progressivism, Leuchtenburg argues, that "By 1920 he was crying against 'Organized labor's assault on American institutions,' interspersing speeches against the League of Nations with demands for the repeal of the excess profits tax. Inflation was caused by the drawing of money to Europe through foreign propaganda and the unreasonable demands of labor unions for higher wages. Once more Beveridge's views on domestic and foreign policy had merged, and this new outlook persisted until his death."[11]

The story of Beveridge is, in an exaggerated form, the story of the Progressive Party, Leuchtenburg maintains. Embarrassed by Wilson's record on domestic affairs, progressives had to choose between joining him, presenting more radical domestic alternatives, or fighting him on foreign policy grounds. Largely nationalistic and imperialistic since 1898, it was not difficult for them to choose the last of these. "For the first time in the history of the Progressive movement foreign affairs determined the line of direction, and by 1916 the Progressives were completely absorbed with foreign policy issues and their movement was moribund."[12] Significantly, as of 1915 "Not only had foreign policy become a key issue, but it had been linked by now with the need for high tariff walls, a prophecy of the economic policy of Warren G. Harding and Herbert Hoover." The fault, Leuchtenburg finds, is hardly accidental, but characterized much of western thought.

> In the final analysis the Progressive movement suffered from a contradiction between humanistic values and nationalistic aspirations, which,

if not inherent, had certainly beset other democracies from the time of the wars of the French Revolution. In arguing for a positive national government, the followers of Croly ultimately lost sight of the distinction between the state as an instrument and the state as an end. The consequences were not only the endorsement of an imperialistic foreign policy but the death of the Progressive Party in the interest of their national zeal.[12]

Leuchtenburg's view is another that tends to see at least a substantial part of progressivism's decline rooted in its own pre-war days. It is, however, a highly controversial argument. Mowry describes Theodore Roosevelt drifting away from his Progressive Party associates in 1915 and 1916 partly because he found so many of the progressives insufficiently belligerent. By contrast, Roosevelt found himself again allied with his erstwhile conservative enemies on the common ground of nationalism. Walter Trattner argues that progressivism had virtually achieved consensus status by 1912 and that the progressives were therefore as divided on foreign policy as were the American people generally. Howard Allen, moreover, finds no pattern in the voting of progressive Republican Senators between 1913 and 1917 to confirm Leuchtenburg's thesis.[13]

A different aspect of the thinking especially evident among some of the New Nationalist intellectuals has received much more attention from historians explaining the decline of the Progressive movement. I refer to the outlook called relativism. While the evil effects attributed by some historians to relativism occurred during the war, the roots of the new way of thought are viewed as developing prior to American involvement. Moreover, relativism, the by-product of Darwinism and pragmatism as many historians view it, is seen as a major causal factor in progressivism's acceptance of the war and all that war entailed. From this perspective, the war was not an external factor that came and destroyed progressivism. Rather, pre-war progressivism moved at least half-way to meet the war. Progressivism made its own fate. In this indictment of relativism, scholars like Morton White, Daniel Aaron, Eric Goldman and Charles Forcey seem now to accept the views of the anti-war progressives Randolph Bourne and Harold Stearns.[14] As Aaron views it, the philosophy of adaptation or adjustment leads to preoccupation with techniques to the exclusion of ends, and doesn't even achieve the adjustment desired.[15] The view is familiar and needs no elaboration.

David Noble, while agreeing that relativism had a corrosive effect on progressivism, causing for Carl Becker a "numbing, debilitating stage of self-doubt," offers a different explanation for the rise of relativism, also based on pre-war thought. The new relativism sprang not from the gradual impact of evolutionary theory, but from the loss of faith in progress. Noble writes:[16]

> Men, suggested Becker, will always . . . live in unreal worlds which have no solid foundation in truth when they do not follow the scientific method to its logical extreme. In retrospect, this was the error of Becker and his progressive contemporaries before 1914. More sophisticated than the Enlightenment thinkers, they had openly confessed that science could not create positive values. But no more sophisticated than the philosophes, they followed the same Goddess of Progress and believed that men could find universally verifiable standards for progress in a past that he created himself. Suddenly it had become obvious to Becker that when man knows only specific nonvaluational facts through science and creates his own subjective definition of progress through his personal creation of a history that does have values, there is no real progress.

Noble goes on to ask:

> Is this, then, the true history of the dramatic breakdown of liberal morale after 1914? The liberal generation did not lose all of the past through abstract education in the implications of Darwinian evolution, but rather it lost a past, a past of inevitable progress imposed on history by a blind faith in progress—so that it can be argued that relativism came not by the route of philosophy, but the end of a belief which had previously ordered the world.[17]

Perhaps the most thorough study of progressive thought in transition is Henry May's *The End of American Innocence.*[18] May details not only the roots and development of new outlooks, but the nature of the older view, seemingly dominant as of 1912, and the interaction between new and old. Thus May writes:

> Suppose . . . that people were to ask whether corruption really mattered, or whether good government made men happier, or whether a future of ordered peace and prosperity really satisfied human needs. If such questions were to be asked seriously and often, the whole progressive movement might collapse.

"Though most Americans did not know it, such questions had actually been raised."[19] The three great bastions of the older progressive thought were Moralism, Progress and Culture. By 1917, attacked from within the ramparts of progressivism and from without, the old views had been, if not destroyed, at least rendered aggressively defensive. Relativism, generated by William James and John Dewey, among others, led the way, the more effectively for being part of the Progressive movement at the outset and therefore heard. But many other bodies of thought together with certain social developments enter into the argument as well, ranging from the rise of W. C. Handy's jazz through the preaching of Billy Sunday to the poetry of Baudelaire.

Those who discuss the rise of relativism and of a new body of thought generally find that if the war didn't begin the decline of progressivism, it certainly accelerated it. In May's view, the war brought the intellectual and social conflict of the pre-war years to a climax. The old thought, the Wilsonian ideology, after a last gasp counter-attack, was toppled, but the newer varieties of progressive thought, as expressed in the pre-war Liberation, likewise lost force. The conflict is best described in May's own words:

> Most of the custodians of culture, beset already by intellectual attack and worried by signs of sexual, racial and other kinds of insurrection, linked the Allied Cause with the defense of all they valued, and thereby added the last element needed to produce a really big explosion.[20]

To most historians, it has seemed a paradox that during a war for freedom and democracy, civil liberties should have been the victim of what Goldman calls a "contagion of suppression." May would explain the seeming paradox in terms of pre-existing tensions. The war was for the defenders of Moralism, Progress and Culture an opportunity to strike at the enemies of the dominant civilization, the radicals, foreigners, believers in new ideas; it was a last chance to restore idealism, true religion and morality, and promote a new and nobler national literature.[21]

Many of those in the middle between the old culture and the new, progressives of a new view, such as Croly, Lippmann, Dewey, Beard and La Guardia, embraced the idealism and nationalism of the wartime Wilson. For these, the effect of war was not so much suppression as disillusionment.

Hofstadter presents a view that dovetails with May's: "Participation in the war put an end to the Progressive movement. . . . And yet the wartime frenzy of idealism and self-sacrifice marked the apotheosis as well as the liquidation of the Progressive spirit."[22] Post-war reaction was inevitable in any case, he argues, but "by linking the foreign crusade as intimately as possible to the Progressive values and the Progressive language, he [Wilson] was unintentionally insuring that the reaction against Progressivism and moral idealism would be as intense as it could be."[23] Yet that linking was no accident, in May's view, but a result of the tensions and conflicts within progressive thought.

Eric Goldman finds in progressive thought an explanation for the disillusionment that greeted the Versailles Treaty. The Treaty, he argues, was especially disillusioning to progressives because it sprang from premises which they themselves had endorsed. The Wilsonian phrases, self-determination, democracy and international law and order were applications on the international level of a laissez faire liberalism characteristic of Schurz and Tilden but long since repudiated by progressives. "Could it be," Goldman asks rhetorically, "that progressives had proclaimed an essentially conservative peace program and then were indignant when they got an essentially conservative peace?"[24] The sub-conscious knowledge of their own complicity, due in part to the pragmatic frame of mind, sent progressives in search of a scapegoat. Lord Keynes' book *The Economic Consequences of the Peace* came along at the opportune time to meet the need of an intelligentsia already "desperately anxious to deny Wilson."[25]

Our focus of attention on intellectual factors allegedly involved in the decline of the Progressive movement has carried us not only into the war period but beyond it. A considerable measure of reconciliation can be effected, however, between the arguments stressing the pre-war decline of the movement and those that take the story into the wartime and postwar years. Leaving aside the cyclical theory, the argument for the pre-war decline of the movement is essentially that progressivism in its Wilsonian mainstream involved a rather limited set of goals and once they were achieved in the first Wilson administration, there was no more reason for existence. Hofstadter, who seems to put forth this view, is not repudiating it entirely but only amending it somewhat when he argues that the Wilsonians did find in foreign affairs a new avenue for the expression of the same general principles. May seems to agree, viewing the Great Crusade as not simply an expression of Wilsonian progressive ideals on the level of international policy but a defense of the very limitations of the older progressivism against innovators. And the anti-relativists imply that progressive thought as formulated prior to 1917 was as much responsible as were external factors for the decline of progressivism in the war and Reconstruction years.

The whole subject has been regarded from an entirely different perspective by a number of historians, including John Blum, Arthur Link and George Mowry. While using intellectual factors in their analyses, these men have viewed the decline of the movement primarily from the standpoint of politics. They too, though, seem to see the decline of progressivism more in terms of internal limitations than of external blows.

Link establishes the ground rules for this type of analysis when he writes: "Since national progressivism was never an organized or independent movement (except imperfectly and then only temporarily in 1912), it could succeed only when its constituent elements formed a coalition strong enough to control one of the major parties."[26] From this perspective, the decline of the Progressive movement sprang from the failure of progressives to control or successfully utilize the Republican, Democratic or Progressive Parties.

Prominent Bull Moose Party leaders such as Amos Pinchot and Harold Ickes laid much of the blame for the demise of their party on George Perkins. Perkins, they claimed, financed the party in order to control it for the ends of J. P. Morgan and Company, U.S. Steel and International Harvester.[27] Contemporary historians disagree. Perkins' biographer, John A. Garraty, describes Perkins as sincere in his political efforts;[28] Helene Hooker, in her introduction to Amos Pinchot's history of the party, demurs from Pinchot's charge by offering a more fundamental alternative: "How far or how effectively," she asks, "could the Progressives have fought in view of the gains created by the Democratic reform and the additional crisis of a world war?"[29] Mowry, who traces the decline of the party in some detail, does so in terms both of Theodore Roosevelt's shifting sentiments and the inherent difficulties of the situation.[30] John Blum agrees with Mowry that Roosevelt helped to kill the party, but emphasizes the inherent weaknesses that doomed the party from the start:

> It was a party with only three assets, all transitory, enthusiasm, money and a Presidential candidate. The enthusiasm and the money vanished with defeat. The candidate understood political organization too well to expect a group of ardent amateurs—even wealthy amateurs—running an incomplete ticket, to provide the stuff of victory in 1912 or continuity thereafter. After the election of Woodrow Wilson, Roosevelt was prepared to dissolve the party he had made as soon as it suited his convenience.[31]

The creation of the Progressive Party looms, then, as a major factor in the overall demise of the progressive movement, for, as Mowry puts it: ". . . with the Roosevelt secession radicalism as a potent force within the Republican party was dead for at least thirty years."[32] The baleful effects of this secession caused Mowry to write that ". . . in the end Roosevelt was to be largely responsible for the destruction of progressivism in the Republican Party."[33] To be sure, the argument runs, progressives such as La Follette, Cummins, Hadley, Borah and others remained in the Republican party after the split, but the position of progressives was far weaker than it had been in early 1912, when, with the momentum of Insurgency behind them, they were on the verge of capturing the party. Even the renomination of Taft in 1912 was tolerable, from this perspective, for only their own departure could have prevented the progressives from controlling the party following the inevitable defeat of the President.

Progressive Republican ranks were of course augmented when the Progressive party broke up and the majority of its members returned to the G.O.P. But the terms of reunion established by the Republican leaders were inauspicious for the future of progressive Republicanism. "From all except Roosevelt unconditional surrender was expected," Mowry writes.[34] Garraty tells us that Perkins continued his strenuous efforts in behalf of the ex-Progressives into 1917, but being objectionable to both sides he served only to make an acceptable rapprochement the more difficult.[35]

If the breakup of the Republican Party in 1912 was, as Mowry, Blum and others claim, the fatal blow to progressive Republicanism, then the causes of that breakup become significant factors in the decline of the Progressive movement. Roosevelt's decision to bolt the party following Taft's nomination was the crucial one. Many factors were involved, as Mowry explains it. The pre-convention and convention battling had been extraordinarily bitter, bringing emotions to a boil; Roosevelt and his supporters believed that the nomination had been stolen; Roosevelt was a god to many of his followers, adding to the passion of those who pressed him to lead a new party; while 107 delegates, chiefly office holders, were unwilling to bolt, and remained in the convention and voted for Roosevelt, the majority of Roosevelt delegates, 344, favored a third party and refused to vote on the nomination; sufficient financial support for a third party campaign was promised by Perkins and Munsey; above all, something in Roosevelt's character made him persist—he couldn't be a quitter, he was sincere about his New Nationalism, and he perhaps secretly hoped for victory.[36] Blum agrees with most of Mowry's analysis, but feels that

Roosevelt was moved more by desire to salvage his pride than by hope of victory.[37]

The impossibility of the Progressive Party and loss of the Republican Party to progressivism put the whole burden on the Democratic Party. It proved unequal to the task, historians like Link and Blum tell us, and they advance some explanations for the failure.

The relatively limited ends of the New Freedom of course come into the account. The Wilson described by Link and Blum was, as of 1913 and 1914, a skilled political leader, unsophisticated in economic theory and relatively conservative in the views to which he adhered. This conservatism, moreover, was characteristic of liberals generally, not just Wilson, in the opinion of these historians. "Americans, even liberal Americans, could not agree upon how to discipline their burgeoning economy without inhibiting its productivity," Blum writes.[38] Link notes that ". . . a general reaction against further excursions into reform set in around the beginning of 1914, gradually permeated the administration and the majority membership of Congress, and gained momentum during the summer and early autumn. . . ." The primary cause of "this ebbing of the reform impulse in 1914" was the business slump that had set in late in 1913.[39]

The demands and thinking of the New Nationalism remained, however, and in 1916 Wilson reversed himself and appointed Brandeis to the Supreme Court, supported a rural credits bill, a child labor law, and the Adamson Act, together with other measures advocated by "advanced" progressives. The motive for the switch was largely or wholly political, both Blum and Link indicate, an effort to fashion a new coalition for the 1916 campaign.[40] The effort succeeded, with the building of a progressive coalition made up of "southern and western farmers, organized labor, the social justice elements, and a large part of the independent radicals who had heretofore voted the Socialist ticket."[41] Link, more than Blum, Goldman and other historians, remarks on the continued functioning of this new progressive coalition through the war, giving support for "heavy taxation, relatively stringent controls over business and industry, and extensive new benefits to labor." Indeed, the coalition even survived the Armistice "in a crippled way," putting across

> a program that constituted a sizeable triumph for the progressive movement—continued heavy taxation, the Transportation Act of 1920, the long fight for railroad regulation, a new child labor law, amendments

for prohibition and woman suffrage, immigration restriction, and water power and conservation legislation.[42]

Link admits, however, that despite these measures, the coalition fell apart between 1917 and 1920, making way for the rout of the Democrats in the election of 1920 and the continued weakness of that party as a national organization through the twenties. He joins other historians in search of explanations for the disintegration of the Democratic Party.

The war has been seen by some historians as creating a situation inherently ruinous to progressivism. Russel Nye writes: "Nothing constructive could be done in wartime. . . ."[43] It inevitably brought, some have felt, a shift in the issues away from those of the progressives, what Mowry has called "The disintegrating effects of the great new national issues which came out of the war. . . ."[44] Hofstadter sees the war as breeding an inevitable reaction, not only to itself but to the Progressive movement that preceded it.[45] Forcey and Goldman see a significant shift in power away from the progressive element, and Forcey at least implies that this too was an inevitable concomitant of war. "Though Croly and Lippmann spoke for the ideals and interests of the great liberal middle class, that class no longer had much power in a world ruled by the hard and secret decisions of admirals and generals, diplomats and heads of state."[46] On this last point Hofstadter demurs, arguing that no significant shift in power to the interests the progressives had been fighting could have taken place, "for only on limited issues and in superficial respects had the management of affairs ever been very far out of those hands."[47]

Link, however, is not willing to accept the argument of inevitability.

> The national progressive movement, which had found its most effective embodiment in the coalition of forces that reelected Woodrow Wilson in 1916, was shattered by certain policies that the administration pursued from 1917 to 1920, and by some developments over which the administration had no or only slight control. The collapse that occurred in 1920 was not inevitable and cannot be explained by merely saying that "The war killed the progressive movement."[48]

Link has drawn up a more specific bill of particulars:[49]

> First, the independent radicals and antiwar agrarians were alienated by the war declaration and the government's suppression of dissent and civil liberties during the war and the Red scare. Organized labor was

> disaffected by the administration's coercion of the coal miners in 1919, its lukewarm if not hostile attitude during the great strikes of 1919 and 1920, and its failure to support the Plumb Plan for nationalization of the railorads. Isolationists and idealists were outraged by what they thought was the President's betrayal of American traditions or the liberal peace program at Paris. These tensions were strong enough to disrupt the coalition, but a final one would have been fatal even if the others had never existed. This was the alienation of farmers in the Plains and western states produced by the administration's refusal to impose price controls on cotton while it maintained ceilings on the prices of other agricultural commodities, and especially by the administration's failure to do anything decisive to stem the downward plunge of farm prices that began in the summer of 1920. Under the impact of all these stresses, the Wilsonian coalition gradually disintegrated from 1917 to 1920 and disappeared entirely during the campaign of 1920.

Blum agrees in stressing the disaffection of the western farmer. The disproportionate power that Wilson permitted to the southern segment of the party caused, he claims, the politically ruinous farm policy. It was also in part responsible for wartime prohibition, which was anathema to urban workers and the city machines, "whose captains never forgave the rural evangelicals."[50] Blum, like Link and others, notes also the alienation of the intellectual on civil liberties issues.

Much of the blame for the wartime and postwar breakup of the progressive coalition within the Democratic party has been placed on Woodrow Wilson. "The attention Wilson gave to his splendid international purpose was needed equally at home," Blum writes. But "It was not in Wilson's power to provide it. He lost himself, as he had at times before, in a transcendent faith so dear to him he could not think that others did not partake of it. . . ."[51]

The analysis of progressive thought reenters the political analysis at this point, as at many others. Wilson was not alone at fault. Progressives generally had been reluctant from the first to embrace the demands of labor and the social welfare advocates. Amidst the heightened fear of radicalism in 1919 and 1920, such coalitions were doubly difficult. Writing of the California progressives, but generalizing also about the national movement, Mowry writes:

> When witch-hunters and reactionaries sought to stamp out all deviations from their creed they inevitably attacked Progressives and pro-

> gressive principles. But even more disastrous to the reform movement was the tendency of progressive leaders to fall prey to the same spirit themselves.[52]

David Burner stresses another factor: ". . . after 1918 Wilson could not satisfactorily direct his own administration." The 1918 election had not been ruinous, Burner argues. The loss of twenty-three House seats to the Republicans was less than the average loss sustained by the party in power in an off-year election. The election did not, moreover, signal any national disaffection but only the alienation of many in the Midwest. But, to a party that had become habituated to strong Presidential leadership in domestic and political affairs, the loss of Wilson's firm hand, first to the Versailles conference, then to the League of Nations fight, and finally to a near-fatal stroke, was disastrous.[53]

A final factor relating to the failure of the Democratic party as a vehicle for progressivism is suggested by Link, among others, when he writes: "When the progressive coalition of 1916 was destroyed in 1920, progressives reverted to their traditional voting habits."[54] We are reminded that since the Civil War the Democratic Party had been the minority party. Only the Republican schism of 1912, healed by 1920, had permitted the Democrats to regain the Presidency after a twenty year drought. The burden of championing progressivism might have rested more lightly on the Republican Party.

In addition to commentary on the fate of each of the three parties discussed above, historians have offered opinions on the progressive decline from an overall political perspective. They are agreed that progressivism involved a coalition of diverse elements. It is natural, therefore, that they should account for its decline partly in terms of schismatization. Progressives were divided between at least three parties (some would include the Socialist party and say four), and divided also on occupational, social and ideological lines. Such a loose coalition was inherently unstable, it has been suggested, and there was little that could be done about it.

Attention has also focused, however, on the failings of individuals like Roosevelt and Wilson and La Follette. They are blamed for augmenting the natural disunity of the movement through their personal animosities, jealousies and drives for power.[55] Implied in such analysis is the notion that the leaders of the Progressive movement might have been of a different character, and had they been something other than what they were, the ultimate fate of progressivism might have been different.

Mowry questions the accidental character of what might be called the personality factor:

> In California, as in the nation, one of the more potent reasons for the decline of progressivism was the sharp personal conflicts among its leaders. If an average can be struck on such elusive matters, the national Progressive leader was extraordinarily individualistic and his character was marked by a pronounced ambitious and competitive strain. He was usually highly intolerant of opposition either within or without his own ranks. After he had held his first important office he seemed to demand a fealty from his supporters which they were often unable or unwilling to give. . . .[56]

It was then, from this viewpoint, perhaps not inevitable that potent leaders of progressivism should have been highly individualistic and prone to schismatizing actions, but statistically highly probable that any given one of them should have been of such a character.

Mowry offers another general factor applicable especially to the years 1916 to 1920—the self-perpetuating properties of failure and defeat. Discouragement led progressives to abandon the pattern of thought and action that had characterized their progressivism. Thus, "many progressives lost all hope of concerted action and were ready to withdraw from the reform crusade. . . ." And,

> As despair succeeded hope in the progressives, their fine progressive rationale of a decade earlier eroded. Gone was their firm belief in the ultimate success of moral values. Gone was their complete faith in democracy, and thus their confidence in politics. Gone was their once tenaciously held conviction of the essential goodness of man and his capacity to improve.[57]

Whatever the explanation emphasized, historians seem to be generally agreed that the Progressive movement was over by 1920. The view is not unanimous, however. Again, it is Link who issues a sharp dissent. Progressivism had declined, to be sure, but it had by no means disappeared. Its apparent demise, he argues, was due to the fact that the several elements could no longer coalesce into a national majority capable of electing a President. One of the weaknesses referred to above concealed tenacious strength.

> When the progressive coalition of 1916 was destroyed in 1920, progressives reverted to their traditional voting habits in the national elections of 1920, 1924, and 1928 and were never able to combine to capture the presidency. On the other hand, they combined in Congress to control the legislative branch during practically all of the 1920's, to thwart the conservative executive leadership, and to push through a remarkable progressive legislative program, the most advanced parts of which were nullified by presidential vetoes.[58]

Kenneth C. MacKay lends support to this view in his book *The Progressive Movement of 1924.* "One purpose of this history," MacKay writes, "is to demonstrate that—far from being dead—the progressive movement, supported by agrarian malcontents, militant labor forces, and far-visioned socialists and intellectuals, remained alive and energetic throughout the Twenties." MacKay develops this view by describing La Follette's campaign as springing from groups and ideas prominent in the earlier progressive movement.[59]

Samuel Lubell disagrees with MacKay.

> The 4,800,000 votes which La Follette got in 1924 were often described loosely as the irreducible minimum of liberal strength in America. Much of the vote, representing approval of La Follette's opposition to war with Germany actually had nothing to do with liberalism.

Ethnic origin, for Lubell, has been the key factor in American politics from the outbreak of World War One.[60] Hofstadter sides with Lubell on the specific issue of the meaning of La Follette's 1924 vote and disputes Link's emphasis on progressive continuity in the 1920's. He points to the progressive consensus in 1912, when Taft, the lone candidate regarded as a conservative, did so poorly, and says that "It is the disappearance of this progressive consensus of 1912 that seems most significant." The Congressional progressives of the twenties, with the exception of Norris, he puts down as "a fake." The nub of the matter, for Hofstadter as for others, is this: Progressivism had been founded on a mood, and with the reaction that followed the war that mood was dissipated."[61]

While some difference of opinion continues as to whether progressivism was alive or dead during the 1920's, historians agree that the movement had declined significantly by 1920. A wide variety of explanations have been offered for its decline, but certain broad themes have received special emphasis.

It has been argued that the Progressive movement suffered certain grave blows from the outside, chiefly the advent of World War One. The war inevitably diverted attention, raised new and divisive issues, and shifted power into non-progressive hands.

While by no means disparaging the importance of war, most recent history emphasizes the character of the Progressive movement itself. Schlesinger's cyclical theory retains adherents who see decline as inherent in any reform movement. A good deal of attention has been devoted to the intellectual content of progressivism, resulting in several different, though not always incompatible, explanations for the decline of the movement. Stress has been laid on the limited goals of the dominant strain of the movement, which is generally seen as the Wilsonian. The effect alleged was, among other things, to cause progressives to run out of issues and to draw away from reform when challenged by more radical elements from within and without. Attention has been directed also to a new mode and body of thought arising in pre-war years, including relativism. Some have indicted relativism for promoting a philosophy and psychology of acquiescence. May, especially, focuses attention on the ruinous conflict between the old ideology reflected in Wilson's New Freedom and the varied body of new thought which at first was largely within the shelter of the Progressive movement.

For the most part, arguments relating to the intellectual content of progressivism depict the movement declining in the war and postwar period. The war is seen, nevertheless, as simply accelerating a decline that was already underway due to internal intellectual factors.

A related block of opinion, similarly focusing mainly on internal weaknesses, traces the decline in political terms. Failure of progressives to control a major political party is the fundamental weakness pointed to and explained. The Progressive Party is not seen as a major one, however. Though Leuchtenburg discusses a shift within the Progressive Party away from domestic progressive issues, the majority view is one of unconcern about the internal functioning of the party. The failure of the Progressive Party was virtually unavoidable, Blum and others argue, hence the basic fault was creation of it. The schism of the Republican party in 1912, giving birth to the Bull Moose effort, has been seen as the big event in the decline of progressive Republicanism. With respect to the Democratic Party, decline came in the years 1917 to 1920, it is widely asserted. Internal diversity and disharmony, worsened by the rise of new problems with the war, a discriminatory farm policy, and other failures of leadership are especially blamed.

Certainly the views available are sufficient for creation of one or several comprehensive syntheses on the subject of the decline of the Progressive movement. But would such a view stand the test of empirical inquiry? As this writer has not undertaken a thorough bibliographical study, but only a survey of prominent contemporary historical opinion, it would be presumptuous to suggest that more monographic study is needed within the general area of the decline of progressivism. Certain needs are, however, apparent even at this point.

Above all, study of progressivism on the state and local level needs to be not only fuller in quantity, but broader in scope. Are the intellectual factors really evident? Were progressive Republicans really materially weaker after the 1912 schism? Are there additional factors in the decline of progressive Democracy, such as the long run effects of Wilson's conservative patronage policy? Does the election of 1916 in its non-presidential aspects reveal anything about progressive strength prior to American involvement in the war? Is it true that progressivism had little appeal for the immigrant?

National questions that need further exploration include the following: What was the background, political and otherwise, of the men brought into government during the war? (Was there really a significant influx of conservatives?) Just how heterogeneous was the Progressive movement? For example, just how different were the economic views of Brandeis and Perkins, Wilson and Roosevelt? Were the progressives more nationalistic than conservatives in the period 1898–1916? Did nationalism divert progressives from reform, or did the two dovetail?

Pending completion of a large number of monographic studies, especially on the state and local level, no truly definitive history of the decline of progressivism can be written. Certainly, however, a large number of potentially fruitful and not entirely unrelated hypotheses are now available as a guiding framework within which such efforts of detailed inquiry may be pursued.

NOTES

1. George E. Mowry, *Theodore Roosevelt and the Progressive Movement,* Madison, 1946, 378.
2. Charles Forcey, *The Crossroads of Liberalism,* New York, 1961, xv, xvi.
3. Arthur M. Schlesinger, Sr., *New Viewpoints in American History,* New York, 1922.

4. *Ibid.*, 110, 123, 112, 121.
5. John M. Blum, *Woodrow Wilson and the Politics of Morality,* Boston, 1956, 79.
6. John M. Blum, *Joe Tumulty and the Wilson Era,* Boston, 1951, 257. For a similar view, see Walter I. Trattner, "Progressivism and World War I: A Reappraisal," MID-AMERICA, 44 (July, 1962), 131–145, 134.
7. Arthur Mann, "The Progressive Tradition," in John Higham, ed., *The Reconstruction of American History,* New York, 1962, 162.
8. Richard Hofstadter, *The Age of Reform,* New York, 1956, 184, 195.
9. George E. Mowry, *The California Progressives,* Berkeley, 1951, 297.
10. William Leuchtenburg, "Progressivism and Imperialism: The Progressive Movement and American Foreign Policy, 1898–1916," *Mississippi Valley Historical Review,* XXXIX (December, 1952), 484.
11. *Ibid.*, 485.
12. *Ibid.*, 492, 494, 503.
13. Mowry, *Theodore Roosevelt and the Progressive Movement,* 321; Trattner, *loc. cit.*, 144; Howard W. Allen, "Republican Reformers and Foreign Policy, 1913–1917," MID-AMERICA, 44 (October, 1962), 222–229.
14. Morton G. White, *Social Thought in America,* New York, 1949; Daniel Aaron, *Men of Good Hope,* New York, 1951; Eric Goldman, *Rendezvous With Destiny,* New York, 1956; Charles Forcey, *Crossroads of Liberalism;* White has subsequently modified his opinions considerably; see the preface and epilogue to the 1961 edition.
15. Aaron, *Men of Good Hope,* 285–286.
16. David Noble, *The Paradox of Progressive Thought,* Minneapolis, 1958, 28–29.
17. *Ibid.*, 33.
18. Henry May, *The End of American Innocence,* New York, 1959.
19. *Ibid.*, 28.
20. *Ibid.*, 254.
21. *Ibid.*, 388.
22. Hofstadter, *Age of Reform,* 273.
23. *Ibid.*, 276.
24. Goldman, *Rendezvous With Destiny,* 209.
25. *Ibid.*, 208.
26. Arthur S. Link, "What Happened to the Progressive Movement in the 1920's?" *American Historical Review,* LXIV (July, 1959), 833–851, 838.
27. Harold L. Ickes, "Who Killed the Progressive Party?", *American Historical Review,* XLVI (1941), 306; Amos R. E. Pinchot, *History of the Progressive Party, 1912–1916,* ed. by Helene M. Hooker, New York, 1958.
28. John A. Garraty, *Right-Hand Man: The Life of George W. Perkins,* New York, 1960.
29. Helene M. Hooker, in Pinchot, *History of the Progressive Party,* 59.
30. Mowry, *Theodore Roosevelt and the Progressive Movement,* 284–366.
31. John M. Blum, *The Republican Roosevelt,* Cambridge, 1961.
32. Mowry, *Theodore Roosevelt and the Progressive Movement,* 252.
33. *Ibid.*, 208.

34. *Ibid.*, 367.
35. Garraty, *Right-Hand Man,* 361.
36. Mowry, *Theodore Roosevelt and the Progressive Movement,* 237–255.
37. Blum, *The Republican Roosevelt,* 149.
38. Blum, *Woodrow Wilson and the Politics of Morality,* 79.
39. Arthur S. Link, *Wilson: The New Freedom,* Princeton, 1956, 445.
40. Arthur S. Link, *Woodrow Wilson and the Progressive Movement,* New York, 1954, 223–241.
41. Link, "What Happened to the Progressive Movement," *loc. cit.,* 838.
42. *Ibid.*
43. Russel B. Nye, *Midwestern Progressive Politics,* East Lansing, 1959, 287.
44. Mowry, *The California Progressives,* 278.
45. Hofstadter, *Age of Reform,* 276.
46. Forcey, *Crossroads of Liberalism,* 275; see also Goldman, *Rendezvous With Destiny,* 196.
47. Hofstadter, *Age of Reform,* 279.
48. Link, "What Happened to the Progressive Movement, *loc. cit.,* 850.
49. *Ibid.,* 838.
50. Blum, *Woodrow Wilson and the Politics of Morality,* 152.
51. *Ibid.,* 155–156.
52. Mowry, *The California Progressives,* 293.
53. David Burner, "The Breakup of the Wilson Coalition of 1916," MID-AMERICA, 45 (January, 1963) 18–35, 18–24.
54. Arthur S. Link, *American Epoch,* New York, 1956, 255.
55. With respect to La Follette, see Robert S. Maxwell, *La Follette and the Rise of the Progressives in Wisconsin,* Madison, 1956, 173–194.
56. Mowry, *The California Progressives,* 291–292.
57. *Ibid.,* 299, 301.
58. Link, *American Epoch,* 255.
59. Kenneth Campbell MacKay, *The Progressive Movement of 1924,* New York, 1947, 12–13; 22–91.
60. Samuel Lubell, *The Future of American Politics,* second ed., revised, Garden City, 1956, 149, 137–167.
61. Hofstadter, *Age of Reform,* 281, 283, 280.

5 ∽ The Campaign of 1928 Re-Examined: A Study in Political Folklore*

[Author's Note] *One conclusion commonly drawn from the election of 1928 is that Alfred E. Smith was defeated because he was a Roman Catholic. During the campaign of 1960, an old sore was reopened as the chances of a Catholic being elected President were debated once more. The affirmative answer to the question given by the electorate in 1960 inspired Paul A. Carter to re-examine the Hoover-Smith confrontation, since it has contributed so much dialogue in political folklore. Carter waxes optimistic in his conclusion concerning toleration, finding that the 1928 campaign cannot be reduced to one between snobs and plain people, "wets" and "drys," liberals and conservatives or even Protestant against Catholic. If the anti-Smith forces were united, they were held together by the general fear of the urban East that existed in the American hinterland, a fear that John F. Kennedy also faced thirty-two years later.*

At an early stage in the presidential campaign of 1960, Denis Brogan, interpreting that campaign from a foreign perspective, wrote: "American politicians live to an extraordinary degree by historical shorthand, by the memory of past . . . episodes that 'prove' that this *must* happen or that this *cannot* happen. And high on the list of such political rules of thumb

* By Paul A. Carter. Reprinted with permission from *The Wisconsin Magazine of History,* XLVI (Summer, 1963), pages 263–272.

is the belief that 'Al' Smith was defeated in 1928 because he was a Catholic."[1]

Up until election night of 1960, and indeed in some worried minds up until the meeting of the electoral college in December, the conclusion commonly drawn from this rule of thumb was that any Catholic American who sought the Presidency could expect the same fate as Smith. But even before the nomination and election of John F. Kennedy as the first Catholic President of the United States, the rule of thumb had begun to be challenged. Richard Hofstadter, for example, said in an article published early in 1960: "There was not a Democrat alive, Protestant or Catholic, who could have beaten Hoover in 1928." John D. Hicks in a review in 1958 declared: "Had Smith been nominated in 1932, he would almost certainly have won."[2] And in 1952 Samuel Lubell, in an arresting sentence which is already reshaping the historiography of the 1920's, maintained that the 1928 election demonstrated, not the fatal weakness of a Catholic candidate for the Presidency, but precisely the reverse: "Before the Roosevelt Revolution there was an Al Smith revolution."[3]

Yet political folklore dies hard. As recently as 1956, the year in which the American Catholic who now occupies the White House began his spectacular drive to power, Edmund A. Moore examined the 1928 presidential campaign and warned that the supposed "unwritten law" against Catholic Presidents might still be in effect; therefore, politicians who were Catholics would be better advised to aim at the relatively modest office of the Vice-Presidency as a more realistic personal and political goal. Two years later, in the *dénouement* of his lucid and moving biography of Al Smith, Oscar Handlin wrote that at the time of Smith's death "no Catholic . . . could aspire to be President, whatever other avenues of advance might be open."[4]

"Can a Catholic be President?" As early as 1924, at least one American Catholic, Martin Conboy, put the question in such a way as to imply the answer "yes." In that era, when Alfred E. Smith was Governor of the nation's most populous state, there had already been a number of Catholic Governors and Senators, and two Chief Justices of the United States: "Short of the Presidency, Catholics have held every position of importance within the gift of their fellow citizens"—therefore, Conboy reasoned, why not the Presidency?[5] The closing of the question in the affirmative as of 1960 invites at least a re-examination of the question as of 1924 and especially as of 1928.

One of the discoveries of the 1960 election has been that when Americans ask themselves the question "Can a Catholic be President of the United States?" it is necessary to specify what kind of Catholic. During 1959 and 1960, the thought of John F. Kennedy as a prospective President prompted all kinds of misgivings, among both liberals and conservatives, which had nothing whatever to do with religion.[6] *Mutatis mutandis,* the same may be presumed of Al Smith in his day—although the misgivings roused by the man from Fulton Street would have been of a different sort from those roused by the man from Hyannis Port. One of President Kennedy's pre-election critics, for example, summed up his impression of the candidate in the title of an article: "The Cool Eye of John F. Kennedy."[7] It is difficult to imagine anyone making precisely this assessment of Smith. Stock campaign jokes of 1960 about the Democratic candidate's Harvard accent and his father's millions—related no doubt to the "country squire" stereotype of Franklin Roosevelt still popular among aging Republicans—are a far cry indeed from the Al Smith portrayed in some of the more savage political cartoons of 1928: a bibulous, ungrammatical roughneck.

Professor Moore in his study of the 1928 campaign has shown that the anti-Smith feeling contained a considerable element of sheer social snobbery, connected perhaps with the traditional middle-class Republican image of the Opposition as shiftless good-for-nothings—the image classically set forth in 1896 in the editorial "What's the Matter with Kansas?"[8] "Can you imagine Al Smith in the White House?" the Republican National Committeewoman for Texas asked a W.C.T.U. meeting in Houston, visualizing for them a President Smith committing *gaucheries* of grammar and etiquette; and, more to the point for that audience, "Can you imagine *Mrs.* Smith in the White House?"[9] Those last words would have rather a different ring had they been said about the former Jacqueline Bouvier!

While Moore's point on the effect of snobbery in the 1928 election is well taken, mere snobbism can not fully account for the detestation of Smith on the part of many who, like Al, could claim a heritage from the wrong side of the tracks. The most militant of all the anti-Smith forces, the Klansmen, liked to think of themselves as plain and even poor people (which some of them were), "open to the charge of being 'hicks' and 'rubes' and 'drivers of secondhand Fords.' "[10] For such voters to concur with W.C.T.U. ladies from Houston, there had to be something more than simple social condescension to unite them.[11] The common bond most frequently assumed has been anti-Catholicism. But the Woman's Christian

Temperance Union had quite another primary concern, and the members of the Ku Klux Klan spent a part of their energies in destroying whisky stills. An inescapable political issue throughout the 1920's for any candidate, regardless of his church or his manners, was Prohibition.

Common causes which unite rather widely disparate kinds of Americans—anti-Masonry, Free Soil, free silver, world peace, and most recently anti-subversion—are of course an old chapter in the republic's history. When they have been comparatively short-lived, or when they have not seemed clearly related to issues which are alive for a later generation, the emotions which such movements can arouse have often seemed inexplicably intense. Robert Moats Miller has wisely noted: "Nothing is more difficult than for an individual indifferent to a certain issue to appreciate that to others it might be of transcendent importance."[12] It can only be said again that Prohibition *was* deemed to be of transcendent importance by millions of Americans both "wet" and "dry"; the sheer bulk of serious public discussion of the issue during the 1920's is enough to document the point. Since the antiliquor crusade of the twentieth century emerged from nineteenth-century conflicts which pitted Protestant against Protestant, it would be begging the question to insist that the prohibitionist case against Smith was nothing but a cover for anti-Catholicism. Hoover was "sound" on liquor; Smith was not. For many a voter the issue was as simple as that.

Edmund A. Moore, in the able study of the 1928 election previously referred to, up to a certain point makes this same judgment: "There can be no doubt that the enforcement, by statute, of the ban on alcoholic beverages was an issue of great importance in its own right."[13] But he warns us that "Prohibition . . . was often made to play hide-and-seek with the religious issue," and suggests that the extensive debate on Prohibition may have been a sublimated version of a debate on Catholicism, frank discussion of which was "limited by a widespread sense of delicacy and shame."[14]

But to speculate on what discussants *may* have meant—on the "latent" as opposed to the "manifest" content of their discussion, so to speak—is to play a very dangerous historiographic game indeed.[15] Having in mind some of the imputations of religious prejudice in the 1960 campaign, as for example the journalistic treatment of the West Virginia presidential primary,[16] the historian of the 1928 campaign ought perhaps to be less concerned with searching out anti-Catholicism assumed to be masquerading as something else than with avoiding the error of assuming what might be called "anti-Catholicism by association." This effort, which would now be superfluous in the case of John Kennedy, is still necessary when discussing Al Smith.

And yet a further pitfall awaits the historian of Prohibition, after he has disentangled it from anti-Catholicism: the temptation to construe such a question in terms of equivalent *political* ideas, so that the Wets become "liberal" and the Drys become "conservative." This reading of the question then becomes assimilable to a liberal-versus-conservative reading of the Smith-Hoover campaign more generally, especially when one notices that four of the conservative "solid-South" states carried by Herbert Hoover were subsequently to be twice carried by Dwight Eisenhower, and three of them again by Richard Nixon. But in the case of Prohibition, at least, these "left"—"right" categories of political ideology break down; the present writer has shown elsewhere that a progressive, social-welfare, and even radical outlook pervaded the anti-liquor movement at least in its incipient stages and to some extent throughout its existence.[17] So unquestionably liberal a journal as the *Christian Century* justified supporting Hoover in 1928 on prohibitionist grounds;[18] and one social radical in 1932, finding the Democrats, the Republicans, and the Socialists either insufficiently liberal, insufficiently "dry," or both, by process of elimination voted Communist![19]

Conversely, there were "wet" conservatives. Senator Oscar Underwood, for example, in his later years condemned the Eighteenth Amendment because it "challenged the integrity of the compact between the States" and compelled men "to live their lives in the mold prescribed by the power of government." The Alabama Senator argued, furthermore, that the Drys could no more force their interpretation on the Eighteenth Amendment on the Wets than the North could force its interpretation of the Fourteenth Amendment on the South.[20] When one reflects that this same conservative Southern Senator had courageously denounced the Ku Klux Klan at the Democratic Convention of 1924 and thereby ruined his own chances of being a presidential nominee, the campaign of 1928 which followed becomes even harder to see in "liberal" versus "conservative" terms.

Yet Smith himself is persistently seen by his latter-day admirers as a "liberal" who became "conservative" only upon the failure of his "liberal" expectations. He was not always seen in this light, However, by his contemporaries; Walter Lippmann wrote in 1925: "[Smith] is really a perfectly conservative man about property. . . . He believes in the soundness of the established order. . . . He is what a conservative ought to be always if he knew his business."[21] When one finds a *New York Times* story on June 27th, the second day of the 1928 Democratic National Convention, headlined "Stocks up in 'Smith Market' as Raskob tells business it need not fear the governor," one begins to understand what Lippmann was talking about: "Market leaders such as General Motors, United States Steel, Anaconda Copper, Allied Chemical and New York Central, had a sharp run-up. . . . Buying orders poured in so rapidly . . . that Wall Street began talking of a 'Smith market.' Friends of the Governor were said to be actively in the market, prepared to demonstrate that the financial and business interests are not hostile to his candidacy."

One of these friends of the Governor was John J. Raskob, whose remarks, the *Times* noted apparently without irony, "frequently have stimulated buying enthusiasm in the stock market." Franklin Roosevelt, among others, had serious misgivings about Smith's choice of Raskob as Democratic national chairman, largely on account of this Wall Street taint[22]—yet some of Smith's putative liberalism has rubbed off on the General Motors financier, who is described in Oscar Handlin's biography of Al Smith as "another poor boy who had come up in the world." Raskob grew up, Handlin writes, in "the free-and-easy atmosphere of Detroit where religious prejudice seemed altogether out of place."[23] Remembering the notorious anti-Semitism of the then president of the leading competitor of General Motors, one is a little surprised at hearing Detroit described as being a city altogether free of religious prejudice; here is another indication that a straight liberal/conservative interpretation of the campaign of 1928 must be burdened with more ideological freight than it can carry.

Moore, in contrast to Handlin, sees Raskob's role in the campaign in terms not of liberalism but of expediency: the Democrats had to win some of the business community away from its prosperous love affair with Hoover Republicanism, and Raskob was their instrument for this purpose. But had not the candidacies of stanch "gold standard" advocate Alton B. Parker in 1904 and corporation counsel John W. Davis in 1924 demonstrated that Democratic attempts to beat Republican conservatism at its own game usually failed? Moore does note that Raskob's appointment as national chairman "seemed like an insult to the dry, Protestant, rural South";[24] was it not equally an insult to the Democratic Party's anti-corporate, anti-speculative Progressives and liberals?

If, then, the campaign of 1928 will not reduce to a campaign between liberals and conservatives, snobs and plain people, or Wets and Drys, are we then left with Protestant against Catholic by process of elimination? Not necessarily. Let us return again to the contemporary assessment of Smith by Walter Lippmann: "The Governor's more hasty friends show an intolerance when they believe that Al Smith is the victim of purely religious prejudice. . . . There is an opposition to Smith which is as authentic and, it seems to me, as poignant as his support. It is inspired by the feeling that the clamorous life of the city should not be acknowledged as the American ideal."[25]

Closely allied to the image of the corner saloon in American folklore has been the image of the Eastern city slicker. It is a venerable one; dissipated urban vice in contrast to abstemious rural virtue are themes as old in history as are cities themselves. In America, as witness Jefferson's *Notes on Virginia* and Royall Tyler's play *The Contrast,* they antedate the Constitution. There is also a long-standing tradition of the South and the West perennially arrayed politically against the urban East, almost regardless of the specific political issues confronting America at any given moment. The anti-Smith country in the election of 1928 was, by and large, the old Bryan country—which suggests that the Prohibition issue, and the Klan issue, and possibly even the Catholic issue, were surface stirrings of animosities of another kind. It may be noted in passing that this same trans-Mississippi Bryan country of 1896, which had become Hoover country by 1928,[26] was to become Nixon country in 1960 and Goldwater country in the maneuverings which followed; so perhaps President Kennedy and Governor Smith had more in common as actors of an American political role than simply their religion, or their status as (by definition) liberal Democrats.

"The principal obstacle in Smith's way," wrote a contemporary observer of the preconvention maneuverings of 1928, "never becomes palpable. . . . It lies in the fact that to millions of Americans he . . . embodies something alien. Not something alien in race or religion, but something alien to themselves . . . something they do not understand and which they feel does not understand them. . . . Some of the perturbed Methodist clergymen in the South opposed to Smith's nomination unconsciously revealed what really moves them most profoundly . . . when they said he was 'New York minded.' "[27]

Had these words been written by one of those same perturbed Methodist clergymen, or indeed by any other Protestant, or even by a secularist liberal such as Lippmann, [28] they could be cited as merely an unusually tortuous rationalization for anti-Catholicism. But they were written *by a Catholic,* and were printed in the Catholic liberal weekly *Commonweal.* And, conscious that bogeymen are not slain by one magazine article, the writer, Charles Willis Thompson, returned to the fray some months later in the *Catholic World,* with a piece entitled "The Tammany Monster." This second article was a ringing defense of the "monster" against attacks by the kind of outlander (Thompson mentioned Iowa, Nebraska, Oklahoma, and Little Rock, Arkansas) who viewed the mysterious East and all its works as evil, saying: "Tammany and Wall Street are the same thing, aren't they?"[29]

Smith's own managers and friends were aware of this widespread fear of the urban East in the American hinterland. Norman Hapgood and Henry Moskowitz, in their campaign biography of Smith in 1927 (significantly titled *Up From the City Streets*), faced the problem squarely. The story of Al Smith, they wrote, "suggests that in the future our vast cities may do better by humanity than we have feared." Specifically, the politics characteristic of great cities, abhorred by some as "machine" or "Tammany" politics, might have creative possibilities undreamed of in the Mississippi Valley. Smith, in particular, "has been a product of the machine and . . . has remained a member of it, and at the same time has become a leader of the most progressive thought of the United States." Corner saloon politics, these authors argued, were not in essence very different from country store politics. Far from regarding "the machine" as oppressive and corrupt, the urban poor among whom Al Smith had grown up "were convinced that Tammany Hall was kind to them." Pressing this interpretation perhaps a shade too far in their enthusiasm, Hapgood and Moskowitz defined machine politics as "neighborliness—which on election day is translated into votes."[30]

For the rural voter, who on successive days during the spring of 1928 might have seen headlines such as "Chicago's Election Starts with Kidnapping" and "Deneen Ticket Leads; His Candidate Slain," such a concept of big-city neighborliness was rather hard to take.[31] New York was, of course, not Chicago, especially in 1928 when the Capone organization was near its peak; but to the rural mind one big city was much like another.[32] With this problem in mind, local leaders in some rural areas —not all of them Democrats—strove to bridge the chasm between their constituents' world and Al Smith's.

One of the most interesting of these attempts, particularly in the light of what happened later in the campaign, was made by the Republican editor of the Emporia *Gazette,* William Allen White. Writing to Franklin D. Roosevelt on February 11, 1928, on behalf of the Kansas State Editorial Association, White invited Al Smith to come out to Kansas, "the center of the world which Smith does not know and which does not know Smith." "Smith is supposed to have horns and a tail out west," he wrote, and a confrontation between the New York Governor and a bipartisan group of Western newspaper editors "would do more for him politically than any other one thing he might possibly do."[33] Frank Freidel has noted that Roosevelt tried to persuade Smith to accept this invitation, but failed;[34] in that failure may lie a subtle indication of one reason for the failure of Smith's entire campaign.

The aftermath of this friendly gesture was saddening and distasteful. Throughout his life, William Allen White was the kind of partisan who can be a man of good will toward the Opposition "three and a half years out of every four," as Franklin Roosevelt himself later put it.[35] As the campaign grew hotter than it ever could have been in February, even in 1928, an organization man "regular" enough to have supported Harding and Coolidge when the time came[36] could have been expected to be drawn into the fray against Smith, even though White credited Al with "one of the important brains now functioning in American politics."[37] But, as Professor Moore has shown at length in his study of the campaign, White's attacks on Smith went far beyond the generally acceptable limits of campaign behavior. White wrote that Smith's record as governor showed the New Yorker to be "soft" not only on Prohibition but also on gambling and prostitution. Worse, when he realized the enormity of such a charge when unproven, his retraction was grudging and ambiguous.[38] It was, Moore concludes, a shocking lapse in a theretofore conspicuously honorable political career.

Professor Moore conjoins William Allen White's charges against the Governor with those of the Fundamentalist Baptist leader in New York City, the Rev. John Roach Straton—a conjunction which strongly implies that White's and Straton's warfare with Smith comes down essentially to the same thing, namely, anti-Catholicism. White in this period of the campaign saw Al Smith as a threat to "the whole Puritan civilization which has built a sturdy, orderly nation";[39] and Moore comments: "Of course one important facet of the 'whole Puritan civilization' was its stanchly Protestant character." Moore finds this attitude of the Kansas editor particularly "confused and distressing" because White, in a book which was already in press while these attacks were going on, "was about to present Smith in an essentially favorable light."[40]

A re-reading of *Masks in a Pageant,* the work referred to, leads the present writer to a conclusion somewhat different from Professor Moore's. References to "Puritanism" and "a Puritan civilization" occur throughout White's writings in contexts having little or nothing to do with Smith or Catholicism. His apt characterization of Calvin Coolidge as "a Puritan in Babylon," for example, loses all its bite if the most cautious of all of America's Presidents is made merely a *Protestant* in Babylon. And parenthetically it may be observed that President Kennedy has had some notoriously kind words to say about Puritanism.[41] What worried White far more than Al Smith's religious affiliation, or even his "wet" sympathies, was the old Jeffersonian bugbear of the great city as an enemy of liberty. In *Masks in a Pageant,* White was trying not only to reassure his readers about Smith but also to reassure himself about Smith's background.

William Allen White was aware that great cities had brought forth American Presidents before, and he cited Theodore Roosevelt—whose faithful vassal he himself had been—and Chester A. Arthur. But neither of these two men "was purely urbanite" (recall Mark Hanna's "damn cowboy" epithet hurled at T.R., for example), whereas Al Smith was "urbanite with an urbanity unstrained . . . city born, city bred, 'city broke,' city minded, and city hearted." And, White's urban reader might well have asked, why not? The Kansas editor did his best to agree: "There is no reason why the back alley cannot produce as good moral, spiritual, mental, and physical timber for politics as the backwoods. . . . The streets educated [Smith] as the woods and fields educated Lincoln." And yet, backwoods and back alley were inevitably headed for conflict in the twentieth century; "industrial democracy" was destined to "struggle for supremacy with . . . rural democracy—the America of our past."[42]

As a determined political progressive, White was intellectually on the side of the new order; as a product of the Kansas frontier he was emotionally drawn to the old. The most revealing fact about the Al Smith sketch in White's *Masks in a Pageant* is that the author grouped it at the end of the book in a section titled "The Young Princes of Democracy"—and his other young prince was Mayor William Hale "Big Bill" Thompson of Chicago. The Al Smith essay *was,* in the main, favorable to Smith; but Al and Big Bill were of the same species in White's mind. In the epigraph to that part of the book, White wrote: "When we have sloughed off our rural philosophy—our fundamental Puritanism—we shall crown the young princes. In the meantime the warning is plain: 'Put not your trust in princes!' "[43]

With mistrust of White's sort rampant throughout the Bryan country, it is understandable that practicing Democrats in the spring of 1928 might have cast about for a candidate who could hold Al Smith's constituents without alienating William Allen White's; ideally, a Catholic who was not one of the young princes. Predictably, some of them found him, in a state even more rural than Kansas. On March 4, Senator Thomas J. Walsh of Montana tossed his hat into the ring.[44] On May 1, he was knocked out of the running in the California presidential primary;[45] but in the meantime he had posed a major obstacle for the hypothesis of an "unwritten law" governing Catholic candidates. What is one to make of the fact that, in Professor Moore's words, "The two leading candidates for the Democratic nomination in 1928 were Catholic [and] one of them was nominated"?[46] If the Walsh candidacy was a stalking-horse to divide the Catholic vote, as has been suggested,[47] clearly the effort was unsuccessful; and if it was a serious bid for the Presidency, then the "unwritten law" was already well on the way to being a dead letter. In either case, conclusions about toleration in American life more optimistic than those which have been customarily drawn for the 1920's would seem to be in order.

NOTES

NOTE: This article originated as a paper read before the meeting of the Mississippi Valley Historical Association at Detroit, Michigan, April 21, 1961. A portion of the paper dealing with the preconvention presidential candidacy of Senator Thomas J. Walsh of Montana has been omitted.

1. D. W. Brogan, "The Shadow of Al Smith," in the *Manchester Guardian Weekly,* May 19, 1960.
2. Richard Hofstadter, "Could a Protestant Have Beaten Hoover in 1928?," *The Reporter,* 22: 31*ff*. (March 17, 1960); John D. Hicks reviewing Oscar Handlin, *Al Smith and His America,* in the *American Historical Review,* XLIV:203 (October, 1958); see also Robert K. Murray reviewing Edmund A. Moore, *A Catholic Runs for President,* in the *Mississippi Valley Historical Review,* XLIII:516 (December, 1956): " 'Bible Belt' Republicans were not the only political species who sought the demise of the former employee of the Fulton Fish Market."

3. Samuel Lubell, *The Future of American Politics* (2nd ed. rev., New York, 1956), 36. See also the earlier judgment by Roy V. Peel and Thomas C. Donnolly, *The 1928 Campaign: An Analysis* (New York, 1931), 171.
4. Edmund A. Moore, *A Catholic Runs for President: The Campaign of 1928* (New York, 1956), 200; Oscar Handlin, *Al Smith and His America* (Boston, 1958), 189.
5. Martin Conboy, "Can a Catholic be President?", in the *Forum,* LXXII:76*ff.* (July, 1924); Professor Moore (*op. cit.,* 30) discusses this article but draws from it a conclusion different from that of the present paper.
6. A characteristic liberal example is Margaret Halsey, "I'm Not All Right, Jack," in *Frontier: The Voice of the New West,* XI:5*ff.* (September, 1960). A characteristic conservative example is the lead editorial, "Jack Should Worry, Jack Should Fret," Chicago *Tribune,* July 26, 1960.
7. Douglass Cater, "The Cool Eye of John F. Kennedy," in *The Reporter,* 21:27*ff.* (December 10, 1959).
8. This anti-Populist, anti-Bryan editorial has been widely reprinted both in its own day and in ours; *vid., e.g.,* William Allen White, *Autobiography* (New York, 1946), 280*ff.*
9. Quoted in Moore, *op. cit.,* 159. Italics supplied.
10. Hiram Wesley Evans, Imperial Wizard of the Ku Klux Klan, quoted by Richard Hofstadter in *The Age of Reform: From Bryan to FDR* (New York, 1955), 294. Professor Hofstadter uses the same quotation again in *Anti-Intellectualism in American Life* (New York, 1963), 124. Evans' statement originally appeared in the *North American Review,* CCXXIII:38*ff.* (March–April–May, 1926).
11. And yet, paradoxically, the Klan-minded *were* susceptible to snobbism, as is shown by the cartoon which appeared in the KKK's Washington organ, *Fellowship Forum,* November 3, 1928. This may be involved in the psychology of a proletarianized, yet status-conscious American extreme Right, a phenomenon which has been noted by Hofstadter, Daniel Bell, Peter Viereck, and others.
12. Robert Moats Miller, "A Footnote to the Role of the Protestant Churches in the Election of 1928," *Church History,* XXV:149 (June, 1956). Substantially this same essay appears as Chapter IV of Miller, *American Protestantism and Social Issues, 1919–1939* (Chapel Hill, 1958), 48*ff.*
13. Moore, *op. cit.,* 39, 117.
14. *Ibid.,* 41. Professor Kenneth K. Bailey, in a paper read before the American Historical Association on December 28, 1960, titled "Southern White Protestantism and the Campaign of 1928," dwelt at some length on prohibitionism as a politically unifying (and divisive!) force among Southern churchmen, but nevertheless concluded that "the corporate churches and their spokesmen cannot be absolved from complicity in the smear campaign often imputed to the Ku Klux Klan fringe of Protestantism," thereby aligning himself more nearly with Professor Moore's point of view than with Professor Miller's or my own. In a letter to the author of the present paper, March 20, 1961, he elaborated: "My feeling is that the religious question was much more vital in the South than the churches and churchman admitted. . . . It was one of those issues, like race, which didn't have to be talked about much to carry great weight."
15. The present writer is fully aware that he is himself on record as holding views similar to Professor Moore's and Professor Bailey's; *vid.* P. A. Carter, *The*

Decline and Revival of the Social Gospel (Ithaca, N.Y., 1956), 40. He now regards himself, along with others of the guild who too uncritically accepted the "unwritten law" hypothesis as having been mistaken.

16. *Vid.* discussion of Joseph Alsop's treatment of the West Virginia campaign in the *New Republic,* 142:5 (April 25, 1960); reply by Alsop in *ibid.,* May 2, 1960, 11*f.* The editors of the *New Republic* noted, May 9, 1960, not only that the convincing Kennedy victory in West Virginia refuted Alsop's charges of bigotry in 1960, but also that Al Smith, running against a Baptist, Senator Reed, had carried this same West Virginia presidential primary in 1928. That observation would seem to support the general thesis of the present paper.
17. Carter, *op. cit.,* Chap. III: "Prohibition, Left and Right." Professor Miller comes to essentially the same conclusion in the essay cited, note 12, *supra.* And *cf.* Walter G. Muelder, *Methodism and Society in the Twentieth Century* (New York and Nashville, 1961), 56: "Both Prohibition and Woman Suffrage were heralded as victories for purer politics, a cleaner national life, and an effective public control of political life. They were thus not isolated issues, but integral parts of the inclusive reform programs of the Progressive Era."
18. *Christian Century,* XLV:530*f.,* 594*f.,* 818*ff.* (1928), cited by Donald B. Meyer, *The Protestant Search for Political Realism, 1919–1941* (Berkeley and Los Angels, 1960), 429n, 112.
19. *Ibid.,* 179. Meyer cautions (p. 435) that "the case was not quite clear," inasmuch as the man in question had been a socialist anyway; but it is significant that he nevertheless felt constrained to offer a "dry" rationale for his action, not only in the *Christian Century* but also in the *New Leader,* XIII:6 (1932), as cited by Meyer.
20. Oscar W. Underwood, *Drifting Sands of Party Politics* (New York and London, 1928), 365, 376, 391.
21. Walter Lippmann, *Men of Destiny* (New York, 1927; the essay on Smith originally published December, 1925), 4*f.*
22. Frank Freidel, *Franklin D. Roosevelt: The Ordeal* (Boston, 1954), 246, citing Roosevelt to Daniels, July 20, 1928; Moore, *op. cit.,* 122*f.,* citing the same letter.
23. Handlin, *op. cit.,* 127, 128.
24. Moore, *op. cit.,* 121.
25. Lippmann, *op. cit.,* 8.
26. But, pursuant to Mr. Lubell's "Al Smith revolution," it should be pointed out that, whether or not it was true that Smith "had not fully studied the farm problem" (Moore, *op. cit.,* 119; Handlin, *op. cit.,* 129, disagrees), nevertheless the Democrats in 1928 made some inroads into traditional Republican strength even in farm areas. On this point *vid.* Gilbert C. Fite, "The Agricultural Issue in the Presidential Campaign of 1928," in the *Mississippi Valley Historical Review,* XXXVII:653*ff.,* (March, 1951).
27. Charles Willis Thompson, "The Unseen Factors in Politics," *Commonweal,* VIII:95 (May 30, 1928).
28. The writer classifies Lippmann as a "secularist" at this period because he was about to publish *A Preface to Morals* (1929). Whether the term "liberal" is fully applicable to Lippmann at that time is perhaps open to question.
29. Charles Willis Thompson, "The Tammany Monster," in the *Catholic World,* CXXVIII:1–9 (October, 1928). Thompson is described by the editors of that

journal as a Republican (*ibid.*, 111); his defense of Tammany may therefore be presumed a reasonably disinterested one.

30. Norman Hapgood and Henry Moskowitz, *Up from the City Streets: A Life of Alfred E. Smith* (New York, 1927), 3, 95, 45, 42.
31. Great Falls (Montana) *Tribune*, April 10 and 11, 1928.
32. C. W. Thompson, in the *Catholic World* article cited previously (note 29, *supra*), tried to distinguish between the governments of New York and of other large cities, as well as between the party organizations in each of New York's own five boroughs.
33. White to Roosevelt, February 11, 1928; reprinted in Walter Johnson, ed., *Selected Letters of William Allen White* (New York, 1947), 282.
34. Freidel, *op. cit.*, 229n.
35. Walter Johnson, *op. cit.*, 13*f.*, quoting FDR.
36. On White's rationalized support of Harding in 1920 (having opposed him at the nominating convention), *vid.* W. A. White, *Autobiography*, 596*f.*; on his support of Coolidge in 1924, *vid.* Johnson, *op. cit.*, 12. When an election was not actually under way White could be remarkably detached about politicians (always excepting Theodore Roosevelt); *cf.* the appraisal of Harding in the *Autobiography*, Chap. LXXXVI ("An American Tragedy"), and of Coolidge in White's *A Puritan in Babylon* (New York, 1938).
37. White to Roosevelt, as cited in note 33, *supra.*
38. This episode is discussed and described in Moore, *op. cit.*, 129–136.
39. *Ibid.*, 131, citing AP dispatch (July 15, 1928) which thus quoted White.
40. Moore, *op. cit.*, 129*f.*
41. Examples: the discussion of the cultural heritage of John Quincy Adams in *Profiles in Courage* (New York, 1956), Chap. 2; the praise of the "courage—judgment—integrity—dedication" of the builders of the Bay colony by the President-elect before the Massachusetts General Court on January 9, 1961 (*New York Times*, January 10, 1961).
42. William Allen White, *Masks in a Pageant* (New York, 1928), 465*f.*, 473*ff.*, 479.
43. *Ibid.*, 462.
44. L. C. Speers, "Walsh of Montana Throws in His Hat," *New York Times*, March 11, 1928.
45. Walsh attributed his defeat, under California's cross-filing and cross-voting system, to "thirsty Republicans and misguided Drys." AP dispatch, May 2, 1928. The Senator, it may be noted, was a teetotaler, though a Catholic—a factor which had contributed to his initial availability.
46. Moore, *op. cit.*, 93. Moore believes that "an attack on Walsh as a Catholic would surely have been made had he been nominated"; but he concedes that "except in a most indirect and farfetched way, Walsh could not have symbolized, as did Al Smith, the insistent claims for more recognition of the newer and urban population groups."
47. This charge was made, *e.g.*, in the *Catholic World*, CXXVII:104 (April, 1928). But J. Leonard Bates, who is writing a scholarly biography of the Senator, has the impression that Walsh "wanted the nomination pretty badly." Bates to author, January 28, 1961.

III ~ *The Diplomacy of the 1920's: Isolationist?*

6 ~ The House Divided*

[Author's Note] *After a careful mining of important sources, Selig Adler, Samuel Paul Capen Professor of History at the State University of New York at Buffalo, finds that internationalism in the twenties was relative rather than absolute. Although he views the twenties as basically isolationist, Adler recognizes a plethora of internationalist groups and individuals who were, albeit largely ineffective because of their inability to unite upon a program, certainly conspicuous on the American scene.*

"I suppose," wrote Elihu Root in 1922, "that the people of the United States have learned more about international relations within the past eight years than they had learned in the preceding eighty years. They are, however, only at the beginning of the task."[1] Root might have added that the war had taught many people how to rationalize their isolationist convictions. On the other hand, the years of strife had also reinforced internationalist thinking. Before 1914, the masses had been indifferent and only a few cosmopolites were aware that vital American interests had been projected far beyond the water's edge. Despite the vigor of the new isolationist coalition, the friends of international organization were more numerous, more vocal, and more potent in the 1920s than they had ever been in the quiet years before the holocaust. "The literature of 'Internationalism,' " complained the editor of the Grand Rapids *Herald*, Arthur H. Vandenberg, in 1925, "continues at flood-tide."[2]

Thus the postwar decline in internationalist zeal was relative rather than absolute. Educators, liberal clergymen, club women, idealistic

* Reprinted from *The Isolationist Impulse* by Selig Adler. Pages 118–136. By permission of Abelard-Schuman, Ltd.

journalists, public officials, and enlightened businessmen challenged the basic concepts of the renovated isolationism. After the war, crucial decisions in American foreign policy could be made only after both sides had had their say.

The isolationists were trying to hold back the integrating forces of the twentieth century. Once the United States had been initiated into the wiles of power politics, there was no turning back, for the lessons of the war had been too encompassing. At home and abroad horizons were steadily widening. Provincialism was lessened by trips in Model T Fords, by movies filmed in Hong Kong or Timbuktu, and by radio broadcasts tuned in through crystal sets from the capitals of the world. Foreign correspondents, books, and magazines all stressed European and Asiatic affairs. Although soldiers brought back stout prejudices, they also returned with a more cosmopolitan outlook. Isolationism now had to be defended, something quite unnecessary when the policy reflected genuine salt-water insulation. The philosophy no longer enjoyed a monopoly of thought, for it now had to contend with rival attitudes based upon more realistic foundations. As rapid transportation and communication brought the nations together, it became increasingly apparent that war could not be quarantined. The march of science had undermined the Irreconcilable position.

The isolationists, nevertheless, still held certain great advantages. Their gospel was simple, direct, and easy to comprehend. They followed in the footprints of what had once been a great and universally popular tradition. Isolationist rural areas were over-represented in Congress, thanks to the workings of the Constitution. Above all, the isolationists were better able to settle basic differences among themselves than were the internationalists. It is always easier to unite against something than to muster unity for so specific a cause as the League of Nations, and the internationalists were unable to do even that.

The array of internationally minded men and organizations of the twenties is large and impressive. Their effectiveness, however, was seriously hindered by failure to agree upon a program. The only feasible and tangible peace plan in the postwar years was the League. Yet many internationalists could not overcome their initial distaste for any organization that sanctioned the use of force. This was tantamount to spurning any program that held a reasonable expectation of success.

Some of the most stalwart opponents of the League were, in theory, internationalists rather than isolationists. Liberal and pacifist critics of the Covenant were often willing to sacrifice aspects of national sovereignty in the interests of peace. But in effect they were isolationists because they opposed all peace efforts related to the League. Nor were these theoretical internationalists able to agree among themselves on an alternate peace formula. Frequently, confirmed internationalists made common cause with the Irreconcilables in order to defeat some specific proposal. Circumstances had made the League the object of a tug of war, and there were strange partners on each end of the rope.

Many of the internationalists were only half-hearted converts to the cause. Deep down in their hearts they still clung to the old belief that the United States would always be safe and secure regardless of the outcome of their efforts. Therefore, many of their campaigns lacked a sense of urgency, for peace in Europe was not seriously threatened until the next decade. While a majority of the internationalists remained true to the League ideal, there were those who wanted the impossible—a maximum amount of world leadership with a minimum risk of foreign entanglements.

Another factor in the perplexity of the twenties was derived from the nature of our government. Congress and public opinion always had to be taken into consideration, and both were afflicted with "insular sclerosis." Shortsighted political bromides were found to yield more votes than candid disclosures of unpleasant facts to an electorate eager to enjoy the new affluence. (Perhaps there is something to Clement Attlee's observation that our Constitution was designed for an "isolationist state.") Yet despite all the smugness, men sought to influence the formation of foreign policy as never before. Secretary of State Charles Evans Hughes later complained of the telegrams that fell like snowflakes in a thick storm, clouding each issue with diverse opinions. He commented upon the great amount of knowledge needed to appraise even a single diplomatic decision.[3] This was a new dilemma for the modern democracies, for streamlined pressure techniques threatened to destroy the time-honored *in camera* habits of the statesmen. Diplomacy, too, was in danger of becoming socialized.

Elihu Root cautioned that if the masses insisted upon influencing foreign policy, they must learn the facts lest ignorance and error should govern our decisions. To be sure, international affairs were studied now as never before—in schools, colleges, service clubs, press columns, and institutes. Often, however, confusion was only intensified. Peace, rather than national security in the broadest sense, was made the goal. Headlines and digests oversimplified complex situations. Commentators seldom made allowance for the temper of less fortunate nations and cavalierly assumed that Americans had cornered the market on international morality. Only a minority recognized that the world's best chance for peace lay in an effective association that must necessarily include the United States. Hence the contradiction: as American political, economic, and moral influence penetrated to all parts of the globe, we withdrew into the cocoon of a rejuvenated isolationism and left the peace to the safekeeping of other nations.

Educators and liberal ministers rose to expose this inconsistency. Frederick Jackson Turner stated that a shrinking earth was compelled by irrepressible forces to exercise restraint, to associate, agree, and adjust, or to commit suicide. It was pointed out by Dean Frank Thilly of Cornell that whether the people would admit it or not, every disturbance in the economic, political, and social arrangements of other states would inevitably affect our national life. Former Harvard President Charles W. Eliot, long an internationalist crusader, spent his octogenarian years denouncing those senators who beguiled the masses with specious words.

Foundation lectures, designed to dispense information leading to a more enlightened world order, were the current fad. Edward W. Bok, the Dutch immigrant boy who became a famous editor, helped to launch the new Walter Hines Page School of International Relations at Johns Hopkins. In nearby Washington, Georgetown University had its School of Foreign Service, and the Jesuit Fathers sponsored popular lectures. Current events, and sometimes even American diplomatic history, were emphasized in high school classrooms.

International education, in the modern sense, dates from the establishment of the Rhodes Scholarships in 1904. At the end of the First World War, Nicholas Murray Butler, Elihu Root, and Professor Stephen P. Duggan of the City College of New York fostered the movement by establishing an Institute of International Education. Founded on a shoestring, the Institute acted as a clearing house for American students who wished to study abroad, and encouraged public and private groups to subsidize international cultural exchange. (The program of the Institute was given a tremendous fillip when, in 1946, Congress passed the Fulbright Act which authorized the Secretary of State to use funds from the sale of surplus war materials to finance American students studying abroad and to bring foreign students to our own universities. Later, Congress expanded the plan in order to facilitate the exchange of teaching personnel throughout the free world. In 1956, the Ford and Rockefeller Foundations and the Carnegie Corporation gave over five million dollars to the Institute of International Education. Between 1919 and 1955, 212,696 persons from some 151 countries and political areas left their homelands to further their education.)

Prior to the Second World War, however, if faculty and students on campuses throughout the world showed interest in the fitful progress of the League of Nations, their voices were smothered by the hordes of Babbitts who surrounded the cloistered walls of the universities.

In the religious world, while American Catholics tended to be anti-League because of Irish and sometimes German affinities, worldly Protestant clergymen were usually international cooperationists. Their motives were varied. In some cases the old missionary spirit called for a League of Nations to save the Armenians from the hands of the atrocious Turks. Modernists projected their evangelical impulses in a move to spread the benefits of American education, science and sanitation to far away countries. Such ministers were advocates of a social gospel that sublimated into humanitarian channels the energy that had once been used to fight the Devil. Religion's paramount duty, they said, was to conquer war by teaching the necessity for cooperation among nations. Unfortunately, there was no real coordination of effort or general agreement on program. Time and again disjointed action was to foil the efforts of the internationalists.

The Federal Council of Churches of Christ in America (now the National Council of the Churches of Christ in the United States of America) emerged from the war as the most powerful pressure group of its kind. Its Commission on International Justice and Goodwill flooded the country with propaganda. Originally the Federal Council blessed Geneva as an agent of Christian unity, but it retreated to preach internationalism while seldom mentioning the League by name. The World Alliance for International Friendship through the Churches, a wartime offshoot of Andrew Carnegie's Church Peace Union, followed a somewhat similar policy. Two groups, however, continued to call for American entry into the Covenant—the Methodist Episcopal Church, one of the two largest Protestant sects in the country, and the National Synod of the Reformed Presbyterian Church. Such a step was also urged by the nationally prominent Episcopal Bishop of Western New York, Charles H. Brent.

There was a marked tendency toward pacifism in some religious circles. In 1925, the Central Conference of American Rabbis (constituting the liberal wing of Jewish religious thinking) created a Commission on Justice and Peace. The Commission, which showed a penchant for pacifism, avoided the divisive League issue, and urged policies upon the Conference that would strike at war in other ways. The current movement to outlaw war made powerful inroads among all religious groups. Fundamentalist Christians proclaimed that this was God's world and the war system must go along with slavery and the saloon.

Additional pro-peace sentiment came from the distaff energy released when the women's suffrage movement terminated logically with the adoption of the Nineteenth Amendment. Limitation of families, urban apartments, prepared foods, and labor-saving household gadgets found increasing numbers of college-bred women with too much leisure time on their hands. While the League idea enjoyed great popularity among the silk-stocking women, it was by no means acceptable to all. The newly formed League of Women Voters discovered that disarmament held out a far better promise of rallying its membership behind a peace program. Why, asked *The Woman Citizen,* descend into the valley of the shadow of death to bear a son to be sacrificed to Mars in 1940? The *Ladies' Home Journal,* as well, campaigned for the scrapping of arms. While these forces were not necessarily anti-Geneva, it was another case of not pushing the one plan that *might* have worked. Some women were not satisfied with merely ignoring collective security, and Jeannette Rankin (the first woman who was elected to Congress and who voted against entry into both World Wars) helped organize the American Women Opposed to [the] League of Nations.[4]

The press reflected the quickened interest in foreign affairs. Three factors influenced newspaper treatment of international relations: completion of the pre-war trend of consolidation of independent dailies into huge chains; the increasing importance of the foreign correspondent; and the rising popularity of the columnist. All over the country newspapers were becoming standardized by using the same syndicated pieces. The consolidated press wielded a terrific influence on the dispensation of news and the consequent formation of public opinion.

Despite some important exceptions, most of the newspaper chains had strong isolationist leanings. Even among papers that remained independent, there was a large overturn in ownership. Frequently, affluent Republicans bought up tottering journals in order to nurse them back to health. They, or their editors, accepted the new isolationism as a tenet of G.O.P. orthodoxy. There was an increasing tendency toward a one-party press. "Democrats everywhere," complained a citizen of Iowa, "are compelled to read Republican daily newspapers. They have no choice."[5] In Coolidge's day, Minnesota and Iowa had hardly a single Democratic journal of any importance.[6] Even Chicago was said to be without a Democratic daily and, in the hinterland, the few remaining rural papers were being rapidly absorbed by owners with Republican leanings.

Among the press moguls were veteran enemies of the League of

Nations. Frank A. Munsey had done yeoman work for the Irreconcilables. One of his Washington correspondents served as Borah's walking encyclopaedia, while another kept up a running correspondence with Beveridge. Munsey had regarded the whole League plan as a dangerous scheme to gratify the whims "of the greatest autocrat of all time."[7] His newspaper empire grew rapidly after the war. By 1923 he controlled the *Sun, Telegram, and Herald* in New York alone, and was about to absorb the *Globe,* the *Evening Mail,* and the *Commercial Advertiser.* Obviously all of these papers could not pay, so Munsey merged a number of them and, in the journalistic world, his touch was held to be the kiss of death. To him, any traffic with the League was equivalent to a surrender of independence.

Munsey's counterpart was William Randolph Hearst, who, wrote William Allen White in a private letter, "is my idea of a rattlesnake crossed with the smallpox . . . I would not work for him for any money on earth."[8] Part of Hearst's exasperating chauvinism was a cover-up for his reluctance to fight Germany. As he expanded his empire in the twenties, there was no deviation from this narrow patriotism. His newspapers listed a circulation of 3,400,060 in 1923 and the chain was still growing! One American family in four, it was said, regularly read a Hearst publication. With his own morning and evening news service, and control of the King Features Syndicate, Hearst was almost invulnerable. Lloyd George was enticed into writing for him, and newspaper feature syndicators, who despised his methods, accepted his contracts. Unpredictable on many subjects, impossible to type as a conservative, liberal, racist, imperialist or anti-imperialist, Republican or Democrat, Hearst's only consistency was a vicious type of parochial isolationism. He even regarded naval disarmament as a British-Japanese plot to scuttle the American fleet. He was, however, willing to make an agreement among the English-speaking peoples to keep peace among themselves and to promote it in the world. Probably Hearst and Munsey reflected, rather than shaped, the opinions of many of their readers; yet both dabbled in politics to strengthen the isolationist congressional clique. They certainly nurtured the prevailing tendency with their editorials contrasting our own moral superiority with the congenital wickedness of other folk.

More middle-of-the road was the Scripps-Howard (formerly Scripps-McRae) chain which controlled over two dozen dailies scattered from the Denver *Rocky Mountain News* to the Washington *News.* Edward W. Scripps was rough and somewhat ruthless, but unlike Hearst or Munsey, he was restrained by unusually clear and shrewd insights. Much of Roy W.

Howard's acerbity came only after the New Deal, and in the twenties, the Scripps-Howard papers favored international cooperation short of joining the League. Frank E. Gannett, who branched out of Elmira to acquire ten papers, was internationally minded in the twenties. (He later swung to the extreme Republican line in general repudiation of both the foreign and domestic policies of the second Roosevelt.) Cyrus H. K. Curtis, of *Saturday Evening Post* and *Ladies' Home Journal* fame, started with the Philadelphia *Public Ledger* and later picked up the venerable New York *Evening Post.* Curtis developed a widely syndicated foreign news service, which along with his papers held to a mildly pro-League point of view.

The stronger papers remained independent despite steadily rising costs of production. The Chicago *Tribune* and the Kansas City *Star,* two of the most important isolationist journals of the interior states, penetrated the countryside far from their home offices. Colonel Robert R. McCormick's *Tribune* could be found on every train, in every leading hotel, and on the Main Street newsstands of every town within hundreds of miles of Chicago. Like Hearst, McCormick had to live down a pro-German reputation. His cynicism, arrogance, militarism, and pretentious patriotism perhaps were affected in order to assure the world of his unadulterated Americanism.[9] The rest was that the *Tribune* carried the most erratic and inconsistent editorial column in the country. The Kansas City *Star,* on the other hand, commanded the respect of its competitors and critics. William Allen White, who disagreed with the *Star's* isolationism, called the paper "clean, brave and fair." Yet, as it was circulated in Kansas, Oklahoma, northern Texas, Colorado, and even New Mexico, it advocated no political ties with the League. William Rockhill Nelson, the owner and founder, believed that he was carrying out the last wishes of his friend, Theodore Roosevelt.

There were, of course, some strongly internationalist journals. No paper fought more vigorously for the League of Nations than Adolph Och's New York *Times.* Its editorial page reflected the views of the eastern business groups and intelligentsia who had both economic and cultural affinities beyond the sea. When Munsey sold the *Herald* to Ogden M. Reid, the newly combined *Herald Tribune* joined the *Times* in pleading for a broader world outlook.

In the midwest, Victor Fremont Lawson, owner of the Chicago *Daily News,* tried valiantly to neutralize the prejudice of the *Tribune.* Lawson, a successful journalist of the old school, had pioneered in foreign reporting since the days of the Russo-Japanese war. In 1914, he had a European service ready to take advantage of the big story. Headed by Edward Price

Bell, such able men as Raymond Gram Swing and the two Mowrer brothers, Paul Scott and Edgar Ansel, worked for the *Daily News's* syndicated service. A few big scoops advertised the usefulness of these dispatches and increased the market for the releases. Lawson was genuinely interested in world organization, and at times the foreign service was run at a loss for the sake of creating enthusiasm for international organization. In order to combat Colonel McCormick's growing influence in the corn belt, Lawson sent Bell on a lecture tour. As part of this campaign, Bell used the radio and the subject of his first broadcast was "If Not a League—What?" The *News's* foreign service, avowedly dedicated to breaking down international misgivings, was at one time used by almost one hundred papers. After Lawson's death, his successors, first Walter A. Strong and then the redoubtable Colonel Frank Knox, continued to beard the *Tribune*. Other important world-minded papers in the Mississippi Valley were the Chicago *Evening Post,* the Wichita *Eagle,* White's Emporia *Gazette,* The St. Louis *Globe-Democrat,* and ex-Senator Gilbert M. Hitchcock's Omaha *World-Herald*.

Except for the Lawson correspondents and the European staff of the New York *Times,* the foreign news guild sent home chits which often bristled with prejudice. Denunciation of Europe made lively reading and, more often than not, conformed to local inclinations. Since those American newspapers that were opposed to the League were violently so, while those that supported it were often lukewarm, it paid correspondents who wanted to sell syndicated dispatches to write disparagingly. It became axiomatic among the journalists abroad that kind words for Geneva or its undertakings just did not help business. Generally speaking, then, American correspondents exaggerated the faults of the League and minimized its achievements. Reports on foreign convulsions were interlarded with prayers of thanks for the wise statesmanship that had spared American composure. Many lazy news gatherers took only enough time off from wine and song to make carbon copies of each other's communications. Such cribbers were dubbed the "black sheet gang."[10]

The rise of the newspaper columnist centered the interest of readers on foregn affairs. The old-time personal journalism, with its lively vituperative editorials, had given away to a deceivingly objective listing of facts. The reader was left adrift without a compass to guide his reflections on complicated problems. The answer to the confusion was the syndicated column, which has done so much to shape opinion in America. The first of these modern publicists were Arthur Brisbane, Heywood Broun, and Walter Lippmann. Brisbane's "Today" began in 1917 and William Randolph Hearst pushed the column so that it eventually reached millions of Americans. Coating his views with a religious unction, Brisbane echoed Hearst's bumptiousness, militarism, and indubitable isolationism. What a far cry from his famous father, Albert Brisbane, who had returned from Europe in 1834 to spread utopian socialism! Lippmann and Broun were much more world-minded than Arthur Brisbane. They were, however, frequently censorious of Europe, and their readers remembered the barbs rather than the occasional reminders that other countries also might be honestly groping for the path to peace.

To sum up, it is apparent that the isolationists enjoyed most of the advantages of a good press. The pro-League papers, foreign correspondents, and urbane columnists were not commensurate with the Irreconcilable big chains, independently owned dailies that made a fetish of isolationism, and the multitude of conforming Republican editors. The internationalist papers were more often apologetic than scintillating. The press, that did so much to mold American opinion before the age of radio and television, helped on balance to argue the isolationist case.

Newspapers, nevertheless, did stimulate interest in foreign affairs. This concern was abetted by a new type of organization which came into being to provide neutral, non-partisan information to its constituents. Thus the Foreign Policy Association and the Council on Foreign Relations evolved from wartime groups. The former, the old League of Free Nations Association, adopted in 1921 the name by which we know it today. For about a year the revamped group pressed for naval disarmament and for joining the World Court, but then abandoned propaganda for purely educational activities. Branches were established in leading cities, a speakers' bureau was set up, and the organization grew. The F. P. A. published weekly bulletins, supported a research department, and opened a Washington bureau. In leading cities, luncheon, dinner and evening meetings were devoted to discussions of world affairs.[11]

Whereas the F. P. A. actively sought members, the Council on Foreign Relations limited its numbers. The dues were high, and membership came only on invitation from the Board of Directors. In 1920, the Council merged with the American Institute of International Affairs, which had been formed in Paris during the Peace Conference. The following year the group took over publication of an established journal, and changed its name to *Foreign Affairs*. The new editor was Hamilton Fish Armstrong, who had learned his way around Europe as a military attaché and foreign correspondent. The Council promoted an objective and non-partisan study of American foreign policy by publications, educational dinners, the formation of study groups, and the establishment of a library in New York. It is significant that neutrality on the League question did not make for complete unity. Apparently it was difficult for the internationalists to agree, even where the goal was enlightenment rather than action.

The Institute of Politics, which opened its first annual meeting in Williamstown, Massachusetts, on July 29, 1921, was of more ephemeral importance. Each summer brought leading European and American thinkers to the pleasant Berkshire town for round-table discussions and formal lectures. The Institute's Board of Advisors contained both friends and critics of the League as well as some whose position was difficult to define. All participants were supposedly thirsting for peace, but liberals were suspicious of the generals and admirals who came to lead the talks on disarmament. Frequently, these Williamstown round-tables stimulated isolationist talk when they made the news headlines. This was particularly true when the gray-bearded Englishman, James Bryce, long beloved for his interest in American problems, called the Treaty of Versailles more wicked than the settlement which had ended the Napoleonic wars. Although able opponents of this view had ample opportunities to refute it, this singular assertion struck a responsive chord.

The World Peace Foundation, which had been established in 1910 by the textbook king, Edwin Ginn, found a certain amount of neutrality on vital issues necessary. The Foundation did, however, become the official distributor of League of Nations publications. The Carnegie Endowment for International Peace also leaned unofficially toward the League. The war had increased the value of Carnegie's initial gift of ten million dollars in United States Steel bonds, so now the Endowment had more money than ever with which to pursue its elusive goal. Thus *International Conciliation* was distributed at nominal rates, one thousand International Relations Clubs were sponsored, and the "International Mind" alcoves in small libraries were well stocked.[12] Both Nicholas Murray Butler, president of the Carnegie Endowment, and James T. Shotwell, director of its Division of Economics and History, were friends of international organization. Butler rued his 1920 stand because he realized that the progress of the League was retarded by American abstention. Shotwell, Canadian-born Columbia specialist in intellectual history, worked quietly but incessantly to awaken the American international conscience. The Carnegie Endowment sent selected groups to Europe and Asia and generally arranged stop-overs at the League in Geneva and the World Court at The Hague.

The Endowment's Division of International Law was headed by a friend of world organization, James Brown Scott, who had often served the State Department.

The National Civic Federation was more nearly neutral on the League issue. Its Committee of One Hundred on Foreign Relations merely sought to present non-controversial material to the American public. The very fact that institutions designed to promote international accord had to treat the League so gingerly is a pointed reflection of the spirit of the times. The front door to Geneva had been barred by politics, with the result that would-be American consociates had to search for a side entrance.

For a century the organized America peace movement had run a familiar course, gaining ground between wars that always managed to appear different and therefore justifiable. George Haven Putnam, the publisher who had fought his way from private to major in the Civil War, was re-elected a vice-president of the American Peace Society while clamoring for war against Germany.[13] The less bellicose officers and members of this venerable society opposed collective security of the League variety because they could not give approbation to any plan which rested upon coercion. They denounced the League as wrong in principle, contrary to the teachings of history, and dangerous to the peace of the world. Dr. Arthur Deerin Call, secretary of the organization, used the *Advocate of Peace* to attack the League and to broach impossible substitutes.

These castle-building American internationalists failed to realize that they were aiding the isolationists by attacking the one existing world organization potentially capable of settling major disputes. In Europe, the desolation of war had convinced realistic men of the necessity of the League. Hence peace organizations abroad invariably championed the tangible, while American peace groups, paradoxically larger and more powerful than those in Europe, were torn by divided counsels and fragmentary plans. Too little thought was given to the practical implementation of attractive but visionary proposals. It was naively supposed that the will for peace, like love, could conquer all things.

As American organizations pursued the dove of peace, reports, inquiries, and recommendations multiplied. What did all of this fact-finding accomplish? From the published data men usually selected parts which buttressed their own previous convictions. Frequently, societies interested in foreign relations prompted celebrated debates in which the internationalist contenders were more often apologetic than enthusiastic about the League. Yet some positive achievements are evident. By their very existence, the internationalist organizations kept the country from sinking even farther into a twentieth-century variant of know-nothingism. In the schools and among the intellectually curious they built attitudes that were later to pay dividends in hard-fought battles against invincible ignorance.

Thus organizations mushroomed with obtrusive names, gaudy stationery, voluble fund-raising campaigns, inane conventions, and annoying pressure techniques. These societies were studded with peace bureaucrats—men and women who ran the organizations while their constituents pursued happiness and prosperity. Frequently, hired personnel and fanatical volunteer staffs resisted concerted action that might threaten the autonomy of their own groups. And always they gave more thought to program than to ultimate ends.[14] Their leaders failed to comprehend that the primary task was to make a parochial people understand that modern science had changed our problem of defense in both space and time relationships.

There were many other schemes to bring about the golden age. Conservative religious leaders called for a revival that would span the boundaries of nations and by its impact would force the League to respect moral values. Some even argued that a universal grass roots reform movement would make peace machinery superfluous, for the newly inspired peoples would prevent their governments from going to war. Even so seasoned a thinker as the veteran correspondent, Frank H. Simonds, held that the pronouncements of righteous judgments would be more effective in keeping the peace than any form of compulsion.

The demand for the enthronement of international law came from experts rather than dilettantes. Deeply ingrained in the American mind was the belief that the codification of international law would eliminate war by substituting judicial settlement. Thus there were insistent requests for a new meeting at The Hague to continue the work started at the two prewar conferences in that city. This third Hague meeting, it was predicted, would systematize the law of nations and replace League power politics with international morality. (As a postscript one might add that when the United States, backed by the League, eventually did convoke a Third Hague Conference, the net result was a "Protocol Relating to Military Obligations in Certain Cases of Double Nationality.") Totalitarianism had not yet demonstrated that brutality, inhumanity, and fiendish ambitions could not be curbed by incantations, codification of international law, and wishful thinking. A persisting nineteenth-century optimism over-estimated the better side of human nature, and obscured the fact that only force could checkmate force. A curious mixture of idealism and irresponsibility was an intrinsic ingredient of American thought of the period.

The uncompromising pacifists formed a small but clangorous minority.

Their solution to the problem of war was as simple as it was unrealistic: let the United States resolve never again to resort to armed strife. Frequently they made common cause with militaristic ultra-nationalists to denounce all rapport with the League and its agencies. The English pacifist, Arthur Ponsonby, helped the Women's Peace Union (affiliated with the War Resisters' International), in its effort to create enough conscientious objectors to frustrate any war effort. The quadrennial Convention of Student Volunteers, meeting at Indianapolis, took the pledge never to aid, directly or indirectly, in the prosecution of war. The pacifists celebrated "No More War Days," their handbills demanded "Disarm or Die," and they held endless discussions and prayer meetings.

The real issue of American help in the preservation of world order was thus obscured by a plethora of plans. There was a major split between those who wanted to enforce peace and those who eschewed coercion whether used by a nation, alliance, or international body. The former were usually outright leaguists, or men who hoped some day to rewrite the Covenant to suit American specifications. The opponents of the use of force were prone to cull ancient peace schemes from the tomes of history. The American Association for International Conciliation held that a sincere effort to build opon our treaties of arbitration and conciliation would solve the problem. To add to the confusion, the same Chicago *Tribune,* that so often championed the mailed fist, turned to twenty-eight existing pacification treaties as an American rather than an Old World remedy for war. Few took the trouble to point out that while these agreements had gathered dust in the State Department's files, bloody wars had rocked the world.

There was more general agreement on disarmament than on any other specific program. In the early twenties the peace societies momentarily buried their differences and concentrated on the scrapping of arms. The new coalition contained some outright pacifists and a conservative element that wanted only such disarmament as was consistent with security. The front was broad enough to include both isolationists and those discouraged leaguists who preferred American leadership in disarmament to a seat on the sidelines. Joseph Pulitzer's New York *World* launched a sweeping crusade that made newspaper history. Even Hudson Maxim, of smokeless powder fame, lent his support to the *World's* "disarmament editor."

The movement was given terrific impetus in 1921 when President Harding convened the Washington Naval Arms Conference. . . . An analysis of the disarmament combine is pertinent here, however, for it will elucidate the workings of the American peace organizations. The most effective body was the National Council for the Limitation of Armament, a union of religious, farm, labor, and educational groups. Frederick J. Libby, a Congregationalist minister turned Quaker, was its executive secretary and presiding genius. Started as a temporary medium to facilitate the work of the 1921 conclave, it organized permanently as the National Council for Prevention of War, with headquarters in Washington. Guided by the pacifist Libby, it raised a good deal of money and, at the height of its power, sent out 430,000 pieces of anti-war material in a single month.[15] Libby's convictions made him an avowed enemy of the League of Nations, but he did urge American adherence to the World Court.

The NCPW's work was paralleled by two women's organizations which were founded in the belief that the new female voting power would make war politically impossible. Jane Addams, pioneer settlement worker, dominated the WILPF-US, the American branch of the Women's International League for Peace and Freedom. Like Libby, Miss Addams condemned the League of Nations because the Covenant approved of war to deter aggression. Interestingly enough, WILPF members attached to their income tax returns the following reservation: "That part of this income tax which is levied for preparation for War is paid only under Protest and Duress."[16]

Devotion to the cause of peace did not preserve tranquillity within the sanctum of the WILPF-US. Mrs. Carrie Chapman Catt's ambitions had been whetted by the triumph of the prohibition and suffrage movements and her personal success as a popular lecturer. She contested Miss Addams's leadership and walked out of the WILPF-US to federate nine women's groups into the National Council on the Cause and Cure of War. The new organization was far less inclined toward pacifism than the WILPF-US. At the very first meeting of the Council, the square-jawed and fiery Rabbi Stephen S. Wise denounced the enemies of collective security with every suitable adjective in the English language. Within a short time a pro-League faction captured control of the organization and proceeded to castigate the country's provincialism.

Neither the pacifists nor the more moderate disarmament leaders caused the isolationist rebound. Many in both camps were internationalists who were not in accord with the League bond of world union. Their organizations, however, incessantly scolded Europe for its standing armies, viewed unrealistically the problem of security, and erred in oversimplifying the complex causes of and remedies for world disorder. Their commotion and fanfare helped delay American acceptance of the responsibilities of a major power in an imperfect world.

The number of crackpot schemes for peace in the twenties was legion. They defy classification, but some common tendencies are apparent. Men of good will sought immortality by trying to solve the problem of peace that had daunted the best minds of generations. The belief persisted that heroic individual efforts would find the answer. Sincere but unsophisticated thinking led to romantic and utopian recipes for ending global turmoil. The new formulas often spliced together shopworn peace plans, forming a maze of contradictions and absurd suggestions.

One of the most persistent would-be architects of a new world order was Samuel Colcord of New York. He had enough money, septuagenarian energy, and contacts to promote his plans. After beginning as a League reservationist, he quickly gave ground in the face of Republican opposition. He then argued that we should police the western hemisphere for the League, freeing ourselves, at the same time, of all European pitfalls. Through a front organization called the Committee on Educational Publicity in the Interests of World Peace, with William Allen White as chairman and Henry L. Stimson on the board, Colcord worked to unite the various groups that favored the outlawry of war. His technique was to deluge prominent officials, from the President down, with personal appeals and circulars. Neither cold silence nor studied incivility was able to dampen his zeal.

The manuscript collections of the period are replete with the peace activities of fleeting organizations, unknown personages, and public figures. The Michigan Council For Peace worked out a plan for world government. A Committee of One Hundred staged a demonstration in Washington "For Law Not War." One Benjamin Blumenthal drafted the outlines of a League of People's Peace. The socially prominent Mrs. Frank A. Vanderlip planned a Peace Pageant called the March of Mankind. William Jennings Bryan, with three unsuccessful tries for the White House and service as Secretary of State behind him, gave some thought to the peace problem. He urged the adoption of a constitutional amendment that would make the declaration of war, except in case of invasion, subject to a popular referendum. This was three years prior to his burial in the full regalia of a colonel of Nebraska Volunteers!

These grandiose schemes mirrored the American thought of the day—isolationist, unrealistic, peace-loving, and for all that unwilling to make genuine sacrifices to secure an ordered world. All groups, including the isolationists, wished to follow the arrow marked "To Peace." Because the country seemed secure, the more world-minded felt free to engage in a Donnybrook Fair among themselves. Despite their cosmopolitan talk, they did not realize the immediate need for American action to stabilize the world. They shared, perhaps far more than they themselves comprehended, the isolationist delusion of American invulnerability. It was in this fog of wistful thought that the Republican statesmen of the twenties were to grope their way in the post-Versailles world.

NOTES

1. "A Requisite for the Success of Popular Democracy," *Foreign Affairs,* I (September 15, 1922), 3–10.
2. Arthur H. Vandenberg, *The Trail of a Tradition* (New York, 1926), Foreword, VII.
3. Ms. of a speech delivered at Hotel Astor, New York City, November 10, 1925. Hughes MSS., Library of Congress.
4. Emma Wold told William E. Borah of the new organization in a telegram, October 13, 1919. Borah MSS., Library of Congress.
5. Samuel F. McConnell to F. D. R., December 18, 1924. Roosevelt MSS., Group 11. Franklin D. Roosevelt Library, Hyde Park.
6. Ray G. Farrington to F. D. R., December 18, 1924. F. D. Roosevelt MSS.
7. Editorial in New York *Sun,* March 17, 1919.
8. White to Guy T. Visknisski, September 9, 1921. White MSS., Library of Congress.
9. Oswald G. Villard, "The World's Greatest Newspaper," *Nation,* CXIV (February 1, 1922), 116–118.
10. Constance Drexel, "The Foreign Correspondent," *New Republic,* XXXVII (January 30, 1924), 252–254.
11. Paul U. Kellogg, *Ten Years of the Foreign Policy Association* (n. p., 1929), 14.
12. Robert H. Ferrell, *Peace in Their Time* (New Haven, 1952), 21.
13. Putnam to Villard, January 27, 1928. Villard MSS., Harvard University.
14. A convenient list of the peace societies of the 1920s is in Ferrell, *Peace in Their Time,* 13–30.
15. Lyman B. Burbank, "Internationalism in American Thought: 1919–1929," (Ms. doctoral dissertation, New York University, June, 1950), p. 58ff.
16. Ferrell, *Peace in Their Time,* 29.

7 ~ The Legend of Isolationism in the 1920's*

[Author's Note] *William Appleman Williams, of the University of Wisconsin, like Adler, revises the traditional interpretation of American foreign policy in the twenties but he uses very different evidence to support his conclusions. American foreign policy was not isolationist, contends Williams, because the United States intervened in affairs throughout the world to preserve peace, weaken radical movements, and maintain prosperity. Stressing expansion by American businessmen, the author finds that a positive foreign policy was present throughout the twenties by the transposition of corporatist principles to other countries.*

The widely accepted assumption that the United States was isolationist from 1920 through 1932 is no more than a legend. Sir Francis Bacon might have classed this myth of isolation as one of his Idols of the Market-Place. An "ill and unfit choice of words," he cautioned, "leads men away into innumerable and inane controversies and fancies."[1] And certainly the application of the terms *isolation* and *isolationism* to a period and a policy that were characterized by vigorous involvement in the affairs of the world with consciousness of purpose qualifies as an "ill and unfit choice of words." Thus the purpose of this essay: on the basis of an investigation of the record to suggest that, far from isolation, the foreign relations of the United States from 1920 through 1932 were marked by express and ex-

* By William A. Williams. Reprinted with permission from *Science and Society,* XVII, No. 1 (Winter, 1954), Pages 1–20.

tended involvement with—and intervention in the affairs of—other nations of the world.

It is both more accurate and more helpful to consider the twenties as contiguous with the present instead of viewing those years as a quixotic interlude of low-down jazz and lower-grade gin, fluttering flappers and Faulkner's fiction, and bootlegging millionaires and millionaire bootleggers. For in foreign policy there is far less of a sharp break between 1923 and 1953 than generally is acknowledged. A closer examination of the so-called isolationists of the twenties reveals that many of them were in fact busily engaged in extending American power. Those individuals and groups have not dramatically changed their outlook on foreign affairs. Their policies and objectives may differ with those of others (including professors), but they have never sought to isolate the United States.

This interpretation runs counter to the folklore of American foreign relations. Harvard places isolationism "in the saddle." Columbia sees "Americans retiring within their own shell." Yale judges that policy "degenerated" into isolation—among other things.[2] Others, less picturesque but equally positive, refer to a "marked increase of isolationist sentiment" and to "those years of isolationism." Another group diagnoses the populace as having "ingrained isolationism," analyzes it as "sullen and selfish" in consequence, and characterizes it as doing "its best to forget international subjects." Related verdicts describe the Republican party as "predominantly isolationist" and as an organization that "fostered a policy of deliberate isolation."[3]

Most pointed of these specifications is a terse two-word summary of the diplomacy of the period: "Isolation Perfected."[4] Popularizers have transcribed this theme into a burlesque. Their articles and books convey the impression that the Secretaries of State were in semi-retirement and that the citizenry wished to do away with the Department itself.[5] Columnists and commentators have made the concept an eerie example of George Orwell's double-think. They label as isolationists the most vigorous interventionists.

The case would seem to be closed and judgment given if it were not for the ambivalence of some observers and the brief dissents filed by a few others. The scholar who used the phrase "those years of isolationism," for example, remarks elsewhere in the same book that "expansionism . . . really was long a major expression of isolationism." Another writes of the "return to an earlier policy of isolation," and on the next page notes a "shift in policy during the twenties amounting almost to a 'diplomatic revolution'." A recent biographer states that Henry Cabot Lodge "did not propose . . . an isolationist attitude," but then proceeds to characterize the Monroe Doctrine—upon which Lodge stood in his fight against the League of Nations treaty—as a philosophy of "isolation." And in the last volume of his trilogy, the late Professor Frederick L. Paxton summed up a long review of the many diplomatic activities of the years 1919–1923 with the remark that this was a foreign policy of "avoidance rather than of action."[6]

But a few scholars, toying with the Idol of the Market-Place, have made bold to rock the image. Yet Professor Richard Van Alstyne was doing more than playing the iconoclast when he observed that the "militant manifest destiny men were the isolationists of the nineteenth century." For with this insight we can translate those who maintain that Lodge "led the movement to perpetuate the traditional policy of isolation." Perhaps William G. Carleton was even more forthright. In 1946 he pointed out that the fight over the League treaty was not between isolationists and internationalists, and added that many of the mislabeled isolationists were actually "nationalists and imperialists." Equally discerning was Charles Beard's comment in 1933 that the twenties were marked by a "return to the more aggressive ways . . . [used] to protect and advance the claims of American business enterprise." All these interpretations were based on facts that prompted another scholar to change his earlier conclusion and declare in 1953 that "the thought was all of keeping American freedom of action."[7]

These are perceptive comments. Additional help has recently been supplied by two other students of the period. One of these is Robert E. Osgood, who approached the problem in terms of *Ideals and Self-Interest in American Foreign Relations*.[8] Though primarily concerned with the argument that Americans should cease being naive, Osgood suggests that certain stereotypes are misleading. One might differ with his analysis of the struggle over the Treaty of Versailles, but not with his insistence that there were fundamental differences between Senators Lodge and William E. Borah—as well as between those two and President Woodrow Wilson. Osgood likewise raises questions about the reputed withdrawal of the American public. Over a thousand organizations for the study of international relations existed in 1926, to say nothing of the groups that sought constantly to make or modify foreign policy.

Osgood gives little attention to this latter aspect of foreign relations, a surprising omission on the part of a realist.[9] But the underlying assumption of his inquiry cannot be challenged. The foreign policy issue of the twenties was never isolationism. The controversy and competition were waged between those who entertained different concepts of the national interest and disagreed over the means to be employed to secure that objective. Secretary of State Charles Evans Hughes was merely more eloquent, not less explicit. "Foreign policies," he explained in 1923, "are not built upon abstractions. They are the result of practical conceptions of national interest arising from some immediate exigency or standing out vividly in historical perspective."[10]

Historian George L. Grassmuck used this old-fashioned premise of the politician as a tool with which to probe the *Sectional Biases in Congress on Foreign Policy*. Disciplining himself more rigorously in the search for primary facts than did Osgood, Grassmuck's findings prompted him to conclude that "the 'sheep and goats' technique" of historical research is eminently unproductive. From 1921 to 1933, for example, the Republicans in both houses of Congress were "more favorable to both Army and Navy measures than . . . Democrats." Eighty-five percent of the same Republicans supported international economic measures and agreements. As for the Middle West, that much condemned section did not reveal any "extraordinary indication of a . . . tendency to withdraw." Nor was there "an intense 'isolationism' on the part of [its] legislators with regard to membership in a world organization."[11] And what opposition there was seems to have been as much the consequence of dust bowls and depression as the product of disillusioned scholars in ivory towers.

These investigations and correlations have two implications. First, the United States was neither isolated nor did it pursue a policy of isolationism from 1920 to 1933. Second, if the policy of that era, so generally accepted as the product of traditional isolationist sentiment, proves non-isolationist, then the validity and usefulness of the concept when applied to earlier or later periods may seriously be challenged.

Indeed, it would seem more probable that the central theme of American foreign relations has been the expansion of the United States. Alexander Hamilton made astute use of the phrase "no entangling alliances" during the negotiation of Jay's Treaty in 1794, but his object was a *de facto* affiliation with the British Fleet—not isolation.[12] Nor was Thomas Jefferson seeking to withdraw when he made of Monticello a counselling center for those seeking to emulate the success of the American Revolution. A century later Senator Lodge sought to revise the Treaty of Versailles and the Covenant of the League of Nations with reservations that seemed no more than a restatement of Hamilton's remarks. Yet the maneuvers of Lodge were no more isolationist in character and purpose than Hamilton's earlier action. And while surely no latter-day Jefferson, Senator Borah was anything but an isolationist in his concept of the power of economics and ideas. Borah not only favored the recognition of the Soviet Union in order to influence the development of the Bolshevik Revolution and as a check against Japanese expansion in Asia, but also argued that American economic policies were intimately connected with foreign political crises. All those men were concerned with the extension of one or more aspects of American influence, power, and authority.

Approached in this manner, the record of American foreign policy in the twenties verifies the judgments of two remarkably dissimilar students: historian Richard W. Leopold and Senator Lodge. The professor warns that the era was "more complex than most glib generalizations . . . would suggest"; and the scholastic politician concludes that, excepting wars, there "never [was] a period when the United States [was] more active and its influence more felt internationally than between 1921 and 1924."[13] The admonition about perplexity was offered as helpful advice, not as an invitation to anti-intellectualism. For, as the remarks of the Senator implied, recognition that a problem is involved does not mean that it cannot be resolved.

Paradox and complexity can often be clarified by rearranging the data around a new focal point that is common to all aspects of the apparent contradiction. The confusion of certainty and ambiguity that characterizes most accounts of American foreign policy in the twenties stems from the fact that they are centered on the issue of membership in the League of Nations. Those Americans who wanted to join are called internationalists. Opponents of that move became isolationists. But the subsequent action of most of those who fought participation in the League belies this simple classification. And the later policies of many who favored adherence to the League casts serious doubts upon the assumption that they were willing to negotiate or arbitrate questions that they defined as involving the national interest. More pertinent is an examination of why certain groups and individuals favored or disapproved of the League, coupled with a review of the programs they supported after that question was decided.

Yet such a re-study of the League fight is in itself insufficient. Equally important is a close analysis of the American reaction to the Bolshevik Revolution. Both the League Covenant and the Treaty of Versailles were written on a table shaken by that upheaval. The argument over the ratification of the combined documents was waged in a context determined as much by Nikolai Lenin's *Appeal to the Toiling, Oppressed, and Exhausted Peoples of Europe* and the Soviet *Declaration to the Chinese People* as by George Washington's Farewell Address.[14]

Considered within the setting of the Bolshevik Revolution, the basic question was far greater than whether or not to enter the League. At issue was what response was to be made to the domestic and international division of labor that had accompanied the Industrial Revolution. Challenges from organized urban labor, dissatisfied farmers, frightened men of property, searching intellectual critics, and colonial peoples rudely interrupted almost every meeting of the Big Four in Paris and were echoed in many Senate debates over the treaty. And those who determined American policy through the decade of the twenties were consciously concerned with the same problem.

An inquiry into this controversy over the broad question of how to end the war reveals certain divisions within American society. These groupings were composed of individuals and organizations whose position on the League of Nations was coincident with and part of their response to the Bolsheviks; or, in a wider sense, with their answer to that general unrest, described by Woodrow Wilson as a "feeling of revolt against the large vested interests which influenced the world both in the economic and the political sphere."[15] Once this breakdown has been made it is then possible to follow the ideas and actions of these various associations of influence and power through the years 1920 to 1933.

At the core of the American reaction to the League and the Bolshevik Revolution was the quandary between fidelity to ideals and the urge to power. Jefferson faced a less acute version of the same predicament in terms of whether to force citizenship on settlers west of the Mississippi who were reluctant to be absorbed in the Louisiana Purchase. A century later the anti-imperialists posed the same issue in the more sharply defined circumstances of the Spanish-American War. The League and the Bolsheviks raised the question in its most dramatic context and in unavoidable terms.

There were four broad responses to this reopening of the age-old dilemma. At one pole stood the pure idealists and pacifists, led by William Jennings Bryan. A tiny minority in themselves, they were joined, in terms of general consequences if not in action, by those Americans who were preoccupied with their own solutions to the problem. Many American businessmen, for example, were concerned primarily with the expansion of trade and were apathetic toward or impatient with the hullabaloo over the League.[16] Diametrically opposed to the idealists were the vigorous expansionists. All these exponents of the main chance did not insist upon an overt crusade to run the world, but they were united on Senator Lodge's proposition that the United States should dominate world politics. Association with other nations they accepted, but not equality of membership or mutuality of decision.

Caught in the middle were those Americans who declined to support either extreme. A large number of these people clustered around Woodrow Wilson, and can be called the Wilsonites. Though aware of the dangers and temptations involved, Wilson declared his intention to extend American power for the purpose of strengthening the ideals. However noble that effort, it failed for two reasons. Wilson delegated power and initiative to men and organizations that did not share his objectives, and on his own part the president ultimately "cast in his lot" with the defenders of the status quo.[17]

Led by the Sons of the Wild Jackass, the remaining group usually followed Senator Borah in foreign relations. These men had few illusions about the importance of power in human affairs or concerning the authority of the United States in international politics. Prior to the world war they supported—either positively or passively—such vigorous expansionists as Theodore Roosevelt, who led their Progressive Party. But the war and the Bolshevik Revolution jarred some of these Progressives into a closer examination of their assumptions. These reflections and new conclusions widened the breach with those of their old comrades who had moved toward a conservative position on domestic issues. Some of those earlier allies, like Senator Albert J. Beveridge, continued to agitate for an American century. Others, such as Bainbridge Colby, sided with Wilson in 1916 and went along with the president on foreign policy.

But a handful had become firm anti-expansionists by 1919.[18] No attempt was made by these men to deny the power of the United States. Nor did they think that the nation could become self-sufficient and impregnable in its strength. Borah, for example, insisted that America must stand with Russia if Japan and Germany were to be checked. And Johnson constantly pointed out that the question was not whether to withdraw, but at what time and under what circumstances to use the country's influence. What these men did maintain was that any effort to run the world by establishing an American system comparable to the British Empire was both futile and un-American.

In this they agreed with Henry Adams, who debated the same issue with his brother Brooks Adams, Theodore Roosevelt, and Henry Cabot Lodge in the years after 1898. "I incline now to anti-imperialism, and very strongly to anti-militarism," Henry warned. "If we try to rule politically, we take the chances against us." By the end of the first world war another generation of expansionists tended to agree with Henry Adams about ruling politically, but planned to build and maintain a similar pattern of control through the use of America's economic might. Replying to these later expansionists, Borah and other anti-expansionists of the nineteen-twenties argued that if Washington's influence was to be effective it would have to be used to support the movements of reform and colonial nationalism rather than deployed in an effort to dam up and dominate those forces.

For these reasons they opposed Wilson's reorganizations of the international banking consortium, fearing that the financiers would either influence strongly or veto—as they did—American foreign policies. With Senator Albert B. Cummins of Iowa they voted against the Wilson-approved Webb-Pomerene Act, which repealed the anti-trust laws for export associations. In the same vein they tried to prevent passage of the Edge Act, an amendment to the Federal Reserve Act that authorized foreign banking corporations.[19] Led by Borah, they bitterly attacked the Versailles Treaty because, in their view, it committed the United States to oppose colonial movements for self-government and to support an unjust and indefensible status quo. From the same perspective they criticized and fought to end intervention in Russia and the suppression of civil liberties at home.[20]

Contrary to the standard criticism of their actions, however, these anti-expansionists were not just negative die-hards. Senator Cummins maintained from the first that American loans to the allies should be considered gifts. Borah spoke out on the same issue, hammered away against armed intervention in Latin America, played a key role in securing the appointment of Dwight Morrow as Ambassador to Mexico, and sought to align the United States with, instead of against, the Chinese Revolution. On these and other issues the anti-expansionists were not always of one mind, but as in the case of the Washington Conference Treaties the majority of them were far more positive in their actions than has been acknowledged.[21]

Within this framework the key to the defeat of the League treaty was the defection from the Wilsonites of a group who declined to accept the restrictions that Article X of the League Covenant threatened to impose upon the United States. A morally binding guarantee of the "territorial integrity and existing political integrity of all members of the League" was too much for these men. First they tried to modify that limitation. Failing there, they followed Elihu Root and William Howard Taft, both old time expansionists, to a new position behind Senator Lodge. Among those who abandoned Wilson on this issue were Herbert Hoover, Calvin Coolidge, Charles Evans Hughes, and Henry L. Stimson.

Not all these men were at ease with the vigorous expansionists. Stimson, for one, thought the Lodge reservations "harsh and unpleasant," and later adjusted other of his views.[22] Hoover and Hughes tried to revive their version of the League after the Republicans returned to power in 1920. But at the time all of them were more uneasy about what one writer has termed Wilson's "moral imperialism."[23] They were not eager to identify themselves with the memories of that blatant imperialism of the years 1895 to 1905, but neither did they like Article X. That proviso caught them from both sides, it illegalized changes initiated by the United States, and obligated America to restore a status quo to some aspects of which they were either indifferent or antagonistic. But least of all were they anxious to run the risk that the Wilsonian rhetoric of freedom and liberty might be taken seriously in an age of revolution. Either by choice or default they supported the idea of a community of interest among the industrialized powers of the world led by an American-British entente as against the colonial areas and the Soviet Union.

This postwar concept of the community of interest was the first generation intellectual off-spring of Herbert Croly's *Promise of American Life* and Herbert Hoover's *American Individualism*. Croly's opportunistic nationalism provided direction for Hoover's "greater mutuality of interest." The latter was to be expressed in an alliance between the government and the "great trade associations and the powerful corporations."[24] Pushed by the Croly-Hoover wing of the old Progressive Party, the idea enjoyed great prestige during the twenties. Among its most ardent exponents were Samuel Gompers and Matthew Woll of the labor movement, Owen D. Young of management, and Bernard Baruch of finance.

What emerged was an American corporatism. The avowed goals were order, stability, and social peace. The means to those objectives were labor-management co-operation, arbitration, and the elimination of waste and inefficiency by closing out unrestrained competition. State intervention was to be firm, but moderated through the cultivation and legalization of trade associations which would, in turn, advise the national government and supply leaders for the federal bureaucracy. The ideal was union in place of diversity and conflict.[25]

Other than Hoover, the chief spokesmen of this new community of interest as applied to foreign affairs were Secretaries of State Hughes and Stimson. In the late months of 1931 Stimson was to shift his ground, but until that time he supported the principle. All three men agreed that American economic power should be used to build, strengthen, and maintain the co-operation they sought. As a condition for his entry into the cabinet, Hoover demanded—and received—a major voice in "all important economic policies of the administration."[26] With the energetic assistance of Julius Klein, lauded by the National Foreign Trade Council as the "international business go-getter of Uncle Sam," Hoover changed the Department of Commerce from an agency primarily concerned with interstate commerce to one that concentrated on foreign markets and loans, and control of import sources.[27] Hughes and Stimson handled the political aspects of establishing a "community of ideals, interests and purposes."[28]

These men were not imperialistic in the traditional sense of that much abused term. All agreed with Klein that the object was to eliminate "the old imperialistic trappings of politico-economic exploitation." They sought instead the "internationalization of business."[29] Through the use of economic power they wanted to establish a common bond, forged of similar assumptions and purposes, with both the industrialized nations and the native business community in the colonial areas of the world. Their deployment of America's material strength is unquestioned. President Calvin Coolidge reviewed their success, and indicated the political implications thereof, on Memorial Day, 1928. "Our investments and trade relations are such," he summarized, "that it is almost impossible to conceive of any conflict anywhere on earth which would not affect us injuriously."[30]

Internationalization through the avoidance of conflict was the key objective. This did not mean a negative foreign policy. Positive action was the basic theme. The transposition of corporatist principles to the area of foreign relations produced a parallel policy. American leadership and intervention would build a world community regulated by agreement among the industrialized nations. The prevention of revolution and the preservation of the sanctity of private property were vital objectives. Hughes was very clear when he formulated the idea for Latin America. "We are seeking to establish a *Pax Americana* maintained not by arms but by mutual respect and good will and the tranquillizing processes of reason." There would be, he admitted, "interpositions of a temporary character"—the Secretary did not like the connotations of the word intervention—but only to facilitate the establishment of the United States as the "exemplar of justice."[31]

Extension to the world of this pattern developed in Latin America was more involved. There were five main difficulties, four in the realm of foreign relations and one in domestic affairs. The internal problem was to establish and integrate a concert of decision between the government and private economic groups. Abroad the objectives were more sharply defined: circumscribe the impact of the Soviet Union, forestall and control potential resistance of colonial areas, pamper and cajole Germany and Japan into acceptance of the basic proposition, and secure from Great Britain practical recognition of the fact that Washington had become the center of Anglo-Saxon collaboration. Several examples will serve to illustrate the general outline of this diplomacy, and to indicate the friction between the office holders and the office dwellers.

Wilson's Administration left the incoming Republicans a plurality of tools designed for the purpose of extending American power. The Webb-Pomerene Law, the Edge Act, and the banking consortium were but three of the more obvious and important of these. Certain polishing and sharpening remained to be done, as exemplified by Hoover's generous interpretation of the Webb-Pomerene legislation, but this was a minor problem. Hoover and Hughes added to these implements with such laws as the one designed to give American customs officials diplomatic immunity so that they could do cost accounting surveys of foreign firms. This procedure was part of the plan to provide equal opportunity abroad, under which circumstances Secretary Hughes was confident that "American businessmen would take care of themselves."[32]

It was harder to deal with the British, who persisted in annoying indications that they considered themselves equal partners in the enterprise. Bainbridge Colby, Wilson's last Secretary of State, ran into the same trouble. Unless England came "to our way of thinking," Colby feared that "agreement [would] be impossible." A bit later Hughes told the British Ambassador that the time had come for London's expressions of cordial sentiment to be "translated into something definite." After many harangues about oil, access to mandated areas, and trade with Russia, it was with great relief that Stimson spoke of the United States and Great Britain "working together like two old shoes."[33]

Deep concern over revolutionary ferment produced great anxiety. Hughes quite agreed with Colby that the problem was to prevent revolutions without making martyrs of the leaders of colonial or other dissident movements. The despatches of the period are filled with such expressions as "very grave concern," "further depressed," and "deeply regret," in connection with revolutionary activity in China, Latin America, and Europe.[34] American foreign service personnel abroad were constantly reminded to report all indications of such unrest. This sensitivity reached a high point when one representative telegraphed as "an example of the failure to assure public safety . . . the throwing of a rock yesterday into the state hospital here." Quite in keeping with this pattern was Washington's conclusion that it would support "any provisional government which gave satisfactory evidence of an intention to re-establish constitutional order."[35]

Central to American diplomacy of the twenties was the issue of Germany and Japan. And it was in this area that the government ran into trouble with its partners, the large associations of capital. The snag was to convince the bankers of the validity of the long range view. Hoover, Hughes and Stimson all agreed that it was vital to integrate Germany and Japan into the American community. Thus Hughes opposed the French diplomacy of force on the Rhine, and for his own part initiated the Dawes Plan. But the delegation of so much authority to the financiers backfired in 1931. The depression scared the House of Morgan and it refused to extend further credits to Germany. Stimson "blew up." He angrily told the Morgan representative in Paris that this strengthened France and thereby undercut the American program. Interrupted in the midst of this argument by a trans-Atlantic phone call from Hoover, Stimson explained to the president that "if you want to help the cause you are speaking of you will not do it by calling me up, but by calling Tom Lamont." Stimson then turned back to Lamont's agent in Europe and, using "unregulated language," told the man to abandon his "narrow banking axioms."[36]

Similar difficulties faced the government in dealing with Japan and China. The main problem was to convince Japan, by persuasion, concession, and the delicate use of diplomatic force, to join the United States in an application of its Latin American policy to China. Washington argued that the era of the crude exploitation of, and the exercise of direct political sovereignty over, backward peoples was past. Instead, the interested powers should agree to develop and exercise a system of absentee authority while increasing the productive capacity and administrative efficiency of China.

Japan seemed amenable to the proposal, and at the Washington Conference, Secretary Hughes went a great distance to convince Tokyo of American sincerity. Some writers, such as George Frost Kennan and Adolf A. Berle, claim that the United States did not go far enough.[37] This is something of a mystery. For in his efforts to establish "cooperation in the Far East," as Hughes termed it, the Secretary unconsciously gave Japan "an extraordinarily favorable position."[38]

Perhaps what Kennan and Berle have in mind is the attitude of Thomas Lamont. In contrast to their perspective on Europe, the bankers took an extremely long range view of Asia. Accepting the implications of the Four and Nine Power Treaties, Lamont began to finance Japan's penetration of the mainland. Hughes and Stimson were trapped. They continued to think in terms of American businessmen taking care of themselves if given an opportunity, and thus strengthening Washington's position in the world community. Hughes wrote Morgan that he hoped the consortium would become an "important instrumentality of our 'open door' policy.[39] But the American members of the banking group refused to antagonize their Japanese and British colleagues, and so vetoed Washington's hope to finance the Chinese Eastern Railway and its efforts to support the Federal Telegraph Company in China.

In this context it is easy to sympathize with Stimson's discomfort when the Japanese Army roared across Manchuria. As he constantly reiterated to the Japanese Ambassador in Washington, Tokyo had come far along the road "of bringing itself into alignment with the methods and opinion of the Western World."[40] Stimson not only wanted to, but did in fact give Japan every chance to continue along that path. So too did President Hoover, whose concern with revolution was so great that he was inclined to view Japanese sovereignty in Manchuria as the best solution. Key men in the State Department shared the president's conclusion.[41]

Stimson's insight was not so limited. He realized that his predecessor, Secretary of State Frank B. Kellogg, had been right: the community of interest that America should seek was with the Chinese. The Secretary acknowledged his error to Senator Borah, who had argued just such a thesis since 1917. Stimson's letter to Borah of February 23, 1932, did not say that America should abandon her isolationism, but rather that she had gone too far with the wrong friends. The long and painful process of America's great awakening had begun. But in the meantime President Hoover's insistence that no move should be made toward the Soviet Union, and that the non-recognition of Manchuko should be considered as a formula looking toward conciliation, had opened the door to appeasement.

NOTES

1. F. Bacon, *Novuum Organum,* Headlam's translation as revised by C. P. Curtis and F. Greenslet, *The Practical Cogitator* (Boston, Houghton Mifflin Co., 1945), p. 14–16.
2. A. M. Schlesinger, *Paths to the Present* (New York, The Macmillan Co., 1949), 69, 201; L. M. Hacker, "American International Relations," in *The United States and Its Place in World Affairs,* 1918–1943, ed. by A. Nevins and L. M. Hacker, (Boston, D. C. Heath and Co., 1943) p. 166; S. F. Bemis, "The Shifting Strategy of American Defense and Diplomacy," in *Essays in History and International Relations in Honor of George Hubbard Blakeslee,* ed. by D. E. Lee and G. E. McReynolds (Worcester, Clark University, 1949), p. 9.
3. In sequence, these quotations come from S. Adler, "The War-Guilt Question and American Disillusionment, 1919–1928," *The Journal of Modern History,* XXIII, No. 1 (March, 1951), p. 27; A. K. Weinberg, *Manifest Destiny. A study of Nationalist Expansion in American History* (Baltimore, Johns Hopkins Press, 1935), p. 473; L. M. Hacker and H. S. Zahler, *The United States in the 20th Century* (New York, Appleton-Century-Crofts, Inc., 1952). p. 278, 302; W. Wilson, quoted in Weinberg, *Manifest Destiny,* p. 473; F. D. Roosevelt, *Foreign Affairs,* VI, No. 4 (July, 1928), p. 577; W. Johnson, *The Battle Against Isolation* (Chicago, Chicago University Press, 1944), p. 132. For similar expressions see S. F. Bemis, *A Diplomatic History of the United States* (3rd ed., New York, Henry Holt and Co., 1950), p. 705; J. D. Hicks, *The American Nation* (Boston, Houghton Mifflin Co., 1949), p. 565; D. Perkins, *The Evolution of American Foreign Policy* (New York, Oxford University Press, 1949), p. 110; and A. Nevins, *America in World Affairs* (London, Oxford University Press, 1941), p. 80.
4. D. F. Fleming, *The United States and World Organization, 1920–1933* (New York, Columbia University Press, 1938), title of Chapter VI.
5. This literature is far too vast to cite, but even a perusal of *The Reader's Guide to Periodical Literature* will indicate the great volume of such material. It is vital to note however, that the so-called disillusionment writers did not make this mistake—whatever their other errors. They criticized the policies of the time, but documented, in such journals as *The Nation,* the active character of the diplomacy.
6. Quotations, in order, from Weinberg, *Manifest Destiny,* p. 473, 454; H. U. Faulkner, *American Political and Social History* (6th ed., New York, Appleton-Century-Crofts, Inc., 1952) p. 700, 701; J. A. Garraty, *Henry Cabot Lodge. A Biography* (New York, Alfred A. Knopf, 1953), p. 348, 364–65; F. L. Paxton, *American Democracy and the World War. Postwar Years. Normalcy, 1918–1923* (Berkeley, University of California Press, 1948), p. 367. For other examples of this ambiguity see D. Perkins, *The American Approach to Foreign Policy* (Cambridge, Harvard University Press, 1952), p. 26; T. A. Bailey, *A Diplomatic History of the American People* (4th ed., New York, Appleton-Century-Crofts, Inc., 1950, p. 682—where he says that the Harding Administration "retreated into what ex-President Wilson described as 'sullen and selfish isolation' "; H. J. Carman and H. C. Syrett, *A History of the American People* (New York,

Alfred A. Knopf, 1952, p. 264–65, and title of Chapter XII; S. E. Morrison and H. S. Commager, *The Growth of the American Republic* (4th ed., New York, Oxford University Press, 1950), Volume II, p. 497; and H. B. Parkes, *The United States of America* (New York, Alfred A. Knopf, 1953).

7. R. W. Van Alstyne, "The Significance of the Mississippi Valley in American Diplomatic History, 1686–1890," *Mississippi Valley Historical Review,* XXXVI, NO. 2 (September, 1949), 238; L. L. Leonard, *Elements of American Foreign Policy* (New York, McGraw-Hill Book Co., Inc., 1953), p. 220; among the many others who characterize Lodge in this manner is S. Adler in his recent article on isolation, "Isolationism Since 1914," *The American Scholar,* XXI, NO. 3 (Summer, 1952), p. 340; W. G. Carleton, "Isolationism and the Middle West," *Mississippi Valley Historical Review,* XXXIII, NO. 3 (December, 1946), p. 381–82; C. A. and M. R. Beard, *The Rise of American Civilization* (New Edition. Two Volumes in One. Revised and Enlarged. New York, The Macmillan Co., 1933), p. 681–83; and compare D. Perkins, *The American Approach to Foreign Policy,* 26, with D. Perkins, "The Department of State and Public Opinion," Chapter IX in *The Diplomats* 1919–1939, ed. by G. A. Graig and F. Gilbert (Princeton, Princeton University Press, 1953), p. 308. Interestingly enough, both Carleton and Van Alstyne addressed their remarks to meetings of the Mississippi Valley Historical Association, and their articles later appeared as lead articles in the *Review.* On the same program with Van Alstyne, furthermore, was Professor Richard Leopold, whose comments were of a similar nature and whose paper was also printed. This professional audience seems to have ignored their keen suggestions. Professor Weinberg's article, "The Historical Meaning of the American Doctrine of Isolation," *The American Political Science Review,* XXXIV (1940), p. 539–47, offers certain concepts that would go far to resolve the contradictions in his earlier *Manifest Destiny,* but he did not apply the ideas to any later period. H. Feis writes of America's active foreign economic policy in *The Diplomacy of the Dollar, First Era, 1919–1932* (Baltimore, Johns Hopkins Press, 1950), but fails to note that these facts contradict the idea of isolation. The same approach is taken by G. Soule, *Prosperity Decade. From War to Depression: 1917–1929* (New York, Rinehart and Co., Inc., 1947), p. 252–74. Far more stimulating than either Feis or Soule is S. Kuznets, "Foreign Economic Relations of the United States and Their Impact Upon the Domestic Economy," Chapter 11 in his *Economic Change* (New York, W. W. Norton and Co., 1953), p. 296–333. See also the neglected work of A. D. Gayer and C. T. Schmidt, *American Economic Foreign Policy. Postwar History, Analysis, and Interpretation* (New York, no publisher given, 1939), especially p. 11–17.

8. R. E. Osgood, *Ideals and Self-Interest in America's Foreign Relations. The Great Transformation of the Twentieth Century* (Chicago, University of Chicago Press, 1953).

9. This is strange for a realist trained in the school of Professor Hans J. Morgenthau's *Realpolitik.* For the realists emphasize the fact that the relationship between power and ideals is reciprocal. Not only do ideas fail to have consequences without power, but the sources and the nature of the power have some correlation with the character of the ideals. Thus it would seem doubly unrealistic to slight the sources of power and at the same time discuss the ideas without reference to the private as well as the public record of the groups and individuals in question.

10. C. E. Hughes, "The Centenary of the Monroe Doctrine," *The Annals of the American Academy of Political and Social Science,* Supplement to Volume CXI (January, 1923), p. 7.

11. G. L. Grassmuck, *Sectional Biases in Congress on Foreign Policy* (Baltimore, Johns Hopkins Press, 1951), p. 32, 93, 162, 49.

12. Hamilton to the British Minister, as quoted by S. F. Bemis, *Jay's Treaty. A Study in Commerce and Diplomacy* (New York, Macmillan and Co., 1924), p. 246.

13. R. W. Leopold, "The Mississippi Valley and American Foreign Policy, 1890–1941: an Assessment and an Appeal," *Mississippi Valley Historical Review,* XXXVII, NO. 4 (March, 1951), p. 635; H. C. Lodge, "Foreign Relations of the United States, 1921–1924," *Foreign Affairs,* II, NO. 4 (June, 1924), p. 526.

14. None of the authors cited above makes this association of events central to their discussion of the League issue. Few of them even connect the two. The integration has, of course, been made: most notably by E. H. Carr, *The Soviet Impact on the Western World* (New York, The Macmillan Co., 1947); M. Dobb, *Political Economy and Capitalism. Some Essays in Economic Tradition* (New York, International Publishers, 1945), Chapter VII, and *Studies in the Development of Capitalism* (New York, International Publishers, 1947), Chapter VIII; H. J. Laski, *Reflections on the Revolution of Our Time* (New York, 1947); Sir L. Namier, *Conflicts. Studies in Contemporary History* (London, The Macmillan Co., 1942), Chapter I; and, of especial significance, H. Hoover, *American Individualism* (Garden City, Doubleday, Page and Co., 1923).

15. W. Wilson, remarks to the Council of Ten, January 16, 1919, *Papers Relating to the Foreign Relations of the United States. Paris Peace Conference* (13 vols., Washington, D.C.), III, p. 583.

16. See the excellent essay by J. H. Foote, "American Industrialists and Foreign Policy, 1919–1922. A Study in Attitudes," Master's Thesis, University of Wisconsin, Madison, 1947; for a typical expression see the remarks of Senator Walter E. Edge—"we wasted, practically wasted, two years of the opportunity presented to us at that time, unequaled, as I say, in the history of the world"—in National Foreign Trade Council, *Official Report of the Eighth National Foreign Trade Convention, 1921* (New York, 1921), p. 553.

17. W. Wilson, remarks to the Big Five, February 14, 1919, *Foreign Relations. Russia, 1919* (Washington, D.C., 1937), p. 59.

18. C. Vevier reviewed these early expansionist sympathies of the Progressives in "The Progressives and Dollar Diplomacy," Master's Thesis, University of Wisconsin, Madison, 1949. W. E. Leuchtenburg later published a summary of his own study of the same question as "Progressivism and Imperialism: The Progressive Movement and American Foreign Policy, 1898–1916," *Mississippi Valley Historical Review,* XXXIX NO. 3 (December, 1952), p. 483–504. It would seem, however, that Leuchtenburg missed the split within the Progressives over Wilson's foreign policy. For in note 38, page 493, he considers it "remarkable" that the Progressives fought Wilson in view of the degree to which the president "was involved with American imperialist aspirations." This writer's information on the division comes from the manuscript papers of Calvin Coolidge, William E. Borah, William Judson, Samuel N. Harper, Theodore Roosevelt, Alexander Gumberg, Raymond Robins, and Woodrow

Wilson; from the materials in the National Archives; and the *Congressional Record.*

19. See, for example, the debates on the Webb-Pomerene Act in *Congressional Record,* Volume 56, Part 1, p. 69–71; and the votes on the same legislation, p. 168, 186.

20. Especially pertinent are the remarks of Borah, *Congressional Record,* V54:1:636; V57:1:190, V58:3:3143–44; and his letter to F. Lynch, August 1, 1919, *Papers of William E. Borah,* Library of Congress, manuscript Division, Washington, D.C. Also important are the comments of Senator Hiram Johnson, *Congressional Record,* V53:1:503, 505. Eric Goldman's penetrating study of the Progressives, *Rendezvous With Destiny. A History of Modern American Reform* (New York, Alfred A. Knopf, 1952), completely misses this development. On p. 273–74, Goldman remarks that the "most striking deviation of American progressivism in foreign affairs from its attitudes in domestic affairs was the enthusiasm for international order in the form of the League of Nations." He proceeds, then, to argue that if the progressives had applied the same criticism to the League as they had to its laissez faire counterpart in domestic affairs "they could hardly have emerged with a favorable attitude." But the key point is that the hard core of the Progressives did exactly this and came out in opposition to the League.

21. This paragraph is based on much the same material cited in note 18. But see, as representative, Cummins' remarks on the loans, *Congressional Record,* V5511:757, 762; Borah on economic factors, V64:1:930–31; and the parliamentary maneuvers over the Liberian Loan, V63:1:287–88.

22. Stimson, Diary entry of December 3, 1919, quoted in H. L. Stimson and McGeorge Bundy, *On Active Service in Peace and War* (New York, Harper and Brothers, 1948), p. 104.

23. H. F. Cline, *The United States and Mexico* (Cambridge, Harvard University Press, 1953), p. 141.

24. H. Croly, *The Promise of American Life* (New York, The Macmillan Co., 1909); H. Hoover, *American Individualism,* p. 43; and Hoover, quoted in Goldman, *Rendezvous With Destiny,* p. 309. Goldman makes this identification between Croly and Hoover, but does not develop it, either as corporatism or in foreign affairs. Other Americans had spoken the language of the community of interest. J. P. Morgan used it to describe his ideal in the economic realm. Brooks Adams warned Theodore Roosevelt that such coordination at the national level was necessary to insure American supremacy in the world. The Adams argument emphasized the need for an intellectual and political elite chosen from the upper classes to supervise the community of interest through control of the national government.

25. American corporatism is a neglected field. This writer is greatly indebted to Professor Paul Farmer, University of Wisconsin, for many long discussions of the question. Farmer brought to these conversations his intimate and extended knowledge of French corporative theory and practice as it developed to and culminated in the Vichy Government. His insights into the American scene were equally penetrating. At a later date M. H. Elbow, *French Corporative Theory, 1789–1948. A Chapter in the History of Ideas* (New York, Columbia University Press, 1953), was helpful in review. Of other published material, the following were most helpful: S. D. Alinsky, *Reveille For Radicals* (Chicago, University of Chicago Press, 1946); G. A. Almond, "The Political Attitudes of Wealth,"

Journal of Politics, VII, NO. 3 (August, 1945); R. A. Brady, *Business as a System of Power* (New York, Columbia University Press, 1938); R. Bendix, "Bureaucracy and the Problem of Power," *Public Administration Review,* V, NO. 3 (Summer, 1945); J. A. C. Grant, "The Guild Returns to America," *Journal of Politics,* IV, NOS. 3 AND 4 (August, November, 1942); W. E. Henry, "The Business Executive: the Psycho-Dynamics of a Social Role," *American Journal of Sociology,* LIV, NO. 1 (January, 1949); E. J. Howenstine, "Public Works Policy in the Twenties," *Social Research,* XII (December, 1946); F. Hunter, *Community Power Structure. A Study of Decision Makers* (Chapel Hill, University of North Carolina Press, 1953); R. S. Lynd, "Power Politics and the Post War World," in *The Postwar World. The Merrick Lectures for 1944* (New York, Abingdon-Cokesbury Press, 1945); and M. Weber, *The Theory of Social and Economic Organization,* trans. by A. M. Henderson and T. Parsons, ed. by T. Parsons (New York, Oxford University Press, 1947). For a revealing glimpse of the later bi-partisan movement toward corporatism, and the consequences thereof, see *The Welfare State and the National Welfare. A Symposium on Some of the Threatening Tendencies of Our Times,* ed. by S. Glueck (Cambridge, Addison-Wesley Press, Inc., 1952); and the last chapter in Goldman, *Rendezvous With Destiny.*

26. *The Memoirs of Herbert Hoover. The Cabinet and the Presidency, 1920–1933* (New York, The Macmillan Co., 1952), p. 36.
27. *Official Report of the 18th Foreign Trade Convention, 1931* (New York, 1931), p. 287.
28. C. E. Hughes, remarks concerning a substitute for Article X of the League Covenant, Union League Club Speech, New York, March 26, 1919.
29. J. Klein, *Frontiers of Trade* (New York, The Century Co., 1929), p. 40, 46.
30. C. Coolidge, Address of May 30, 1928, *Congressional Record,* V69:10:10729.
31. C. E. Hughes, "Centenary of the Monroe Doctrine," *Annals,* p. 17; and Hughes, remarks to the Havana Conference, 1928.
32. The story of the fight over diplomatic immunity for consular officers can be followed in *Foreign Relations, 1925,* p. 211–54; the quote from Hughes is by J. Butler Wright, in *Official Report of the 12th National Foreign Trade Convention, 1925,* (New York, 1925), p. 165.
33. Colby to Wright, November 5, 1920, *National Archives of the United States* (hereafter cited as *NA*), 574.D1/240b; Hughes, Memorandum of conversation with Geddes, September 20, 1921, *NA,* 500.A 4/190.5; Stimson, Memorandum of July 20, 1931, *NA,* 462.00 R 296/4594.5.
34. Colby to Russell, August 13, 1920, *NA,* 333.3921 L 96/3; Hughes to Cottrell, April 9, 1923, *NA,* 824.51/174; Hughes to Morales, June 30, 1923, *NA,* 815.00/2609; same to same, May 15, 1923, *NA,* 815.00/2574.
35. Kodding to Hughes, October 10, 1924. *NA,* 375.1123 Coleman and Delong/89; Hughes to Welles, April 10, 1924, *NA,* 815.00/3077a supplement.
36. Stimson, Memorandum of talks with representatives of J. P. Morgan and Co., Paris, July 17, 1931, *NA,* 462.00 R 296/4587.5.
37. G. F. Kennan, *American Diplomacy, 1900–1950* (Chicago, University of Chicago Press, 1951), p. 82; A. A. Berle, Jr. review of H. Feis, *The China Tangle,* in the *New York Times,* Book Review Section, October 4, 1953.
38. Hughes to Judge Hiscock, April 24, 1924, quoted in M. J. Pusey, *Charles Evans Hughes* (2 vols., New York, The Macmillan Co., 1951), II, p. 516; Hughes to

Bell, October 22, 1924, *NA,* 893.51/4699; Hughes, Memorandum of conversations with Kato and Balfour, December 2, 1921, *NA,* 500.A4b/547.5.

39. Hughes to Morgan, August 8, 1921, *NA,* 861.77/2184.
40. Stimson, Memorandum of November 21, 1931, *NA,* 793.94/2865; and see Stimson, Memorandum of February 27, 1933, *NA,* 793.94/5953, for a clear review of his changing attitudes.
41. This writer is greatly indebted to Professor Richard N. Current, University of Illinois, for sharing his extended knowledge of the Manchurian Crisis. Professor Current's study will be published in the spring of 1954 by Rutgers University Press.

IV ∽ *The Economy: Paralysis Or Prosperity?*

8 ∽ Business Thought in the Twenties: Social Responsibility*

[Author's Note] *The legacy of business thought in the 1920's is viewed positively by Morrell Heald of Case-Western Reserve University. Far from being an "impregnable citadel of the older values," the author recognizes significant efforts on the part of the business community to adopt a new social role suited to the changing nature of society. If business thought was, at times, conflicting, Heald argues that such contradictions merely reflected the uncertainties of the times.*

Much of the appeal which the decade of the 1920's exerts for Americans stems from its dramatic location in time. An era of rapid material progress and intriguing social high jinks stands in sharp contrast to the earnest reformism of the Progressive years and the desperate, but exhilarating, salvage effort of the New Deal. We have learned a great deal, to be sure, from thoughtful contrasts of the spirit and achievements of the twenties with other periods of our recent history. Now, new perspectives on this era are emerging. Scholars are pursuing the influences and remnants of Progressivism ever further into the postwar years.[1] Studies of the age of Franklin D. Roosevelt have shown how much its origins, its philosophy and its measures derive from the period presided over by Harding, Coolidge and Hoover. We are coming to see the twenties not alone as an era of rampant materialism, reaction and individualism but as a troubled decade in which old and new were inextricably intermingled and confronted. It was a time of deep uncertainty and conflict: of faltering efforts to face—or

* By Morrell Heald. Reprinted with permission from *American Quarterly* (published by the University of Pennsylvania), XIII (Summer, 1961), Pages 126–139. Copyright, 1961, Trustees of the University of Pennsylvania.

sometimes to avoid—the fact of change. It was an age, as we have come to understand, not so very different from our own.

Behind the bright façade of "normalcy" some perplexed Americans were awakening to a realization that normalcy would not return. Indeed, the term was peculiarly ill-fitted to years so characterized by sweeping economic and social change. Only by a desperate effort of will could the values and virtues of the old order be made to appear fully adequate for postwar America. Increasingly evident imbalances of urban industrial life demanded attention and provoked thought. Significant efforts to adapt existing institutions to new and pressing needs were undertaken even within the business community itself, that lofty and apparently impregnable citadel of the older values and source of so much that was calling them into question. For example, a broadening concept of the social role of corporate enterprise had appeared even before the war; but the twenties produced a more self-conscious and persistent concern with this question on the part of business leadership, as well as a notion of managerial trusteeship which has become a favorite theme in recent business literature.[2] No clearly-formulated doctrine of social responsibility had emerged by the end of the decade, if, indeed, one exists today. Nevertheless, men such as Gerard Swope and E. A. Filene were striving for a new understanding of business institutional relationships in a mass production economy. The forces underlying their search were diverse. Taken together, they included some of the most basic social tendencies of a dynamic, divided America.

Prominent among them was a spirit of idealism and sacrifice in the common interest which had been aroused and only partially satisfied by the war. Without recognition of the influence of this sentiment, its frustration and distortions in the course of the decade, no understanding of the twenties is complete. Its impact on business thought can be traced in the record of the term, "service." Charles Cason, vice-president of the Chemical National Bank of New York struck a note echoed in innumerable business editorials, speeches, articles and advertisements:

> "Today, there is a new point of view. We know that real success in business is not attained at the expense of others. Business can succeed only in the long run by acquiring and holding the good will of the people. To do this, it is necessary to render honest, intelligent service at a fair price . . . The best upper class men in business are really genuine in their belief in it [service] and are consistent in its practice. Most of them would not consider a policy which enriched them or their company and was at the same time against the public interest."[3]

Others—clergymen, journalists, politicians—joined in proclaiming "service" to be the chief aim and justification of American business. Henry Ford asserted that, "Service as a basis for profit-making is coming to be recognized as the true motive for creative industry."[4] Probably no single motto or slogan exercised more appeal within and beyond the business community. For many the service motif helped justify and reconcile the peacetime pursuit of profit with the war-awakened sense of community, although as time passed some prophets and practitioners of service seemed to find it more attractive as a sales slogan than as a standard for practical policy-making.[5] Still, whatever their source, the many changes rung upon the theme kept the notion of public service in the forefront of business thinking.

If the service ideal came to be seized upon and exploited chiefly for propaganda purposes, it could hardly have escaped the consequences of management's awakening interest in the cultivation of friendly and favorable public opinion. Like so much that attracted notice in the twenties, the public relations movement had its origins in the prewar era. Now it found an eager audience and ready customers among the executives of large corporations. The reasons for this interest are complex and only some of the major factors can be noted here. Although the American public was generally complacent and uncritical, the rise of the Soviet state was an ominous portent. At home, the Red Scare and the obvious disenchantment of some writers and intellectuals were hardly calculated to promote peace of mind in conservative circles. The irreverent image of businessmen as Babbitts rankled more than many were willing to admit. Although the Federal government was in friendly hands, the expansion of its functions continued; and state governments increased their expenditures even more rapidly. Underlying these factors and of even greater immediacy was recognition that the spread of mass production and economic concentration made business more than ever dependent on a favorable public image of its institutions and its products. Often managers tended to consider good public relations simply in terms of support and acceptance for their policies; but some acknowledged that public approval must be earned, not simply manipulated. Walter S. Gifford, for example, wrote,

> ". . . not only our stockholders, but the public generally, are entitled to know how we are carrying on our stewardship. . . . It is our further purpose to conduct the affairs of the Bell System in accordance with American ideals and traditions, so that it may continue to merit the confidence of the people of the country."[6]

Mass production and the centralization of decision-making through the growth of corporations, holding companies and trade associations were among the most highly visible economic developments of the 1920's. Less immediately obvious was the threat these tendencies posed for traditional values and practices. Business executives, close to powerful sources of change, were sometimes more perceptive than others in sensing their implications. ". . . The machinery of modern business does make the whole world one, . . . we are mutually dependent and must, if we are to give expression to our very will to live, go in with all our heart for mutual service," wrote E. A. Filene, a point of view other businessmen found increasingly relevant to problems of sales, capital and credit, as well as to industrial and community relations.[7] As J. H. Tregoe, Secretary-Treasurer of the National Association of Credit Men, put it in 1922:

> With the geographical separation of seller and buyer that followed this large-scale manufacture and large-scale distribution, commerce done on the principle of caveat emptor was on a precarious basis. Selling and buying needed a confidence and warmth which the principle of caveat emptor did not supply. Goods could not move freely if the buyer had continually "to beware." The compulsion was laid on the seller to make his goods of such quality as to remove the suspicion of the buyer and to insure his confidence in the goods.[8]

Managers often acknowledged that their growing interest in harmonious relations with employees, stockholders, customers and the public resulted quite as much from the exigencies of profit under changing economic conditions as from moral or social concerns.

It was, perhaps, in their altered relationship to the stockholders whose properties they managed that corporation managers faced most directly the broad implications of institutional change. As stock ownership became more widespread, management found itself increasingly free to set its own policies and define its own responsibilities. Executives of large corporations spoke deferentially of obligations to their employers, but already stockholders were coming to be considered as simply one among a variety of interests and participants in the enterprise whose claims management must recognize and reconcile. Arthur Pound, describing the changing nature of this relationship from the perspective of 1936, wrote,

> The American way is to pay the stockholder well, to treat him honestly and gently, but to keep him in his place, so that he has neither the de-

> sire nor the extended opportunity to interfere with operations and policies.[9]

Owen D. Young, whose career with General Electric coincided with and helped to clarify the shift in corporate leadership and responsibility, saw the issues it presented. Young acknowledged the ambiguities of policy-making in an institution in which ownership was divorced from direct participation. Only managers could be held responsible for business policies, he stated,

> . . . it makes a great difference in my attitude toward my job as an executive officer of the General Electric Company whether I am a trustee of an institution or an attorney for the investor. If I am a trustee of the institution, who are the beneficiaries of the trust? To whom do I owe my obligation?[10]

Young, as did other executives of the twenties, concluded that his obligation extended to include the workers, the customers and the general public. Management's task as trustee for these parties, he believed, involved maintenance of the good credit of the institution, provision of healthy working conditions and the production of a high-quality product, meeting the corporation's duties as a "good citizen." Thus, a counterpart of management's growing independence from owner domination was its recognition of the claims of other interest groups including that vague entity, the community at large.

The new generation of independent corporate managers which came to power and prominence in the 1920's was more than ever before a professional group. Many of its members had received advanced training in American universities and colleges. Young and Gary were lawyers, although Gary represented in most respects an earlier phase in the evolution of management. Swope and Sloan were engineers. Among such men, owner-entrepreneur Henry Ford was becoming an anachronism despite the impetus he had given to the remodeling of the industrial order. The influence of advanced professional training on business executives deserves closer analysis than it has so far received. Arthur Pound's claim that ". . . the legal influence introduced the idea of justice, the habit of compromise, and the institutional idea into American industry" was seconded by businessmen who asserted that the educational backgrounds of the newer corporate managers tended to produce a broader understanding of the ramifications and social relations of their companies.[11] It seems likely that training in other professions than the law supported and strengthened this shift in attitudes. The advantages of such preparation were apparent to the growing number of men who attended business and professional schools. Additional evidence that management approved such training can be found in the burgeoning of night school, summer school and other special courses provided by the colleges with the encouragement and sometimes the direct support of business. Through these programs young businessmen came into contact with psychology and sociology, as well as more orthodox business and economics subjects. Northwestern University, for example, offered under the sponsorship of the Chamber of Commerce and the American Trade Association Executive a series of two-week summer sessions which included courses on civic affairs and problems of the community. Business support for research, a growing practice at this time, reflected still further in awakening to the need for systematic study of social and economic problems.[12] A quite different, and highly informal, experience which surely influenced the thinking of business leaders was the fact that many had come to maturity during the Progressive period, with its critique of traditional business ethics and its drive for higher standards of public and private ethics. Both Gerard Swope and Walter Gifford, to cite an unusual example, had lived and worked with Jane Addams at Hull House. This was direct education, not easily forgotten.[13]

Emphasis on the role of ethics in business came also from a quite different direction. As part of the "self-regulation" movement led by trade associations and chambers of commerce, formulating and promulgating codes of ethics became one of the more popular business pastimes of the period. Serving to justify the elimination of "unfair" competition, it demonstrated the concern of an increasingly centralized economic system for careful cultivation of its public relations. Whether seriously intended and consequently practiced or not, these codes by their sheer numbers kept before the business community an ideal, however vague, of accountability to the public. As early as 1922, F. M. Feiker, vice president of the McGraw-Hill Company and an associate of Secretary of Commerce Hoover, argued on behalf of trade associations that, ". . . sooner or later such associations become professionally conscious . . . set up for each member standards of practice or codes of ethics which, broadly speaking, constitute a great structure, with the service motive as the standard of conduct. . . ."[14] In 1925 the President of the U.S. Chamber of Commerce proudly reported that its statement of "Principles of Business

Conduct," adopted the previous year, had been subscribed to by over seven hundred and fifty member organizations representing more than three hundred thousand businessmen. "I find," he complimented his constituents, "no such recognition of obligation to the public among the other blocs or factions in this country."[15]

The new roles and responsibilities of corporate managers, as these men interpreted their own functions, were most fully summed up, perhaps, in the idea of trusteeship. The concept coupled with broad authority an ill-defined commitment to consideration of the public interest in the making of business policy. A typical formulation was that of the Chamber of Commerce Committee on Business Ethics:

> The primary obligation of those who direct and manage a corporation is to its stockholders. Notwithstanding this, they act in a representative capacity, and in such a capacity owe obligations to others—to employees, to the public which they serve, and even to their competitors. . . .[16]

Gerard Swope, a notable advocate of this view of management's role, put it even more succinctly when he said, "Today a much higher proportion of corporate leaders realize their responsibilities as trustees of other people's money, their obligation of service to the public, and their duty to their employees."[17] While the spokesmen for this "managerial" viewpoint were chiefly representatives of the larger corporations, trade associations and chambers of commerce, their prestige and authority were greater than their numbers. Their statements set a standard with which the wider business community could hardly avoid comparing its policies.

To what extent were these concepts of social responsibility and trusteeship translated into actual practice by business firms during the 1920's? Their influence can be seen in a number of policies initiated at this time as well as in a new impetus or direction given to older practices. Especially noteworthy were developments in three areas; industrial relations, publicity and education, and corporate philanthropy. Of these, industrial relations attracted the widest attention. Company-sponsored unions, employee stock-ownership plans, industrial pension and welfare programs, while hardly new, experienced a sudden spurt of interest and support in management circles. By inference, at least, such programs conceded that the existing order did not adequately provide for the needs and desires of an industrial labor force. Many were based upon the paternalistic assumption that the employer knew what was best for his help. Yet the failures of "industrial democracy" or "welfare capitalism," 1920's style, need not blind us to their significance as steps toward recognition of management's stake in the security and satisfaction of the worker.[18] More questionable and, ultimately, even less successful were the efforts of some business groups to promote what they considered to be a friendly climate of public opinion. Led especially by the utility companies, these propaganda ventures became involved, among other things, in efforts to silence criticisms of the business system in the press and the schools. In the long run, of course, they failed dismally. The depression revealed weaknesses in the system no propaganda campaign could conceal. Yet this movement, too, with all its shortcomings, was an important step in a new direction. Those who backed such campaigns recognized, in effect, the dependence of business upon public approval and support.[19]

The third, and in some ways the most fruitful, of the areas in which business executives explored the limits of their social obligation, was the donation of corporate funds to hospitals, community chests and similar welfare agencies. Here there was no sudden, spectacular campaign, no flurry of interest or "all-out" drive. Rather, the record shows modest, but steadily increasing, support for philanthropic and welfare work. Even the depression, while it retarded the movement, did not destroy it. Only toward the end of the decade did thoughtful men begin to see that a transformation in the concept of the modern business corporation was involved. A paternal management interest in the order, stability and welfare of the communities from which it drew workers was, again, not new. In Pullman, Aliquippa, Gary and many other company towns employers, both for highly moral and severely practical reasons, had long recognized their stake in the social conditions surrounding their plants.[20] Had the postwar years seen only an expansion of these policies, they would have marked merely the unchecked growth of a benevolent business autocracy. But such was not the case. Simultaneously with the growth of management's sensitivity to social conditions had emerged a well-organized, professionally trained, and ably led social work movement. Increasingly united for fund-raising and the interpretation of community needs through the community chest movement, welfare work in the twenties was achieving a professional competence of its own. Community chests appealed to businessmen on grounds of efficiency and promised to relieve them from the necessity for evaluating the many appeals received from individual agencies. Chest leaders, too, were conscious of their stake in the interest and support of business. Managers found themselves serving in increasing numbers as board members or as active fund raisers for chest agencies. Indeed, the success of the community chest movement was, to a considerable degree, the result of collaboration between these two increasingly professionally-minded groups.[21]

Statistics can indicate the dimensions, but scarcely the true significance, of this joint approach to problems of community welfare. Here business leaders were confronted with the consequences of industrialization as interpreted by independent experts. Here they could participate in an exchange of views and a definition of responsibilities which held the promise, at least, of a larger concept of community welfare and business contributions to it. Many difficult problems were involved. The right of corporate management to spend company funds for community purposes had to be clarified, a lengthy and laborious process in law and policy-making. In addition to the right, the advisability of making donations remained very much a question in the minds of many executives. Standards for measuring the extent of responsibility were unclear. The relationship of corporate gifts to the power of determining allocation of chest funds was in dispute. None of these issues was resolved by the end of the decade, nor, indeed, have some been settled today. Still, important beginnings were made. By 1928, business and community chest leaders at both the local and national levels were jointly striving for mutually acceptable solutions to these problems. In this context, the social responsibility of business enterprise was on the way to being recognized, not as an issue to be resolved by management alone, but as itself a community problem.

The emergence of the idea that corporate profits might properly be devoted to community welfare projects is difficult to reconcile with the notion of the twenties as a time when business with singleminded intensity pursued the almighty dollar. The sunny climate of prosperity undoubtedly encouraged experiments in corporate giving. In this sense corporate philanthropy may well have been an unrecognized stepbrother of the more frenzied and widely publicized speculative booms of the period. As our understanding of the decade deepens, however, the contribution of other factors mentioned here becomes more apparent. The ideal of service, the drive for public approbation and support, the consequences of mass production and large-scale organization, and the emergence of a professional management group of self-designated "trustees" all contributed impulses and opportunities for which corporate philanthropy provided convenient satisfactions. Concern for the social responsibilities of their enterprises was clearly more than a luxury item on the list of problems pondered by business executives. To be sure, the depression of 1921–23 squeezed much of the idealism out of the postwar concern for "service." Similarly, many of the hastily assembled, largely paternalistic employee welfare programs collapsed—victims of economic pressure and their own failure to meet the true needs of the worker. Much that was ill-conceived and partisan in the social policies of business failed to survive the even more severe test of 1929–33. On the whole, the programs that weathered the storm were those which met fundamental problems of economic security and social welfare in realistic, generally acceptable terms. In its efforts to evaluate its social role and responsibilities, business leadership learned most and achieved most when it worked *with,* rather than merely *for,* other interest groups.[22]

The point to be noted, however, is that a variety of ideas and practices did survive. Some businessmen did sense the fact of change and the need to face new problems with new social techniques. Behind the optimism and confidence of the official organs of business opinion lurked a number of ill-defined but insistent issues: the meaning of the nationalization of economic power and social control, the social consequences of large-scale organization and the emergence of an apparently chronic problem of economic insecurity in a technically progressive, industrial society. If America was, as some sensed, in the process of a major social and economic upheaval, workable solutions for these problems must be found. The practice of corporate philanthropy as it developed during the twenties grew in part out of a desire to cope with, or to stave off, the consequences of social change dimly seen and imperfectly understood.

Yet corporate philanthropy by no means won unanimous approval even among "progressive" business leaders. One of the most thoughtful, E. A. Filene, sharply challenged the philosophy and practice of corporate giving, re-asserting in broadened terms the traditional justification of business enterprise. Donations to charity, Filene felt, indicated "often a supine acquiescence in the assumption that the poor are always going to be with us and that nothing can be done about it." The true responsibility of the businessman was not to alleviate poverty, but to abolish it. "It is my belief that business men can best serve the cause of social progress through activities in their own field—by advancing their own self-interest."[23] Henry Ford agreed. "It is easy to give; it is harder to make giving unnecessary," he wrote. "I have no patience with professional charity or with any sort of commercialized humanitarianism. . . . Industry organized for service removes the need for philanthropy. Philanthropy, no matter how noble its motive, does not make for self-reliance. We must have self-reliance."[24] In this view, economic self-interest remained the key to social welfare; but Filene was no simple conservative. Rather, he saw management's role as dynamic: the creation of an increasingly efficient and productive economy in the social interest. In contrast to Filene's view that business was most responsible when most intent on its own internal problems were the more sweeping, if not more ambitious, ideas of corporate responsibility this paper has summarized. As Henry D. Sharpe, president of Brown and Sharpe, expressed them, "Directors may think of themselves merely as trustees of property interests and ignore the social conditions of the community from which their corporation draws its labor and its patronage. Not at all in an invidious sense, this is a narrow concept of responsibility."[25]

The issue posed by these conflicting viewpoints has been clarified, if not resolved, by the passage of time. If profit alone does not define the limits of managerial responsibility, where is the line to be drawn? Or is management properly free to define and undertake obligations throughout the length and breadth of society, in education, the arts and politics no less than in community welfare?[26] The legacy of business thought in the 1920's lies precisely in its recognition of the changing nature of corporate enterprise and its posing of a problem whose significance has become increasingly evident.

Business ideas about the social role and responsibility of corporate management, then, reflected the uncertainties of the times. In its mixture of old and new ideas, its simultaneous tendencies to conserve and to experiment, business thought was conflicting—and typical. Nowhere is the confusion and divergence of views more evident than in discussions of the issue of social responsibility. Certainly, the traditional belief that management's chief duty was to earn profits experienced no sudden eclipse. Yet, even its most ardent defenders laid increased stress on the social justification of profit as contributing to the welfare of the community at large. On the other hand, the conviction was spreading that management must think more than ever before of the social implications of its policies. Far from being completely immobilized in adulation of the status quo, business leadership was exploring new solutions for new, or recently recognized, problems. It was a period of trial and error. If the errors and shortcomings were numerous, the trials—the new ventures in business thought and practice—were of equal importance for the future of business and American society.

NOTES

1. Arthur S. Link, "What Happened to the Progressive Movement in the 1920's" *American Historical Review,* LXIV (July 1959), 833–51. Research for this paper has been made possible in part by the Research Fund of Case Institute of Technology.
2. Morrell Heald, "Management's Responsibility to Society: The Growth of an Idea," *Business History Review,* XXXI (Winter, 1957), 375–79.
3. *Commercial and Financial Chronicle,* CXXV (November 12, 1927), 2625–26. See also: *Nation's Business,* XII (June, 1924), 16; XIII (January, 1925), 18–20; XV (March, 1927), 95–96; XV (May, 1927), 15 ff.; *World's Work,* LII (March, 1927), 556–61; United States Chamber of Commerce, *Report of the Thirteenth Annual Meeting . . .* (1925), pp. 16–17. Compare James Warren Prothro, *The Dollar Decade, Business Ideas in the 1920's* (Baton Rouge, La., 1954), pp. 46, 54–59, *passim.* The influence of war-time idealism on the formulation of the business concept of service in the twenties can be traced in the following: George W. Perkins, "We Are as Unprepared for Peace as We Are for War" (New York, n.d. [1915]), p. 21; John D. Rockefeller, Jr., *The Personal Relation in Industry* (New York: Boni & Liveright, 1923), pp. 11–13, 21, 83, 116, *passim.;* U.S. Chamber of Commerce, *Report of the Seventh Annual Meeting . . .* (1919), p. 45; Lucius E. Wilson, *Community Leadership, The New Profession* (New York, 1919), pp. 63–66; *Forbes Magazine,* VI (May 1, 1920), 51; B. C. Forbes, *Finance, Business and the Business of Life* (New York, 1915), *passim.*
4. F. M. Feiker, "The Profession of Commerce in the Making," *Annals of the American Academy of Political and Social Science,* CI (May, 1922), 203–7; Henry Ford in cooperation with Samuel Crowther, *My Life and Work* (New York: Doubleday, Page & Co., 1922), p. 20.
5. William Nelson Taft, "Shouting 'Service' as a Battle Cry," *Nation's Business,* XIII (April, 1925), 37–39. See also XIV (April, 1926), 104 and XIV (October, 1926), 120.
6. Quoted in Arthur Pound, *The Telephone Idea* (New York: Greenberg, 1926), n., p. 21. Business leaders, of course, had no intention of abdicating all management's prerogatives in order to court public favor. See Alfred P. Sloan, Jr., "Modern Ideals of Business," *World's Work,* LII (September, 1926), 694–97; *Forbes Magazine,* XIV (May 10, 1924), 178; Samuel Insull, *Public Utilities in Modern Life* (Chicago, 1924), p. 262. Thomas C. Cochran, *The American Business System* (Cambridge, 1957), p. 155, has held that businessmen conceived of public relations in the twenties as consisting primarily in the dissemination of favorable publicity and in silencing critics. He has suggested that the concept of public relations as a "two-way street" did not win acceptance until later. This is largely true; but it should not obscure the fact that many business spokesmen of the period *said* that their companies were trying to deserve the confidence

they desired. See Sloan, *World's Work,* LII, 694–97; *Forbes Magazine, XIV* (May 24, 1924), 215; Edwin B. Parker, "The Fifteen Commandments of Business," *Nation's Business,* XII (June, 1924), 16; David Loth, *Swope of G. E.* (New York, 1958), pp. 129–32. For statements revealing reasons for the growing interest in public relations, see S. T. Scofield, "Business is Getting Public," *Advertizing and Selling,* X (February 22, 1928), 28 ff.; *Forbes Magazine,* III (February 8, 1919), 771; VI (October 2, 1920), 456; XIV (May 24), 218; XIV (June 21, 1924), 367, and *passim.; Nation's Business,* XV (March, 1924), 10, 95–96, and *passim.;* U.S. Chamber of Commerce, *Report of the Twelfth Annual Meeting . . .* (1924), p. 19, *Report of the Sixteenth Annual Meeting . . .* (1928), p. 43; N. R. Danelian, *A. T. and T.; The Story of Industrial Conquest* (New York, 1939), pp. 285–86; John A. R. Pimlott, *Public Relations and American Democracy* (Princeton, 1951), p. 235.

7. E. A. Filene, *Successful Living in the Machine Age* (New York: Simon & Schuster, 1931), pp. 80–81.

8. J. H. Tregoe, "Canons of Commercial Ethics," *Annals . . .,* CI (May, 1922), 208. See also, Mark Wiseman, "Why I Stay in Business," *Survey,* LXV (February 1, 1931), 469–72; E. A. Filene, "A Simple Code of Business Ethics," *Annuals . . .,* CI (May, 1922), 223–28; Arundel Cotter, *United States Steel, A Corporation with a Soul* (New York, 1921), pp. 185–96; John D. Rockefeller, Jr., *The Personal Relation in Industry,* p. 15.

9. Arthur Pound, *Industrial America, Its Way of Work and Thought* (Boston, 1936), pp. 16–17; *Nation's Business,* XVII (March, 1929), 11; David Loth, *Swope,* pp. 129 ff.; Owen D. Young, "Business—The Newest Profession," *Aera,* XVIII (October, 1927), 301–6; Arthur Pound, *The Telephone Idea,* p. 16; Whiting Williams, "Business Statesmanship, A New Force in Business," *Magazine of Business,* LVIII (April, 1929), 388 ff.; Ida M. Tarbell, *Owen D. Young, a New Type of Industrial Leader* (New York, 1932), p. 233; *Iron Age,* CXVII (February 25, 1926), 523–24; Sloan, *World's Work,* LII, 694–98.

10. *Nation's Business,* XVII (March, 1929), 161–64; Whiting Williams, "What Makes Business an Institution," *Magazine of Business,* LV (June, 1929), 658–59; John H. Sears, *The New Place of the Stockholder* (New York, 1929), pp. 26–27.

11. Pound, *Industrial America,* pp. 10–13; Tarbell, *Owen D. Young,* pp. 62, 92–94; Loth, *Swope,* p. 21, 129 ff.; Tom M. Girdler, in collaboration with Boyden Sparks, *Bootstraps, The Autobiography of Tom M. Girdler* (New York, 1943), p. 158; Owen D. Young, *Aera,* XVIII, 301–6; Whiting Williams, *Magazine of Business,* LV, 388–90; *Commercial and Financial Chronicle,* CXXV, 2625–26.

12. Dean W. Malott, "Business Advancing as a Profession," *Iron Trade Review,* LXXIV (June 12, 1924), 1564–65; Josiah H. Penniman, "Business and Higher Learning," *Nation's Business,* XIII (November, 1925), 56 ff.; *Nation's Business,* XIV (April, 1926), 58–60; Glenn Frank, "Needed: A New Man of Business," *Magazine of Business,* LII (November, 1927), 565–67; Rockefeller, *The Personal Relation in Industry,* p. 46.

13. Zona Gale, "Great Ladies of Chicago," *Survey,* LXVII (February 1, 1932), 482; Loth, *Swope,* pp. 21, 31–38, 48–51, *passim.*

14. Feiker, *Annals of American Academy of Political and Social Science,* CI, 203–7.

15. U.S. Chamber of Commerce, *Report of the Thirteenth Annual Meeting . . .* (1925), pp. 16–17. See also, *Nation's Business,* XII (June, 1924), 5, 7–9;

Forbes Magazine, XXII (October 15, 1928), 60; U.S. Chamber of Commerce, *Report of the Sixteenth Annual Meeting . . .* (1928), p. 13.

16. Edwin B. Parker, "The Fifteen Commandments of Business," *Nation's Business,* XII (June, 1924), 16 ff. See also, *Nation's Business,* XVII (March, 1929), 9, 142–46; Insull, *Public Utilities . . .,* p. 262; Loth, *Swope,* p. 162; Pound, *Industrial America,* pp. 26–27, Tarbell, *Owen D. Young,* pp. 155–56, 232; E. H. Gary, "Principles and Policies of the United States Steel Corporation," n. p., n. d. (1921), pp. 5–6; *Forbes Magazine,* XIV (April 26, 1924), 113. Gary, more clearly than the others, strongly hinted at the right of management to exercise independent judgment as to what constituted the public interest. John D. Rockefeller, Jr., on the other hand, perhaps because he was less directly involved in the day-to-day problems of management himself, proposed "adequate representation of the four parties [capital, management, labor and the public] in the councils of industry." *The Personal Relations in Industry,* pp. 12–21. Sometimes "the public" was subdivided into two groups: consumers, and the community at large.

17. Gerard Swope, "What Big Business Owes to the Public," *World's Work,* LIII (March, 1927), 556–61.

18. Tarbell, *Owen D. Young,* p. 150, 227, ff.; *Survey,* LXIV (July 15, 1930), 340; Beulah Amidon, "Ivorydale, A Payroll That Floats," *Survey,* LXIV (April 1, 1930), 18 ff.; Loth, *Swope,* pp. 153, 167–72.

19. Sloan, *World's Work,* LII, 694–96; Lucius E. Wilson, *Community Leadership, The New Profession* (New York, 1919), pp. 63–66; *Nation's Business,* XVII (August, 1929), 13; Danelian, *A. T. and T.,* pp. 284–92; *Forbes Magazine,* III (January 25, 1919), 724; XIV (May 24, 1924), 215, 218, 226; XIV (June 7, 1924), 310; XIV (June 21, 1924), 367; Loth, *Swope,* p. 134.

20. Of Aliquippa in 1914, Tom M. Girdler later wrote, ". . . I became an unofficial caliph, an American Haroun-al-Raschid obliged by my office in a big corporation to consider a whole community as my personal responsibility." *Bootstraps . . .,* pp. 165–66.

21. Pierce Williams and Frederick E. Croxton, *Corporate Contributions to Organized Community Welfare Services* (New York, 1930), 56–93; F. Emerson Andrews, *Corporation Giving* (New York, 1952), pp. 15–39; "Multiplicity of Community Chest Appeals Source of Vexation to National Business Concerns," American Association for Community Organization, *Bulletin #30,* January, 1927; Paul A. Schoellkopf, "The Corporation and Its Community," *Survey,* LX (September 1, 1928), 540 ff.; Helen B. Leavens, "A Social Worker in Prosperity Land," *Survey,* LXI (March 15, 1929), 789–91; Arthur J. Todd, "Corporations as Givers," *Survey,* LXIV (August 15, 1930), 424–25; F. S. Tisdale, "Winning Ways of the Charity Fakers," *Nation's Business,* XIV (August, 1926), 26 ff.; XIV (February, 1926), 67. Extensive data on the interaction between business leadership and community chest officials can be found in the files of the United Community Funds and Councils of America, Inc., New York City, where the writer has had access to them through the courtesy of Mr. Ralph Blanchard, Executive Director, and Miss Fay Webb, Director of Reference Services. See especially "Big Business and Community Chests," Association of Community Chests and Councils, *Minutes . . .,* I (April 10, 1928), 419; *Minutes . . .,* I (January 12, 1925), 5; Mark M. Jones. "Corporate Contributions to Community Welfare Agencies" (New York, 1929), File Box 72: "Corporate Gifts—Tax Deduction."

22. Beulah Amidon, *Survey,* LXIV, 20; Tarbell, *Owen D. Young,* p. 224. It is interesting to find the president of the U.S. Chamber of Commerce in his 1922 address stating, "What is not for the public good is not for the good of business," and emphasizing "the obvious fact that business alone cannot be the final judge of what is for the public good." U.S. Chamber of Commerce, *Report of the Tenth Annual Meeting . . .* (1922), pp. 7–8.
23. E. A. Filene, "I Believe in Working with Others," *Nation's Business,* XVII (April, 1929), 179 ff. See also, *Successful Living in the Machine Age, passim.; Annals . . .,* CI, p. 223–28; *Survey,* LXXIII (October, 1937), 318–19.
24. Henry Ford, *My Life and Work,* pp. 206–10; see also *Fortune,* VII (June, 1933), 50 ff.
25. Henry D. Sharpe, "What Business Owes the Town," *Nation's Business,* XVII (October, 1929), 47 ff.
26. Suggestions as to the directions in which "broad construction" of the responsibility of business might lead can be found in Merwin K. Hart, "Next Job for Business Leadership," *Magazine of Business,* LV (January, 1929), 40 ff., and Julius H. Barnes, "Growing Responsibility of Business," *Nation's Business,* XVII (May, 1929), 15 ff. Both Hart and Barnes believed business leadership ready and able to resolve pressing national and international problems. It was Barnes's view that, ". . . if America translates into the conduct of world enterprise the ethics and standards of American business today it will more directly establish the welfare of uncounted millions than any other crusade in history." On the other hand, John Ihlder, of the U.S. Chamber of Commerce, recognized the danger of business domination and the need for joint participation in social programs. "The Business Man's Responsibility," *Nation's Business,* XIII (November, 1925), 52 ff. For recent discussions of this issue, see Theodore Levitt, "The Dangers of Social Responsibility," *Harvard Business Review,* XXXVI (September–October, 1958), 41–50; O. A. Ohmann, "Search for a Managerial Philosophy," *Harvard Business Review,* XXXV (September–October, 1927), 41–51; Raymond Moley, "Good Gulf Citizenship," *Newsweek* (July 20, 1959), p. 100; Peter F. Drucker, "The Responsibilities of Management," *Harper's Magazine,* CCIX (November, 1954), 67–72; Edward S. Mason, "The Apologetics of 'Managerialism,'" *Journal of Business,* XXXI (January, 1958), 1–11.

9 ~ Labor and Bolshevism*

[Author's Note] *Inextricably linked to the Red Scare of 1919 was the position of organized labor. The Seattle strike led to a spate of anti-union propaganda. Before 1919 was out, much of the concern over domestic radicalism centered around arguments over the merits of collective bargaining. Robert K. Murray of Pennsylvania State University attaches great import to the link that existed in the public mind between labor and Bolshevism and hence the paralyzed state of the unionization movement throughout the twenties. While basic conservatism dominated organized labor in the post-Versailles era, Murray finds that public confidence in the movement declined in response to some of labor's actions. This lack of confidence was nursed along by employers determined to halt the war-time gains of the workingman.*

In any careful analysis of a social phenomenon like hysteria, one always finds in operation a tangled mass of deep-seated causative factors which interact to produce the ultimate manifestation of aberrant response.

This was certainly true in the case of the United States following World War I. As we have seen, by mid-1919 there were a host of factors in existence which were establishing the conditions necessary for the development of national psychoneurosis. The contemporary postwar scene with its war-born emotionalism, its misguided desire for normalcy, and its political and economic instability represented one such factor. The rise of Russian bolshevism, the affinity of domestic radicals for the Bolshevik doctrine, the Seattle strike, the riots, and the bombs constituted still others. Also significant were the various investigations, the sensationalism of the

* *Red Scare: A Study in National Hysteria, 1919–1920* by Robert K. Murray. Pages 105–121. University of Minnesota Press, Minneapolis. Copyright 1955 by University of Minnesota.

press, and the activities of certain politicians, employers, veterans, and super-patriots.

However, in probing into the causes for hysteria, one also is likely to discover one factor which more than any other acts as the trigger mechanism that throws the whole complex reaction of stimulus and response into operation. By mid-1919 there was one such factor in the American scene which did act as the prime mover because upon it the "scare" effectiveness of the other factors was largely dependent and by it the average American squared his thinking on the seriousness of the radical menace.

It involved the position of organized labor.

Because of such incidents as the Seattle strike and the growing success of antiunion propaganda, by mid-1919 much of the concern over domestic radicalism centered around organized labor. It was generally agreed that if domestic radicalism would succeed at all it would succeed first within the ranks of the laboring man; hence the activities of labor were watched carefully as a barometer to the real extent of radicalism in the nation. Public stability, in turn, depended in large measure upon the results of such observations, for as long as the public retained confidence in the fidelity of labor there was scant opportunity for hysteria to emerge.

Organized labor tried from the beginning to entrench itself in the public mind as one of the nation's chief bulwarks against the philosophy of bolshevism. This should not have been difficult to do. The AFL was avowedly a nonrevolutionary organization; indeed, led by Samuel Gompers and organized generally along craft lines, it was highly conservative. Its patriotism during the war had been unexcelled and its wartime cooperation with both government and industry had been unusually consistent. This is not to say that the AFL was apathetic to the workers' cause. On the contrary, it had constantly fought for higher wages, shorter hours, and union recognition, and in order to secure such gains had often used the weapon of the strike. Nevertheless, the AFL had always worked within the framework of the existing economic order and was a firm supporter of the capitalistic system. This fact had already prompted many of those who desired more aggressive action on behalf of the working class to remain outside the AFL and adhere to such other organizations as the IWW. As far as the basic conservatism of the American worker was concerned, one need only recall that while the IWW had 60,000 members at its peak, the AFL had more than 4,000,000.

In spite of later charges, basic conservatism was still the trademark of the AFL in the Red Scare era. As a matter of fact, the organization had already evidenced this when, in June 1918, it announced that although it would continue its crusade in the postwar period for the workers' right to organize and bargain collectively with employers for an adequate living wage and shorter hours of work, it would do so only within the existing fabric of the free enterprise system and without any overtones of radicalism whatsoever.[1] Obviously, a labor organization could not possibly have adopted a more inoffensive postwar program, and it was upon this basis that the historic struggle between American capital and labor was renewed.

It was true that there were a few within the ranks of organized labor in 1919 who did not share the AFL's interest in conservative action. Impressed by the recent Bolshevik Revolution in Russia, they either sympathized with the new Bolshevik philosophy or openly championed it. This was particularly the case with certain members of the various city labor councils and with recent immigrants to this country who had since made their way into the numerous unions of the AFL. Such persons believed that the AFL was moving too slowly and that the announcement of 1918 was not indicative of what the workers really wanted. James Duncan of the Seattle Central Labor Council was an example of those who entertained such beliefs.[2]

Besides these individuals, there were also some unions in 1919 which were out of sympathy with the AFL's conservative policies. Organizations such as the Amalgamated Clothing Workers, Amalgamated Textile Workers, Needle Trades International, and International Ladies' Garment Workers either refused to affiliate with the AFL because of its conservatism, or although belonging to the organization, openly opposed its postwar program. Within such unions there were indications that pro-Bolshevik radicals exerted some influence.[3]

Having already displayed an uncompromising attitude toward the Bolshevik doctrine, conservative AFL officials watched these indications of labor radicalism with growing apprehension and took immediate steps to combat it. The reasons for their resultant antiradical campaign were twofold. First of all, in view of widespread antiunion propaganda, AFL officials desired to remove from organized labor all possible taint of "bolshevism"; secondly, being conservatives themselves, they had a natural distrust and hatred for all radical labor theory.

Leading the attack was Samuel Gompers, who constantly attempted to keep union labor conservative and prevent deviations from the AFL's postwar program. Supported in this fight by other labor leaders, such as

Daniel J. Tobin, Timothy Healey, Matthew Woll, and John L. Lewis, Gompers was especially caustic in his denunciation of Bolshevik sympathizers and most outspoken in his warnings to union men. Through his close relationship with Ralph Easley, Gompers drew heavily upon the propaganda of the National Civic Federation to help him in this antiradical campaign. In fact, the AFL willingly joined the super-patriotic crusade!

It is certainly ironical that at a time when antiunion elements were already meeting with some success in identifying unionism with bolshevism, organized labor cooperated with them in digging its own grave. Union journals were just as quick as employer magazines to attach any unorthodox labor procedure, such as the general strike, to the Communist philosophy, and they bitterly attacked all such innovations as "monuments of folly" and "revolutionary provoking instruments." Along with this scathing criticism, these labor journals also warned union members of the danger of "borers from within" and called upon all local unions to purge these individuals from their membership rolls immediately. The *American Federationist* and the *United Mine Workers' Journal* consistently cautioned union workers against those within the movement who wanted to plunge labor into "a sea of turmoil, hatred, and possible bloodshed."[4]

In making this attack on labor radicalism, union officials and magazines were always careful to emphasize the fact that organized labor as a whole was uninfected. There can be little doubt that most such assurances were designed specifically to offset the growing antiunion propaganda of employers. The *American Federationist,* in particular, had this as its primary goal. The magazine reiterated time and again that despite what some people said, the American trade union movement could never be "sidetracked or befogged by economic theories," and although the nation might experience some labor unrest, it would never be based on the demand for a "dictatorship of the proletariat." "American labor is loyal and true," said the journal, "and can not be swerved . . . by any such impracticable and puerile visions as are entertained by the bolshevists of Russia or of any other land." To further buttress its argument, the *American Federationist* spoke of the "Safety of Trade Unionism" and claimed that organized labor was America's chief barrier against bolshevism because workers within the trade unions were immune to that doctrine.[5]

During 1919 there were many indications that what organized labor claimed for itself was essentially true. Radicals themselves attested to the conservative tendencies of the AFL by frequently referring to the organization as the "American Fakirization of Labor" and characterizing its leaders as "traitors to the workers' cause." Moreover, many pro-Bolshevik radicals, who earlier had hoped to "bore from within," had come to realize what a difficult job it was and by the summer of 1919 had dropped out of the AFL altogether. As a further testimony to the unshakable conservatism of the organization and its leaders, no less than Lenin, himself, remarked that the AFL had to be discounted as a factor in the American radical movement. Gompers, said Lenin, was merely an "agent of the bourgeoisie."[6]

Perhaps an even better indication of the organization's conservatism was its annual convention of 1919. Convening on June 13 at Atlantic City, this gathering was permeated with an antiradical spirit from the start and indicated by its deliberations that it held no brief for Communist ideas. On the question of recommending the recognition of Soviet Russia, the delegates voted against it in no uncertain terms. The convention also refused to sanction the adoption of certain resolutions which asked for the removal of American troops from Siberia. Moreover, the assembly voted against AFL participation in a proposed general strike for Thomas Mooney, a labor radical convicted for the famous 1916 San Francisco Preparedness Day bombing. Finally, the convention reiterated the AFL's opposition to the "one big union" concept, advocated more stringent immigration laws, and overwhelmingly re-elected Samuel Gompers as president.[7]

Before the convention adjourned, however, it tempered this prevailing conservatism somewhat by espousing a few liberal ideas which, although offering no consolation to radicals, subsequently caused consternation in conservative quarters. The assembly urged the repeal of the wartime Espionage and Sedition acts and the shortening of the terms of certain political prisoners. It also unanimously adopted a resolution which stated that "the power of our courts to declare legislation enacted unconstitutional and void is a most flagrant usurpation of power and authority." In addition, over the protests of conservative leaders, the delegates endorsed the controversial Plumb Plan for government ownership of the railroads and put the convention on record as favoring the "use of every legitimate endeavor to promote the enactment of this plan into law."[8]

Nevertheless, the action of the convention as a whole was so clearly an indication of organized labor's conservatism that it could not escape general notice. Most newspapers hailed the work of the convention by contending that "reason rules American labor" and "the conservatism of American labor is a fact, not a theory." The *Literary Digest* proclaimed that organized labor had "set its face firmly against . . . a revolutionary policy," and, indeed, even the most die-hard radicals now openly admitted they saw little hope for their doctrines within the AFL. John Reed curtly described the assembly as "The Convention of the Dead," while Max Eastman declared Gompers' success in getting the delegates to adhere so closely to his policies marked the climax to "a brilliant career in the misguidance of labor."[9]

Strangely enough, at the very moment when much of the press was praising organized labor for its conservative position, some journals were claiming that union labor was actually in the hands of unscrupulous men whose "principles stand on all-fours with those of Lenin and Trotsky."[10] The reason for this contradiction does not readily appear unless the other phase of organized labor's activities in 1919 is understood. It must be remembered that while the AFL was interested in combating radicalism, it was equally interested in securing new gains from employers and its action along this line was just as aggressive.

The 1918 pronouncement of the AFL had already set forth organized labor's postwar desire for new concessions from capital and in February 1919 the *American Federationist* reiterated this position by declaring that workers had the "right to associate and organize into trade unions and to endeavor collectively to attain that economic independence essential to their welfare." A short time later, Samuel Gompers issued an open warning that labor did not intend to lose the advantages it had won during the Progressive Era and the war. "If any employer believes that industrial autocracy is going to prevail in America," he declared, "he is counting without his Host."[11]

Running headlong into the obstinacy of employers, particularly on the matter of collective bargaining, organized labor quickly girded itself for battle. Despite the unfortunate consequences attendant upon the Seattle strike in February, organized labor now relied heavily on the strike weapon, although not the general strike, to bolster its position. Resulting industrial disturbance was nothing short of phenomenal. The strike picture appeared as follows: in March there were 175 strikes; in April, 248; May, 388; June, 303; July, 360; and August, 373. The extent of this unrest was not concentrated in any special areas but was nation-wide. Woolen operatives struck in Passaic, New Jersey, in March; telephone operators in New England in April; carpenters in Columbus, Ohio, and machinists in Toledo in May; workers in the building trades of Dallas in June; Atlantic coast marine workers and Chicago street railwaymen in July; tobacco workers in Philadelphia and Allentown also in July; and silk workers in Paterson in August. In New York City alone, 20,000 harbor workers struck in March, 50,000 cloak and suit makers in May, 25,000 shirt makers and 40,000 tobacco workers in July, and 14,000 painters and 15,000 streetcar men in August.

The average number of days involved in each of these strikes was thirty-four, although a few strikes lasted more than a hundred. Actually, the total number of strikes was less than in comparable periods of 1916 and 1917, but the total number of workers involved in 1919 was much greater. As a result, there was also a much greater loss in workdays, in profits, and in wages. However, there was less loss of life in the turbulence of 1919 than in any previous comparable period of labor unrest in the nation's history.[12]

Although a few of the strikes were "illegal" and appeared to contain some evidences of radical influence, the vast majority were supported by the AFL and centered solely around the demand for higher wages, shorter hours, and collective bargaining. In many of these strikes the workers won concessions on either higher wages or shorter hours, or both, but only rarely did they succeed in securing the right of collective bargaining.[13] Employers were adamant in their stand on the latter demand, bitterly opposing it in the fear that "recognition means closing."

Though it was true that most of the strikes were orthodox and not radical in any way, the amount of unrest coupled with increasing antiunion propaganda made the public uneasy and re-emphasized the suspicions which had arisen during the ill-fated Seattle venture. Constant assurances by the AFL concerning labor's fidelity managed for a time to hold the line and "revolution hunters" had a rather difficult job in convincing anyone but themselves that any immediate danger existed. But unfortunately for the cause of organized labor one strike which occurred in May was made to order for those who were attempting to prove that labor was dangerously radical. Though not involving American labor per se, this struggle had serious repercussions on the domestic labor scene and constituted one of the gravest indications that growing antiunion charges might be true.

Just fifteen days after the May Day riots and bombs had electrified the nation, the Winnipeg Trades and Labor Council called a general strike in sympathy with the striking workers of the metal and building trades of that Canadian city. As 30,000 workers left their jobs, postal and telegraphic communication, fire and sanitary protection, transportation, and industrial production were either directly suspended or seriously curtailed. The city government ultimately fell into the hands of a strike committee which established press censorship and allowed the resumption of police and fire protection only upon its authority. A preponderance of evidence indicates that the policy of this committee was set largely by syndicalists who had hopes for radical changes in the existing economic order and employed "one big union" tactics in order to achieve that goal.[14]

Winnipeg was dominated by this strike committee for more than two weeks before the legal city council regained its lost power, and it was not until June 20 that the general strike movement collapsed. Although proponents of the strike labeled all ensuing charges of revolution as "sheer unadulterated moonshine," Canadian authorities remained convinced that the strike had been a Bolshevik experiment and, indeed, was but a continuation of the affair in Seattle. In fact, it was freely stated in the Canadian press that radical leaders, failing in Seattle, had come to Canada to try their luck and that the strike in Winnipeg had been financed and led by radical labor groups from the United States. Although this was simply not the case, in the record time of one hour the Canadian Parliament passed an emergency measure on June 6 to permit the immediate deportation of the miscreants to the United States should they be apprehended.[15]

In the United States, meanwhile, the Winnipeg incident was reported in a most sensational manner. Eight-column headlines announced to a shocked public the events taking place there, and wide circulation was given exaggerated Canadian press releases which described babies suffering from lack of milk and the city's inhabitants living in filth because of the suspension of sanitation services.

Naturally, the whole affair was bitterly denounced. American newspapers called the venture "Russian sickness" and a "Bolshevist interim." Most other agents of public expression readily admitted that the Winnipeg struggle was radicalism at its worst. Labor journals, in particular, vehemently criticized the action of Winnipeg labor. The *United Mine Workers' Journal* called the "one big union" concept, which underlay the strike, the "One Big Failure," and Samuel Gompers in the *American Federationist* labeled the Winnipeg affair "evil," "ill-advised," and "a complete fiasco."[16]

In spite of America labor's rabid denunciations of the Winnipeg incident, the damage had been done, and suspicious eyes once again turned in organized labor's direction. It is understandable why some citizens by midsummer 1919 held a highly suspicious attitude concerning the aims of organized labor. It is equally understandable how such suspicions could be held in spite of labor's professed conservatism and its antiradical crusade. Constantly open to attack because of its insistence upon labor's rights, organized labor found its support waning as antiunion conservatives made the most of labor's peculiar dilemma. And at a time when general strikes, riots, and bombs were much in evidence it was easy for the enemies of unionism to connect industrial unrest with radicalism and thus cover the whole organized labor movement with the Communist label.

The Winnipeg strike was only the first, and least important, of three major factors operating in the summer of 1919 which helped to crystallize attitudes on the position of organized labor and undermine public faith in its essential soundness. The other two were organized labor's relationship to the proposed nation-wide general strike for Thomas Mooney, and labor's insistence on the Plumb Plan for government ownership of the nation's railroads.

Throughout the spring of 1919, plans for a nation-wide strike had been discussed by radicals and various liberal labor groups as a protest against the allegedly unjust conviction of Mooney, a radical labor agitator who along with Warren K. Billings had been arrested in July 1916 and sentenced to death for a bomb explosion during a San Francisco Preparedness Day parade in which nine persons were killed and forty wounded. With their sentences later commuted to life imprisonment and because of lingering doubts concerning even their guilt, these two men, particularly Mooney, had become a symbol of the working class's fight for equal justice. Radicals especially had embraced Mooney's cause, and it was felt that a general strike, more than any other action, might force his early release.

Pressure had been applied on the AFL for its aid in conducting this strike, but from the beginning that organization expressed antipathy to the scheme. Conservative AFL officials had refused to sanction any consideration of the general strike action, and, in April, the *American Federationist* illustrated this sentiment by denouncing the whole project.[17] At its convention in Atlantic City in June, the position of the AFL was further clarified by the defeat of the general strike resolution and the organization thereafter officially washed its hands of the entire matter.

The defeat of this proposal, however, indicated only the sentiment of the central organization, not that of the individual unions. Under the rules, the Federation had no power either to call or to forestall a strike of its member unions and hence the latter were still free to handle the Mooney situation in any way they chose. As a result, there was some doubt as to what the separate unions would do, especially since there was considerable sympathy for Mooney among their members.

The Mooney general strike had been set for July 4 and for weeks prior to Independence Day newspapers and conservative labor journals cautioned workers against any participation in this folly. As the day drew nearer and radical agitation for the general strike increased, their appeals became all the more insistent. The public press, meanwhile, burdened its readers with wild stories about the horrible event to come, with the result that the public became greatly alarmed. Having already experienced two general strikes, the public could easily believe a new and more terrible one was on the way. Furthermore, since it had but recently witnessed two horrifying bomb plots, the public could also imagine that the July 4 strike would probably be accompanied by renewed attacks on property and life. A reflection of the rising fear appeared in newspaper headlines: "REIGN OF TERROR PLANNED," "STOLEN EXPLOSIVES TO BE USED," and "PLANS FOR WIDESPREAD VIOLENCE AND MURDER."[18]

As a result of these unsubstantiated warnings, many citizens and public officials actually became so terrified that they frantically prepared for the July 4 onslaught. In New York City, 11,000 police and detectives were kept on twenty-four-hour duty, guarding all federal, state, city, and county buildings, as well as the Stock Exchange and the homes of prominent men. Hundreds of private citizens were sworn in as special deputies and all meetings of an emotional nature were suspended for the day. Indeed, so great was the fear of the city's authorities that they even refused the use of Carnegie Hall to the American Defense Society because its proposed Independence Day rally might incite both radicals and patriotic partisans to lawlessness.[19]

The pattern was essentially the same in other American cities. In Chicago, two companies of the Fourteenth Infantry were brought into the city to forestall possible trouble, and the entire police force plus 1000 volunteers were placed on the alert. In Boston, thirty armed soldiers were stationed at the Federal Building. In Philadelphia the streets were literally "filled with policemen." In San Francisco, special precautions were taken in view of the city's connection with the Preparedness Day bombing and the Mooney trial, and in Oakland known Reds were arrested and incarcerated for the day as an "insurance device." Meanwhile, in the Pacific Northwest whole areas were alerted against threatened Wobbly uprisings and federal agents were stationed there to meet any emergency which might arise.[20]

What happened was anticlimactic. Independence Day came and went.

Nowhere in the nation was there any undue disturbance. Liberal labor elements and radicals remained quiet and let the Eagle scream. The Mooney general strike with its attendant bombings and bloodshed simply failed to materialize. Even in the two areas of the country where one might have expected some disorder, none was forthcoming. In both Seattle and San Francisco the day passed quietly except for the usual sounding of exploding fireworks.

Blushingly, most newspapers tossed off the fact that nothing had happened with the claim that widespread precautionary measures had prevented outbreaks. But a few journals were frankly skeptical. These implied that the whole sensational situation might have been built up by conservative interests for its calculated effect on the public mind. Said the *Christian Register:* "The preponderance of evidence leads to the conclusion that the predictions of an organized assault upon American institutions on the occasion of the anniversary of American independence had been considerably overemphasized in an attempt to impress public opinion with the gravity of an ultimate danger."[21]

Since no general strike occurred, public confidence in the conservatism of American workers should have been quickly restored. But the mere possibility of the general strike had given antilabor elements such an excellent opportunity to lodge their propaganda more firmly in the public mind that suspicion of labor actually increased. Furthermore, the sensationalism of the press in promoting the July 4 scare so heightened antiradical emotions that the adverse effect on public faith in the fidelity of labor did not quickly disappear.

This situation was further worsened by the fact that organized labor was currently championing the controversial Plumb proposal for government ownership of the nation's railroads. This plan, drafted by Glenn R. Plumb, a counsel for the Railroad Brotherhoods, first received wide attention in February 1919. It called for the purchase of the railroads by the United States government, the establishment of an operating corporation of fifteen men (five representing the public, five management, and five labor), and the division of the profits between the government and managerial and classified employees.[22] The four Railroad Brotherhoods had immediately endorsed this plan, as did all others who, on principle, desired government displacement of private control. And while the liberal press hailed such action by claiming that the railroad unions had "stuck in their thumbs and pulled out a Plumb," the conservative press branded the scheme " 'Plumb' Bolshevistic."[23]

Throughout the spring of 1919, the Railroad Brotherhoods vigorously defended the proposal while conservatives continued to take pot shots at the program. Plumb wrote and spoke in behalf of his project and strongly urged all labor to support it. By the summer of 1919, the proponents of the plan claimed it had at least three million supporters and a Plumb Plan League was formed to elicit even more support. The primary objective, of course, was to secure the backing of the AFL and considerable pressure was brought to bear on that organization. Conservative AFL officials were not sure they wanted to associate with the project and Samuel Gompers openly opposed it. But favorable sentiment among organized labor in general proved too much for AFL leaders, and at its June convention, as we have seen, the AFL endorsed the scheme. Of all the decisions made by the convention, this one seemed to many conservatives to be the most onerous. "Better things were to have been expected of the American Federation of Labor," complained the *Wall Street Journal*.[24]

In the meantime, Congress itself was wrestling with the knotty railroad problem. It seemed only logical that the government, which had seized the railroads during the war, should return them once again to their private owners. There was considerable hostility even in Congress against the railroad companies because of their previous mishandling of the lines. However, even though many congressmen insisted that certain public safeguards be established before the return of the railroads, few subscribed to the Plumb Plan. Indeed, many members thought the plan "might well have been formulated by a Lenin or a Trotsky," and some simply called it "a bold, bald, naked attempt to sovietize the railroads of this country."[25]

Despite such opposition, the Plumb movement snowballed, and, on August 2, a bill embodying the plan was formally introduced in Congress by Representative Thetus W. Sims of Tennessee. The Railroad Brotherhoods backed this action and made it increasingly clear they would fight with everything at their disposal to prevent the return of the railroads to private ownership. They immediately asked their members to contribute $2,500,000 for a Plumb Plan sinking fund and announced they would elect a "Plumb Plan Congress" if necessary. According to Plumb, there were roughly eight million workmen in August 1919 who were fighting for his plan and he warned that unless his proposal or something like it was adopted, there might be serious trouble. Other spokesmen for public ownership darkly prophesied that even if the roads were returned to their owners, "they wouldn't stay there very long."[26]

But by this time conservative and antiunion elements had fully mustered their forces and through their own publications and their chief ally, the general press, unleashed a murderous counterattack. The railroad companies themselves undertook a vigorous advertising campaign against the plan, calling it the first step along the road to bolshevism. Employer and business magazines urged the nation to resist firmly such a "revolutionary proposal." Editorials appearing in the public press echoed these assertions and further suggested that the principle might next be applied to banks, natural resources, and public utilities. Meanwhile, the very opposition which conservative AFL officials displayed toward the whole project served to accent these charges.[27]

By the close of the summer, organized labor was definitely on the defensive with respect to charges of "bolshevism." Despite its many endeavors to prove that American labor was basically antiradical, its own actions in some respects seemed to contradict its protestations. By continuing its relentless crusade against employers and by underwriting such proposals as the Plumb Plan, labor created situations which worked seriously to its disadvantage. The large body of sentiment which had hailed organized labor's conservatism at the time of the AFL convention rapidly disappeared as antiunion groups met with increased success in their attempt to connect organized labor's postwar program with the radical philosophy of bolshevism.

This decline in public confidence could not have come at a more unfortunate time since labor was just then in the process of intensifying its drive against organized capital for higher wages, shorter hours, and the right of collective bargaining. It undoubtedly would have been wiser for labor leaders to have kept rein on their unions and bided their time until a later date. Their success might have been better; at least it could have been no worse. Under the circumstances it is difficult to see how labor could have expected much public support for its undertakings and it was a mistake for labor leaders not to have realized it.

At the same time, there were also other factors working against labor's chances for success. In September, in connection with the birth of the two Communist parties, many radicals who heretofore had remained aloof from the trade union movement now reversed their position and began to assume a more direct interest in organized labor's affairs. Under the guidance of the two Communist factions, these radicals, along with the radical press, began to identify themselves with organized labor's efforts to wring concessions from employers. Indeed, the Communists championed all the major fall strikes no less vigorously than if such struggles had been their own in the hope that they might turn them to good advantage. Said the Communist party Manifesto: "Strikes of protest develop into general political strikes and then into revolutionary mass action for the conquest of the power of the State. . . . The Communist Party shall participate in mass strikes, not only to achieve the immediate purposes of the strike, but to develop the revolutionary implications. . . ."[28]

Although such radicals still bitterly opposed the conservatism, leaders, and structural arrangement of the AFL, the fact that they now openly supported organized labor's strike actions made the public even less receptive to labor's insistent claims concerning its fidelity. Quite naturally, antiunion groups seized this new opportunity to undermine still further public support for union labor. Meanwhile, constant warnings by conservative labor leaders to "pay no attention to agitators who are now trying to disrupt our splendid movement," were taken as additional proof that radicalism, and not justifiable demands, was to blame for much of the labor unrest.

Thus, having attempted from the beginning to run with the hounds on the issue of domestic radicalism, by the fall of 1919 organized labor found itself identified with the hare instead. Its position had become increasingly precarious as the disappearance of public confidence made even the wildest antiunion charges seem believable. In fact, by the fall of 1919 all strikes, regardless of their nature, had come to be considered "crimes against society," "conspiracies against the government," and "plots to establish communism."

NOTES

1. John R. Commons, *Trade Unionism and Labor Problems* (Boston, 1921), 563–69.
2. Lewis Lorwin, *American Federation of Labor: History, Policies, and Prospects* (Washington, D.C., 1933), 191.
3. See David J. Saposs, *Left Wing Unionism* (New York, 1926), *passim.* This work is particularly good on radical labor unions.
4. For labor opinion see the *American Federationist,* XXVI, pt. 1 (March 1919), 237, and XXVI, pt. 1 (April 1919), 316–18; see also "Advocates of Disorder," *United Mine Workers' Journal,* XXX (April 1, 1919), 7.
5. Editorial, *American Federationist,* XXVI, pt. 1 (February 1919), 149; "This Thing Called Bolshevism," *ibid.* (March 1919), 237; Matthew Woll, "American Labor Is True to Democracy," *ibid.* (April 1919), 318–20; "Safety of Trade Unionism," *ibid.* (May 1919), 398–400.

6. Stanley Frost, *Labor and Revolt* (New York, 1920), 181. This source must be used with caution.
7. *Report of the Proceedings of the Thirty-Ninth Annual Convention of the American Federation of Labor, 1919* (Washington, D.C., 1919), 324, 333–39. Hereafter cited as *Report of the Proceedings, 1919.*
8. *Ibid.*, 328, 361, 391, 396.
9. Newspaper comment from "American Labor and Bolshevism," *Literary Digest,* LXI (June 21, 1919), 9–10; "The Convention of the Dead," *Liberator,* II (August 1919), 12.
10. New York *Sun,* June 21, 1919, p. 7; New York *World,* June 22, 1919, editorial section, p. 2.
11. Editorial, *American Federationist,* XXVI, pt. 1 (February 1919), 151; "American Labor and Bolshevism," *Literary Digest,* LXI (June 21, 1919), 11, quoting Gompers.
12. For complete strike statistics see "Strikes and Lockouts," *Monthly Labor Review,* X (June 1920), 199–218.
13. *Report of the Proceedings, 1919,* 43–45, table of gains and losses.
14. "Canada's One Big Union," *Dial,* LXVII (September 20, 1919), 135; "The Winnipeg General Strike," *Independent,* XCVII (June 7, 1919), 344; Arthur E. Darby, "Winnipeg's Revolution," *New Republic,* XIX (July 9, 1919), 310.
15. "The Causes of the Winnipeg General Strike," *New Statesman* (London), XIII (July 26, 1919), 413.
16. Reports and opinion are found in the New York *Times,* issues May 22–23, 1919; "One Big Union," *Saturday Evening Post,* CXCII (July 26, 1919), 26; "The 'One Big Failure'," *United Mine Workers' Journal,* XXX (July 15, 1919), 7; editorial, *American Federationist,* XXVI, pt. 2 (October 1919), 961.
17. "No Room for Destructionists in Our Movement," *American Federationist,* XXVI, pt. 1 (April 1919), 318.
18. For anti-Mooney opinion see "Against Mooney Strike," *United Mine Workers' Journal,* XXX (June 1, 1919), 6; the example of exaggerated newspaper reporting is from the Chicago *Tribune,* June 8, 1919, p. 1; the headlines appeared in the San Francisco *Examiner,* July 4, 1919, p. 1, and Cincinnati *Enquirer,* July 4, 1919, p. 1.
19. New York *Times,* July 4, 1919, p. 4; New York *Call,* July 4, 1919, p. 1.
20. Chicago *Tribune,* July 4, 1919, p. 13; Boston *Evening Transcript,* July 3, 1919. p. 1; Philadelphia *Public Ledger,* July 5, 1919, p. 3; Los Angeles *Times,* July 4, 1919, p. 1; Portland *Oregonian,* July 4, 1919, p. 1.
21. "News of the Week," *Christian Register,* XCVIII (July 10, 1919), 652.
22. Glenn R. Plumb, "Plan of Organized Employees for Railroad Organization," *Public,* XXII (March 29, 1919), 427–29.
23. Boston *Evening Transcript,* February 25, 1919, p. 10; Howard Brubaker, "May I Not," *Liberator,* II (October 1919), 25.
24. New York *Wall Street Journal,* June 13, 1919, p. 1; for examples of labor support, see the April, May, and June issues of *Railway Carmen's Journal.* See also the editorial in *Railway Carmen's Journal,* XXIV (September 1919), 1315–20.
25. See *Cong. Record,* 66 Cong., 1 Sess., 3765, 4089, for examples of congressional opinion.

26. New York *Times,* August 6, 1919, p. 15; *ibid.,* August 9, 1919, p. 4; Salt Lake *Tribune,* August 4, 1919, pp. 1–2; New York *World,* August 8, 1919, p. 1.
27. Robert Dunn, ed., *The Palmer Raids* (New York, 1948), 23, quotes employer magazine; see also the issues of August 4–6, 1919, of the New York *Times,* Boston *Evening Transcript,* Atlanta *Constitution,* and Salt Lake *Tribune.*
28. "Communist Party's Attitude toward Strikes," *Monthly Labor Review,* X (April 1920), 220, quoting the Manifesto.

10 ~ Vision and Boundless Hope and Optimism*

[Author's Note] *The superficial optimism of the twenties is a subject that has been almost exhuasted by historians who are highly critical of a self-deluded business culture that ushered in the Depression. The attempt of the historian to explain the causes of the Depression, however, too often becomes submerged by his attacks on the false prophets of the era. It is for this reason that the famed Harvard economist, John Kenneth Galbraith, in* The Great Crash, *contributed a welcome addition to the growing corpus of literature on the Depression. Rejecting a simplistic approach, Professor Galbraith isolates the deep-seated factors at work that finally brought the economy tumbling down in the fateful October of 1929.*

On December 4, 1928, President Coolidge sent his last message on the state of the Union to the reconvening Congress. Even the most melancholy congressman must have found reassurance in his words. "No Congress of the United States ever assembled, on surveying the state of the Union, has met with a more pleasing prospect than that which appears at the present time. In the domestic field there is tranquility and contentment . . . and the highest record of years of prosperity. In the foreign field there is peace, the goodwill which comes from mutual understanding . . ." He told the legislators that they and the country might "regard the present with satisfaction and anticipate the future with optimism." And breaking sharply with the most ancient of our political conventions, he omitted to attribute

* *The Great Crash, 1929* copyright 1954, 1955 by John Kenneth Galbraith, pages 6–16. Reprinted by permission of the Publisher, Houghton Mifflin Company.

this well-being to the excellence of the administration which he headed. "The main source of these unexampled blessings lies in the integrity and character of the American people."

A whole generation of historians has assailed Coolidge for the superficial optimism which kept him from seeing that a great storm was brewing at home and also more distantly abroad. This is grossly unfair. It requires neither courage nor prescience to predict disaster. Courage is required of the man who, when things are good, says so. Historians rejoice in crucifying the false prophet of the millennium. They never dwell on the mistake of the man who wrongly predicted Armageddon.

There was much that was good about the world of which Coolidge spoke. True, as liberal misanthropes have insisted, the rich were getting richer much faster than the poor were getting less poor. The farmers were unhappy and had been ever since the depression of 1920–21 had cut farm prices sharply but left costs high. Black people in the South and white people in the southern Appalachians continued to dwell in hopeless poverty. Fine old-English houses with high gables, leaded glass, and well-simulated half-timbering were rising in the country club district, while farther in town one encountered the most noisome slums outside the Orient.

All this notwithstanding, the twenties in America were a very good time. Production and employment were high and rising. Wages were not going up much, but prices were stable. Although many people were still very poor, more people were comfortably well-off, well-to-do, or rich than ever before. Finally, American capitalism was undoubtedly in a lively phase. Between 1925 and 1929, the number of manufacturing establishments increased from 183,900 to 206,700; the value of their output rose from $60.8 billions to $68.0 billions.[1] The Federal Reserve index of industrial production which had averaged only 67 in 1921 (1923–25=100) had risen to 110 by July 1928, and it reached 126 in June 1929.[2] In 1926, 4,301,000 automobiles were produced. Three years later, in 1929, production had increased by over a million to 5,358,000,[3] a figure which compares very decently with the 5,700,000 new car registrations of the opulent year of 1953. Business earnings were rising rapidly, and it was a good time to be in business. Indeed, even the most jaundiced histories of the era concede, tacitly, that times were good, for they nearly all join in taxing Coolidge for his failure to see that they were too good to last.

This notion of an iron law of compensation—the notion that the ten good years of the twenties had to be paid for by the ten bad ones of the thirties—is one to which it will be worthwhile to return.

II

One thing in the twenties should have been visible even to Coolidge. It concerned the American people of whose character he had spoken so well. Along with the sterling qualities he praised, they were also displaying an inordinate desire to get rich quickly with a minimum of physical effort. The first striking manifestation of this personality trait was in Florida. There, in the mid-twenties, Miami, Miami Beach, Coral Gables, the East Coast as far north as Palm Beach, and the cities over on the Gulf had been struck by the great Florida real estate boom. The Florida boom contained all of the elements of the classic speculative bubble. There was the indispensable element of substance. Florida had a better winter climate than New York, Chicago, or Minneapolis. Higher incomes and better transportation were making it increasingly accessible to the frost-bound North. The time indeed was coming when the annual flight to the South would be as regular and impressive as the migrations of the Canada Goose.

On that indispensable element of fact men and women had proceeded to build a world of speculative make-believe. This is a world inhabited not by people who have to be persuaded to believe but by people who want an excuse to believe. In the case of Florida, they wanted to believe that the whole peninsula would soon be populated by the holiday-makers and the sun-worshippers of a new and remarkably indolent era. So great would be the crush that beaches, bogs, swamps, and common scrubland would all have value. The Florida climate obviously did not insure that this would happen. But it did enable people who wanted to believe it would happen so to believe.

However, speculation does not depend entirely on the capacity for self-delusion. In Florida land was divided into building lots and sold for a 10 per cent down payment. Palpably, much of the unlovely terrain that thus changed hands was as repugnant to the people who bought it as to the passer-by. The buyers did not expect to live on it; it was not easy to suppose that anyone ever would. But these were academic considerations. The reality was that this dubious asset was gaining in value by the day and could be sold at a handsome profit in a fortnight. It is another feature of the speculative mood that, as time passes, the tendency to look beyond the simple fact of increasing values to the reasons on which it depends greatly diminishes. And there is no reason why anyone should do so as long as the supply of people who buy with the expectation of selling at a profit continues to be augmented at a sufficiently rapid rate to keep prices rising.

Through 1925 the pursuit of effortless riches brought people to Florida in satisfactorily increasing numbers. More land was subdivided each week. What was loosely called seashore became five, ten, or fifteen miles from the nearest brine. Suburbs became an astonishing distance from town. As the speculation spread northward, an enterprising Bostonian, Mr. Charles Ponzi, developed a subdivision "near Jacksonville." It was approximately sixty-five miles west of the city. (In other respects Ponzi believed in good, compact neighborhoods; he sold twenty-three lots to the acre.) In instances where the subdivision was close to town, as in the case of Manhattan Estates, which were "not more than three fourths of a mile from the prosperous and fast-growing city of Nettie," the city, as was so of Nettie, did not exist. The congestion of traffic into the state became so severe that in the autumn of 1925 the railroads were forced to proclaim an embargo on less essential freight, which included building materials for developing the subdivisions. Values rose wonderfully. Within forty miles of Miami "inside" lots sold at from $8000 to $20,000; waterfront lots brought from $15,000 to $25,000, and more or less bona fide seashore sites brought $20,000 to $75,000.[4]

However, in the spring of 1926, the supply of new buyers, so essential to the reality of increasing prices, began to fail. As 1928 and 1929 were to show, the momentum built up by a good boom is not dissipated in a moment. For a while in 1926 the increasing eloquence of the promoters offset the diminishing supply of prospects. (Even the cathedral voice of William Jennings Bryan, which once had thundered against the cross of gold, had been for a time enlisted in the sorry task of selling swampland.) But this boom was not left to collapse of its own weight. In the autumn of 1926, two hurricanes showed, in the words of Frederick Lewis Allen, "what a Soothing Tropic Wind could do when it got a running start from the West Indies."[5] The worst of these winds, on September 18, 1926, killed four hundred people, tore the roofs from thousands of houses, and piled tons of water and a number of elegant yachts into the streets of Miami. There was agreement that the storm had caused a healthy breathing spell in the boom, although its resumption was predicted daily. In the *Wall Street Journal* of October 8, 1926, one Peter O. Knight, an official of the Seaboard Air Line and a sincere believer in the future of Florida, acknowledged that some seventeen or eighteen thousand people were in need of assistance. But he added: "The same Florida is still there with its magnificent resources, its wonderful climate, and its geographical position. It is the Riviera of America." He expressed concern that the solicitation of Red Cross funds for hurricane relief would "do more damage permanently to Florida than would be offset by the funds received."[6]

This reluctance to concede that the end has come is also in accordance with the classic pattern. The end had come in Florida. In 1925 bank clearings in Miami were $1,066,528,000; by 1928 they were down to $143,-364,000.[7] Farmers who had sold their land at a handsome price and had condemned themselves as it later sold for double, treble, quadruple the original price, now on occasion got it back through a whole chain of subsequent defaults. Sometimes it was equipped with eloquently named streets and with sidewalks, street lamps, and taxes and assessments amounting to several times its current value.

The Florida boom was the first indication of the mood of the twenties and the conviction that God intended the American middle class to be rich. But that this mood survived the Florida collapse is still more remarkable. It was widely understood that things had gone to pieces in Florida. While the number of speculators was almost certainly small compared with the subsequent participation in the stock market, nearly every community contained a man who was known to have taken "quite a beating" in Florida. For a century after the collapse of the South Sea Bubble, Englishmen regarded the most reputable joint stock companies with some suspicion. Even as the Florida boom collapsed, the faith of Americans in quick, effortless enrichment in the stock market was becoming every day more evident.

III

It is hard to say when the stock market boom of the nineteen-twenties began. There were sound reasons why, during these years, the prices of common stocks should rise. Corporate earnings were good and growing. The prospect seemed benign. In the early twenties stock prices were low and yields favorable.

In the last six months of 1924, the prices of securities began to rise, and the increase was continued and extended through 1925. Thus at the end of May 1924, the *New York Times* average of the prices of twenty-five industrial stocks was 106; by the end of the year it was 134.[8] By December 31, 1925, it had gained very nearly another 50 points and stood at 181. The advance through 1925 was remarkably steady; there were only a couple of months when values did not show a net gain.

During 1926 there was something of a setback. Business was off a little in the early part of that year; it was thought by many that values the year before had risen unreasonably. February brought a sharp fall in the market, and March a rather abrupt collapse. The *Times* industrials went down from 181 at the beginning of the year to 172 at the end of February, and then dropped by nearly 30 points to 143 at the end of March. However, in April the market steadied and renewed its advance. Another mild setback occurred in October, just after the hurricane blew away the vestiges of the Florida boom, but again recovery was prompt. At the end of the year values were about where they had been at the beginning.

In 1927 the increase began in earnest. Day after day and month after month the price of stocks went up. The gains by later standards were not large, but they had an aspect of great reliability. Again in only two months in 1927 did the averages fail to show an increase. On May 20, when Lindbergh took off from Roosevelt Field and headed for Paris, a fair number of citizens were unaware of the event. The market, which that day was registering another of its small but solid gains, had by then acquired a faithful band of devotees who spared no attention for more celestial matters.

In the summer of 1927 Henry Ford rang down the curtain on the immortal Model T and closed his plant to prepare for Model A. The Federal Reserve index of industrial production receded, presumably as a result of the Ford shutdown, and there was general talk of depression. The effect on the market was imperceptible. At the end of the year, by which time production had also turned up again, the *Times* industrials had reached 245, a net gain of 69 points for the year.

The year 1927 is historic from another point of view in the lore of the stock market. According to a long accepted doctrine, it was in this year that the seeds of the eventual disaster were sown. The responsibility rests with an act of generous but ill-advised internationalism. Some—including Mr. Hoover—have thought it almost disloyal, although in those days accusations of treason were still made with some caution.

In 1925, under the aegis of the then Chancellor of the Exchequer, Mr. Winston Churchill, Britain returned to the gold standard at the old or pre-World War I relationship between gold, dollars, and the pound. There is no doubt that Churchill was more impressed by the grandeur of the traditional, or $4.86, pound than by the more subtle consequences of overvaluation, which he is widely assumed not to have understood. The consequences, nonetheless, were real and severe. Customers of Britain had now to use these costly pounds to buy goods at prices that still reflected wartime inflation. Britain was, accordingly, an unattractive place for foreigners to buy. For the same reason it was an easy place in which to sell. In 1925 began the long series of exchange crises which, like the lions in Trafalgar Square and the street walkers in Piccadilly, are now an established part of the British scene. There were also unpleasant domestic consequences; the bad market for coal and the effort to reduce costs and prices to meet world competition led to the general strike in 1926.

Then, as since, gold when it escaped from Britain or Europe came to the United States. This might be discouraged if prices of goods were high and interest rates were low in this country. (The United States would be a poor place in which to buy and invest.) In the spring of 1927, three august pilgrims—Montagu Norman, the Governor of the Bank of England, the durable Hjalmar Schacht, then Governor of the Reichsbank, and Charles Rist, the Deputy Governor of the Bank of France—came to the United States to urge an easy money policy. (They had previously pled with success for a roughly similar policy in 1925.) The Federal Reserve obliged. The rediscount rate of the New York Federal Reserve Bank was cut from 4 to 3.5 per cent. Government securities were purchased in considerable volume with the mathematical consequence of leaving the banks and individuals who had sold them with money to spare. Adolph C. Miller, a dissenting member of the Federal Reserve Board, subsequently described this as "the greatest and boldest operation ever undertaken by the Federal Reserve System, and . . . [it] resulted in one of the most costly errors committed by it or any other banking system in the last 75 years!"[9] The funds that the Federal Reserve made available were either invested in common stocks or (and more important) they became available to help finance the purchase of common stocks by others. So provided with funds, people rushed into the market. Perhaps the most widely read of all the interpretations of the period, that of Professor Lionel Robbins of the London School of Economics, concludes: "From that date, according to all the evidence, the situation got completely out of control."[10]

This view that the action of the Federal Reserve authorities in 1927 was responsible for the speculation and collapse which followed has never been seriously shaken. There are reasons why it is attractive. It is simple, and it exonerates both the American people and their economic system from any substantial blame. The danger of being guided by foreigners is well known, and Norman and Schacht had some special reputation for sinister motives.

Yet the explanation obviously assumes that people will always speculate if only they can get the money to finance it. Nothing could be farther from the case. There were times before and there have been long periods since when credit was plentiful and cheap—far cheaper than in 1927–29—and when speculation was negligible. Nor, as we shall see later, was speculation out of control after 1927, except that it was beyond the reach of men who did not want in the least to control it. The explanation is a tribute only to a recurrent preference, in economic matters, for formidable nonsense. . . .

NOTES

1. U.S. Department of Commerce, Bureau of the Census, *Statistical Abstract of the United States, 1944–45.*
2. *Federal Reserve Bulletin,* December 1929.
3. Thomas Wilson, *Fluctuations in Income and Employment,* 3rd ed. (New York: Pitman, 1948), p. 141.
4. These details are principally from two articles on the Florida land boom by Homer B. Vanderblue in *The Journal of Land and Public Utility Economics,* May and August 1927.
5. *Only Yesterday* (New York: Harper, 1931), p. 280. Other details of the damage resulting from the hurricane are from this still fresh and lively book.
6. Vanderblue, *op. cit.,* p. 114.
7. Allen, *op. cit.,* p. 282.
8. Throughout . . . I have used the *New York Times* industrial averages as the short-hand designation of the level of security prices. This series is the arithmetical, unweighted average of the prices of twenty-five of what the *Times* describes as "good, sound stocks with regular price changes and generally active markets." The selection of the *Times* averages in preference to the Dow-Jones or other averages was largely arbitrary. The *Times* averages are the ones I have watched over the years; they are somewhat more accessible to the non-professional observer than the Dow-Jones averages. Also, while the latter are much better known, they carry in their wake a certain lore of market theory which is irrelevant for present purposes. The industrial rather than the railroad or combined average is cited because industrial stocks were the major focus of speculation and displayed the widest amplitude of movement. Unless there is indication to the contrary, values given are those at the close of the market for the date indicated.
9. Testimony before Senate Committee, quoted by Lionel Robbins, *The Great Depression* (New York: Macmillan, 1934), p. 53.
10. *Ibid.,* p. 53.

11 ~ Cause and Consequence*

What, then, are the plausible causes of the depression? The task of answering can be simplified somewhat by dividing the problem into two parts. First there is the question of why economic activity turned down in 1929. Second there is the vastly more important question of why, having started down, on this unhappy occasion it went down and down and down and remained low for a full decade.

As noted, the Federal Reserve indexes of industrial activity and of factory production, the most comprehensive monthly measures of economic activity then available, reached a peak in June. They then turned down and continued to decline throughout the rest of the year. The turning point in other indicators—factory payrolls, freight-car loadings, and department store sales—came later, and it was October or after before the trend in all of them was clearly down. Still, as economists have generally insisted, and the matter has the high authority of the National Bureau of Economic Research,[1] the economy had weakened in the early summer well before the crash.

This weakening can be variously explained. Production of industrial products, for the moment, had outrun consumer and investment demand for them. The most likely reason is that business concerns, in the characteristic enthusiasm of good times, misjudged the prospective increase in demand and acquired larger inventories than they later found they needed. As a result they curtailed their buying, and this led to a cutback in production. In short, the summer of 1929 marked the beginning of the familar inventory recession. The proof is not conclusive from the (by present standards) limited figures available. Department store inventories, for which figures are available, seem not to have been out of line early in the

* *The Great Crash, 1929* copyright 1954, 1955 by John Kenneth Galbraith, pages 179–191. Reprinted by permission of the Publisher, Houghton Mifflin Company.

year. But a mild slump in department store sales in April could have been a signal for curtailment.

Also there is a chance—one that students of the period have generally favored—that more deep-seated factors were at work and made themselves seriously evident for the first time during that summer. Throughout the twenties production and productivity per worker grew steadily: between 1919 and 1929, output per worker in manufacturing industries increased by about 43 per cent[2] Wages, salaries, and prices all remained comparatively stable, or in any case underwent no comparable increase. Accordingly, costs fell and with prices the same, profits increased. These profits sustained the spending of the well-to-do, and they also nourished at least some of the expectations behind the stock market boom. Most of all they encouraged a very high level of capital investment. During the twenties, the production of capital goods increased at an average annual rate of 6.4 per cent a year; non-durable consumers' goods, a category which includes such objects of mass consumption as food and clothing, increased at a rate of only 2.8 per cent.[3] (The rate of increase for durable consumers' goods such as cars, dwellings, home furnishings, and the like, much of it representing expenditures of the well-off to well-to-do, was 5.9 per cent.) A large and increasing investment in capital goods was, in other words, a principal device by which the profits were being spent.[4] It follows that anything that interrupted the investment outlays—anything, indeed, which kept them from showing the necessary rate of increase—could cause trouble. When this occurred, compensation through an increase in consumer spending could not automatically be expected. The effect, therefore, of insufficient investment—investment that failed to keep pace with the steady increase in profits—could be falling total demand reflected in turn in falling orders and output. Again there is no final proof of this point, for unfortunately we do not know how rapidly investment had to grow to keep abreast of the current increase in profits.[5] However, the explanation is broadly consistent with the facts.

There are other possible explanations of the downturn. Back of the insufficient advance in investment may have been the high interest rates. Perhaps, although less probably, trouble was transmitted to the economy as a whole from some weak sector like agriculture. Further explanations could be offered. But one thing about this experience is clear. Until well along in the autumn of 1929 the downturn was limited. The recession in business activity was modest and underemployment relatively slight. Up to November it was possible to argue that not much of anything had happened. On other occasions, as noted—in 1924 and 1927 and of late in 1949—the economy has undergone similar recession. But, unlike these other occasions, in 1929 the recession continued and continued and got violently worse. This is the unique feature of the 1929 experience. This is what we need really to understand.

V

There seems little question that in 1929, modifying a famous cliché, the economy was fundamentally unsound. This is a circumstance of first-rate importance. Many things were wrong, but five weaknesses seem to have had an especially intimate bearing on the ensuing disaster. They are:

1) The bad distribution of income. In 1929 the rich were indubitably rich. The figures are not entirely satisfactory, but it seems certain that the 5 per cent of the population with the highest incomes in that year received approximately one third of all personal income. The proportion of personal income received in the form of interest, dividends, and rent—the income, broadly speaking, of the well-to-do—was about twice as great as in the years following the Second World War.[6]

This highly unequal income distribution meant that the economy was dependent on a high level of investment or a high level of luxury consumer spending or both. The rich cannot buy great quantities of bread. If they are to dispose of what they receive it must be on luxuries or by way of investment in new plants and new projects. Both investment and luxury spending are subject, inevitably, to more erratic influences and to wider fluctuations than the bread and rent outlays of the $25-a-week workman. This high-bracket spending and investment was especially susceptible, one may assume, to the crushing news from the stock market in October of 1929.

2) The bad corporate structure. In November 1929, a few weeks after the crash, the Harvard Economic Society gave as a principal reason why a depression need not be feared its reasoned judgment that "business in most lines has been conducted with prudence and conservatism."[7] The fact was that American enterprise in the twenties had opened its hospitable arms to an exceptional number of promoters, grafters, swindlers, impostors, and frauds. This, in the long history of such activities, was a kind of flood tide of corporate larceny.

The most important corporate weakness was inherent in the vast new structure of holding companies and investment trusts. The holding companies controlled large segments of the utility, railroad, and entertainment business. Here, as with the investment trusts, was the constant danger of devastation by reverse leverage. In particular, dividends from the operating companies paid the interest on the bonds of upstream holding companies. The interruption of the dividends meant default on the bonds, bankruptcy, and the collapse of the structure. Under these circumstances, the temptation to curtail investment in operating plant in order to continue dividends was obviously strong. This added to deflationary pressures. The latter, in turn, curtailed earnings and helped bring down the corporate pyramids. When this happened, even more retrenchment was inevitable. Income was earmarked for debt repayment. Borrowing for new investment became impossible. It would be hard to imagine a corporate system better designed to continue and accentuate a deflationary spiral.

3) The bad banking structure. Since the early thirties, a generation of Americans has been told, sometimes with amusement, sometimes with indignation, often with outrage of the banking practices of the late twenties. In fact, many of these practices were made ludicrous only by the depression. Loans which would have been perfectly good were made perfectly foolish by the collapse of the borrower's prices or the markets for his goods or the value of the collateral he had posted. The most responsible bankers—those who saw that their debtors were victims of circumstances far beyond their control and sought to help—were often made to look the worst. The bankers yielded, as did others, to the blithe, optimistic, and immoral mood of times but probably not more so. A depression such as that of 1929–32, were it to begin as this is written, would also be damaging to many current impeccable banking reputations.

However, although the bankers were not unusually foolish in 1929, the banking structure was inherently weak. The weakness was implicit in the large numbers of independent units. When one bank failed, the assets of others were frozen while depositors elsewhere had a pregnant warning to go and ask for their money. Thus one failure led to other failures, and these spread with a domino effect. Even in the best of times local misfortune or isolated mismanagement could start such a chain reaction. (In the first six months of 1929, 346 banks failed in various parts of the country with aggregate deposits of nearly $115 million.)[8] When income, employment, and values fell as the result of a depression bank failures could quickly become epidemic. This happened after 1929. Again it would be hard to imagine a better arrangement for magnifying the effects of fear. The weak destroyed not only the other weak, but weakened the strong. People everywhere, rich and poor, were made aware of the disaster by the persuasive intelligence that their savings had been destroyed.

Needless to say, such a banking system, once in the convulsions of failure, had a uniquely repressive effect on the spending of its depositors and the investment of its clients.

4) The dubious state of the foreign balance. This is a familiar story. During the First World War, the United States became a creditor on international account. In the decade following, the surplus of exports over imports which once had paid the interest and principal on loans from Europe continued. The high tariffs, which restricted imports and helped to create this surplus of exports remained. However, history and traditional trading habits also accounted for the persistence of the favorable balance, so called.

Before, payments on interest and principal had in effect been deducted from the trade balance. Now that the United States was a creditor, they were added to this balance. The latter, it should be said, was not huge. In only one year (1928) did the excess of exports over imports come to as much as a billion dollars; in 1923 and 1926 it was only about $375,000,000.[9] However, large or small, this difference had to be covered. Other countries which were buying more than they sold, and had debt payments to make in addition, had somehow to find the means for making up the deficit in their transactions with the United States.

During most of the twenties the difference was covered by cash—i.e., gold payments to the United States—and by new private loans by the United States to other countries. Most of the loans were to governments—national, state, or municipal bodies—and a large proportion were to Germany and Central and South America. The underwriters' margins in handling these loans were generous; the public took them up with enthusiasm; competition for the business was keen. If unfortunately corruption and bribery were required as competitive instruments, these were used. In late 1927 Juan Leguia, the son of the President of Peru, was paid $450,000 by J. and W. Seligman and Company and the National City Company (the security affiliate of the National City Bank) for his services in connection with a $50,000,000 loan which these houses marketed for Peru.[10] Juan's services, according to later testimony, were of a rather negative sort. He was paid for not blocking the deal. The Chase extended President Machado of Cuba, a dictator with a marked predisposition toward murder, a generous personal line of credit which at one time reached $200,000.[11] Machado's son-in-law was employed by the Chase.

The bank did a large business in Cuban bonds. In contemplating these loans, there was a tendency to pass quickly over anything that might appear to the disadvantage of the creditor. Mr. Victor Schoepperle, a vice-president of the National City Company with the responsibility for Latin American loans, made the following appraisal of Peru as a credit prospect:

> Peru: Bad debt record, adverse moral and political risk, bad internal debt situation, trade situation about as satisfactory as that of Chile in the past three years. Natural resources more varied. On economic showing Peru should go ahead rapidly in the next 10 years.[12]

On such showing the National City Company floated a $15,000,000 loan for Peru, followed a few months later by a $50,000,000 loan, and some ten months thereafter by a $25,000,000 issue. (Peru did prove a highly adverse political risk. President Leguia, who negotiated the loans, was thrown violently out of office, and the loans went into default.)

In all respects these operations were as much a part of the New Era as Shenandoah and Blue Ridge. They were also just as fragile, and once the illusions of the New Era were dissipated they came as abruptly to an end. This, in turn, forced a fundamental revision in the foreign economic position of the United States. Countries could not cover their adverse trade balance with the United States with increased payments of gold, at least not for long. This meant that they had either to increase their exports to the United States or reduce their imports or default on their past loans. President Hoover and the Congress moved promptly to eliminate the first possibility—that the accounts would be balanced by larger imports—by sharply increasing the tariff. Accordingly, debts, including war debts, went into default and there was a precipitate fall in American exports. The reduction was not vast in relation to total output of the American economy, but it contributed to the general distress and was especially hard on farmers.

5) The poor state of economic intelligence. To regard the people of any time as particularly obtuse seems vaguely improper, and it also establishes a precedent which members of this generation might regret. Yet it seems certain that the economists and those who offered economic counsel in the late twenties and early thirties were almost uniquely perverse. In the months and years following the stock market crash, the burden of reputable economic advice was invariably on the side of measures that would make things worse. In November of 1929, Mr. Hoover announced

a cut in taxes; in the great no-business conferences that followed he asked business firms to keep up their capital investment and to maintain wages. Both of these measures were on the side of increasing spendable income, though unfortunately they were largely without effect. The tax reductions were negligible except in the higher income brackets; businssmen who promised to maintain investment and wages, in accordance with a well-understood convention, considered the promise binding only for the period within which it was not financially disadvantageous to do so. As a result investment outlays and wages were not reduced until circumstances would in any case have brought their reduction.

Still, the effort was in the right direction. Thereafter policy was almost entirely on the side of making things worse. Asked how the government could best advance recovery, the sound and responsible adviser urged that the budget be balanced. Both parties agreed on this. For Republicans the balanced budget was, as ever, high doctrine. But the Democratic Party platform of 1932, with an explicitness which politicians rarely advise, also called for a "federal budget annually balanced on the basis of accurate executive estimates within revenues . . ."

A commitment to a balanced budget is always comprehensive. It then meant there could be no increase in government outlays to expand purchasing power and relieve distress. It meant there could be no further tax reduction. But taken literally it meant much more. From 1930 on the budget was far out of balance, and balance, therefore, meant an increase in taxes, a reduction in spending, or both. The Democratic platform in 1932 called for an "immediate and drastic reduction of governmental expenditures" to accomplish at least a 25 per cent decrease in the cost of government.

The balanced budget was not a subject of thought. Nor was it, as often asserted, precisely a matter of faith. Rather it was a formula. For centuries avoidance of borrowing had protected people from slovenly or reckless public housekeeping. Slovenly or reckless keepers of the public purse had often composed complicated arguments to show why balance of income and outlay was not a mark of virtue. Experience had shown that however convenient this belief might seem in the short run, discomfort or disaster followed in the long run. Those simple precepts of a simple world did not hold amid the growing complexities of the early thirties. Mass unemployment in particular had altered the rules. Events had played a very bad trick on people, but almost no one tried to think out the problem anew.

The balanced budget was not the only strait jacket on policy. There was also the bogey of "going off" the gold standard and, most surprisingly, of risking inflation. Until 1932 the United States added formidably to its gold reserves, and instead of inflation the country was experiencing the most violent deflation in the nation's history. Yet every sober adviser saw dangers here, including the danger of runaway price increases. Americans, though in years now well in the past, had shown a penchant for tinkering with the money supply and enjoying the brief but heady joys of a boom in prices. In 1931 or 1932, the danger or even the feasibility of such a boom was nil. The advisers and counselors were not, however, analyzing the danger or even the possibility. They were serving only as the custodians of bad memories.

The fear of inflation reinforced the demand for the balanced budget. It also limited efforts to make interest rates low, credit plentiful (or at least redundant) and borrowing as easy as possible under the circumstances. Devaluation of the dollar was, of course, flatly ruled out. This directly violated the gold standard rules. At best, in such depression times, monetary policy is a feeble reed on which to lean. The current economic clichés did not allow even the use of that frail weapon. And again, these attitudes were above party. Though himself singularly open-minded, Roosevelt was careful not to offend or disturb his followers. In a speech in Brooklyn toward the close of the 1932 campaign, he said:

> The Democratic platform specifically declares, "We advocate a sound currency to be preserved at all hazards." That is plain English. In discussing this platform on July 30, I said, "Sound money is an international necessity, not a domestic consideration for one nation alone." Far up in the Northwest, at Butte, I repeated the pledge . . . In Seattle I reaffirmed my attitude . . .[13]

The following February, Mr. Hoover set forth his view, as often before, in a famous letter to the President-elect:

> It would steady the country greatly if there could be prompt assurance that there will be no tampering or inflation of the currency; that the budget will be unquestionably balanced even if further taxation is necessary; that the Government credit will be maintained by refusal to exhaust it in the issue of securities.[14]

The rejection of both fiscal (tax and expenditure) and monetary policy amounted precisely to a rejection of all affirmative government economic policy. The economic advisers of the day had both the unanimity and the authority to force the leaders of both parties to disavow all the available steps to check deflation and depression. In its own way this was a marked achievement—a trumph of dogma over thought. The consequences were profound. . . .

NOTES

1. Geoffrey H. Moore, *Statistical Indications of Cyclical Revivals and Recessions, Occasional Paper 31,* National Bureau of Economic Research, Inc. (New York, 1950).
2. H. W. Arndt, *The Economic Lessons of the Nineteen-Thirties* (London: Oxford, 1944), p. 15.
3. E. M. Hugh-Jones and E. A. Radice, *An American Experiment* (London: Oxford, 1936), 49. Cited by Arndt, *op. cit.,* p. 16.
4. This has been widely noted. See Lionel Robbins, *The Great Depression* (New York: The Macmillan Co., 1934), p. 4, and Thomas Wilson, *Fluctuations in Income,* p. 154 ff., and J. M. Keynes, *A Treatise on Money* (New York: Harcourt, Brace, 1930), II, 190 ff.
5. Perhaps I may be permitted to enlarge on this in slightly more technical terms. The interruption could as well have been caused by an insufficient rate of increase in consumer spending as by a failure in the greater rate of increase of capital goods spending. Under-consumption and under-investment are the same side of the same coin. And some force is added to this explanation by the fact that spending for one important consumers' durable, namely houses, had been declining for several years and suffered a further substantial drop in 1929. However, the investment function we still suppose to be less stable than the consumption function, even though we are less assured of the stability of the latter than we used to be. And in the present case it seems wise to attach causal significance to the part of the spending which had to maintain the largest rate of increase if total spending were to be uninterrupted. The need to maintain a specific rate of increase in investment outlay is insufficiently emphasized by Mr. Thomas Wilson in his book which I have so frequently cited and to which students of the period are indebted.
6. Selma Goldsmith, George Jaszi, Hyman Kaitz, and Maurice Liebenberg, "Size Distribution of Income since the Mid-Thirties," *The Review of Economics and Statistics,* February 1954, pp. 16, 18.
7. *Weekly Letter,* November 23, 1929.
8. Compiled from *Federal Reserve Bulletin,* monthly issues, 1929.
9. U.S. Department of Commerce, Bureau of Foreign and Domestic Commerce, *Statistical Abstract of the United States,* 1942.

10. *Stock Exchange Practices* Report, 1934, pp. 220–21.
11. *Ibid.*, p. 215.
12. *Stock Exchange Practices,* Hearings, February–March 1933, Pt. 6, p. p. 2091 ff.
13. Lawrence Sullivan, *Prelude to Panic* (Washington: Statesman Press, 1936), p. 20.
14. William Starr Myers and Walter H. Newton, *The Hoover Administration: A Documented Narrative* (New York: Scribners, 1936), pp. 339–40.

V ~ *A Time of Tensions: The Rural-Urban Conflict: A Crisis in Values?*

12 ~ Sources and Nature of Intolerance in the 1920's*

[Author's Note] *The study of intolerance in the twenties raises questions in the mind of Paul L. Murphy of the University of Minnesota as to how the historian can gain essential information when his lack of data makes any analysis of bigotry unsuitable to quantitative investigation. Regardless of the incompleteness of the data available, Murphy finds "that many interwoven factors produced a concatenation of syndromes which made the country a peculiarly fertile seedbed both for intolerance and its shrewd manipulation." Professor Murphy's study adds to our understanding of a decade marked by the resurgence of the Ku Klux Klan, Henry Ford's experiment in propagating anti-Semitism, and the strong opposition of small-town America against "rum and Romanism."*

In approaching the seamy side of the national character which periodically displays broad-scale intolerance, prejudice, nativism, and xenophobia, many American historians have sought in recent years to draw upon the findings of scholars in related disciplines in their attempts at meaningful analysis. Especially suggestive in this area has been recent work in sociology, social psychology, cultural anthropology, and American studies.[1] Differences exist, however, as to how such findings can actually aid the historian

* By Paul L. Murphy. Reprinted with permission from *The Journal of American History,* LI (June, 1964), pages 60–76.

and the degree of reliance he can confidently place upon them. Given the fact that the average historian must work in a past context in which precise empirical research is impossible, particularly as it applies to a broad spectrum of public attitudes, and given the fact that modern social science studies draw the great body of their evidence from current materials, a question of relevance is raised. How safe is it for the historian to project such modern findings backwards in an attempt better to understand and grasp the tensions and pressures of a prior era? Are modern social science techniques reliable in the analysis of imprecise historical materials?

Some members of the historical guild feel that such borrowing of either materials or techniques is too dangerous to be acceptable. Others at times have relied too heavily upon such interdisciplinary aids in order to validate general presumptions otherwise difficult of documentation. Still others have used such materials cautiously and carefully, so cautiously and so carefully that they have come to differ among themselves concerning their applicability. In the study of past intolerance, for example, there have been those who drew heavily upon a sociologically oriented emphasis on status rivalries and who have emphasized ongoing tensions ever present in the slow process of ethnic integration in our dynamic society.[2] Yet such persons have subsequently been challenged to explain the plausibility of the cyclical nature of waves of intolerance and its frequently differing character as unique situations have produced unique expressions geared to immediate needs. Others who have made careful use of stereotyping or who have placed reliance upon ideological factors have been questioned. So too have those who have focused upon the concrete facts of the immediate situation, especially upon the influence of men of passion with ability to create or nurture moods of alarm by exploiting irrational myths. This has forced such persons to de-emphasize the constant factor of human irrationality in normal times even though it is always basic in assessing causation in all historical events.[3]

In many ways the study of intolerance in the 1920s raises in exaggerated form both a question of the applicability of related materials and of proper permissible use of such materials. That decade, despite its surface prosperity and supposed gaiety and exuberance, was characterized by waves of public intolerance seldom felt in the American experience. Much of this intolerance was merely an outbreak of familiar subsurface prejudices with antecedents in earlier expressed antipathies toward radicals, Catholics, Jews, Negroes, Orientals, and other minority groups. Yet such intolerance was not traditional. Fostered frequently, although seldom led directly by an apprehensive business community or aggravated by men seeking gratuities as brokers for that community or as brokers for men of property, it quickly gained its sanctions from that national consensus so clumsily branded "normalcy" and involved many Americans previously immune to its toxicity. As such it was an integral part of the 1920s, participated in consciously or unconsciously by the great majority of Americans. That it took on a changing character as the decade advanced is apt testimony to its virulence. That it either disappeared or took on different forms with the depression seems to reveal that it was specially suited to the peculiar culture and society of the jazz age.

The historian would be delighted if by merely adding the materials and utilizing the techniques of the social scientists he could say precise and scientific things both about the roots, nature, and manifestations of intolerance at this time. Yet, despite the siren's call of being able through empirical social research to reach quantitative answers, he is tempted to concentrate on the imprecise approaches of history, relying upon interdisciplinary tools as analytical devices only when they seem to have an obvious relation to known and documentable reality.

Clearly the sources of the intolerance of the 1920s can be traced to at least the late Progressive period with obvious roots in the immediately preceding years. Clearly such intolerance had a relation to growing Progressive apprehensions over alarming developments which did not seem to be responding to normal controls. The IWW, the first effectively organized movement of militant workingmen to challenge the whole American economic system, sent chills through the hearts and outrage through the souls of upper and middle class Americans. Here in the early years of the century was a group with the effrontery to make demands no decent citizen could honor and employ techniques no moral American could tolerate. But worse than this, these people and their Socialist "cousins" rejected the premises upon which the American system rested, namely that rights and privileges were open in a free society to anyone who was willing to work up patiently within the system. Or if the individual was incapable of utilizing this technique he would eventually be taken care of in a spirit of paternalism by the affluent class, as long as he stood with his hat in his hand and patiently waited. The alarming fact was that the IWWs and Socialists were no longer willing to wait. They were unwilling to accept the fact that only after one had gained a stake in society was he warranted in becoming a critic or a reformer. As one Progressive editor wrote during the Lawrence textile strike of 1912 (at the point which Paul Brissenden called "the high tide of the I.W.W. activity"):

On all sides people are asking, Is this a new thing in the industrial world? . . . Are we to see another serious, perhaps successful, attempt to organize labor by whole industrial groups instead of by trades? Are we to expect that instead of playing the game respectably, or else frankly breaking out into lawless riot which we know well enough how to deal with, the laborers are to listen to a subtle anarchistic philosophy which challenges the fundamental ideas of law and order, inculcating such strange doctrines as those of "direct action," "sabotage," "syndicalism," "the general strike," and "violence"? . . . We think that our whole current morality as to the sacredness of property and even of life is involved in it.[4]

Also involved in it was the IWW practice of utilizing the rhetoric of American democracy as a device for obtaining their ends. The "free-speech fight" which assumed national proportions after 1910 was distressingly successful at times and was painfully difficult to counteract. For while many Americans could argue that utilizing free speech to gain personal economic ends was an abuse of American ideals, the alternative of arbitrary suppression hardly preserved them.

For those in this dilemma World War I afforded a satisfying rationalization for suppression. Woodrow Wilson's prediction, "once lead this people into war and they'll forget there ever was such a thing as tolerance,"[5] was clairvoyant, as the government quickly set out to turn the President's words into official policy that succeeded frighteningly well. Every element of American public opinion was mobilized behind "my country, right or wrong," dissent was virtually forbidden, democracy at home was drastically curtailed so that it could be made safe abroad, while impressionable children were either "educated" in Hun atrocities, or their time was employed in liberty loan, Red Cross, war saving stamp, or YMCA campaigns. It was not difficult then to channel an aroused nation's wrath against earlier boatrockers—a development made easier by the fact that many IWWs and Socialists stood out boldly against the war from the start. The Espionage Act of 1917, while ostensibly a measure to strike at illegal interference with the war effort, was so worded that it could be, and was, used to stamp out radical criticism of the war. Its subsequent 1918 amendment, the Sedition Act, was a less subtle device. Passed by the pressure of western senators, and modeled after a Montana IWW statute, its purpose was to undercut both the performance and advocacy of undesirable activity. There was a clear implication that people who utilized speech as a means of gaining improper ends had to be restricted.[6] And with the subsequent federal prosecution of 184 members of the IWW in 1918 and 1919,[7] to say nothing of a crackdown on Socialists, German-Americans, conscientious objectors, and Non-Partisan Leaguers, the intent of the federal legislative and administrative program became crystal clear.

With peace and the end of conservative labor's wartime honeymoon, there was renewed fear on the part of the reinvigorated business community that an unholy union of dissident malcontents and elements of more orthodox labor, now feeling callously betrayed, was not only possible but probable. The strikes of the immediate postwar period could only be rationalized by business in these terms. And to create further alarm, not only was Bolshevism a reality in Russia, but American workers and even some influential leaders were studying its economic and political implications with interest if not with admiration. Catholics, when under fire in the past, had consistently denied their allegiance to the Vatican, but some of these Bolshevik admirers even proclaimed proudly and openly their allegiance to a new order functioning from the Kremlin.[8]

Fear led to irrationality and business found it impossible to analyze the meaning and implications of these developments or to understand what Gutzon Borglum called in 1919 the "real labor problem," which was labor's dependent condition. In response to a speech by Nicholas Murray Butler, rebuking labor for its lack of "reasonableness,"[9] Borglum wrote:

> Labor's recent political activity is due to a deep consciousness of the necessity of self-reliance to secure any and all improvement in its condition. And further, the political color that has recently appeared in its methods, is forced because of the utter faithlessness and failure of partisan government to give it relief.[10]

But to conservative leaders, protection was more important than understanding. With the wartime legislation now generally inapplicable, they sought to get onto the statute books peacetime sedition and criminal syndicalism laws to take its place. To accomplish this, business was frequently able to transfer its own fears of Bolshevism both to a broader public and to state legislators who served that public. The result was that such propagandizing, plus added apprehensions triggered by frequently specious bomb scares, produced wide demand for restriction. Thus, although much of the new legislation was enacted in a sincere desire to control agitators and dangerous seditionists, other more responsive legislators took care to be sure that resultant laws were carefully worded and did not appear to be class legislation. By 1920 thirty-five states had enacted some form of restrictive, precautionary legislation enabling the rapid crackdown on speech that might by its expression produce unlawful actions geared toward stimulating improper political or economic change. Such legislation was couched in terms which in Connecticut permitted punishment of "disloyal, scurrilous, or abusive language about the form of government of the United States," and in Colorado, "advocacy by word or in print of forcible resistance to constituted government either as a general principle, or in particular instances as a means of affecting governmental, industrial, social or economic conditions."[11]

That there was no legal need or justification for such legislation (the criminal codes of the states adequately covered conspiracy and libel)[12] further underlined the fact that its purpose was devious. It constituted intimidating legislation by which business subtly sought to institutionalize forms of prior curtailment and thereby free itself from the necessity of having personally to restrict those it considered a threat to the existing order. Henceforth such restriction and subtle regimentation could be left to the discretion of administrative officials who could develop standards to fit immediate and local needs,[13] and who, as the decade progressed, were to add the injunction as a further precautionary weapon.

Although this legislation was quickly implemented in 1919 in a number of states, it did not quiet malcontents. Prompted by a multiplication of strikes and labor discontent, the more hysterical began to fear that local sanctions were not enough and proceeded to advocate a form of federal "direct action." Powerful federal activity such as the Palmer raids, the army-conducted deportation of 249 "dangerous Reds" aboard the "Soviet Ark" *Buford,* the contemporaneous effort of representatives and senators to rush through a federal peacetime sedition act, while a product of and response to excessive public hysteria should also be understood as the partial culmination of an increasingly more pressing apprehensiveness which had obsessed conservatives for well over a decade. And the fact that many Americans were at the time able to rationalize and condone the most disgraceful, wholesale departure from fundamental guarantees of basic liberty and due process of law in American history further underscores the extent of their fears.[14]

Yet the Red scare of the 1920s introduced a new permanent dimension of intolerance. This was the aspiring, self-seeking individual or special interest group which sought to exploit the hysteria and intolerance of the moment for personal advantage. Such individuals and groups were not new in American history.[15] But the breadth of their operations was more sweeping in the 1920s, and the ambitiousness of their calculations was greater, as was the number of Americans they sought to affect. For aggressive politicians like A. Mitchell Palmer, Leonard Wood, or Albert S. Burleson, the ability to project themselves into the role of master defender of the endangered order could mean nomination to high office, hopefully the presidency. To an Anthony Caminetti, the first person of Italian extraction to be elected to Congress and by then Commissioner of Immigration, this was an opportunity to demonstrate that he, as well as others of his national origin, were fully 100 percent American. To an aggressive bureaucrat like William J. Flynn, head of the Bureau of Investigation, or J. Edgar Hoover, head of the Bureau's newly created General Intelligence (antiradical) Division, here was a chance to enhance the power of the Bureau, and his own power and domain simultaneously.[16] To Flynn's successor, William J. Burns, the ability to guide public fears and even create fears where only apprehensions had existed was also an opportunity to stimulate a brisk private business for the Burns International Detective Agency until an increasingly more hostile public forced a curtailment and a housecleaning in the Department of Justice.[17]

At the group level motivations were equally divergent. The American Legion epitomized the service-oriented organizations, obligated to deliver a variety of specific benefits to its wide membership. To do this entailed sufficient flattering and assisting of those in power to convince them that the organization deserved favors. But to write the Legion off as "apple-polishing, flag-wavers of patriotism" is to miss the fact that most legionnaires received great satisfaction from ousting "Reds" and Americanizing everyone completely. Such patrioteering afforded an opportunity for members to demonstrate and articulate their faith and allegiance to basic ideals and institutions and thereby to gain acceptance and status with those who felt a similar need.[18] Thus in this and similar organizations there was a natural tie between aiding the "establishment" and crusading to save America. The professional patriots, on the other hand, had simpler and even less commendable motives. Primarily propaganda organizations, and the mouthpieces of single leaders or small cabals, their purpose was to ingratiate themselves with large private or corporate donors and thereby insure their continuation. This meant showing results, not only in broad distribution of literature but in providing speakers to help in mobilizing large elements of the general public against all manner of enemies of "the American way." Thus Harry A. Jung of the powerful National Clay Products Industries Association and later the American Vigilant Intelligence Federation could write to a potential subscriber:

> We cooperate with over 30 distinctly civic and patriotic organizations. . . . It would take me too long to relate how I "put over" this part of our activities, namely, "trailing the Reds." Should you ever be in Chicago, drop in and see me and I will explain. That it has been a paying proposition for our organization goes without saying. . . .[19]

And again, Fred R. Marvin, head of the Keymen of America, could for six dollars per annum supply potential private radical hunters with his *Daily Data Sheets* which conveyed the doings of the Bolsheviks and parlor pinks to nervous and apprehensive individuals.[20] It was Marvin's aim to inspire the leadership of such a group as the DAR to draw up and enforce a national "black-list" of undesirable speakers that included such public disturbers of the peace as Jane Addams, Sherwood Eddy, James Harvey Robinson, and William Allen White.[21] In all, over thirty such ultra-patriotic organizations came and went in the 1920s, all to a greater or lesser degree dependent upon the success with which they could mobilize and direct public intolerance and intemperance.[22]

In this context the Ku Klux Klan played a unique role. Although it was geared to financial gain, especially as the decade progressed and its leadership fell more and more into the hands of those who sought to utilize it solely for personal profit, it was content to draw its money and support largely from private citizens in small towns and rural communities, a fact which set it apart from most other intolerance purveyors in the 1920s. This also meant, however, that it operated upon poorly underpinned grounds, a fact graphically illustrated by its rapid collapse well before the onset of the economic crisis of the depression years.

The success which all these individuals and groups achieved would still not have been possible if great segments of the American public had not been highly susceptible to the various types of appeal which they made. The source of this susceptibility was neither simple, nor always rational. It stemmed from the turbulence of the decade as value patterns underwent modification from the impact both of external pressures and internal conflict. When the German sociologist Ferdinand Tönnies delineated in his 1926 volume[23] between what he called Gemeinschaft-Gesellschaft social structure, he inadvertently suggested the root of one of the sources of the chronic distress of the American middle class mind. Tönnies' Gemeinschaft structure well described that segment of American society which was basically rural or rural oriented, homogeneous in its ethnic and religious structure and values, a society which functioned through traditional status arrangements and which was characterized by low mobility.

The members of such a society had always in America fought off what they considered the deleterious effect of foreign values endemic in a Gesellschaft structure with its urban orientation, secular focus, heterogeneous ethnic makeup, its preference for ordering social and economic relations through contract, and its tradition of high mobility which too often seemed to operate on questionable standards. In fact, the decade had opened on the crest of a successful counterattack of superimposed Gemeinschaft values in the "noble experiment," prohibition. But such a victory was a nervous one as open defiance and hostility grew and as erosion seemed to be occurring elsewhere with the nation succumbing to the excitement and immediacy of a new, generally urban dispersed popular culture. Formerly insulated value orientations now were subjected to the lure of new behavioral patterns suggested by the radio, the movies, romance magazines, and national service clubs. Moreover, the automobile, and in time the airplane, were affording the physical mobility which inevitably speeded up actual social contact with those whose values may earlier have only been slightly known.[24] This does not suggest that either form of social organization was bound to prevail. What it does suggest is that with the pressures to standardize, elements of formerly isolated groups were being subjected to a new challenge to modify the intensity with which they held to their own unique ways as the only acceptable ones.

Those who were thus disturbed accepted dominant American values. However, they found that their interpretation of these values or the techniques that they found acceptable in attaining them frequently had to undergo more modification than they found comfortable. Yet "normalcy," incorporating as it did a multitude of simple virtues along with carefully contrived selfish ends, proved an acceptable home for most rural Victorians and Babbitts alike. Their concern, and often it was held with equal intensity by each, was not the system, but the deviator, who for one reason or another was unwilling to accept the system with its fairly rigid formulae as to how to succeed and who might succeed. Here two types of troublemakers invariably stood out. The one was made up of those who sought unjustifiably to reach the pinnacle of full attainment of the success symbols which the system held out. The other consisted of those whose hierarchy of values and, of necessity, methods for attaining them were totally at odds with the standards of the day. In the former group one inevitably found the targets of Klan antipathy, for example: the ambitious immigrant, non-Anglo-Saxon, non-Protestant, whose frequent tendency to "overachieve" led to actions to "keep him in his place." But the quiet "consensus" of the 1920s backed up the Klan's overt censuring with a type of silent coercion which was often far more effective, especially if a Jew wanted admission to the local country club, or a Catholic wanted the presidency of the nation. Although Americans may never be fully ready for "the functionally strategic convergence of the standards by which conduct is evaluated," to use Robin Williams' phrase,[25] they were not ready in the 1920s even to consider such a possibility as a desirable national objective. The deviators, although small in number, were even more of a threat. Radicals, militant labor leaders, other loud and unreasonable critics of the system, and the honest and misguided average citizens whom they seemed to be perverting, had to be clamped into place even more quickly and thoroughly and by virtually any means possible. In this many welcomed the aid of any and all self-proclaimed champions of 100 percent Americanism.[26]

This position constituted an interesting modification of an earlier confidence in progress through broad public participation and discussion, a process long boasted as inherent in American institutions. In 1931 Roger Baldwin attributed this to the manifestly declining postwar faith in democracy.[27] Others attributed it to the general insecurity of all Americans and especially the chronic dissatisfaction with what many had been led to believe would be the glorious life of a postwar world.[28] Regardless of the cause, the effect was to undercut one of the potentially important sources which might have brought significant relief. Having convinced themselves that deviators from the status quo were potential Bolsheviks, many Americans found it a simple step to renounce the mildest type of reformer or reform program, a view in which they had the most thorough encouragement from the self-seeking patriots of the decade. An organization like the American Civil Liberties Union, the Federal Council of Churches, various social justice elements within specific religious groups,[29] explicit social reform organizations like the American Birth Control League, the Consumer's League, the National Child Labor Committee, although in reality seeking to strengthen the system by eliminating its many defects, found basic communication difficult with a public conditioned to look askance at any but practitioners of normalcy.[30]

Despite the general similarity through the decade of the sources of broad scale intolerance, its public manifestations took a variety of changing forms. The early fears of Bolshevism could not be exploited indefinitely especially when the sins committed in the name of its suppression were revealed and its purveyors were shown to be using it as a device for unscrupulous personal gain. Public indignation toward the excesses of the Palmer raids, for example, came quickly following the issuance by the

National Popular Government League of the devastating report on the *Illegal Practices of the United States Department of Justice* in late May 1920.[31] Such indignation was sufficient to drive those who might have sought to extend similar techniques to adopt far more subtle and clandestine modes of approach, and also to turn hysteria-making over to the private professional patriot organizations. Thus, William J. Burns, for example, after carefully instituting the Bridgeman raids of August 1922 turned to Ralph Easley of the National Civic Federation, Richard M. Whitney of the American Defense Society, and Joseph T. Cashman of the National Security League to arouse the public to a fever pitch over their implications.[32]

Yet even Burns's string ran out in 1923–1924 as the misrule of the Department of Justice could no longer be ignored[33] and as antiradicalism (labor by this time having been quite thoroughly tamed) was becoming a tiresome broken record. This is not to say, as Sidney Howard wrote bitterly at the time, that certain business interests might not find it useful to tar their critics by turning to the "services of radicalism in almost any one of their patriotic clashes with social liberalism or rambunctious unions, or, even, child labor reformers."[34] But for the moment different targets were needed.

For those distressed with the growing disruption of their Gemeinschaft society, the Ku Klux Klan offered avenues for assaulting those most surely responsible. And while all Americans might not have agreed with C. Lewis Fowler, editor of the *American Standard,* that a heinous conspiracy to destroy America was afoot between Roman Catholicism and anti-Christian Jewry,[35] the irrational myths and stereotyping surrounding these groups were sufficient to convince many they needed surveillance, if not repression. The Klan also impressed many with its pious objectives of uplifting the nation's morality through attacking its immoral desecrators. Atypical of the conservative, service-and-fellowship oriented organizations, or the professional patriot groups, stemming primarily from outside the urban business community, the Klan, nonetheless, for three or four years in the mid-1920s successfully attacked and insidiously exploited the shattering of old moral standards. Thereby the Klan could resort to direct action against progenitors of public immorality, as it did in the case of Judge Ben "Companionate Marriage" Lindsey in Denver.[36] Indirectly, it could also inspire others to heed the clarion call to expose the evil forces which had to be behind the callous disregard of traditional ways, a call answered by Calvin Coolidge, for example, in his public exposé of "Reds" in our women's colleges,[37] or by Texas representaive Thomas L. Blanton's public assault on the ACLU which he branded the "UnAmerican Criminal License Union."[38]

For those patriots seeking essentially to play a broker's role for powerful interests, intriguing new opportunities were opening up in antipacifism and the baiting of antimilitarists. The official demise of Burns left the tradition of his office to the War Department. By that time the department was growing more apprehensive over the potential threat to its authority from antiwar sentiments that were increasingly prevalent as disillusion with the war experience intensified. As early as 1923, General Amos Fries, head of the Chemical Warfare Service, had publicly committed the government to support Preparedness Day, and by inference the continuation of an expanded military establishment. Fries had also encouraged Mrs. Lucia R. Maxwell, librarian of the Service, to prepare and circulate the famed "Spider Web Chart," which purported to study women's peace organizations in the United States and show, by ramification and association, that they were all Bolshevik inspired or at least deep pink.[39] Although the War Department eventually ordered retraction, and directed Fries to inform persons to whom the chart had been circulated that its information was erroneous, the retraction fell on few careful ears. The chart was still being used by the Legion and the DAR in the early 1930s as an authentic exposé of the enemies of America. Such sentiments were also purveyed by such a professional militarist as General John J. Pershing, who in a series of lectures for the American Defense Society warned that "our situation is seriously complicated by the teachings of numerous pacifist organizations. . . ."[40]

The concern with pacifism does not imply, however, that earlier hostility toward radicals, social reformers, and other public disrupters had ended. On the contrary, the development of pacifism as a term of opprobrium was merely adding another liability to the large series of undesirable personality traits that these enemies of America were supposed to possess, one which could be stressed more strongly when public apprehensions of radicalism were relatively deflated. Certainly as explosive public episodes developed—the Passaic Textile Strike,[41] the furor over New York City's Stuyvesant High School, and by implication to use of any public building as a public forum even for liberals,[42] the Colorado Mine War of late 1927,[43] and above all the execution of Sacco and Vanzetti,[44]—the "Reds" and their dupes were held largely to blame, both for the episodes and for any number of people taking a remotely liberal view on the questions they raised. However, the dangers of such people could be brought home to a far more diversified audience if one talked of the "whole Pacifist-Radical-Communist movement in America [which] is foreign in its conception, if not actually under foreign influence, direction and control,"[45] or referred to such a leader as Roger Baldwin as a "slacker, radical, draft evader, and Leavenworth ex-convict."[46]

And the most effective agents of intolerance came more and more to have this focus. By 1925, the heyday of the Klan was over. The enactment of the National Origins Act in 1924, internal strife (endemic in the order from its beginnings), and burgeoning prosperity, all undercut prior strength. In its annual report for 1927, the American Civil Liberties Union announced that the principal purveyors of intolerance in the country were the War Department, the American Legion, and professional patriot societies. It declared that the American Legion had by then "replaced the Klan as the most active agency of intolerance and repression in the country."[47] The report was editorially criticized by Joseph Pulitzer's liberal New York *World* for such a value judgment, stating: "With scores of different organizations seeking to curtail liberty in scores of different ways, it is a wise man who can say that one is more active than any of the others."[48] To which Forrest Bailey, Director of the ACLU, responded by merely pointing out that this was the consensus of all the state units reporting to national headquarters for the year.[49]

It is not the purpose of this paper to attempt to explain the effect of the depression upon what had become fairly standard patterns of intolerance and intolerance-making. Nonetheless, certain clear developments can be recognized. On one hand, the professional patriots quickly found their traditional sources of income drying up. The National Civic Foundation, for example, previously one of the bellwethers of such groups, was reduced to such belt-tightening by 1930 and the years following that its activities had to be cut to virtual ineffectiveness.[50] Other comparable groups collapsed completely. Faced with similar problems the American Legion and the DAR found it expedient to do some of their cutting back in the area of antiradical activity. Pacifist-baiting no longer seemed a highly meaningful or relevant response to public problems.

On the other hand, vast evidence suggests that many businesses stepped up their antiradical activity. Deserting the intolerance purveyors who had formerly performed the function of subtly undermining and discrediting their critics, they now preferred to spend their money for direct action in the form of company guards, labor spies, strike breakers, and arms. Thus the American Civil Liberties Union could report a vast increase in the number of cases it received in the early depression years and generally the greatest suppression of individual liberties in the country since the days of the Red scare. Similarly, the number of instances of police brutality and flagrant abuse of local governmental power were well known.[51]

If one is to talk in terms of meaningful and internally consistent cycles of public intolerance, an era ends in 1929–1930. By this time, to defend the status quo as unassailable was to make oneself ludicrous, since a casual glance revealed the magnitude of its defects. Significantly, when Representative Hamilton Fish auspiciously launched a series of congressional investigations in 1930 in an attempt to throw the blame for the depression on domestic "Reds,"[52] the results of his crusade were to produce either large-scale public apathy or large-scale public antipathy.

The imperfect public record of the 1920s then would seem to reveal that many interwoven factors produced a concatenation of syndromes which made the country a peculiarly fertile seedbed both for intolerance and its shrewd manipulation. These undoubtedly included the tensions of economic dynamism, grossly unequal distribution of wealth, enhanced urbanization with the dislocation it produced both in the urban area and in its rural recruitment grounds, virulent disillusionment with democracy, and the confusing and contradictory assumptions concerning the increasingly unpopular war experience.

A moot question still exists as to whether more precise results could not have been reached by placing heavier reliance on social science. Undoubtedly if public opinion poll information were available or if scientific attempts had been made at the time to quantify a variety of public attitudes, the record would be more approachable. Certainly steeping ourselves in a more sophisticated analysis of present and future events enhances the understanding of social and human processes in general and affords a more precise appreciation of human behavior in a past context. Certainly the types of questions which the empirical social researcher is currently asking can be asked of that decade and the historian is derelict if he fails to ask them. Yet the basic problem is still how to gain essential information now lacking and difficult or impossible to obtain. The social science researcher is not much help here. In fact, he operates on the assumption that unless sufficient information is available to permit arrival at quantitative answers, little of value can be produced and one's energies are wasted in the effort.

The historian, proceeding on the assumption that almost all important questions are important precisely because of their subtle implications and overtones, their complexities, ambiguities, and ambivalences—because in other words, they are not susceptible to quantitative answers—then must plod on his dogged and imperfect way. He must approach incomplete materials not only semi-analytically, but impressionistically and eclectically, even at times attempting to devise his own ways to evaluate a great divergency of data which the social scientist scarcely feels worth considering due to its impreciseness and unsuitability to quantitative analysis. But the historian likes to feel that only if serious attempt is made to assess all the data, regardless of its nature or its incompleteness, can anything resembling past reality possibly be attained. And as a humanist viewing essentially human phenomena, even if in so imprecise a fashion, the historian also likes to feel that he may, as Arthur M. Schlesinger, Jr., has suggested, "yield truths about both individual and social experience which quantitative social research by itself could never reach."[53]

NOTES

1. Particularly suggestive in this regard are the works of Gordon Allport, Bruno Bettelheim, Kenneth B. Clark, Allison Davis, E. Franklin Frazier, Marie Jahoda, Morris Janowitz, Clyde Kluckhohn, Kurt Lewin, Herbert Muller, Gunnar Myrdal, Arnold Rose, Gerhart Saenger, Edward A. Shils, James Vander Zanden, Robin Williams, and J. Milton Yinger.
2. For example, John Higham, "Another Look at Nativism," *Catholic Historical Review,* XLIV (July 1958), 150, in denigrating an ideological approach, argues: "Except on the subject of race (and in related forms anti-Semitism), the kind of accusations which nativists leveled against foreign elements remained relatively constant. . . . For the history of nativism, therefore, emotional intensity provided the significant measure of change."
3. David B. Davis confronts this dilemma with healthy open-mindedness in "Some Themes of Counter-Subversion: An Analysis of Anti-Masonic, Anti-Catholic, and Anti-Mormon Literature," *Mississippi Valley Historical Review,* XLVII (Sept. 1960), 205–24.
4. "After the Battle," *Survey,* XXVIII (April 6, 1912), 1–2. Such attitudes are explored in provocative detail in Reinhard Bendix, *Work and Authority in Industry: Ideologies of Management in the Course of Industrialization* (New York, 1956), 254–340.
5. Ray Stannard Baker, *Woodrow Wilson, Life and Letters* (8 vols., New York, 1927–1939), VI, 506–07. On the persecution of anti-war groups generally, see H. C. Peterson and Gilbert C. Fite, *Opponents of War: 1917–1918* (Madison, 1957), and O. A. Hilton, "The Minnesota Commission of Public Safety in World War I, 1917–1919," *Bulletin of the Oklahoma Agricultural and Mechanical College,* LXVIII (May 15, 1951).
6. Zechariah Chafee, Jr., *Free Speech in the United States* (Cambridge, 1941), 39–41.

7. Philip Taft, "The Federal Trials of the IWW," *Labor History,* III (Winter 1962), 57–91.
8. Roger N. Baldwin, "The Myth of Law and Order," in Samuel D. Schmalhausen, ed., *Behold America!* (New York, 1931), 660–61. The appeal of the Soviet experiment in its early years stands out in various liberal organs. See, for exmple, *The Advance* (New York), 1919–1923. See also Matthew Josephson, *Sidney Hillman: Statesman of American Labor* (Garden City, 1952), 274 ff., and Christopher Lasch, *The American Liberals and the Russian Revolution* (New York, 1962).
9. Nicholas Murray Butler, *The Real Labor Problem* (n.p., [1919]), an address delivered before the Institute of Arts and Sciences, Columbia University, October 13, 1919, and published as a pamphlet.
10. Gutzon Borglum, *The Real Labor Problem* (n.p., [1919]), a confidential pamphlet, privately printed.
11. See Fund for the Republic, *Digest of the Public Record of Communism in the United States* (New York, 1955), 266 ff. For a detailed history of this legislation and a careful state-by-state record of its framing see Eldridge F. Dowell, "A History of the Enactment of Criminal Syndicalism Legislation in the United States" (2 vols., doctoral dissertation, Johns Hopkins University, 1936).
12. "Criminal Syndicalism," *Columbia University Law Review,* XX (Feb. 1920), 232. The point was made regularly by liberals in the 1920s. See, for example, Brandeis' famous concurring opinion in the Whitney case (1927), 274 U.S. 357, 372 ff.
13. American Civil Liberties Union, *The Police and Radicals: What 88 Police Chiefs Think and Do About Radical Meetings* (New York, 1921). See also *Investigation of Communist Propaganda. Hearings before a Special Committee to Investigate Communist Activities in the United States.* House Exec. Docs., 71 Cong., 2 Sess., Pt. IV, Vol. I, 3; Vol. II, 574 ff. (1930).
14. National Popular Government League, *To the American People: Report upon the Illegal Practices of the United States Department of Justice* (Washington, 1920). On the impact of the report see Robert K. Murray, *Red Scare: A Study in National Hysteria* (Minneapolis, 1955), 255.
15. One is immediately reminded of the careful attempt of the Adams Federalists to exploit the half-war with France in 1798, Know-Nothingism in various periods of American History, bloody-shirt waving in the post-Civil War years, among other things. See James M. Smith, *Freedom's Fetters: The Alien and Sedition Laws and American Civil Liberties* (Ithaca, 1956).
16. Max Lowenthal, *The Federal Bureau of Investigation* (New York, 1950), 71–72, 90, 298 ff.
17. Don Whitehead, *The F.B.I. Story* (New York, 1956), 55–59; Alpheus T. Mason, *Harlan Fiske Stone: Pillar of the Law* (New York, 1956), 149–50; Methodist Federation for Social Service, *The Social Service Bulletin* (Feb. 1920), 1–4; *ibid.* (Sept. 1924), 1–4; Dowell, *Criminal Syndicalism Legislation,* 1026, 1129.
18. Rodney G. Minott, *Peerless Patriots: Organized Veterans and the Spirit of Americanism* (Washington, 1963), 112 ff.
19. Jung to Henry E. Niles, March 23, 1926, American Civil Liberties Union Collection, Microfilm Reel 333 (New York Public Library). The ACLU files are filled with material concerning the various professional patriot groups.

20. There is a complete run of the *Daily Data Sheets* in the ACLU Collection, Microfilm Reel 332.

21. On the blacklist see Martha Strayer, *The D.A.R., An Informal History* (Washington, 1958), 133 ff., and Walter Johnson, ed., *Selected Letters of William Allen White, 1899–1943* (New York, 1947), 278–83.

22. Norman Hapgood, ed., *Professional Patriots* (New York, 1927), concentrates on twenty-five or so of the major ones, although Fred R. Marvin, *Our Government and Its Enemies* (New York, 1932), by adding a variety of local auxiliaries, lists fifty-four organizations as making up the American Coalition of Patriotic Societies at the height of the movement.

23. Ferdinand Tönnies, *Gemeinschaft und Gesellschaft,* translated and edited by Charles P. Loomis (East Lansing, 1957). The danger for the historian in utilizing such a concept is well delineated by Robin M. Williams, Jr., *American Society* (2nd rev. ed., New York, 1960), 482–83. Highly provocative in this context is the assessment of value orientation within a culture in Florence R. Kluckhohn and Fred L. Strodtbeck, *Variations in Value Orientation* (Evanston, 1961), 24 ff., 340–44.

24. A perceptive contemporary understanding of this development was given by Judge Learned Hand in 1930; see Irving Dilliard, *The Spirit of Liberty: Papers and Addresses of Learned Hand* (New York, 1960), 66–83.

25. Williams, *American Society,* 557. In this regard see John P. Roche, *The Quest for the Dream* (New York, 1963), 261 ff.

26. Such champions sometimes used aggressive campaigns of "Americanization" geared especially toward education. See "Program for Promoting American Ideals," *American Bar Association Journal,* VIII (Sept. 1922), 587. See also Bessie L. Pierce, *Public Opinion and Teaching of History in the United States* (New York, 1926), and the same author's *Citizens' Organizations and the Civic Training of Youth* (New York, 1933).

27. Baldwin, "Myth of Law and Order," 658–59.

28. Walter Lippmann, whose own writings had reflected intense disillusionment with the "phantom public," attempted to analyze the general disillusionment of the decade in his volume, *A Preface to Morals* (New York, 1929). Revealing in this regard is the broad study of Joseph E. Clark, "The American Critique of the Democratic Idea, 1919–1929" (doctoral dissertation, Stanford University, 1958).

29. The Methodist Federation for Social Service, Unitarian Fellowship for Social Justice, Church League for Industrial Democracy (Episcopal), National Catholic Welfare Council, and Central Conference of American Rabbis are leading examples.

30. Clarke A. Chambers, "Creative Effort in an Age of Normalcy, 1913–1933," *The Social Welfare Forum* (1961), 252–71.

31. See National Popular Government League, *To the American People.*

32. Burns's dealings with Easley are revealed in some detail in the files of the National Civic Federation. See Easley to Howard E. Coffin, Oct. 9 and 19, 1922, National Civic Federation Collection (New York Public Library). See also Richard M. Whitney, *The Reds in America* (New York, 1923), and Joseph T. Cashman, *America Asleep: The Menace of Radicalism* (New York, 1923).

33. American Civil Liberties Union, *The Nation-Wide Spy System Centering in the Department of Justice* (New York, 1924); Mason, *Harlan Fiske Stone;* Whitehead, *F.B.I. Story.*
34. Sidney Howard, "Our Professional Patriots: V, The New Crusade," *New Republic,* XL (Sept. 24, 1924), 93.
35. A typical *American Standard* story caption read: "Ochs (Jew) wants Smith (R.C.): Owner of 'New York Times' Would Give Wet Papist Life Tenure of New York Governorship," Sept. 1, 1925. On the modern Klan and southern racism generally see: James W. Vander Zanden, "The Southern White Resistance Movement to Integration" (doctoral dissertation, University of North Carolina, 1958).
36. Ben B. Lindsey and Rube Borough, *The Dangerous Life* (New York, 1931), 388 ff.
37. Calvin Coolidge, "Enemies of the Republic: Are the 'Reds' Stalking Our College Women?" *The Delineator,* XCVIII (June 1921), 4 ff.
38. *Cong. Record,* LXVII, Pt. 2, 1217 ff. (Dec. 19, 1925). The story of the assault was widely reprinted. Harry A. Jung wrote to 600 trade secretaries urging support for Blanton in his fight against the ACLU. ACLU Collection, Microfilm Reel 333.
39. Howard, "Our Professional Patriots," 94. Howard quotes Fries as referring to "The insidious pacifist, who is more to be feared than the man with the torch, gun or sword."
40. ACLU Collection, Microfilm Reel 331, contains pamphlet reprints of a number of Pershing's public addresses.
41. The material on Passiac is voluminous. See especially Albert Weisbord, *Passaic* (Chicago, 1926); Mary Heaton Vorse, *The Passaic Textile Strike* (New York, 1927); Joseph Freeman, *An American Testament* (New York, 1936), 392 ff.; *American Labor Year Book, 1927* (New York, 1927), 105 ff., 156.
42. The Annual Report of the American Civil Liberties Union for 1927, *Free Speech, 1926* (New York, 1927), referred to the ACLU's struggle with the New York City School Board in the Stuyvesant case as the "most important 'free speech fight' of the year." This struggle revealed the existence of a "blacklist" against individuals whose opinions did not conform to those of board members.
43. American Civil Liberties Union, *The War on Colorado Miners* (New York, 1928); Donald J. McClurg, "The Colorado Coal Strike of 1927: Tactical Leadership of the IWW," *Labor History,* IV (Winter 1963), 68–92; Dowell, "Criminal Syndicalism Legislation," 806 ff.; *The Advance* (New York), Dec. 2, 16, 27, 1929.
44. See especially G. Louis Joughin and Edmund M. Morgan, *The Legacy of Sacco and Vanzetti* (New York, 1948), and Francis Russell, *Tragedy in Dedham* (New York, 1962).
45. Fred R. Marvin, quoted in Marcus Duffield, *King Legion* (New York, 1931), 177–78.
46. This was the standard indictment of Baldwin by his enemies throughout the decade. The quote here is by Col. Leroy F. Smith of the Better America Federation of Los Angeles in an "expose" entitled: *The American Civil Liberties Union: Its Mental Processes, Its Chums, Its Program and Purpose* (Los Angeles, 1930), 1. On the early activities of the Federation see Edwin Layton, "The

Better America Federation: A Case Study of Super-patriotism," *Pacific Historical Review,* XXX (May 1961), 137–47.

47. *Free Speech, 1926,* p. 2.
48. Editorial, "The American Civil Liberties Union," New York *World,* May 17, 1927, p. 12.
49. Letters column, *ibid.,* May 18, 1927, p. 12.
50. Prior to 1929 the organization's subversive activities program was lavishly supported. In that year the only contribution so earmarked was $1,000 from John Hays Hammond. In 1930 the only contribution was $5,000 from Samuel Insull. By 1931 the amount had been reduced to $138, and in 1932, 1933, and 1934 there were no entries of money received for that purpose. National Civic Federation Receipt Book, National Civic Federation Collection.
51. See the popular summarization of the findings of the Wickersham Commission, Ernest J. Hopkins, *Our Lawless Police: A Study of the Unlawful Enforcement of the Law* (New York, 1931).
52. See footnote 13. The *Hearings* of the so-called Fish committee were published in nineteen volumes. The hearings were responsible for a large "Deport the Reds," rally in Carnegie Hall on Jan. 10, 1931. A good cross section of national newspaper opinion on the rally (which was primarily hostile) is in the ACLU Collection, Microfilm Reel 464.
53. Arthur M. Schlesinger, Jr., "The Humanist Looks at Empirical Social Research," *American Sociological Review,* XXVII (Dec. 1962), 771.

13 ∽ The Husbandman*

[Author's Note] *Concern for individual values rather than societal goals was to be the trademark of the post-war era. At the head of the campaign for personal and intellectual freedom was the irreverent Henry L. Mencken, editor of the* American Mercury. *Violently contemptuous of ordinary men, he flailed away unceasingly at the "grasping, selfish and dishonest mammal" known as the farmer. For Mencken, the romantic appeal of the farm as a symbol of democracy—the "myth of the garden"—was non-existent. The sage of Baltimore never recognized the farm or the farmer as the backbone of America.*

A reader for years of the *Congressional Record,* I have encountered in its dense and pregnant columns denunciations of almost every human act or idea that is imaginable to political pathology, from adultery to Zionism, and of all classes of men whose crimes the legislative mind can grasp, from atheists to Zoroastrians, but never once, so far as I can recall, has that great journal shown the slightest insolence, direct or indirect, to the humble husbandman, the lonely companion of *Bos taurus,* the sweating and persecuted farmer. He is, on the contrary, the pet above all other pets, the enchantment and delight, the saint and archangel of all the unearthly Sganarelles and Scaramouches who roar in the two houses of Congress. He is more to them, day in and day out, than whole herds of Honest Workingmen, Gallant Jack Tars and Heroic Miners; he is more, even, than a platoon of Unknown Soldiers. There are days when one or another of these totems of the statesman is bathed with such devotion that it would make the Gracchi blush, but there is never a day that the farmer, too, doesn't get his share, and there is many a day when he gets ten times his share—when, indeed, he is completely submerged in rhetorical vaseline, so that it is hard to tell which end of him is made in the image of God and which is mere hoof. No session ever begins without a grand assault at all arms upon his hereditary foes, from the boll-weevil and the San José scale to Wall Street and the Interstate Commerce Commission. And no session comes to an end without a huge grist of new laws to save him from them—laws embodying the most subtle statecraft of the most daring and ingenious body of law-makers ever assembled under one roof on the habitable globe. One might almost argue that the chief, and perhaps even only aim of legislation in These States is to succor and secure the farmer. If, while the bombs of goose-grease and rockets of pomade are going off in the two Chambers, certain evil men meet in the basement and hook *banderillas* into him—say, by inserting jokers into the chemical schedule of a new tariff bill, or by getting the long-haul rules changed, or by manipulating the loans of the Federal Reserve Banks—then the crime is not against him alone; it is against the whole American people, the common decency of Christendom, and the Holy Ghost. Horn a farmer, and you stand in contumacy to the platforms of all known parties, to the devout faith of all known statesmen, and to God. *Laborantem agricolam oportet primum de fructibus percipere.*

Paul wrote to the Bishop of Ephesus, at the latest, in the year 65 A.D.; the doctrine that I have thus ascribed to the Mesmers and Grimaldis of our politics is therefore not a novelty of their contrivance. Nor is it, indeed, their monopoly, for it seems to be shared by all Americans who are articulate and devote themselves to political metaphysics and good works. The farmer is praised by all who mention him at all, from archbishops to zoölogists, day in and day out. He is praised for his industry, his frugality, his patriotism, his altruistic passion. He is praised for staying on the farm, for laboriously wringing our bread and meat from the reluctant soil, for renouncing Babylon to guard the horned cattle on the hills. He is praised for his patient fidelity to the oldest of learned professions, and the most honorable, and the most necessary to all of us. He takes on, in political speeches and newspaper editorials, a sort of mystical character. He is no longer a mundane laborer, scratching for the dollar, full of staphylococci, smelling heavily of sweat and dung; he is a high priest in a rustic temple, pouring out his heart's blood upon the altar of Ceres. The farmer, thus depicted, grows heroic, lyrical, pathetic, affecting. To murmur against him becomes a sort of sacrilege, like murmuring against the Constitution, Human Freedom, the Cause of Democracy. . . . Nevertheless, being already doomed, I herewith and hereby presume to do it. More, my murmur is scored in the manner of Berlioz, for ten thousand trombones *fortissimo,* with harsh, cacophonous chords for bombardons and ophicleides in the bass clef. Let the farmer, so far as I am concerned, be damned forevermore! To hell with him, and bad luck to him! He is, unless I err, no hero at all, and no priest, and no altruist, but simply a tedious fraud and ignoramus, a cheap rogue and hypocrite, the eternal Jack of the human pack. He deserves all that he suffers under our economic system, and more. Any city man, not insane, who sheds tears for him is shedding tears of the crocodile.

No more grasping, selfish and dishonest mammal, indeed, is known to students of the Anthropoidea. When the going is good for him he robs the rest of us up to the extreme limit of our endurance; when the going is bad he comes bawling for help out of the public till. Has anyone ever heard of a farmer making any sacrifice of his own interests, however slight, to the common good? Has anyone ever heard of a farmer practising or advocating any political idea that was not absolutely self-seeking—that was not, in fact, deliberately designed to loot the rest of us to his gain? Greenbackism, free silver, government guarantee of prices, all the complex fiscal imbecilities of the cow State John Baptists—these are the contributions of the virtuous husbandmen to American political theory. There has never been a time, in good seasons or bad, when his hands were not itching for more; there has never been a time when he was not ready to support any charlatan, however grotesque, who promised to get it for him. Why, indeed, are politicians so polite to him—before election, so romantically amorous? For the plain and simple reason that only one issue ever interests or fetches him, and that is the issue of his own profit. He must be promised something definite and valuable, to be paid to him alone, or he is off after some other mountebank. He simply cannot imagine himself as a citizen of a commonwealth, in duty bound to give as well as take; he can imagine himself only as getting all and giving nothing.

Yet we are asked to venerate this prehensile moron as the *Ur*-burgher, the citizen *par excellence,* the foundation-stone of the state! And why? Because he produces something that all of us must have—that we must get somehow on penalty of death. And how do we get it from him? By submitting helplessly to his unconscionable blackmailing—by paying him, not under any rule of reason, but in proportion to his roguery and incompetence, and hence to the direness of our need. I doubt that the human race, as a whole, would submit to that sort of high-jacking, year in and year out, from any other necessary class of men. When the American railroad workman attempted it, in 1916, there was instant indignation; when a certain small squad of the *Polizei* tried it, a few years later, there was such universal horror that a politician who denounced the crime became President of the United States. But the farmers do it over and over again, without challenge or reprisal, and the only thing that keeps them from reducing us, at intervals, to actual famine is their own imbecile knavery. They are all willing and eager to pillage us by starving us, but they can't do it because they can't resist attempts to swindle each other. Recall, for example, the case of the cotton-growers in the South. They agreed among themselves to cut down the cotton acreage in order to inflate the price—and instantly every party to the agreement began planting *more* cotton in order to profit by the abstinence of his neighbors. That abstinence being wholly imaginary, the price of cotton fell instead of going up—and then the entire pack of scoundrels began demanding assistance from the national treasury—in brief, began demanding that the rest of us indemnify them for the failure of their plot to blackmail us!

The same demand is made almost annually by the wheat farmers of the Middle West. It is the theory of the zanies who perform at Washington that a grower of wheat devotes himself to that banal art in a philanthropic and patriotic spirit—that he plants and harvests his crop in order that the folks of the cities may not go without bread. It is the plain fact that he raises wheat because it takes less labor than any other crop—because it enables him, after working sixty days a year, to loaf the rest of the twelve months. If wheat-raising could be taken out of the hands of such lazy *fellahin* and organized as the production of iron or cement is organized, the price might be reduced by a half, and still leave a large profit for *entrepreneurs*. It vacillates dangerously today, not because speculators manipulate it, but because the crop is irregular and undependable—that is to say, because those who make it are incompetent. The worst speculators, as everyone knows, are the farmers themselves. They hold their wheat as long as they can, borrowing our money from the country banks and hoping prayerfully for a rise. If it goes up, then we pay them an extra and unearned profit. If it goes down, then they demand legislation to prevent it going down next time. Sixty days a year they work; the rest of the time they gamble with our bellies. It is probably the safest gambling ever heard of. Now and then, true enough, a yokel who plunges too heavily comes to grief, and is ingested by the county-town mortgage-shark; now and then a whole county, or State or even larger area goes bankrupt, and the financial dominoes begin falling down all along the line from Saleratus Center to New York. But such catastrophes are rare, and they leave no scars. When a speculator goes broke in Wall Street it is a scandalous matter, and if he happens to have rooked anybody of importance he is railroaded to jail.

But when a speculator goes broke in the great open spaces, there is a great rush of political leucocytes to the scene, and presently it is made known that the sin was not the speculator's at all, but his projected victims', and that it is the prime duty of the latter, by lawful order upon the Treasurer of the United States, to reimburse him his losses and set him up for a new trial.

The notion that wheat would be much cheaper and the supply far more dependable if it were grown, not by a motley horde of such puerile loafers and gamblers, but by competent men intelligently organized is not mine; I borrow it from Henry Ford, a busted seer. Since he betrayed them to Dr. Coolidge for a mess of pottage, the poor Liberals, once so enamored of his sagacity, denounce Ford as an idiot and a villain; nevertheless, the fact remains that his discussion of the wastefulness of our present system of wheat-growing, in the autobiography which he didn't write, is full of a powerful plausibility. Ford was born and brought up on a farm—and it was a farm, as farms go, that was very competently managed. But he knows very well that even the most competent farmer is but seldom more adept than a chimpanzee playing the violin. The Liberals, indeed, cannot controvert his judgment; they have been thrown back upon belaboring his political morals. What he proposes, they argue, is simply the enslavement of the present farmer, now so gloriously free. With capitalism gradually absorbing his fields, he would have to go to work as a wage-slave. Well, why not? For one, I surely offer no objection. All the rubber we use today is raised by slave labor; so is all the morphine consumed at Hollywood. Our children are taught in school by slaves; our newspapers are edited by slaves. Wheat raised by slave labor would be just as nutritious as wheat raised by men earning $10,000 a year, and a great deal cheaper. If the business showed a good profit, the political clowns at Washington would launch schemes to confiscate it, as they now launch schemes to make good the losses of the farmers. In any case, why bother about the fate of the farmer? If wheat went to $10 a bushel tomorrow, and all the workmen of the cities became slaves in name as well as in fact, no farmer in this grand land of freedom would consent voluntarily to a reduction of as much as 1/8 of a cent a bushel. "The greatest wolves," says E. W. Howe, another graduate of the farm, "are the farmers who bring produce to town to sell." Wolves? Let us not insult *Canis lupus.* I move the substitution of *Hyæna hyæna.*

Meanwhile, how much truth is in the common theory that the husbandman is harassed and looted by our economic system, that the men of the cities prey upon him—specifically, that he is the chronic victim of such devices as the tariff, railroad regulation, and the banking system? So far as I can make out, there is none whatever. The net effect of our present banking system, as I have already said, is that the money accumulated by the cities is used to finance the farmers, and that they employ it to blackmail the cities. As for the tariff, is it a fact that it damages the farmer, or benefits him? Let us turn for light to the worst Tariff Act ever heard of in human history: that of 1922. It put a duty of 30 cents a bushel on wheat, and so barred out Canadian wheat, and gave the American farmer a vast and unfair advantage. For months running the difference in the price of wheat on the two sides of the American-Canadian border—wheat raised on farms not a mile apart—ran from 25 to 30 cents a bushel. Danish butter was barred out by a duty of 8 cents a pound—and the American farmer pocketed the 8 cents. Potatoes carried a duty of 50 cents a hundredweight—and the potato growers of Maine, eager, as the phrase has it, to mop up raised such an enormous crop that the market was glutted, and they went bankrupt, and began bawling for government aid. High duties were put, too, upon meats, upon cheese, upon wool—in brief, upon practically everything that the farmer produced. But his profits were taken from him by even higher duties upon manufactured goods, and by high freight rates? Were they, indeed? There was, in fact, no duty at all upon many of the things he consumed. There was no duty, for example, upon shoes. The duty upon woolen goods gave a smaller advantage to the manufacturer than the duty on wool gave to the farmer. So with the duty on cotton goods. Automobiles were cheaper in the United States than anywhere else on earth. So were all agricultural implements. So were groceries. So were fertilizers.

But here I come to the brink of an abyss of statistics, and had better haul up. The enlightened reader is invited to investigate them for himself; they will bring him, I believe, some surprises, particularly if he has been reading the *Congressional Record* and accepting it gravely. They by no means exhaust the case against the consecrated husbandman. I have said that the only political idea he can grasp is one which promises him a direct profit. It is, alas, not quite true: he can also grasp one which has the sole effect of annoying and damaging his enemy, the city man. The same mountebanks who get to Washington by promising to augment his gains and make good his losses devote whatever time is left over from that enterprise to saddling the rest of us with oppressive and idiotic laws, all hatched on the farm. There, where the cows low through the still night, and the jug of peruna stands behind the stove, and bathing begins, as at Biarritz, with the vernal equinox—there is the reservoir of all the nonsensical legislation which now makes the United States a buffoon among the great nations. It was among country Methodists, practitioners of a theology degraded almost to the level of voodooism, that Prohibition was invented, and it was by country Methodists, nine-tenths of them actual followers of the plow, that it was fastened upon the rest of us, to the damage of our bank accounts, our dignity and our ease. What lies under it, and under all the other crazy enactments of its category, is no more and no less than the yokel's congenital and incurable hatred of the city man—his simian rage against everyone who, as he sees it, is having a better time than he is.

That this malice is at the bottom of Prohibition, and not any altruistic yearning to put down the evils of drink, is shown clearly by the fact that most of the State enforcement acts—and even the Volstead Act, as it is interpreted at Washington—permit the farmer himself to make cider as in the past, and that every effort to deprive him of that astounding immunity has met with the opposition of his representatives. In other words, the thing he is against is not the use of alcohol *per se,* but simply the use of alcohol in its more charming and romantic forms. Prohibition, as everyone knows, has not materially diminished the consumption of alcohol in the cities, but it has obviously forced the city man to drink decoctions that he would have spurned in the old days—that is, it has forced him to drink such dreadful stuff as the farmer has always drunk. The farmer is thus content with it: it brings his enemy down to his own level. The same animus is visible in innumerable other moral statutes, all ardently supported by the peasantry. For example, the Mann Act. The aim of this amazing law, of course, is not to put down adultery; it is simply to put down that variety of adultery which is most agreeable. What got it upon the books was simply the constant gabble in the rural newspapers about the byzantine debaucheries of urban Antinomians—rich stockbrokers who frequented Atlantic City from Friday to Monday, vaudeville actors who traveled about the country with beautiful mistresses, and so on. Such aphrodisiacal tales, read beside the kitchen-stove by hinds condemned to monogamous misery with stupid, unclean and ill-natured wives, naturally aroused in them a vast detestation of errant cockneys, and this detestation eventually rolled up enough force to attract the attention of the quacks who make laws at Washington. The result was the Mann Act. Since then a number of the cow States have passed Mann Acts of their own, usually forbidding the use of automobiles "for immoral purposes." But there is nowhere a law forbidding the use of barns, cow-stables, hay-ricks and other such familiar rustic ateliers of sin. That is to say, there is nowhere a law forbidding yokels to drag virgins into infamy by the technic practised since Tertiary times on the farms; there are only laws forbidding city youths to do it according to the technic of the great municipalities.

Here we come to the limits of bucolic moral endeavor. It never prohibits acts that are common on the farms; it only prohibits acts that are common in the cities. In many of the Middle Western States there are statutes forbidding the smoking of cigarettes, for cigarette-smoking, to the louts of those wastes, bears the aspect of a citified and levantine vice, and if they attempted it themselves they would be derided by their fellows and perhaps divorced by their wives, just as they would be derided and divorced if they bathed every day, or dressed for dinner, or attempted to play the piano. But chewing tobacco, whether in public or in private, is nowhere forbidden by law, for the plain reason that nine-tenths of all husbandmen practise it, as they practise the drinking of raw corn liquor. The act not only lies within their tastes; it also lies within their means, and hence within their *mores*. As a consequence the inhabitants of the towns in those remote marches are free to chew tobacco all they please, even at divine service, but are clapped into jail the instant they light cigarettes. The same consideration gets into comstockery, which is chiefly supported, like Prohibition, by farmers and chiefly aimed at city men. The Comstock Act is very seldom invoked against newspapers, for the matter printed in newspapers lies within the comprehension of the peasantry, and hence within their sphere of enjoyment. Nor is it often invoked against cheap books of a frankly pornographic character—such things as "Night Life in Chicago," "Adventures on a Pullman Sleeper" and "The Confessions of an ex-Nun"—for when yokels read at all, it is commonly such garbage that they prefer. But they are hot against the infinitely less gross naughtiness of serious books, including the so-called classics, for these books they simply cannot read. In consequence the force of comstockery is chiefly directed against such literature. For one actually vile book that it suppresses it attempts to suppress at least a dozen good ones.

Now the pious husbandman shows signs of an itch to proceed further. Not content with assaulting us with his degraded and abominable ethics, he begins trying to force upon us his still worse theology. On the steppes Methodism has got itself all the estate and dignity of a State religion; it becomes a criminal offense to teach any doctrine in contempt of it. No civilized man, to be sure, is yet actually in jail for the crime; civilized men simply keep out of such bleak parking spaces for human Fords, as they keep out of Congress and Franz Josef Land. But the long arm of the Wesleyan revelation now begins to stretch forth toward Nineveh. The mountebank, Bryan, after years of preying upon the rustics on the promise that he would show them how to loot the cities by wholesale and *à outrance,* now reverses his collar and proposes to lead them in a *jehad* against what remains of American intelligence, already beleaguered in a few walled towns. We are not only to abandon the social customs of civilization at the behest of a rabble of peasants who sleep in their underclothes; we are now to give up all the basic ideas of civilization and adopt the gross superstitions of the same mob. Is this fanciful? Is the menace remote, and to be disregarded? My apologies for suggesting that perhaps you are one of the multitude who thought that way about Prohibition, and only half a dozen years ago. Bryan is a protean harlequin, and more favored by God than is commonly assumed. He lost with free silver but he won with Prohibition. The chances, if my mathematics do not fail, are thus 1 to 1 that he will win, if he keeps his health, with Fundamentalism—in his own phrase, that God will be put into the Constitution. If he does, then *Eoanthrophus* will triumph finally over *Homo sapiens.* If he does, then the humble swineherd will drive us all into his pen.

Not much gift for Vision is needed to imagine the main outlines of the ensuing *Kultur.* The city man, as now, will bear nine-tenths of the tax burden; the rural total immersionist will make all the laws. With Genesis firmly lodged in the Testament of the Fathers he will be ten times as potent as he is now and a hundred times as assiduous. No constitutional impediment will remain to cripple his moral fancy. The Wesleyan code of Kansas and Mississippi, Vermont and Minnesota will be forced upon all of us by the full military and naval power of the United States. Civilization will gradually become felonious everywhere in the Republic, as it already is in Arkansas. What I sing, I suppose, is a sort of Utopia. But it is not the Utopia of bawdy poets and metaphysicians; it is not the familiar Utopia of the books. It is a Utopia dreamed by simpler and more virtuous men—by seven millions of Christian bumpkins, far-flung in forty-eight sovereign States. They dream it on their long journeys down the twelve billion furrows of their seven million farms, up hill and down dale in the heat of the day. They dream it behind the egg-stove on winter nights, their boots off and their socks scorching, Holy Writ in their hands. They dream it as they commune with *Bos taurus, Sus scrofa, Mephitis mephitis,* the Methodist pastor, the Ford agent. It floats before their eyes as they scan the Sears-Roebuck catalogue for horse liniment, porous plasters and Bordeaux mixture; it rises before them when they assemble in their Little Bethels to be instructed in the word of God, the plots of the Pope, the crimes of the atheists and Jews; it transfigures the chautauquan who looms before them with his Great Message. This Utopia haunts and tortures them; they long to make it real. They have tried prayer, and it has failed; now they turn to the secular arm. The dung-fork glitters in the sun as the host prepares to march. . . .

Well, these are the sweet-smelling and altruistic agronomists whose sorrows are the *leit-motif* of our politics, whose votes keep us supplied with Bryans and Bleases, whose welfare is alleged to be the chief end of democratic statecraft, whose patriotism is the so-called bulwark of this so-called Republic!

14 ~ Closing the Gates*

[Author's Note] *The restrictive immigration laws of the twenties are as much a symbol of the anti-foreign trend that began after World War I as the Ku Klux Klan. John Higham of the University of Michigan, in his* Strangers in the Land, *finds that after the war the debate "no longer concerned the desirability of restriction but simply the proper degree and kind." Nativist movements slackened after 1924 as the country's traditional values and vibrant prosperity served to restrain xenophobia. Professor Higham believes, however, that the basic fabric of American society was irretrievably changed after the acute nativist outbreak that followed World War I.*

The general terms of the great immigration restriction laws of the early twenties stare up at us from the pages of every textbook in American history. We realize that these measures brought to culmination a legislative trend extending back to the 1880's. It is not so obvious perhaps that they belonged equally to a cascade of anti-foreign statutes that began during the war. From the passage of the Espionage Act in 1917 through the tribal reaction of the twenties, state and national governments legislated almost ceaselessly against the successive dangers that seemed to arise from America's foreign population. Immigration restriction marked both the climax and the conclusion of an era of nationalistic legislation.

During the war and its immediate aftermath, interest focused not on the old objective of restriction but rather on new policies of repression, Americanization, and deportation. By 1920, however, about as much official coercion as the United States would tolerate had been undertaken; for some time to come further attempts to impose internal conformity would rest more completely in private hands. By 1920, also, the policies of Americanization and deportation, as massive ventures, were suffering general discredit. Political nativism shifted again toward its traditional goals, by the same maneuver that turned nativist thinking back into racial and religious channels. With new momentum the two main pre-war trends in legislation revived: economic discriminations against aliens, and immigration restriction. In respect to the former, the early twentieth century movement to exclude aliens from a wide range of white-collar jobs went forward again as soon as the war ended, and in the first half of the 1920's these proscriptions accumulated more rapidly and extensively than ever before. Licensing acts in many states barred aliens from practicing medicine, surgery, chiropractic, pharmacy, architecture, engineering, and surveying, from operating motor buses, and from executing wills.[1] These state enactments paralleled the adoption by Congress of a more general kind of restriction: a human blockade sufficiently drastic to be generally considered at the time a permanent solution of the immigration question. And, in truth, the principles then adopted remain the foundation of our immigration law. . . .

The declining Red Scare left an afterglow of vague suspicion that the immigrants harbored subversive designs; yet the passing of the mood of 1919 ended hopes that any quick internal therapy could cure the nation's ills. The collapse of the Americanization movement, which had seemed to many the most positive way to deal with immigration, suggested that only preventive action could preserve the nation; and the failure of the Americanizers to transform the alien seemed ample evidence of his unassimilable nature.[2] In a climate gray with disillusion, a racial nativism pinpointed on the new immigration was coming back in fashion. A growing isolationism poisoned the atmosphere still further, and for many the Jews were becoming a special bogey. When Congress reassembled in November 1920, the occasion had arrived (in the words of a representative from Minnesota) for "a genuine 100 per cent American immigration law."[3]

Without troubling with extended hearings, Johnson's committee* refurbished and reintroduced its two-year suspension bill, softening it somewhat by exempting close relatives of resident aliens. Admittedly, the proposal was a stopgap, designed as such to meet the dread crisis at Ellis Island and allow Congress time to work out a permanent policy. The House of Representatives acted swiftly. It cut the period of suspension to one year and, within the space of a week, passed the bill by an immense

* Editor's note: Albert Johnson became Chairman of the House Committee on Immigration in March, 1919.

bipartisan majority of 296 to 42. All but one of the negative votes came from industrial areas between Chicago and Boston.[4]

Congressional restrictionists knew that public opinion upheld them, even if some of the big city newspapers remained critical. Consequently the supporters of the bill felt little need to engage in elaborate justifications. Was it not enough to realize that a terrible emergency had befallen the nation? The vision of hungry Europe inundating jobless America provided, therefore, the main theme of debate, and enough of the spirit of the Red Scare endured to furnish supplementary reflections on the immigrants' Bolshevistic and disloyal propensities. Apparently the doctrines of racial nativism had not yet regained a wide enough currency to play much part in the discussion. On the other hand, a considerable strain of anti-Semitism was present.

A post war wave of persecution in central and eastern Europe was bringing the United States 119,000 Jews during the fiscal year 1920–21, and the sponsors of the suspension bill made as much of this condition as they dared. From an official in the State Department known as a pronounced anti-Semite, Johnson secured a report paraphrasing comments by American consuls overseas on the pernicious character and gigantic proportions of Jewish emigration. According to this document, America faced an inundation of "abnormally twisted" and "unassimilable" Jews—"filthy, un-American, and often dangerous in their habits." The House Committee on Immigration appended these comments to its own report in favor of the suspension bill and used them to suggest that the present immigration was largely Jewish. This strategy made a strong impression. It left a conviction in various quarters that the chief purpose of the immigration law of 1921 was to keep out the Jews.[5]

Before the Johnson bill could become law, however, it had to clear the Senate and receive executive approval. The Senate proved less responsive than the House to nativist influence. The Republican leadership in the Senate heeded solicitously the counsels of business interests, and prospects of a suspension of immigration, even on a temporary basis, filled employers of foreign labor with dismay. The Senate Committee on Immigration was dominated by eastern Republicans like its chairman, Le Baron Colt of Rhode Island, who kept both the interests of the businessman and the votes of his foreign-born employees in mind. Refusing to grant that a calamity impended, Colt's committee opened leisurely hearings at which southwestern cotton growers, Colorado beet producers, building contractors, the National Federation of Construction Industries, and the National

Association of Manufacturers protested against exclusion. For a while it seemed that all action might be postponed.[6]

Public pressure was too strong to flout, however, and the great majority of Senators shared the popular desire at least to cut down on the new immigration. A moderate restrictionist, Senator William P. Dillingham of Vermont, offered a plan designed to do just that. His scheme would not affect existing arrangements which excluded most Asiatic immigration, nor would it interfere with the unrestricted movement of Canadian and Latin American labor into the United States. But it would limit European immigration during the coming year to 5 per cent of the number of foreign-born of each nationality present in the United States at the time of the last available census, that of 1910. This percentage plan would hold the new immigration to an annual maximum of a quarter of a million without reducing the normal flow from northwestern Europe.[7]

Dillingham, who headed the old prewar United States Immigration Commission, had presented a similar bill back in 1913. The idea probably originated with his able secretary, William Walter Husband, who came to Washington with Dillingham early in the century. Husband had served as executive secretary for the Immigration Commission and was probably responsible for the inclusion, among the commission's recommendations in 191[illegible] the first vague formulation of a percentage plan.[8] But the country [illegible] not ready for it until the twenties.

T[illegible]ingham bill passed the Senate with practically no opposition excep[illegible]thern and western Senators who wanted complete suspension. [illegible] of Representatives then abandoned its suspension plan in fav[illegible]ta system but persuaded the Senate to reduce the quotas from [illegible] 3 per cent of the 1910 census. This would restrict Europ[illegible]igration to a maximum of about 350,000 and assign most of that total to northwestern Europe.[9] So the bill came before Woodrow Wilson in his last days in office. Supported by the adverse recommendation of Secretary of Labor William B. Wilson, the President simply ignored the bill, allowing it to die by withholding his signature. The ailing, rejected chief of state never explained his silent scorn, and his available papers provide no clue to it.[10] Did he still remember his iron-clad promises to the immigrants in 1912? Did his mind turn back to the cosmopolitan ideals that echoed through his earlier vetoes of the literacy test? Whatever the case, Wilson's disapproval was an anachronism in the world of 1921. It may stand as the inarticulate swan song of unrestricted immigration.

This last Presidential veto made no real difference. The die was cast.

The new chief executive, Warren G. Harding, was summoning a special session of Congress, and Harding was a different sort of fellow. The bill that Wilson had blocked was reintroduced in both houses, Johnson now supporting it rather than his own suspension plan. The measure cleared the House in a matter of hours without a record vote, passed the Senate by 78 to 1, and became law in May.[11]

Although adopted as very temporary legislation, the law of 1921 proved in the long run the most important turning-point in American immigration policy. It imposed the first sharp and absolute numerical limits on European immigration. It established a nationality quota system based on the pre-existing composition of the American population—an idea which has survived in one form or another through all subsequent legislation. It ensured especially that the new immigration could not reach more than a small fraction of its prewar level. Above all, the policy now adopted meant that in a generation the foreign-born would cease to be a major factor in American history. . . .

In some respects the waning of American nativism after the early twenties was a familiar phenomenon. Anti-foreign movements had surged and subsided time and again in American history. Each time the stresses that fostered them had eased in a few years, the agitators had sunk into obscurity, the secret societies had dissolved in factional stri[illegible]and the people had recovered their tempers and their aplomb.

The forces that contributed to this down-swing in the [illegible]es were also not entirely unfamiliar; for some of the underlying co[illegible]at had curbed the nativist impulse in earlier periods reasserted [illegible]In the mid-1920's, as in the 1860's and in the late 1890's, a [illegible]sperity washed over and helped to smooth the emotional turm[illegible]eding years. The fabulous economic boom from 1923 to 1929 [illegible]e and more Americans into a hectic kind of confidence in their instit[illegible]ons. If the self-assurance was somewhat more forced and less natural than it once had been, temporarily it had much the same effect. Furthermore, one can scarcely doubt that again, as in previous eras, a democratic balance-wheel, working deep inside the national culture, partially counteracted the nativist movements. Even at the height of the Nordic craze, Congressional nativists could not embrace its premises with an entirely good conscience. And although America felt too well satisfied with itself after 1924 to sheer openly and consciously in another direction, the nation's traditional values undoubtedly exercised a quiet brake on xenophobia.

Whereas both prosperity and democracy had restrained nativism at the turn of the century, a third factor operating in the twenties took the United States all the way back to the atmosphere of the age of confidence. As opposed to 1898, when an exhilarating new issue diverted the crusading impulse, Coolidge's America relapsed into a general indifference toward all big problems, international and internal alike. After more than three decades of practically incessant crusading—for reform, for empire, for world salvation, and for national unity—the time had come for a moral holiday. The related missionary ventures of the postwar era, prohibition and fundamentalism, shared in the desiccation that nativism underwent, and no mass movement, no grander vision, appeared to take their places. If any popular ideal dawned in the late 1920's, it was the cozy image of two chickens in every pot and two cars in every garage. Isolation seemed guaranteed by statesmen's promises never to resort to war again; and the radio blared "It Ain't Gonna Rain No More." Thus, America reverted to the spirit of the early 1880's in bidding farewell to that passion for uplift which stirred both liberal and illiberal movements from the days of the Populist party to those of the Ku Klux Klan.

Still, the real burden of the nativist story transcends its cyclical theme. History may move partly in cycles but never in circles. With every revolution some new direction opens, and some permanent accretion is carried into the next phase. Each upthrust of nativism left a mark on American thought and society. The consequences of the anti-foreign wave that flowed without pause for two decades in the early twentieth century are still too recent to be clearly evident; yet who can doubt their primary significance?

Although that wave resembled its predecessors in some ways and incorporated much of their heritage, it must stand alone in its persistence, in its complexity, and in the massiveness of its institutional deposit. Earlier nativist episodes produced only marginal changes in American life; but now the country would never be the same again, either in its social structure or in its habits of mind. Although immigration of some sort would continue, the vast folk movements that had formed one of the most fundamental social forces in American history had been brought to an end. The old belief in America as a promised land for all who yearn for freedom had lost its operative significance. And the new equation between national loyalty and a large measure of political and social conformity would long outlive the generation that established it.

NOTES

1. For examples see *Session Laws of Arizona,* 1921, p. 175; *Public Acts of Connecticut,* 1921, p. 3282; *Public Acts of Michigan,* 1919, p. 592, and 1925, p. 77; *Laws of New Mexico,* 1921, p. 198; *Cahill's Consolidated Laws of New York,* 1923, p. 711; *Wyoming Revised Statutes,* 1931, pp. 1234, 1830.
2. *Literary Digest,* LXII (July 5, 1919), 29, LXVII (December 18, 1920), 8–9, and LXVII (December 25, 1920), 14; National Education Association, *Proceedings,* 1921, p. 760.
3. *Cong. Rec.,* 66 Cong., 3 Sess., 4550.
4. *Ibid.,* 285–86.
5. *Temporary Suspension of Immigration* (66 Cong., 3 Sess., House Report No. 1109, Washington, 1920); *World's Work,* XLI (1921), 329–30, and XLIV (1922), 144; D. F. Garland, "Immigration and the Labor Supply," *System: The Magazine of Business,* XLIII (1923), 589; *Cong. Rec.,* 66 Cong., 3 Sess., 178–79. On the origin of the State Department report see Louis Marshall to Charles Evans Hughes, April 27, 1921, in Marshall Papers, Box C (Archives of the American Jewish Committee); and *Hearings: Emergency Immigration Legislation* (Senate Committee on Immigration, 66 Cong., 3 Sess., Washington, 1921), 10.
6. *Hearings: Emergency Immigration Legislation,* 1921, pp. 37–39, 87, 117–28; New York *Times,* December 5, 1920, p. 16, and January 12, 1921, p. 14.
7. New York *Times,* December 13, 1920, p. 25. On the pressure for Senatorial action see issues of February 9, 1921, p. 8, February 10, 1921, p. 15, and February 18, 1921, p. 3; and *Literary Digest,* LXVIII (February 26, 1921), 7. Actually the percentage plan applied to Europe, Siberia, Asia Minor, Persia, Africa, Australia, and New Zealand. On the provisions of the law as enacted see Roy L. Garis, *Immigration Restriction: A Study of the Opposition to and Regulation of Immigration into the United States* (New York, 1927), 142–49.
8. *Reports of the Immigration Commission: Abstracts* (61 Cong., 3 Sess., Senate Document No. 747, Washington, 1911), I, 47. For Dillingham's bill two years later see Seattle *Post-Intelligencer,* December 9, 1913. Husband's son, Richard F. Husband, tells me that his father claimed to be the originator of the percentage idea "as well as the author of the law introduced by Senator Dillingham." The fact that Husband presented to the Senate Committee in January 1921 the key testimony explaining the Dillingham bill tends to support this claim. Soon after, the incoming Harding administration rewarded Husband for his long services as an immigration expert by appointing him commissioner of immigration. See *Hearings: Emergency Immigration Legislation,* 1921, 534–44, and the biographical sketch in *National Cyclopaedia of American Biography,* XXXIV, 264.
9. New York *Times,* February 20, 1921, p. 1, and April 7, 1921, p. 29.
10. Secretary of Labor William B. Wilson placed his own opposition to the bill on technical grounds: that no emergency justified it and that it would be exceedingly difficult to administer; William B. Wilson to President Wilson, March 1, 1921, in Labor File 164/14.
11. New York *Times,* March 29, 1921, p. 19; *Cong. Rec.,* 67 Cong., 1 Sess., 589, 968.

15 ~ Introduction*

[Author's Note] *The climax between rural and urban America appropriately enough reached a climax with the Scopes trial at mid-decade in the small town of Dayton, Tennessee. Historians have traditionally regarded World War I as the catalytic agent that precipitated a last stand of rural America against modernism. The late Norman Furniss of Colorado State University agreed that the clouds of controversy first became clearly evident after World War I. He maintained, however, that perception was not a necessary concomitant for existence. Dissidents, argued Furniss, ". . . lacked influence in the councils of their churches but . . . kept alive hostility to the new concepts until the postwar period, when a number of elements combined to make the already strong undercurrent a force to be reckoned with. . . ." The selection which follows is a lively account of the "Monkey Trial." (Strangely enough, in view of all that was said of the biology teacher's heterodoxy, he later was converted to Catholicism.)*

Among the many sensational events of the 1920's, one of the most curious occurred in the small Tennessee town of Dayton, where in the summer of 1925 William Jennings Bryan, self-appointed spokesman for religious conservatives, undertook on the witness stand to defend the faith of his fathers against the harsh, skeptical reasoning of Clarence Darrow. The scene was a part, actually the climax, of the fundamentalist controversy, that acrimonious dispute over evolution in science and modernism in theology which had arisen after the first World War.

By 1925 the Fundamentalists could have taken considerable satisfaction in the success of their efforts to repress ideas hostile to their orthodox dogmas. In several of the denominations they had seriously embarrassed liberal clergymen who tried to bring inherited beliefs into accord with

* Reprinted by permission of Yale University Press from *The Fundamentalist Controversy, 1918–1931* by Norman F. Furniss, Pages 3–13. Copyright 1954 by Yale University Press.

the new knowledge through reinterpretation and relaxation of creeds. But their greatest accomplishments had come in the field of public education. In their conviction that the theory of evolution would destroy acceptance of the Bible as an authoritative guide in religion and conduct, they had sought to make instruction in the biological sciences conform with the narratives found in Genesis. During the years from 1923 to 1925 such pressure had produced favorable results in Oklahoma, Florida, North Carolina, and Texas, where officials had issued temporary orders to enforce orthodox teaching in public schools.

The importance of these preliminary triumphs soon paled, for in Tennessee the Fundamentalists' victory was complete. George Washington Butler, farmer, part-time school teacher, and clerk of the Round Lick Association of Primitive Baptists, had become so alarmed at reports of skepticism among college students of biology that he put himself up for election to the legislature on a platform consisting solely of the pledge to outlaw heretical instruction, which appealed to the theological conservatism of his constituency. Once in the state capitol, Butler dashed off the draft of his promised bill during a period of after-breakfast relaxation and submitted it to the House, where it was approved seventy-one to five. The Senate at first rejected the measure but on reconsideration voted twenty-four to six for acceptance. In March, 1925, Governor Austin Peay made the bill law with his signature. And so it became illegal "for any teacher in any of the universities, normal, and all other public schools of the state, to teach any theory that denies the story of the divine creation of man as taught in the Bible and to teach instead that man has descended from a lower order of animals."[1]

So far little opposition to the Fundamentalists had arisen in Tennessee. Representatives of the churches had shown no displeasure with the anti-evolution statute; newspapers had maintained a discreet silence during the legislature's deliberations; officials of the state, the university, and the Tennessee Academy of Science were apparently not concerned for the cause of academic freedom. But in the small mountain town of Dayton, where large strawberry beds had brought a certain prosperity, there were a few young men with less at stake in a challenge to the Fundamentalists than had the people of higher station who had kept their peace. On an afternoon in the spring of 1925 there gathered in Robinson's Drug Store on Dayton's main street a small group of friends whose habit it was to hold earnest discussion on important topics. Among those present was John T. Scopes, biology teacher and athletic instructor at Central High School, a small, bespectacled person, unexciting in appearance but with the attributes of modesty, sincerity, and humor. With Scopes were George Rappelyea, whose field work had won him the position of manager of a local Cumberland Coal and Iron Company mine, and druggist Robinson, part-time chairman of the Rhea County schoolbook committee.[2]

Over several lemon phosphates the group discussed Scopes' classes in the high school. It was Rappelyea who last pointed out to his companion that his lectures violated Butler's law, which both men considered undesirable, and thus provided the necessary grounds for ascertaining its constitutionality. Mindful that the American Civil Liberties Union had offered to support any Tennessee teacher who would challenge the statute, Rappelyea and Scopes, in a spirit more of playfulness than righteous indignation, formulated a plan of action: Scopes would lecture on some aspect of evolution; Rappelyea would complain to the public officials; and the resulting trial would provide an opportunity for testing the new law. Accordingly, on the next day Scopes lectured from Hunter's *Civic Biology,* and Rappelyea fulfilled his part of the bargain. Shortly thereafter the police haled the young teacher before the justices of the peace, who were compelled to bind him over to a grand jury. Under the direction of Judge John T. Raulston, who defended the law with great vehemence in his instructions, the jury ignored the question of the law's constitutionality and, finding only that its letter had been broken, indicted Scopes. The little scheme so casually formed by the two young men had set the stage for the most bizarre trial of the decade.[3]

As the result of these preliminary activities Dayton suddenly found itself the center of national, even international, attention. Some writers have stated that the townsfolk acted throughout the entire trial with great dignity, hoping only for a chance to gain knowledge, and that the newspapers of the country were the agents responsible for the enormous publicity surrounding the events.[4] The press, with its hundred reporters filing over 150,000 words daily, undoubtedly did much to dramatize the affair, but the people of Dayton were also quick to capitalize upon the incident, which offered obvious commercial advantages. A newly formed Progressive Dayton Club, with $5,000 to spend, planned diversions for the anticipated spectators and announced available accommodations for 30,000. When the editor of a Chattanooga newspaper, making use of a delay in Dayton's legal machinery, endeavored to start a similar trial in his city, a mass protest meeting in Dayton considered a retaliatory boycott of Chattanooga wholesalers, warned other cities not to steal the show, and persuaded

Judge Raulston to call a special session of the grand jury to hasten the indictment of Scopes. In its hurry to launch the business of the day the first jury drew up such a badly worded indictment that the judge had to call another jury.[5]

As Scopes gradually became aware of the national interest in his case, he gathered his attorneys around him. His original plan had been to rely upon the services of a local judge, but he soon received additional assistance from John Randolph Neal, an able constitutional lawyer. Neal was an ideal counsel for the defense: his resignation from the University of Tennessee faculty during 1923 in response to fundamentalist interference and his subsequent humiliating defeat by Peay in the gubernatorial contest the next year had given him an interest in the controversy.[6] Soon other notable men came to Scopes' aid and lent added importance to the trial. When the report was circulated that Bryan would assist the prosecution, Dudley Field Malone, an eminent New York lawyer, Arthur Garfield Hays of the Civil Liberties Union, and finally the disputatious, free-thinking Clarence Darrow offered their talents to the defense. In the end others threw their support behind Scopes—Charles Francis Potter, Henry Fairfield Osborn, and that professional opponent of the Fundamentalists, Maynard Shipley.

On the side of the prosecution there was less prestige, perhaps, but equal zeal. The most prominent among those who rallied to uphold Butler's law and with it their concept of the true faith was, of course, William Jennings Bryan. It was appropriate that Bryan had come to Dayton; it was fitting that he should assist the Fundamentalists in their greatest test of strength. For Bryan had given spirit to their crusade and had made it a potent force in American life by 1925. His prolonged campaign against the theory of evolution, begun early in 1920, had called the orthodox in many parts of the country to a belligerent defense of their beliefs. No other man had been able to tell the people what was Good and what was Evil in such neat phrases spoken in well modulated tones; none but the Peerless Leader of political innovationists and religious conservatives could have directed the energies of the Fundamentalists in a nationwide attack upon the forces undermining their theology. Bryan more than any other person had made the Scopes trial necessary.

As July 10, the day set for the opening of the trial, approached, the strategies of the prosecution and the defense began to take shape. For the former the issue was not an intricate one, since it was only necessary to show that Scopes had broken the law; but the defense had two possible approaches. The first was to prove the law unconstitutional insofar as it violated the state constitution's mandate to the legislature "to cherish literature and science," ran counter to guarantees of religious and intellectual freedom, ignored the Fourteenth Amendment, and failed to live up to existing contracts between the national and state governments. As a second line of attack, perhaps even to be used in conjunction with the first, the defense could also show from the testimony of experts that the theory of evolution was both true and compatible with the Bible.[7]

A spirit of intense excitement pervaded Dayton on the eve of the trial. Emotions became so strained that, when George Rappelyea arose in a civic boosters' meeting to deliver an impromptu address in behalf of evolution, the town barber fell upon him, crying, "You can't call my family monkeys," and sank his teeth into the mining engineer.[8] On all roads into Dayton posters appealed to the skeptical: "Where Will You Spend Eternity?" and "You Need God in Your Business"; others invited: "Sweethearts, Come to Jesus." Hot dog, lemonade, and sandwich stands sprang up along the sidewalks. Little cotton apes appeared in windows, and stores offered pins reading "Your Old Man's a Monkey." Along with the swarm of reporters that descended upon the town came publicity seekers and religious zealots of every description. Circus performers, hoping to be called to testify at the trial, brought two chimpanzees. Lewis Levi Johnson Marshall, "Absolute Ruler of the Entire World, without Military, Naval, or other Physical Force"; Elmer Chubb, who could withstand the bite of any venomous serpent; Wilbur Glenn Voliva, exponent of the flat-earth school of geography, and many others came to Dayton to peddle their especial anodynes.

The fundamentalist overtones, prejudicial to the defense, penetrated the courtroom itself. Judge Raulston, born in the mountain locality of Fiery Gizzard, presided over the court as though he were conducting a religious service, for he opened each session with a prayer intended to convince the defense of its error. He sat under a large banner that urged "Read Your Bible Daily" and, seeing nothing amiss in its presence, removed the emblem only after a vigorous appeal from Darrow. The prosecution made no effort to secure an unbiased jury. Although one candidate for jury duty, a fundamentalist preacher, admitted having frequently inveighed against the theory of evolution, he asserted his ability to study the case equitably and received the approval of the district attorney, A. T. Stewart. But for all their orthodox beliefs the people of Dayton welcomed the lawyers for the defense, whom they considered agnostics at best, with hospitality and even provided Darrow with a house, gifts of delicacies, and the honorary title of colonel.[9]

Throughout most of the trial the events were of a routine nature, not fulfilling the expectations of the reporters and the few citizens who could squeeze into the small courtroom. In the oppressive heat which brought tempers to an edge, only an occasional incident, such as Malone's stirring peroration on the sacredness of Truth, held the attention of the spectators on the proceedings of the trial.[10] Otherwise they watched a limp Bryan try to cool himself with a wicker fan, studied Darrow's bright suspenders, or wondered nervously whether the floor of the old building could support the unusual activity. As the hours dragged slowly by, the audience waited impatiently for the defense to summon its experts to the stand and for the open battle between fundamentalism and evolution to begin. Finally Judge Raulston destroyed even this hope when he unexpectedly ruled that there was no legal necessity for such testimony. The much publicized "monkey trial" appeared to be over without the sensational events anticipated. A number of cotton chimpanzees were still unsold.

Then, as suddenly, the day was saved. Darrow, unable to produce his own witnesses, hit upon the expedient of calling to the stand Bryan himself, who had posed as the Fundamentalists' authority on all questions, whether anthropological or religious. By questioning him, Darrow felt, the defense could perhaps reveal to the orthodox people of the country the fallacy of their position in the controversy over evolution. Bryan accepted the challenge.

In the course of the strange cross-examination Darrow followed two different lines of attack. At the outset he tried to make Bryan acknowledge the existence of errors in the Scriptures when read literally, in hopes that the admission would force him to confess the allegorical nature of many biblical stories, among them the account of man's creation. With this end in mind Darrow brought up one story after another—Joshua and the sun that stood still, Jonah and the whale, the Deluge—shrewdly, sometimes with anger and impatience, following Bryan as he sought to escape the concessions which would have destroyed the Fundamentalists' case. Then, in the middle of the ordeal, while the spectators saw their champion unable to crush this atheist from the North with a clever phrase, and while District Attorney Stewart vainly endeavored to end the exhibition, Darrow changed the nature of his questions, now trying to make Bryan convict himself of colossal ignorance and thus reveal his shallow mentality. In the end the cruel tactics of the lawyer triumphed: Bryan was forced to admit that, although he had undertaken to lead the fight against evolution and modernism, he had never read widely in such essential subjects as comparative religion, ancient history, or philosophy.[11]

Stewart's pleas and the obvious weariness of Bryan finally convinced Judge Raulston that he should postpone the trial until the next day, but the decision came only after the Commoner had made the mistake, fatal to all leaders, of appearing slightly ridiculous to his adherents. In the closing moments of the cross-examination Bryan heard the laughter and hisses of the people who had so recently given him their homage. When the court adjourned it was Darrow who was surrounded by men and women eager to congratulate the victor; Bryan walked away alone. That evening Stewart gave Bryan an even harder blow by informing him that the cross-examination would not be continued.[12] And so the Peerless Leader, who had already drafted a rebuttal to annihilate Darrow and restore his own shaken reputation, was denied a chance to vindicate himself. He was bereft even of prestige among many of his once devoted followers. He had come to town in triumph; few noticed his departure.

The trial that brought Bryan and Darrow face to face provided entertainment for the devotees of the Sunday supplement throughout the nation. But many who read the millions of words filed by enthusiastic reporters were mystified. The United States, they well knew, had entered upon an era in which science, already having disclosed the secrets of the airplane and radio, was hinting at new wonders soon to be revealed. In the midst of this progress the scene at Dayton appeared anachronistic. In another way the Scopes trial was more disturbing than mystifying: it opened the eyes of newspaper readers to the fact that thousands, even millions, of Americans espoused a faith leaving no room for acceptance of the remarkable achievements of the past half-century, Americans who not only deplored the challenges to their orthodox beliefs but were determined to crush those challenges by law and ecclesiastical court. People wondered why the controversy should have burst out so unexpectedly and irrationally after the end of World War I; why the country should have suddenly become involved in a bitter dispute over theology. Such questions revealed a mistaken analysis of the whole affair, for those who assumed that the conflict had broken like a summer thunderstorm, without even a cloud the size of a man's hand on the horizon, were unaware that events had been preparing the way for the phenomenon.

True, the arguments concerning Darwinism and scientific analysis of the Bible, or "higher criticism," as the process was called, which had troubled the churches at the end of the nineteenth century did appear in 1918 to have been settled. The Presbyterians, after suspending or expelling three distinguished scholars between 1893 and 1899, seemed to have found peace. The Methodists had struggled with the "untamed speculation" of Vanderbilt's Alexander Winchell in 1878 and with the unorthodoxy of two professors at Boston University in the decade after 1895 but had left these alarms behind them. Following the "Massachusetts Case" of the 1890's and a quarrel involving Algernon S. Crapsey in 1904 and 1905, the Protestant Episcopal church avoided further debate over higher criticism. The Baptists, later embroiled in the fundamentalist controversy, experienced at the turn of the century only two altercations arising from reinterpretation of doctrine.

But although the great assemblies of the denominations had discovered temporary solutions for internal difficulties, many people remained alarmed with the direction of thought in biology and theology. These dissidents, men who lacked influence in the councils of their churches but who possessed deep convictions and steadfast determination, kept alive hostility to the new concepts until the postwar period, when a number of elements combined to make the already strong undercurrent a force to be reckoned with in church and state.

In addition to such prominent opponents of evolution and higher criticism after the Civil War as Mark Hopkins and Noah Porter, there were among the common folk several progenitors of the Fundamentalists of the 1920's. These individuals felt that the theory of man's development from lower species, if accepted, would destroy the faith of the nation's youth, break down standards of morality, and create a wave of "defalcations and robberies, and murders, and infanticides, and adulteries, and drunkenness, and every form and degree of social dishonor."[13] A flood of pamphlets and books sought to disprove and discredit Darwinism. Opposition to the higher critics also arose at this time, although to a lesser extent than to evolution, since the latter was a more dramatic contradiction of orthodox Christianity.

Resistance to new ideas was not expressed merely in random literary works. During the latter part of the nineteenth century the Fundamentalists (the word had yet to be coined) established inconspicuous groups to voice their discontent more effectively. The Serial Science Society engaged "to meet atheists with their own weapons and upon their own ground" by issuing monthly tracts using "Natural Facts in vindication of Bible Truth."[14] Periodic Bible conferences, those held at Niagara after 1875 being the most important, strengthened the religious conservatism of the people. This polemic and organizational activity directly prepared the way for the fundamentalist movement in later years.

After 1900 new figures and fresh leagues carried on the challenge to scientific and theological innovations. In 1902 George McCready Price produced the first of many works rejecting evolution, proclaiming the Advent of Christ, and propounding the Deluge as the cause of geological formations.[15] Luther Townsend, a Methodist who subscribed to Price's views of geology, in 1904 prophetically warned indifferent liberals that the conservatives were prepared to protect orthodoxy even if the struggle should generate violent conflict in the church.[16] Philip Mauro, a patent lawyer who had left his practice to defend his theological convictions, joined in the attack upon Darwinism. William Bell Riley, a Minneapolis Baptist preacher . . . , turned his attention to modernism in *The Finality of Higher Criticism* (1909), and in the same year *Cosmopolitan* carried an article entitled "Blasting at the Rock of Ages," evidence that many in the nation were greatly alarmed at the trend in religious thinking.[17] Supporting the Fundamentalists in their propaganda efforts was the Bible League of North America, formed in 1902 "to meet and counteract the *Current Destructive Teachings* concerning the truthfulness, integrity, and inspiration of the Bible as the Word of God."[18] With the same fervor the Moody Bible Institute and its West Coast sister, the Bible Institute of Los Angeles, stood squarely for the old faith against the new.

If further proof were needed that the controversy survived despite conciliatory gestures of denominational leaders, it came with the appearance of *The Fundamentals* in 1910. This set of ten small pamphlets, produced through the generosity of two wealthy residents of Los Angeles, Milton and Lyman Stewart, was to be sent free of charge to "every pastor, evangelist, missionary, theological student, Sunday school superintendent, Y.M.C.A. and Y.W.C.A. secretary in the English speaking world, so far as the addresses of these can be obtained."[19] Before the printing of the fifth volume 275,000 people had received the tracts; eventually 3,000,000 copies were distributed. The names of the men connected with the undertaking revealed that the Stewarts had gathered together many able exponents of orthodoxy in the United States, Canada, England, Ireland, and Germany. The work was originally begun under the direction of Amzi Clarence Dixon, a widely traveled Baptist minister; later Reuben A. Torrey, dean of the Los Angeles Bible Institute, assumed the task of supervision. The contributors were equally notable as Fundamentalists, men who had already joined the movement or who subsequently became leaders of it: George F. Wright and Melvin G. Kyle, archaeologists and founders of the Bible League of North America; lawyer Philip Mauro; James M. Gray, dean of the Moody Bible Institute; Robert E. Speer, a Presbyterian who in the 1920's added to the intensity of the dispute in his denomination; Edgar Y. Mullins of the Southern Baptist Convention; and Leander W. Munhall, Methodist evangelist.

True to one objective of the project, many of the essays in *The Fundamentals* condemned higher criticism and Darwinism, declaring as to the former that "A mutilated cento or scrapbook of anonymous compilations . . . is confusion worse confounded,"[20] and of the theory of man's descent: "it becomes evident to every intelligent layman that such a system can have no possible points of contact with Christianity."[21] But the primary importance of the work lay in its doctrinal exposition. In addition to several articles on regeneration, sin, and other tenets, the series expatiated on the "Five Points" that were to become the *sine qua non* of fundamentalism: the infallibility of the Bible, Christ's Virgin Birth, his Substitutionary Atonement, Resurrection, and Second Coming. The conservatives' creed was now reduced to clear essentials; so significant did the undertaking seem that some attributed the start of the fundamentalist movement to the influence of the volumes.

After the appearance of *The Fundamentals* the spokesmen for orthodoxy devoted themselves to defense of the faith with increased determination, writing innumerable tracts and holding Bible conferences. Although this activity was interrupted by the sudden outbreak of the World War, it did not cease altogether. Furthermore, the denominations that had apparently resolved their differences by the turn of the century found themselves once more occasionally disturbed; Northern Presbyterian delegates to the 1910 and 1916 General Assemblies felt called upon to issue two deliverances proclaiming the "Five Points," and the Methodists in 1914 were again occupied with charges of heresy at Vanderbilt.

Thus the people who asked during the Dayton trial why the dispute over evolution and modernism should have come to life again so unexpectedly did not know that the fundamentalist crusade, like Joe Hill, had never died. Under the leadership of resolute men it had, often inconspicuously, continued to attack the new beliefs in science and theology. Until 1918 the movement lacked the requisite strength to become a major issue in American life, but in the years immediately following the war several fresh elements, adding to the power already possessed by the Fundamentalists, were enough to precipitate the conflict.

NOTES

1. Irving Stone, *Clarence Darrow for the Defense* (New York, 1941), p. 433; Maynard Shipley, *The War on Modern Science. A Short History of the Fundamentalist Attacks on Evolution and Modernism* (New York, 1927), p. 193; *Harper's, 151* (1925), 623; *New York Times,* March 24, 1925, July 5, 1925.
2. For comments on Scopes see A. G. Hays, *Let Freedom Ring* (New York, 1928), p. 33; Clarence Darrow, *The Story of My Life* (New York, 1932), p. 248; *Independent, 115* (1925), 650; *Outlook, 140* (1925), 421. For Rappelyea see Stone, *Darrow,* p. 434.
3. Hays, *Let Freedom Ring,* p. 26*n; Independent, 115* (1925), 659; *World's Work, 50* (1925), 326; *Harper's, 151* (1925), 624.
4. Michael Williams, *Catholicism and the Modern Mind* (New York, 1928), pp. 181 ff.; *Nation, 121* (1925), 61.
5. Hays, *Let Freedom Ring,* p. 35; *World's Work, 50* (1925), 327–8; *NYT,* May 20, 1925, July 22, 1925.
6. *Outlook, 140* (1925), 422.
7. R. S. Keebler, *The Tennessee Evolution Case* (p.p., 1925), passim; Darrow, *Story of My Life,* p. 260; Stone, *Darrow,* p. 445; *Nation, 121* (1925), 157–8.
8. *World's Work, 50* (1925), 328.
9. For descriptions of the trial's setting see Williams, *Catholicism,* pp. 180–1; Stone, *Darrow,* pp. 428–35; Hays, *Let Freedom Ring,* pp. 34.7; Darrow, *Story of My Life,* pp. 251–6; *Current History, 22* (1925), 880; *NYT,* July 11, 1925, July 12, 1925.
10. A transcript of the trial may be found in *The World's Most Famous Trial . . . A Complete Stenographic Report* (Cincinnati, 1925).
11. *Current History, 22* (1925), 882.
12. Ibid.
13. S. A. Hodgman, *The Miracle of Creation! Or the Theory of Evolution* (Philadelphia, 1867), p. 21.
14. L. S. Benson, *Topics for Thought in Opposition to Materialistic Teachings* (New York, 1876), p. 28.
15. *Outlines of Modern Christianity and Modern Science* (San Francisco, 1902).
16. *Adam and Eve. History or Myth?* (Boston, 1904), p. ix.
17. *Cosmopolitan, 46* (1909), 665.
18. *Bible Student and Teacher, 9* (1908), 347.
19. *The Fundamentals. A Testimony to the Truth* (Chicago, n.d.), *1,* 4.
20. Ibid., *1,* 109.
21. Ibid., *8,* 28.

16 ∽ Introduction*

[Author's Note] *Prohibition is often viewed as a sad remnant of the reforming energies of the country misdirected by the rural Protestant enthusiasm of the twenties. Typical is the observation of Richard Hofstadter in* The Age of Reform, *that Prohibition "was the skeleton at the feast, a grim reminder of the moral frenzy that so many wished to forget, a ludicrous caricature of the reforming impulse, of the Yankee-Protestant notion that it is both possible and desirable to moralize private life through public action." In contrast, Prohibition is viewed by James H. Timberlake as an integral part of the Progressive Movement stemming from the same moral idealism and seeking to deal with the same basic problems as the "Crusade for Social Justice." Thus, Timberlake feels that Prohibition was a continuing strain in the American reform impulse which attempted to bring about a better society in which each individual would be free to develop himself to the fullest. While the following selection does not deal specifically with the 1920's, its penetrating analysis of the "noble experiment" serves as a challenging revision of the traditional explanation of the "dry aberration."*

Between the accession of Theodore Roosevelt to the presidency in 1901 and the repudiation of Woodrow Wilson in 1919, Americans gave vigorous support to two great crusades: one to preserve democracy at home and the other to make the world safe for democracy. The Progressive Movement of these years came as a reaction to a long period of dominant conservatism during which the nation had undergone a rapid transformation from a predominantly rural to an urban-industrial society. Spreading first from city to state and finally to the national government, this movement embraced not only the long-embattled farmers and urban laborers but also middle-class businessmen, professional men, and white-collar workers. Embodied in the dynamic energy of Roosevelt and the lofty idealism of Wilson, the Progressive Movement endeavored to come to

* By James H. Timberlake. From *Prohibition and the Progressive Movement, 1900–1920* (Cambridge, Harvard University Press, 1963), 1–3.

grips with the two great problems threatening American democracy: the growing power of big business on the one hand, and, on the other, the mounting discontent of the lower classes, especially among urban-industrial workers. It sought to solve these two problems by democratizing the machinery of government and using government to control big business and to improve the lot of the underprivileged.

To achieve these ends, the Progressive Movement embraced a wide variety of individual reforms, one of the more important and least understood of which was prohibition. Although today sometimes regarded as a conservative measure, prohibition was actually written into the Constitution as a progressive reform. As an integral part of the Progressive Movement, prohibition drew on the same moral idealism and sought to deal with the same basic problems. If the Progressive Movement was nourished on a belief in the moral law, so was prohibition, which sought to remove from commerce an article that was believed to despoil man's reason and undermine the foundation of religion and representative government. If progressive America's growing devotion to efficiency also reflected an optimistic belief in the desirability of material progress, the attack on alcoholic beverages as an enemy of efficiency mirrored the same faith. Americans were coming to place more and more faith in the claims of science; they were thus willing to accept its findings that even the moderate use of alcohol was dangerous and ought to be avoided. If progressivism desired to curb the power of an industrial and financial plutocracy, prohibition aimed to remove the corrupting influence of one branch of that plutocracy—the liquor industry. Again, if progressivism represented a quickening of the humanitarian impulse, manifested in redoubled efforts of philanthropists and social workers to banish crime, poverty, and disease from the environment, prohibition was an effort to eliminate one factor that caused them. And, finally, if progressivism sought to improve the status of the lower classes by direct legislation, prohibition sought to uplift them by the same means.

Prohibition did not command universal support, however, for its appeal lay largely with the old-stock, middle-class section of the American community. Other progressives, especially those identified with the urban-labor-immigrant elements, disliked the reform and fought it. Although the two groups often cooperated on other measures, they disagreed on the question of prohibition. But because the old-stock middle class constituted the backbone of the Progressive Movement and wielded disproportionate political power, it was able to overcome the opposition of the urban masses and to impose its own standard of sobriety on the nation by law.

17 ~ The Political Argument*

On its political side, prohibition was one of the reforms of the Progressive Movement, which was attempting to use the power of government as a positive instrument of reform in order, as Woodrow Wilson said, "to square every process of our national life again with the standards we so proudly set up in the beginning and have always carried in our hearts."[1] Prohibition, like the other reforms, sought to deal with the two major problems that had arisen by 1900 and that threatened to undermine and destroy traditional American ideals. These were the growing power of big business on the one hand, and the mounting discontent among the lower classes on the other.

At the turn of the century, Americans were confronted by a new wave of financial and industrial consolidation that surpassed any previous ones. The result was to alarm the middle class thoroughly, for concentration brought monopoly and this meant the decline of that economic opportunity that had so long stood at the center of the American democratic faith.[2] Middle-class Americans had long since come to believe that equal opportunity enabled the average man to get ahead, acquire wealth, prestige, and power, and that the struggle for individual success brought material progress, prosperity, and happiness to the nation as a whole. They had also come to believe that their highly competitive economic order was the foundation of their moral strength; as long as opportunity remained open to all on a relatively equal basis, the test of success was a man's own effort, character, and ability. Since good character led to success and bad character to failure, men were encouraged to develop and practice such virtues as industry, thrift, sobriety, and honesty. The result was not only individual improvement but national greatness.

* By James H. Timberlake. From *Prohibition and the Progressive Movement,* 1900–1920 (Cambridge, Harvard University Press, 1963), 100–102; 105–108; 110–124.

Americans had also come to believe that their free economic order was the foundation of their social and political democracy. Monopolies would create men of great wealth and, by restricting opportunity, would prevent the lowly from rising. This in time, they believed, would create rigid and permanent class distinctions. If allowed to grow unchecked, monopolies would also eventually control the government and transform America from a democracy into a plutocracy.[3]

In addition to the threat from big business, middle-class Americans were haunted by the danger of lower-class unrest and discontent. Labor and agrarian upheavals in the late nineteenth century had already frightened many middle-class Americans. Although the farmers and laborers had gone down to defeat, the middle classes continued to be apprehensive, seeing in the rapid growth of monopoly and the lessening of opportunity an ever-increasing source of revolutionary danger. This apprehension increased as they watched the rapid growth of organized labor, the rise of the Socialist party, and the revolutionary activities of the I.W.W. Fear of lower-class unrest, together with a genuine desire to eliminate the inequities and injustices of the social order and to improve the lot of the underprivileged, propelled many middle-class Americans into the work of reform.

Essentially a middle-class movement, progressivism attempted to preserve economic opportunity and restore social and political democracy so that all Americans might continue along the road to greater progress, prosperity, and happiness. It endeavored to do this in two ways. First, it sought to democratize the machinery of government in order to take politics out of the hands of the special interests and restore it to the people. And, second, it sought to use the government to curb big business and to alleviate the distress of the lower classes.[4] But progressivism could not succeed, many Americans believed, unless it came to grips with one of the most predatory and dangerous of all big businesses—the liquor industry.

. . . Like other big businesses during the Progressive Era, the liquor industry came under fire for its monopolistic tendencies.[5] Among its attackers were certain small businessmen who felt themselves squeezed by its growing power. Typical of these was a Wisconsin manufacturer of alcohol burners and heaters who complained that farmers were reluctant to distill their own grain for fear of antagonizing the distillery trust, and that this in turn prevented him from selling more of his own firm's products. Only by smashing the trust, he believed, would farmers be free to produce their own alcohol cheaply and without restraint. . . .[6]

Had the concentration of economic power been the only charge against the liquor industry, it might have fared no worse than other businesses. But what aroused special hostility was its arrogant and ruthless control of government and its practice of gross political corruption. Like many other businesses, the liquor industry sought to influence or control all levels of government in order to promote its interests and to protect itself against unfavorable legislation. But unlike most businesses, it had a special reason to engage in politics: no other enterprise paid such high taxes or contributed such large sums to government. By 1917 it was contributing $52 million a year to municipal governments, $6.6 million to the counties, $21 million to the states, and $262 million to the federal government. This burden, however, was not without benefit to the industry, for it gave government a vested interest in the business and hence a stake in its preservation.[7]

Three national organizations looked after the economic and political interests of the liquor industry. These were the United States Brewers Association, the National Wholesale Liquor Dealers Association—representing distillers, importers, vintners, and wholesale dealers—and the National Retail Liquor Dealers Association, later renamed the National Liquor League of the United States.[8] Each maintained a well-organized lobby in Washington, D.C., and financed its activities by annual assessments of its members, amounting to 20 cents per 100 barrels in the case of the brewers, and $25 to $50 per member in the case of the distillers. Subordinate to these national organizations were many state and local associations, organized similarly and for the same purpose. . . .[9]

Disadvantageously to themselves, however, the liquor interests were not always scrupulous in their publicity methods. The brewers, for example, established a national press bureau that was suspected of buying and secretly subsidizing news space in country and small-town newspapers. This seemed to be borne out when the St. Joseph, Missouri, *Observer,* in its issue of February 22, 1908, printed a two-column attack on the Anti-Saloon League, "clipped," it said, from a Detroit church paper called *Truth. Truth,* however, was a liquor journal, and the article in question did not appear in it until March 17, 1908, nearly a month after the *Observer* had "clipped" it. . . .[10]

The liquor industry became thoroughly involved in political corruption through its connection with the saloon. The root of the trouble here was that the ordinary saloonkeeper, confronted by overcompetition, was practically forced to disobey the liquor laws and to ally himself with vice and crime in order to survive. Unable to make a living honestly, he did so dishonestly.[11]

One of his chief difficulties was the Sunday-closing laws. These laws, which forbade saloons to sell any liquor on Sunday, reflected the moral standards of middle-class Americans and ran directly counter to the wishes and desires of most city dwellers, especially the Irish and Germans. The result was that the saloonkeeper not only found it profitable to cater to the Sunday demand but had to remain open in order to keep from losing his customers and going out of business.[12] In New York City, for example, over 5,000 of the 5,820 saloons in Manhattan and the Bronx were open each Sunday in 1908 in defiance of the law.[13]

To increase their profits, many saloonkeepers also adulterated drinks or sold cheap whiskey from expensive bottles. Other saloonkeepers encouraged hard drinking among their patrons and sold liquor to anyone who would buy it, including women, children, and known drunkards.[14] Remarked one liquor dealer before the Retail Liquor Dealers Association of Ohio:

> We must create the appetite for liquor in the growing boys. Men who drink . . . will die, and if there is no new appetite created, our counters will be empty as well as our coffers. The open field for the creation of appetite is among the boys. Nickels expended in treats to boys now will return in dollars to your tills after the appetite has been formed.[15]

Some saloonkeepers entered into partnership with prostitution, gambling, and petty crime. By allowing their rooms to be used for informal purposes, they were able to increase their liquor sales and enlarge their profits. In one working class district in Chicago, for example, 34.5 per cent of the saloons investigated in 1900 were found to be frequented by prostitutes. Nearly all of these places exhibited nude pictures, either in the form of costly wall paintings or cards furnished by the brewing companies. In addition to prostitution, some saloons sought to increase their income by permitting gambling on their premises, and, in a few cases, by allowing pickpockets and other petty thieves to operate among their customers.[16]

Although illegal activities enabled saloons to make a profit, they also put them at the mercy of the police and politicians. As it turned out, however, these officials were usually quite willing to allow saloons to break the law, provided the saloon paid them protection and gave them their support. Thus arose a formidable alliance between the liquor interests and the city machines.[17]

For the privilege of breaking the law, saloons delivered to the politicians both money and votes. Money, of course, was needed to finance elections and to satisfy the politicians' more personal needs. The method of collecting this graft and the amount saloons were required to pay varied from place to place. In New York City, for example, a saloon paid $5 a month for Sunday openings, $25 a month for harboring prostitutes, and $25 a month for permitting gambling. These fees were collected by a Tammany wardman who later divided the money with those higher up. The patrolman got his graft from the local retail liquor dealers association, supported by a monthly contribution of about $6.50 from each saloon. . . . [18]

The saloon also provided politicians with votes. As the chief social center of the lower classes, the saloon was a natural and convenient political unit and was able to deliver votes at election time. In general, the political power of a saloon varied with the class it served: those that catered to the respectable middle classes were usually unimportant, whereas those that served the lower classes were usually quite powerful. To politicians the most valuable saloons of all were those that were always able to deliver a dependable bloc of votes. These saloons got their votes from a number of sources. One was the men who lived in their back rooms and slept on the floor; for two or three dollars they would always vote right. Another source was the thieves, pickpockets, and pimps who made the saloon their headquarters. Then there were those fictitious voters whose names were registered and parceled out to neighboring lodging houses and whose existence could be vouched for by their landlords, if necessary. A final source was those voters rounded up by the gangs of "strong-arm gorillas" whose services the saloons were able to mobilize for rough work on election day. . . .[19]

As a social and political center, the saloon served as a natural headquarters for precinct and ward captains and as a meeting place for the city boss and his cabinet. There they held caucuses, drew up lists of acceptable candidates, and held political conventions.[20] During a single year in New York City, for example, the Democratic and Republican parties held 1,002 conventions, of which 633 met in saloons and 96 in places next to saloons.[21]

A key link in the alliance between the saloon and politics was the saloonkeeper. As a friend and confidant of the workingman and as a person of considerable prestige among the immigrant population, the average saloonkeeper commanded the affection, loyalty, and respect of his neighbors and was able to exert a strong influence over them. Many saloonkeepers, in fact, used their position to enter politics themselves.[22] In Milwaukee, for example, 13 out of the 46 members of the city council in 1902 were saloonkeepers.[23] And it was in St. Louis that, according to Lincoln Steffens, a practical joker nearly emptied one house of the municipal assembly by tipping a boy to rush in and call out: "Mister, your saloon is on fire. . . ."[24]

The link between the saloon and the politician alone, however, fails to account for the full power of the liquor industry, for there were other interests whose position and strength made the political machines, on which the liquor interests depended for their security, practically invulnerable. These were businesses that sought and obtained public franchises, grants, and other special favors from government. Chief among these were privately owned utilities and contracting companies. They, in their turn, brought the politicians the respect and influence they wanted and the money they required. Any attack on the saloon and politicians, therefore, was bound to be regarded as a blow at the whole and was certain to bring down the opposition of these interests also.[25]

Thus the liquor industry was not only economically powerful but also politically entrenched. This fact alone would have aroused the ire of middle-class progressives, but what provoked their opposition equally as much was the dangerous consequences of drinking among the lower classes. Fearful of the growing unrest from below, the middle classes became deeply concerned lest the sale of liquor increase this discontent. To most middle-class Americans, this unrest seemed to lie mainly in the cities where the mass of the propertyless poor was concentrated. . . .[26]

Outside the South the problem of lower-class discontent was usually identified with the immigrant masses. To old-stock Americans the sheer force of their numbers was sufficient to cause alarm. Between 1900 and 1917, nearly 14.3 million persons arrived in the United States, averaging in some years more than a million. By 1910 there were 13,345,545 foreign-born in the country and 18,897,837 children of foreign-born. Out of a total population of 91,972,266, therefore, 32,243,382, or 35.2 per cent, were first- or second-generation Americans. Most of these newer Americans, moreover, chose to remain in the cities. By 1910, 68.1 per cent of them were residing in places of over 2,500, compared with 36.1 per cent for the old-stock whites. By 1910 people of foreign stock comprised 51.6 per cent of the total urban population but only about 20 per cent of the rural population.[27]

What made this urban-immigrant population seem such a threat to old-stock Americans was that it represented an element that was becoming increasingly difficult to assimilate or "Americanize." To begin with, the average immigrant was a peasant, and, after the 1880's, more than likely a peasant from southern and eastern Europe. This meant that he brought with him a set of cultural values alien to those held by most middle-class Americans. Having his roots in a peasant economy, with its stable and communal organization, he found it difficult to adjust to the American world of free enterprise, with its individualism, competition, and emphasis on self-help and success. Accustomed to a tightly knit and well-ordered society where his social status was fixed and where authority and hierarchy were taken for granted, he found it hard to accommodate to the American ideal of social mobility and equality. A Roman Catholic, Jew, or nonbeliever, he found himself out of tune with the theology and social ethics of American Protestantism and resisted efforts by revivalists and social gospelers to convert him. Finally, because he had never participated in government and was habituated to looking upon the state as an exploiter, he found it hard to comprehend the American ideal of political equality and of independent and disinterested political action. To the peasant immigrant, politics tended to be not a means of realizing high moral principles and the general welfare, as it was to middle-class progressives, but rather a means of meeting his personal needs, to get for him jobs, relief, favors, and protection. For this reason he gave his loyalty and vote to the local boss who often satisfied these needs.[28]

The result of the rapid influx of millions of foreigners to a new and unfamiliar urban environment was to plant large pockets of alien culture within an already existing and well-defined American culture, and thus to create serious tensions and conflicts. To the immigrant, the establishment of his own institutions in America was a means of orienting his life and helping him adjust to the new and strange environment. To the old-stock American, however, the perpetuation of alien ways was an obstacle to speedy assimilation and a menace to American ideals and institutions. The remedy, in the opinion of many Americans, was to restrict immigration and to Americanize those foreigners who had already arrived.[29]

This conflict between old- and new-stock Americans increased during the Progressive Era by the attack on the city machines, by the identification of the immigrant with municipal corruption, and by the enactment of middle-class reforms that ran counter to immigrant interests. Although the old-stock middle classes and the immigrant population often cooperated to secure labor and other welfare legislation of benefit to the latter, they fought bitterly whenever the middle classes tried to uplift and assimilate the foreign stock against its wishes.[30]

Nowhere were the differences between old and foreign stock more clearly revealed than on the question of temperance reform. To old-stock Americans, liquor demoralized the immigrant, kept him in poverty, intensified his discontent, unfitted him to exercise the duties of responsible citizenship, and prevented him from becoming Americanized. And the institution held to be primarily responsible for this was the saloon. . . .

Although newer Americans found in the saloon one of the institutions that gave their lives meaning and helped them adjust to American ways, the native Protestant middle classes were unable to tolerate this fact. To them the saloon was a demoralizing, disruptive, and reactionary force that kept the foreign stock from becoming Americanized; they thus sought to destroy the saloon in order to "uplift" their countrymen and force them to assimilate. Abolish the saloon, advised one social worker, "and the task of Americanizing the conglomerate foreign population would be lightened 50 per cent."[31] The result, however, was not to hasten assimilation but rather to impede it by antagonizing the newer Americans and by intensifying their alienation.[32]

What the foreign-stock population was to the rest of the country, the Negro and lower-class white was to the South. Practically untouched by the wave of foreign immigration, the eleven states of the old Confederacy contained several million poor whites in 1910 and 7,928,109 of the nation's 9,827,763 Negroes.[33] Unlike the foreign-stock population in the North, however, these Southern lower classes were primarily rural. Southern Negroes, for example, though migrating to the cities in increasing numbers, were only about 18.8 per cent urbanized in 1910.[34]

Taken together, lower-class whites and Negroes posed much the same challenge to middle-class Southerners as the foreign-stock population did to the middle classes elsewhere. And as always, the problem focused on the liquor question. Liquor, Southerners believed, demoralized and debauched the lower classes, kept them from acquiring property, and, what was particularly bad, lowered efficiency and prevented Southern agriculture and industry from achieving a faster rate of growth. Liquor also led to crime, vice, poverty, and suffering, and kept the lower classes from rising and becoming socially respectable. Finally, liquor unfitted them for civic duties and made it easier to buy or control their votes. Although Negroes were politically handicapped by poll taxes and other devices in every

Southern state by 1910, they could still be bought corruptly by paying their poll taxes, giving them a few drinks and a little ready money, and voting them in droves at the polls. By this means, the liquor interests were believed to have defeated dry campaigns in Florida, Texas, and Arkansas.[35]

But above all, Southerners feared that liquor would result in race conflict. The danger spot here, they believed, was the saloon, where the worst elements of both races met and drank, although at separate bars. "It is realized," noted one Southern writer, "that in any Southern community with a bar-room, a race war is a perilously possible occurrence. The danger is not in the upper but in the lower levels of both races."[36] "Two-thirds of the mobs, lynchings, and burnings at the stake," declared another observer, "are the result of whisky drunk by bad black and bad white men. . . ."[37]

The liquor problem, then, was intimately bound up with the two major challenges that by 1900 confronted middle-class Americans: the control of economic and political life by big business, and unrest and discontent among the lower classes. And in responding to these two challenges, middle-class Americans naturally turned to prohibition as one of their remedies. They did so, however, not merely because prohibition would destroy the liquor industry, but because, by removing a key link in the corrupt alliance between business, vice, and politics, it would also help free government from the control of other predatory interests and thus open the way to reform in general. As long as the liquor industry remained entrenched, they believed, no lasting reform was possible.[38]

But if the prohibition campaign helped to pave the way for other reforms, the reverse was also true—other reforms helped clear the way for prohibition. Initiative, referendum, and recall, the direct election of United States Senators, and woman's suffrage were all looked upon to help make it easier for the people to break the shackles of political corruption and to enable their governments to destroy the liquor traffic.[39]

How closely these reforms were related and how they provoked the combined opposition of the liquor industry and its business and political allies, was illustrated by the case of woman suffrage. Most of those who supported woman suffrage believed that the woman's vote would be a power for good and would help bring about progressive legislation and reform, including prohibition. Women would vote dry, they believed, because two of the leading women's organizations, the W.C.T.U. and the General Federation of Women's Clubs, both favored prohibition, and because election returns, wherever open to analysis, showed the great majority of women casting dry ballots. For this reason, the liquor interests and their allies were among the staunchest opponents of the suffragette movement.[40] In Texas, for example, a group of brewers and eighty or more other corporations (including the Gulf Refining Company, the Santa Fe Railroad, the American Express Company, Swift and Company, and the Southwestern States Portland Cement Company) formed the Texas Business Men's Association to promote their interests and prevent hostile legislation. Under the cover of a farmers' union, this association supplied rural newspapers throughout the nation with a series of free "educational" articles, in fact nothing but disguised propaganda against business regulation and woman suffrage.[41]

The opposition of the liquor interests to progressive reform was also seen in their attitude toward the Negro vote in the South. Most Southerners regarded the removal of the mass of illiterate and propertyless Negroes from politics as a progressive measure because it eliminated a source of political corruption, weakened the power of the conservative interests, and opened the way to further reform. The liquor interests, however, opposed Negro disfranchisement because they had generally been able to win or control his vote. Here again, therefore, the liquor interests aligned themselves against the progressive cause.[42]

Middle-class progressives, then, supported prohibition, woman suffrage, and other reforms as a means of democratizing government and securing legislation to curb big business. But this was only half their program, for they also sought to democratize government in order to improve the lot of the lower classes. This was the traditional way of American reform—to respond to a threat from below not by repressing the lower classes but by enabling them to become happy and prosperous themselves. Prohibition was simply a means of helping to force this process.

NOTES

1. Russell B. Nye, *Midwestern Progressive Politics: A Historical Study of its Origins and Development, 1870–1950* (East Lansing, Mich., 1951), p. 300.
2. Eric F. Goldman, *Rendezvous With Destiny,* (New York, 1953), pp. 72–75.
3. This discussion is drawn largely from Irvin G. Wyllie, *The Self-Made Man in America: The Myth of Rags to Riches* (New Brunswick, N.J., 1954).

4. Benjamin Parke DeWitt, *The Progressive Movement* (New York, 1915), pp. 4–5.
5. Anti-Saloon League, *Proceedings, 1906,* p. 12; John Spargo, *Social Democracy Explained: Theories and Tactics of Modern Socialism* (New York, 1918), p. 323; Charles Stelzle, *Why Prohibition!* (New York, 1918), pp. 104–105.
6. W. E. Shaffer to Richmond P. Hobson, April 19, 1909, in Richmond P. Hobson Papers, Library of Congress.
7. Harry S. Warner, *Social Welfare and the Liquor Problem* (rev. ed., Chicago, 1913), pp. 114, 248; *The World's Work,* 34:295 (July 1917).
8. John M. Barker, *The Saloon Problem and Social Reform* (Boston, 1905), pp. 24, 91; National Wholesale Liquor Dealers Association, *Constitution and By-Laws* (n.p., 1896), pp. 5–6; David Stauber, "Attitude of the Distillers and Wholesale Liquor Dealers on the Regulation of the Liquor Traffic," *The Annals of the American Academy of Political and Social Science,* 32:539 (November 1908); D. Leigh Colvin, *Prohibition in the United States: A History of the Prohibition Party and of the Prohibition Movement* (New York, 1926), p. 551.
9. Barker, *The Saloon Problem,* p. 26; National Wholesale Liquor Dealers Association, *Constitution and By-Laws,* p. 15; *idem, Organization and Its Work* (n.p., n.d.), pp. 4–5, 19–20; *Standard Encyclopedia of the Alcohol Problem,* V, 2348–2349; Colvin, *Prohibition in the United States,* p. 551.
10. Will Irwin, "Tainted News Methods of the Liquor Interests," *Collier's Weekly,* 42:27–28 (March 13, 1909).
11. Arthur H. Gleason, "The Saloon in New York," *Collier's Weekly,* 41:12 (May 2, 1908); *idem,* "The New York Saloon," *Collier's Weekly,* 41:16–17 (April 25, 1908); Irwin, in *Collier's,* 41:9; *idem,* "The American Saloon," *Collier's Weekly,* 40:11–12 (February 29, 1908); "The Experiences and Observations of a New York Saloon-Keeper, as Told by Himself," *McClure's Magazine,* 32:301–307, 311–312 (January 1909).
12. Gleason, in *Collier's,* 41:12 (May 2, 1908); "The Experiences and Observations of a New York Saloon-Keeper," in *McClure's,* 32:306; Edwin S. Lane, "Chicago Commission on the Liquor Problem," *National Municipal Review,* 6:447 (May 1917).
13. Gleason, in *Collier's,* 41:12 (May 2, 1908).
14. *Ibid.,* p. 13; "The Experiences and Observations of a New York Saloon-Keeper," in *McClure's,* 32:305, 311–312; *The Independent,* 65:589–592 (September 10, 1908); William H. Tolman, "Competing with the Saloon," *The Outlook,* 76:791 (April 2, 1904).
15. Peter H. Odegard, *Pressure Politics: The Story of the Anti-Saloon League* (New York, 1928), p. 41.
16. Royal L. Melendy, "The Saloon in Chicago," *The American Journal of Sociology,* 6:299–300 (November 1900); Gleason, in *Collier's,* 41:13, 27 (May 2, 1908).
17. A. H. Woodson, "The Model License Law," *Harper's Weekly,* 55:24 (February 11, 1911).
18. Gleason, in *Collier's,* 41:12 (May 2, 1908); Lincoln Steffens, *The Autobiography of Lincoln Steffens* (1 vol. ed., New York, 1931), pp. 231–238, 247–265.
19. Augustus R. Hatton, "The Liquor Traffic and City Government," National Municipal League, *Proceedings, 1908,* pp. 429–430; Irwin, in *Collier's,* 41:11; Gleason, in *Collier's,* 41:27–28 (May 2, 1908).

20. Max B. May, "The Liquor Question," *The Annals of the American Academy of Political and Social Science,* 23:377 (March 1904); F. E. Stevens, "The Liquor Question," *ibid.,* 23:372–373.
21. Barker, *The Saloon Problem,* pp. 31–32.
22. Charles Stelzle, *A Son of the Bowery: The Life Story of an East Side American* (New York, 1926), pp. 47–49; Hatton, in National Municipal League, *Proceedings, 1908,* p. 430; William C. Smith, *Americans in the Making: The Natural History of the Assimilation of Immigrants* (Edward A. Ross, ed., *The Century Social Science Series,* New York, 1939), p. 228; *McClure's,* 21:713 (October 1908).
23. Barker, *The Saloon Problem,* p. 33.
24. Lincoln Steffens, *The Shame of the Cities* (New York, 1904), p. 34.
25. Frank A. Magruder, "Municipal Ownership of Public Utilities," *National Municipal Review,* 7:76 (January 1918); Colvin, *Prohibition in the United States,* pp. 568–570; Steffens, *Shame of the Cities,* pp. 101–143; *idem, Autobiography,* pp. 169–178, 274–291.
26. Colvin, *Prohibition in the United States,* pp. 563–576; Anti-Saloon League, *Proceedings, 1906,* p. 12; *idem, Proceedings, 1917,* p. 147.
27. U.S. Bureau of the Census, *Thirteenth Census of the United States, 1910: Population* (2 vols., Washington, 1912), I, 126, 171, 188–189.
28. Oscar Handlin, *The Uprooted: The Epic Story of the Great Migrations That Made the American People* (Boston, 1951), *passim;* David F. Bowers, ed., *Foreign Influences in American Life: Essays and Critical Bibliographies* (New York, 1952), pp. 50–52, 86–92; Richard Hofstadter, *The Age of Reform: From Bryan to FDR* (New York, 1955), pp. 3–22, chap. v.
29. Goldman, *Rendezvous With Destiny,* p. 78.
30. Handlin, *The Uprooted,* pp. 217–221, 225; Bowers, *Foreign Influences,* p. 89.
31. Paul H. Benjamin, "Disgorging the Saloon," *The Survey,* 35:26 (October 2, 1915).
32. Constantine Panunzio, "The Foreign Born's Reaction to Prohibition," *Sociology and Social Research,* 18:223–225, 228 (January–February 1934).
33. Bureau of the Census, *Thirteenth Census, 1910: Population,* I, 126, 135, 141. The population of the United States in 1910 was divided as follows: native white stock, 53.8 percent; foreign white stock, 35.2 percent; and Negro, 10.7 percent.
34. *Ibid.,* I, 193–194; C. Vann Woodward, *Origins of the New South, 1877–1913* (Wendell H. Stephenson and E. Merton Coulter, eds., *A History of the South,* IX, Baton Rouge, 1951), pp. 299, 354.
35. Irwin, in *Collier's,* 40:10–14; A. J. McKelway, "Local Option and State Prohibition in the South," *Charities and Commons,* 19:1452 (January 25, 1908); Anti-Saloon League, *Proceedings,* 1916, pp. 181–183, 186–187; Manufacturers Record, *The Prohibition Question Viewed from the Economic and Moral Standpoint* (2nd ed., Baltimore, 1922), p. 24; C. Vann Woodward, *The Strange Story of Jim Crow,* (New York, 1955), p. 65; Ferdinand C. Iglehart, "The Campaign Against the Saloon," *The American Monthly Review of Reviews,* 48:80 (July 1913).

36. Samuel C. Mitchell, ed., *History of the Social Life of the South* (The Southern Historical Publication Society, *The South in the Building of the Nation,* Richmond, 1909), X, 576.
37. *Brotherhood of Locomotive Firemen and Enginemen's Magazine,* 45:265 (August 1908), p. 265.
38. Colvin, *Prohibition in the United States,* pp. 569–570; DeWitt, *The Progressive Movement,* pp. 101–104, 108; *McClure's Magazine,* 34:702 (April 1910).
39. Frederick M. Davenport, "The Persistence of the Pioneer Conscience," *The Outlook,* 110:370–371 (June 16, 1915).
40. Ella S. Stewart, "Woman Suffrage and the Liquor Traffic," *The Annals of the American Academy of Political and Social Science,* 56:146, 148–152 (November 1914); Unger, "W.C.T.U.," pp. 100–102, 111–112, 117–119; L. Ames Brown, "Suffrage and Prohibition," *The North American Review,* 203:97–100 (January 1916).
41. *The New Republic,* 4:62–63 (August 21, 1915).
42. Anti-Saloon League, *Proceedings, 1916,* pp. 181–183, 186–187; Woodward, *Origins of the New South,* pp. 254, 256, 276–277, 323; *idem, Jim Crow,* pp. 65, 68, 74; William G. Brown, "The South and the Saloon," *The Century Magazine,* 76:462–463 (July 1908); *The Literary Digest,* 36:815 (June 6, 1908); James B. Sellers, *The Prohibition Movement in Alabama, 1702 to 1943* (The James Sprunt Studies in History and Political Science, XXVI, Chapel Hill, N.C., 1943), pp. 81, 101; Daniel J. Whitener, *Prohibition in North Carolina, 1715 to 1945* (The James Sprunt Studies in History and Political Science, XXVII, Chapel Hill, N.C., 1945), p. 73; Will Irwin, "The American Saloon," *Collier's Weekly,* 40:14 (March 21, 1908); Iglehart, in *The American Monthly Review of Reviews,* 48:80.

18 ~ Segregation in Indiana during the Klan Era of the 1920's*

[Author's Note] *The Ku Klux Klan represents for many the very symbol of intolerance in the twenties. The mass migration of Negroes from the rural south to the cities of the north began with the lure of wartime jobs. In the decade that followed Versailles, the Klan is usually depicted as the prime force in the drive for racial segregation. In this cogent analysis of segregationist practices in Indiana, Emma Lou Thornbrough of Butler University finds small evidence to hold the Klan responsible for this discrimination. Although Klan influence may have played some role in the tightening of racial barriers in the 1920's, the rapid influx of Negroes from the south into urban centers in itself offers the best explanation for the new segregationist measures. The author has wisely chosen Hoosier society for her investigation, since Indiana was the most Klan-ridden state in the twenties.*

During the First World War there began a mass migration of Negroes from the rural South to the cities of the North which was to have marked effects upon the character and institutions of these cities. The number of Negroes moving into Indiana was not as great as the number moving into the neighboring states of Ohio, Michigan, and Illinois, but in the years from 1910 to 1930 the colored population of Indiana doubled.[1] Hopes for economic betterment were probably the most important reason for the migration, but the desire for greater personal freedom, for political and civil rights, and for opportunities to educate their children also brought

* By Emma Lou Thornbrough. Reprinted with permission from *The Mississippi Valley Historical Review,* XLVIII (March, 1961), 594–618.

Negroes northward. In Indiana the newcomers found little of the legalized Jim Crowism which they had known in the South, but they encountered much prejudice and discrimination. Although there were no racial disorders comparable to the riots in East St. Louis, Chicago, and Detroit, the influx of Negroes led to a movement for segregation on a scale previously unknown. In these same years the Ku Klux Klan, an organization which was habitually a strong advocate of white supremacy, was also rising to a position of unprecedented power in Indiana. It is not unusual for present-day commentators to see a close link between these two developments and to conclude that the increase in segregation measures was due primarily to Klan influence. This is a relationship, however, which has never been closely analyzed, and before the nature of the Klan's role can be understood it is necessary to look first at the segregation measures as they were originated in the state in the years following World War I.

These measures were confined for the most part to urban areas, because it was there that the Negro population was concentrated. In an earlier period, Negroes entering the state had settled in Evansville and the other Ohio River communities; but by the time of World War I new arrivals moved farther north, to Indianapolis, in the central part of the state, or to the cities in the Calumet region, especially Gary. The largest number went to Indianapolis, where the colored population increased from 21,816 in 1910 to 43,967 in 1930 (when it comprised about 12 per cent of the total population of the city). A more spectacular increase occurred in the extreme north, where a steel empire was arising on the shores of Lake Michigan. The population of Gary, which was little more than a small town in 1910, had grown to just over 100,000 in 1930. In this same twenty-year period the city's Negroes had increased from 383 to almost 18,000—approximately 18 per cent of the total population. In the neighboring city of East Chicago, where there were only 28 Negroes in 1910, the number had grown to more than 5,000 by 1930. By the latter date nearly 60 per cent of the Negro population of the state was found in Indianapolis and the Gary-East Chicago area. Most of the remainder was in other cities and towns, census figures showing that over 92 per cent of the Negro population lived in urban areas.

Although the new arrivals settled in cities, most of them came from rural areas in the South, and an increasingly large number came from the Lower South. Before 1900 most Negroes migrating to Indiana had come from the Upper South, especially Kentucky, while a very few had come from the Lower South. By 1930, when the census showed that 67 per cent of the total Negro population had been born outside of Indiana, persons from Kentucky still outnumbered by a large margin those from any other single state. In Indianapolis the number of Kentucky-born Negroes was only slightly smaller than the number native to Indiana. But in the Calumet area most Negroes came from the Lower South. In Gary in 1930 the largest single group came from Mississippi, and the second largest from Alabama. Each of these groups was substantially larger than the number born in Indiana. In 1930 more than 86 per cent of the Negroes in the steel city had been born outside of Indiana, and of these an overwhelming majority came from the South.[2]

The problems of assimilation created by the abrupt transition from a simple, rural way of life to the more complex patterns of city life were complicated by Indiana's long tradition of racism. In the pre-Civil War period the Black Code of Indiana had scarcely been equaled in its harshness by the law of any other northern state. In the years following the Civil War the adoption of the Fourteenth and Fifteenth Amendments removed most of the legal disabilities against Negroes in the state,[3] and by the time of the migration of the First World War era only a few remnants of earlier racial distinctions remained in the law code. One of these was a severe prohibition against marriages between white persons and persons with as little as one-eighth Negro blood. Another was the school law, which gave local school authorities the option of maintaining segregated schools or of allowing members of both races to attend the same school.[4]

In spite of the fact that there was little legal segregation, in practice there was little mingling of the races. In the larger cities Negroes were unable to find housing outside of well-defined areas, which were largely slums. Since 1885 there had been a civil rights law prohibiting discrimination in the use of public accommodations, but it was largely a dead letter. Negroes almost never ventured into a "white" hotel or restaurant, and signs announcing that the proprietor "catered to white trade only" were not uncommon. When Negroes went into a theater or concert hall they sat in the gallery. In the rural parts of the state there were many small communities in which a Negro was not allowed to settle or even spend the night.[5]

In Indianapolis, where the bulk of the Negro population lived, race relations were normally peaceful. At least there were few overt signs of antagonisms. The leading Negro newspaper, the *Freeman,* which was far from militant in its editorial policy, frequently asserted that racial harmony prevailed, but some of its content seems to indicate that friction was avoided in part by the failure of Negroes to take advantage of all the rights which were legally theirs. One editorial admitted: "We have learned to forego some rights that are common, and because we know the price. We would gain but little in a way if certain places were thrown open to us. We have not insisted that hotels should entertain our race, or the theaters, rights that are clearly ours." But even the conservative *Freeman* insisted that Negroes could not give up the right to live where they chose.[6]

The rapid increase in Negro population created new tensions, especially in housing. The parts of the city which had been the Negro districts simply could not house both the older residents and the newcomers. As immigrants from the South took over these districts, older residents sought to buy homes in hitherto all-white neighborhoods. The largest concentration of Negroes in Indianapolis had always been just northwest of the downtown business area. After the war this area began to expand northward—toward upper middle class white neighborhoods. Property owners, faced with the prospect of Negro neighbors and fearful of a decline in real estate values, organized themselves into local civic leagues, which had as their chief purpose the barring of Negro residents. One novel device to which one group, the Capitol Avenue Protective Association, resorted was to try to isolate and humiliate Negroes who bought property by building spite fences on either side of the property. But a young Negro dentist, faced with this form of retaliation, obtained an injunction which prohibited the practice.[7]

Sometimes opposition to Negro neighbors took a more sinister form. When, despite warnings, a Negro family moved into a white neighborhood in 1924, a hand grenade was thrown through a window of their house. Following this episode handbills were circulated in an adjacent neighborhood, asking "DO YOU WANT A NIGGER FOR A NEIGHBOR?" The handbills appear to have been the work of a group which unabashedly called itself the White Supremacy League and which had as its objective not only barring Negroes from white neighborhoods but excluding them from most forms of employment as well. Members were bound by oath not to employ Negroes in their homes or trade at stores which employed Negroes.[8] This group represented an extremist element, but its president was also active in the Mapleton Civic Association, an organization which included in its membership eminently respectable businessmen. A printed statement of the aims of the Mapleton group frankly stated: "One of our chief concerns is to prevent members of the colored race from moving into our midst, thereby depreciating property values fifty per cent, or more." Members of the association pledged themselves not to sell or lease property to anyone except a white person. The agreement was reported to have worked so well that for three years no more Negroes had moved into the Mapleton area, and some who were already residents had moved away.[9]

Although private efforts of this sort met with some success in stemming the Negro tide, stronger measures were sought. In response to pressure from civic groups, including particularly the White Citizens Protective League, the Indianapolis city council enacted a residential zoning ordinance in March, 1926. Declaring that "in the interest of public peace, good order and the general welfare, it is advisable to foster the separation of white and negro residential communities," the measure made it unlawful for white persons to establish residence in a "portion of the municipality inhabited principally by negroes," or for Negroes to establish residence in a "white community," except with the written consent of a majority of persons of the opposite race inhabiting the neighborhood.[10]

The measure was sponsored by a Republican member of the council who said he had received petitions containing more than five thousand names asking for the enactment of the ordinance. The only member to oppose it was a Democrat, who insisted that it was unconstitutional and violated "the spirit of American institutions." More than eight hundred cheering, hand-clapping, stamping spectators crowded into the council chambers while the ordinance was under consideration. After the favorable vote the president of the White Citizens Protective League declared with satisfaction: "Passage of this ordinance will stabilize real estate values . . . and give the honest citizens and voters renewed faith in city officials."[11]

The mayor, asserting that it was not the duty of the executive to pass upon the validity of an act of the legislative branch, signed the ordinance, even though he admitted that the entire legal staff of the city was of the opinion that it was unconstitutional. In a lengthy message justifying his action the mayor expressed the opinion that there was no intention to discriminate against either whites or Negroes in adopting the ordinance and that its "tenor" precluded either race from obtaining any advantage over the other. He went so far as to say that if critics would study the law with "open minds" they would "hail with delight this step toward the solution of a problem that has long caused deep thought and serious study by members of both races."[12]

Doubts as to the constitutionality of the ordinance arose because of its similarity to a Louisville ordinance which had been declared unconstitutional by the United States Supreme Court in 1917. Backers of the Indianapolis ordinance, who declared themselves ready to take a test case to the Supreme Court, were not unaware of this precedent, but were hopeful that in the years which had elapsed since the Louisville case the highest tribunal might have changed its mind. The principal reason for their optimism was the fact that the Supreme Court of Louisiana had recently upheld the constitutionality of a New Orleans racial zoning ordinance which had served as a model for the Indianapolis enactment. The court had held that the Louisville precedent did not apply because the New Orleans ordinance (like the Indianapolis ordinance) did not prohibit outright the buying or selling of property but merely restricted the right of purchasers to *occupy* property. They ruled that the ordinance was not discriminatory because it applied equally to whites and blacks and dealt with "social relations" rather than civil or political rights.[13]

The optimism of members of the Protective League proved to be unwarranted. By 1926 there was a vigorous chapter of the National Association for the Advancement of Colored People in Indianapolis, which was eager to take every possible step to invalidate the ordinance. The national office of the NAACP, which had won one of its first victories in the United States Supreme Court in connection with the Louisville case, was also interested in the situation in Indianapolis. Funds amounting to about five thousand dollars were quickly raised to carry on the fight, and a case which bears the signs of having been arranged with the deliberate purpose of testing the ordinance was soon on the docket of a local court. The case arose from the refusal of a Negro physician to fulfill a contract for the purchase of real estate in a predominantly white neighborhood. He based his refusal on the grounds that the zoning ordinance would prevent him from occupying the property. The judge who heard the case ruled in favor of the Negro, declaring the zoning ordinance unconstitutional in the light of the precedent established by the Louisville case. He held that the ordinance deprived a citizen of his constitutional rights by making his right to live in his own property depend upon the consent of other citizens.[14] Hopes of supporters of the ordinance for an appeal to the Supreme Court of the United States were dashed when that tribunal reversed the Louisiana Supreme Court decision as to the New Orleans ordinance.[15]

The successful attack on the zoning ordinance was the only significant legal victory in the fight in Indiana against segregation during the 1920's. On other fronts, and especially in connection with segregation in the schools, there were some serious defeats. In Indianapolis the movement for residential restrictions went hand in hand with a movement to remove

Negroes from hitherto mixed schools. From the time that colored children were first admitted to the city elementary schools in 1869, the general policy had been to require that they attend separate schools, but there had always been a few schools with mixed enrollments. Inasmuch as most Negroes lived in all-Negro neighborhoods children had usually attended the school nearest them, but sometimes there were complaints that children were required to travel long distances to attend Negro schools rather than schools nearer to their homes. Indianapolis high schools had never been segregated. As early as 1872 a Negro student had been admitted to Indianapolis High School, which was later renamed Shortridge High School. Thereafter, although their numbers were not large, there were always Negroes enrolled in the school, which had the reputation of being one of the best public academic institutions in the country. In later years as two new high schools were built, Negroes attended them also. It was always the policy to employ Negro teachers in the all-Negro elementary schools, but Negro teachers were never assigned to the mixed elementary schools or the high schools.[16]

The growth of the Negro population after World War I and the consequent movement of Negroes into new neighborhoods led to demands for a more restrictive policy. Two principal arguments were used by those favoring segregation. First, they insisted that the presence of Negroes in the same schools as the whites menaced the health of the latter and that Negroes should be segregated to protect the white children. Second, they argued that Negroes would benefit from segregation—that in their own schools they would take more pride in their work, their scholarship would improve, and that they would develop more initiative. The latter argument, more than the first, dealt with intangibles, and proponents never made clear how segregation would bring about the desired results. Their conclusions, too, now appear to be completely at variance with the views of the Supreme Court in the segregation cases of 1954 and with a large body of sociological studies.

A resolution presented to the Indianapolis Board of School Commissioners in 1922 on behalf of the Federation of Civic Clubs was a forceful statement of the health argument and a revealing commentary on Negro housing. It pointed out that, while Negroes constituted only about one tenth of the total population of Indianapolis, about one fourth of the deaths in the city were among Negroes. "For years," it asserted, "the Marion County Tuberculosis Society has emphasized the care of incurable consumption among the colored people as the greatest social need in this city." Because crowded housing conditions made it impossible for a tubercular patient to be cared for at home without endangering other members of the family, a large number of cases of incipient tuberculosis were believed to exist among colored school children. For this reason the school board was asked to establish separate schools for all Negro children and to staff them with Negro teachers.[17]

At the same session a letter in support of segregation was presented to the school board on behalf of the Mapleton Civic Association and the White Supremacy League. The contents have not been preserved, but they were of such a nature as to cause the president of the board to remark that the letter "contained such statements as rendered it impossible to properly be received by the Board, without the reservation that its receipt was in no sense to be construed as endorsement on the part of the Board of the sentiments which it contained."[18]

In response to such pressures the Board of School Commissioners set up new boundaries for fourteen elementary schools for Negroes and required that Negroes attend them. Groups of Negro parents protested in vain. When the attorney for the school board ruled that under the law the children could be required to attend the Negro schools even though they had to travel long distances, two parents sought court orders to permit attendance at the schools nearest their homes. But in both cases the court upheld the right of the school board to carry out the transfer.[19] After these transfers, which occurred in 1923, elementary schools were predominantly all white or all Negro. The process of separation of the races was carried almost to completion in 1929 when Negroes were removed from three more schools.[20]

Before the latter date segregationists in Indianapolis had also been successful in removing Negroes from the mixed high schools and putting them in an all-Negro school. The demand for separate high schools was backed by many white groups. Among them was the Indianapolis Chamber of Commerce, which presented a petition to the Board of School Commissioners in September, 1922, setting forth the "necessity" for a "separate, modern, completely equipped and adequate high school building for colored students."[21]

This movement met with strong and bitter opposition in the Negro community. Various delegations representing Negro civic and ministerial groups appeared before the school board, while other groups sent written protests. A petition from the Better Indianapolis Civic League forcefully and eloquently presented the arguments against a separate school. Declaring that the public school system was the most powerful factor in American society for the "engendering and transmission of sound democratic ideals," it emphasized that "no one section of the population" could be isolated and segregated without taking from it the advantages of the common culture." Since money for the public schools came from taxation of all the people it was "unjust, un-American, and against the spirit of democratic ideals that one section of the citizenship should subvert the funds of the common treasury to discriminate against another section solely on the basis of ancestry."[22]

The report which the board adopted on December 12, 1922, recommending a separate school, embodied a different point of view. It declared that the enrollment of over eight hundred Negroes in the city high schools showed a "laudable desire on their part and on the part of their parents" for an education, but that a "new, modern, well equipped high school" of their own would provide them with the "maximum educational opportunity" and the fullest opportunity for the development of initiative, self-reliance, and the other qualities needed for good citizenship.[23]

The movement for a Negro high school was closely linked with the movement to relocate Shortridge High School, which was regarded as the best college preparatory school in the city and which included in its enrollment a number of students from wealthy and influential white families. The school occupied ancient and inadequate buildings in an older part of the city, not far from a Negro slum area. That new quarters for the school were badly needed was undeniable, but the zeal of some of its patrons for a new building and a new location on the north side of the city was clearly motivated by a desire to get rid of Negro students, who constituted 10 to 15 per cent of the enrollment. In a report of a survey of the school, made by one of the leading women's clubs of the city, it was emphasized that one of the reasons for planning a new building was the fact that "there are numbers of colored students packed into crowded class rooms with the white children." The *Freeman* commented bitterly that it was "evidently thought that to call attention to the Negroes as mixed with white children would be the weightiest argument for action on the part of the School Commissioners."[24]

After the school board decided to build both a Negro high school and a new Shortridge at a new location, a delegation of whites appeared before it to request "in the interest of economy" that the old buildings at Shortridge be used for the Negro school, "thus releasing building funds for other construction projects."[25] But the school board, instead of acting on this suggestion, went ahead with the construction of a Negro school, which was substantially equal to new schools being built for white students so far as construction and equipment were concerned. The board no doubt hoped that the new school and the employment of Negro teachers to staff it would make segregation less offensive to the Negro community.[26]

But before the building was started, a group of Negroes, backed by the NAACP, brought suit to enjoin construction on the grounds that the proposed school could not meet the requirements of "equality" under the "separate but equal" doctrine. Lawyers for the Negroes argued that the new school could not be equal to the three Indianapolis high schools already in operation because no single school could offer the range of subjects—academic and technical—which were offered in these schools. To build a Negro school truly equal to the combined three schools would be so expensive as to be prohibitive. After the local court in Marion County refused to grant the injunction an appeal was taken to the Indiana Supreme Court. That court, sustaining the action of the lower court, held that the suit was premature—that the mere fear that the proposed school might not offer courses of equal caliber was no reason for not building it. If, after the school was in operation, a case arose in which a colored pupil was denied some "educational advantage accorded white children of equal advancement," then proceedings could be taken "to secure the constitutional rights of such a child." In the meantime, the court declared, an injunction would not be granted "merely to allay the fears and apprehension of individuals."[27]

As the new school, which was named Crispus Attucks after the Negro of Revolutionary War fame, was nearing completion in 1927 the Board of School Commissioners announced that it would be the policy of the board to require all colored high school students to attend that school.[28] The board, in fact, followed this policy until the state legislature adopted a law in 1949 which required the desegregation of all public schools in the state.

In Gary, where the Negro population was increasing at a faster rate than in Indianapolis, the school segregation provoked a more militant response. In that city there had been a policy since 1908 of maintaining separate elementary schools for Negroes, which were staffed by Negro teachers,[29] but until 1927 Negroes were not required to attend a separate high school. Nearly all of the burgeoning Negro population of Gary was concentrated in the central part of the city, known as "the Patch." In that area was located Froebel High School, a four-year institution, with a racially mixed student body. Some Negroes were also enrolled for the first two years of high school work in two Negro elementary school buildings. A few Negroes—not more than fifty—were scattered in schools in other parts of the city.[30]

Racial tension was occasionally evident at Froebel, but no serious racial disturbances occurred in the Gary schools until September, 1927. These disturbances broke out not at Froebel but at Emerson High School when twenty-four Negroes were transferred there from a Negro school, known as the Virginia Street school. A few days after the transfer white students at Emerson went on strike in protest. About six hundred of them paraded down the main street of the city, some of them carrying placards which said: "We won't go back to Emerson 'til it's white." In spite of the fact that the school principal threatened them with expulsion the number of strikers grew, until by the third day over thirteen hundred were absent from classes. At a mass meeting of students the superintendent of schools and the vice-president of the school board declared that the Negroes must remain at Emerson for the time being, but implied that they would be removed when a new Negro high school could be erected—in two or three years. In the meantime the superintendent indicated that it would not be necessary to include Negro students in the social and athletic activities of the school. The members of the board of education, after a conference with the mayor, also gave assurances that the transfer of the Negro students was intended to be temporary, that there was no intention of making Emerson permanently a mixed school, and gave promises that no more Negroes would be transferred there.[31]

At the end of four days the strike was settled by what the local newspaper referred to as a "peace treaty" between the students and the school and city authorities. The strikers were not to be penalized and the city council voted $15,000 for the purpose of erecting a temporary structure for a Negro school. The appropriation was carried in spite of negative votes of the three Negro members of the council and over the protests of a group of Negroes who crowded into the council chamber.[32]

Plans to remove the Negroes from Emerson to the temporary building ran into a snag when the local branch of the NAACP secured an injunction to prevent the expenditure of funds for that purpose.[33] The authorities then changed their tactics and decided to make some renovations in the school from which the Negroes had been transferred in the first place. At the end of the Christmas vacation, in January, 1928, less than four months after the strike, all Negroes except for three seniors were removed from Emerson and transferred either to the Virginia Street school or to Froebel.

Efforts by Negroes to block the transfer were unsuccessful. One parent, with the backing of the local and the national office of the NAACP sought a mandamus ordering the superintendent of schools to readmit his daughter to Emerson. The lawyers for the Negro student tried to prove that the Virginia Street school, which she was ordered to attend, did not meet the state requirements for a four-year high school, but both a local court and the Indiana Supreme Court rejected their plea.[34] The segregationists won a complete victory so far as Emerson High School was concerned. In addition to transferring the Negroes back to the Virginia Street school, the school board rearranged school districts in such a way as to provide that students who finished the tenth grade in that school would continue at Froebel instead of Emerson. As a final step, the city council appropriated $600,000 to build a high school for Negroes which would be equal in all respects to the other high schools. When completed this school was named Roosevelt and made an all-Negro institution with a Negro faculty. Froebel High School, which was on the same side of the tracks, continued to have a mixed enrollment and to be the only unsegregated school in Gary. Emerson, on the other side of town, remained all white until 1945, when another student strike, this time at Froebel, led to the abandonment of segregation throughout the Gary school system.[35]

Thus in Gary and Indianapolis, two major centers of Negro concentration, the decade of the 1920's saw impressive gains by the advocates of segregation. In the southern part of the state, where Negroes had first settled, the schools had always been completely segregated. A few northern towns, where the number of Negroes was small, moved toward segregation for the first time in this decade. One of these was Elkhart, where the total Negro population was only about five hundred. Other northern cities, including South Bend and East Chicago, where the number of Negroes was larger, never adopted segregation.[36]

It is difficult to generalize on the course of racial discrimination in institutions of higher learning, since the number of Negroes enrolled in them was small. At least one private institution is known to have adopted a quota system in the 1920's limiting the number of Negroes admitted. In the state universities there were no racial restrictions in admission policies, but Negroes were not allowed to live in the residence halls maintained by the institutions and were barred from a number of university activities. At Indiana University a house for Negro women erected with private funds was opened in 1929.[37]

Some of the same discriminatory pattern that developed in the public schools during the 1920's may be discerned also in the city regulations governing places of public accommodation. Although discrimination in such places was prohibited by law, it continued to be customary in the decade for Negroes and whites to patronize different establishments. One place where the color line was drawn for the first time was in the public parks of Indianapolis and Gary. In Indianapolis, Douglass Park was acquired in 1921. It was not officially designated as a park for Negroes, but the swimming pool and playgrounds which were subsequently built there were marked with signs which said "Negroes only." After the opening of this park Negro groups found it impossible to get permission to hold functions in the other city parks. In Gary, one park was divided into two areas with "separate but equal" recreational facilities for members of each race. Negroes were excluded from the only park in the area which had a beach on Lake Michigan, and as a result a group of Negro businessmen leased private property on the lakefront for a beach in 1926.[38]

These illustrations of segregationist practices, whether in places of public accommodation or in the public schools, are evidence of the increasing sharpness of racial discrimination during the 1920's. It was a period, at least in the larger urban areas of Indiana, when the color line seemed marked more indelibly than before. The question which remains is that of the responsibility of the Klan—the extent to which the segregationist measures may be attributed to its influence.

Of the strength of the Klan there can be no doubt. The Klan moved into Indiana in the years following the First World War. By 1923 there were klaverns all over the state, with a membership estimated at between a quarter and half a million. The Klan infiltrated Protestant churches, social organizations, and politics. For a time it dominated the Republican party, which in turn controlled state government. But its heyday was short-lived. It collapsed in the midst of a series of disclosures which shook the complacency of Indianans, even though they were inclined to be fairly tolerant of wrongdoing in political circles. David C. Stephenson, former Grand Dragon and dominant figure in the Klan, was sentenced to life imprisonment for a particularly revolting sex crime. A few months later a whole series of public officials identified with the Klan had been accused of various kinds of malfeasance. Some of them escaped conviction but all were disgraced. Ever since that time politicians have frantically sought to dissociate themselves from any hint of Klan ties. Because the Klan was so thoroughly discredited there has been a tendency in recent years to make it a scapegoat and blame it for segregation measures which a later generation finds discreditable. The evidence in support of this belief, however, is tenuous.

In exploiting popular prejudices the Indiana Klan relied most heavily upon traditional fears of Roman Catholicism.[39] The theme which was harped on most consistently in the pages of the official Klan publication, the *Fiery Cross,* was the alleged desire of the Church of Rome to dominate the government and schools of the United States, a theme in which existing prejudice against foreigners was fully exploited. Appeal to race prejudice, in comparison to the appeal to anti-Catholicism, was relatively slight despite Indiana's long history of racial bigotry. In fact, efforts were sometimes made to convince Negroes that the Klan was their friend.

But white supremacy was one of the avowed tenets of the Klan, and part of the appeal to Hoosiers was the use of the well-worn argument of the necessity of maintaining racial purity. One Klansman explained that in "selling" the Klan to prospective members one approach was to bring up the subject of white supremacy "in this way—not anti-negro, but to keep the black man black and the white man white." A full-page advertisement in the *Fiery Cross* from the Wayne County Klan declared that it unalterably opposed "contamination of the pure blood of the Anglo-Saxon race with an inferior nationality." A Junior Klan had among its ideals, along with "shielding the chastity of the home and the purity of our womanhood" and "the practical value of the Scriptures," a pledge "to maintain forever white supremacy."[40]

At the same time the *Fiery Cross* and Klan spokesmen frequently asserted that they were not enemies of Negroes but were in reality their best friends. One editorial declared: "The fact that the Ku Klux Klan believes in white supremacy has furnished much propaganda for the enemy to use among the negro population, inciting hatred for the Klan in that quarter, although thousands of intelligent negroes realize the meaning of the sentiment expressed by 'white supremacy,' and are not excited by the slanderers of the Klan." It insisted that there were many cases "wherein worthy negroes have been materially aided in time of misfortune by the Klan." One form of aid cited was gifts made to "worthy" Negro churches. It was reported that a gift to the Edinburg Colored Baptist Church was "gratefully received by the secretary of the church, who knows that the Klan is not the enemy of the negro as alien propaganda would have his people believe."[41] The *Fiery Cross* insisted, also, that Klansmen were law-abiding and that they were opposed to lynching. In one instance, it was claimed, members of the Klan were responsible for preventing the lynching of a Negro accused of assaulting a white woman.[42] In spite of these protestations of good will, however, it was well known that processions of white-robed Klansmen sometimes paraded through Negro districts as warning to Negroes to be law-abiding and to "keep in their place."

Attitudes among Negroes toward the Klan were mixed. Because it was identified with Protestantism and was publicly opposed to sin, some Negro clergymen either praised it or refrained from criticism, but other Negro ministers were frankly opposed to it. Negro intellectuals generally were openly suspicious and hostile. Most disturbing to them was the power which the Klan displayed in the Republican party.

The identification of the Klan with the party of Lincoln created a curious dilemma for Negro voters. As a legacy from the days of Reconstruction, Negroes had always retained an unquestioning loyalty to the Republican party. In the Democratic party, which in the South, at least, was the symbol of white supremacy, Negroes were a rarity. The injection of the Klan issue into the 1924 election campaign created the possibility of a change in the traditional political alignment. In the May primaries the Klan-backed candidates on the Republican ticket were victorious almost without exception. No Negro Republicans were nominated, but for the first time in history a Negro Democrat was nominated as a candidate for the Indiana house of representatives. One Negro newspaper, the Indianapolis *Ledger,* was undoubtedly subsidized by the Klan, and its editor was active in support of Ed Jackson, whom the Klan backed for the Republican nomination as governor. In an effort to hold the support of Negroes the Jackson group attempted to promote a kind of Klan for Negroes—an organization called "The Ritualistic Benevolent Society for American Born Citizens of African Blood and Protestant Faith." Members pledged themselves to support the American government, the Protestant faith, "protection of home and chastity of womanhood," free public schools, laws punishing lynching, and immigration laws to check the influx of "undesirables" who threatened the jobs of colored workers. The organization apparently met with little success, and on the day of the primary the Negro vote was light.[43]

From the beginning the *Freeman,* whose owner and publisher, George L. Knox, had been active in Republican politics in an earlier period, was strongly anti-Klan. After the primary it declared: "The Republican party as now constituted is the Ku Klux Klan of Indiana. The nominees for Governor, House, Senate, and County offices with one possible exception are all Klansmen, in fact there is no Republican party." The

Freeman called upon Negroes to support the Democrats; otherwise they would show that they were not worthy to vote. "The ballot is the only weapon of a civilized people and it is up to the Negro to use that weapon as do other civilized groups."[44]

Throughout the campaign the Democratic leaders in Indiana adopted an anti-Klan position. The Democratic state platform condemned efforts to make political issues out of race and religion. While not calling the Klan by name, it declared that the Republican party had been "delivered into the hands of an organization which has no place in politics and which promulgates doctrines which tend to break down the safeguards which the constitution throws around every citizen." The Klan responded by circulating a bulletin during the campaign declaring that the Democratic candidate for governor, Dr. Carleton McCulloch, was "antagonistic" toward the Klan and had "openly and publicly denounced the Klan," and should therefore be defeated.[45]

The Klan issue in Indiana attracted nationwide attention and aroused apprehension among Negroes in other states. During the campaign the *Freeman* asserted that because of the Klan, nationally known Negro Republican leaders refused to come into the state to campaign. At the national convention of the National Association for the Advancement of Colored People, James Weldon Johnson, the executive secretary, declared that the most important issue before Negroes in the coming election was the Klan. In spite of protestations by Klan leaders that it was not anti-Negro, he insisted that if the Klan gained political power the rights of Negroes would be endangered. In Indiana, he declared, it was the plain duty of Negroes to vote against Republican candidates who were "touched with the tar brush of the Ku Klux Klan."[46]

Members of the NAACP in Indiana made strenuous efforts to defeat the Klan-backed candidates and organized an Independent Voters League for this purpose. In October the NAACP and the recently organized League called a meeting in Indianapolis of Negroes from all parts of the state for the purpose of alerting voters to the Klan issue. At a session which several thousand Negroes attended it was voted to endorse the entire Democratic ticket.[47]

Some Negro clergymen were outspoken in their opposition to the Klan. At the general conference of the African Methodist Episcopal Church, meeting in Louisville, Kentucky, a resolution was adopted condemning Senator James E. Watson of Indiana for endorsing Jackson for governor. In Indianapolis, the minister of the leading A.M.E. church was known to be a foe of the Klan. On the other hand, Negro ministers, who were traditionally active in Republican politics, in many instances continued to give their support to that party. Several A.M.E. ministers were listed as speakers by the Republican speakers' bureau. As might be expected, the Negroes most vocal in support of the Republican cause were those holding political jobs. Anti-Klan Negroes were bitter in their denunciation of those "Jim Crow" Negroes who continued to work in the Klan dominated Republican organization.[48]

Democrats tried to convince Negro voters that the real issue in the campaign was not between Democrats and Republicans but between Democrats and the Klan.[49] Republicans tried to hold the Negro vote by pointing up traditional political loyalties. Representative Leonidas C. Dyer, of Missouri, author of an anti-lynching bill in Congress, told Indiana Negroes that their real enemy was the Democratic party. "There is no such thing," he said in Indianapolis, "as a colored man being loyal to his race and at the same time voting the Democratic ticket."[50]

As the campaign wore on Republican leaders apparently began to feel concern over the possibility of a defection of the normally loyal Negroes. The director of the Republican state campaign bureau for Negroes told party workers that the Klan question had frightened Negroes. "The heart of the colored man is with you," he said, "but his mind is confused." The Klan itself was also apprehensive about the Negro vote. One bulletin from Klan headquarters warned that "the amalgamated enemies of the organization [Klan] are influencing the negro and foreigner to such an extent that practically the entire negro and foreign vote will be cast for the anti-Klan candidates. We must overcome this loss by seeing to it that all Protestant people support those candidates whom we favor."[51] Headlines in the *Fiery Cross* proclaimed: "Rome Dictates to Indiana Voters: Attempt Is Made to Stampede the Negro Vote." The paper accused the Democrats of "waging a war of hate, misrepresentation, coercion and party destruction with the hope of driving the Negro out of the Republican party and into the Democratic camp." "Roman agents" were said to be busily trying to create trouble at every Negro political meeting. But the *Fiery Cross* expressed confidence that Negroes were too intelligent to be misled. The agents of Rome, it said, "may control the Roman Catholic vote, but their task of driving like a herd of sheep, the negro voter into the McCulloch fold is too big for the Roman corporation. It can't be done."[52]

In spite of these brave words there were marked defections among

Negro Republicans on election day. In Indianapolis, Negro wards, which normally were solidly Republican, now went Democratic.[53] But these Republican losses were more than offset by the large numbers of white Democrats and independents who voted the Klan-backed Republican ticket. The result was the election of a governor and other state officers who were known to have Klan ties. More than half of the members of the Indiana house of representatives as well as a large number of state senators were elected with Klan support, while innumerable local officials owed their victories in part to the Klan.

During the campaign Democrats had warned Negroes that if the Klan got control of the state government it would enact severe segregation measures, but no such measures materialized. In the 1925 session of the state legislature, in which Klan-supported members were in a majority, several measures were proposed against Roman Catholic influence in the public schools. But not a single segregation measure nor any other proposal to establish racial discrimination was introduced.[54]

By the autumn of 1925, when municipal elections were held in the larger cities in the state, the prestige and influence of the Klan were already badly shaken. The trial of D. C. Stephenson, former Grand Dragon, got under way at the same time as the fall campaigns. But in spite of Stephenson's disgrace the Klan had not yet lost its power in Indianapolis and Gary. In Indianapolis the Republican candidates for mayor and the city council were openly supported by the Klan. In the election of members of the Board of School Commissioners, which was held at the same time as the municipal election, a slate of candidates known as "the United Protestant Clubs ticket" also had Klan backing. Although the election of the school board was supposed to be non-partisan, Republican workers as well as Klan members were active in support of the Protestant ticket. In the closing days of the campaign a huge rally was held at which the Exalted Cyclops of Marion County Klan No. 3 presided. Prayers and speeches were made on behalf of the Republican candidates for mayor and city council and the Protestant school ticket, all of whom were present.[55]

All of the Klan-backed candidates were elected. Negroes do not appear to have been aroused over the Klan issue during the campaign as they had been in 1924. Except for a few party workers, they showed little enthusiasm for the Republican candidates, but neither did they show much disposition to support the Democrats. On election day the Negro vote was light, but the Republicans carried the day. Negro wards which had been Democratic the year before were once again in the Republican column. In Gary, as in Indianapolis, the Klan scored a victory. Floyd E. Williams, who was reputed to be a member of the Klan, was elected mayor, and five members of the Gary city council were persons nominated and elected with Klan support.[56]

There is a widespread belief that the Indianapolis school board elected with Klan backing was responsible for the segregation measures which became so controversial a part of the city's school administration in the remaining years of the decade. A recent book on desegregation in the schools says that "the Klan secured the erection of Crispus Attucks High School in 1927 and established it as a segregated school. In the same year a Klan dominated school board initiated the policy of transporting Negroes away from the elementary school in their neighborhood to more distant schools for Negroes." In a newspaper statement in 1957 the superintendent of the Indianapolis schools also placed the blame for segregation in the schools on the Klan.[57]

The accuracy of these statements is questionable in view of what we know about the development of segregation measures after World War I. Certainly the Klan did not "initiate" the policy of requiring Negro children to travel long distances to Negro schools. Negro parents were complaining about this policy before the Klan made its appearance in Indiana.[58] In September, 1923, as noted above, the policy of requiring elementary school children to attend segregated schools was greatly extended. In December of that same year the building of a Negro high school was authorized. These developments, of course, all took place before 1925, when the Klan-backed school board was elected. In 1923 the board was made up of members nominated and elected with the support of the Citizens School Committee, a group which in 1925 ran candidates in opposition to the Klan-backed slate; in fact, members of the school board who had voted for the segregation measures in 1923 were defeated by Klan-backed candidates in 1925. In 1923, moreover, the Indianapolis school board had been under constant attack by the Klan because of alleged Roman Catholic influence, especially because the president of the board was a Catholic. The *Fiery Cross* regularly published articles and editorials on this subject, charging that Catholic influence was impeding the construction of needed public schools. But during 1923 there was not a single item in the columns of that paper on the subject of segregation in the Indianapolis schools.

The Klan-backed school board elected in 1925 instead of initiating segregation merely carried forward policies begun by its predecessor. In 1927, when the Negro high school, Attucks, was completed, the board adopted a policy which apparently had been intended all along, that all

Negro high school students must attend this school. The action of the board in 1929 in removing Negro pupils from three mixed elementary schools was a continuation of an already established policy. By that year Negro leaders in Indianapolis, including the president of the NAACP, were active in a campaign to defeat the members of this board who were seeking re-election. Publicly, at least, they did not base their opposition on the board's segregationist policies but rather on discrimination against Indianapolis Negroes in the hiring of teachers.[59]

The fact that the Klan did not work openly for the segregation of the Indianapolis schools does not mean that Klan influence was nonexistent. Since Klan membership and Klan influence were pervasive in the early 1920's, undoubtedly Klan views were represented in the Indianapolis Chamber of Commerce and other civic groups which worked for the separation of the races in the schools. By 1926, Klan influence no doubt contributed to passage of the racial zoning ordinance in Indianapolis and the segregation movement in the Gary schools; at that time the influence of the Klan was indirect and covert rather than direct and open. But throughout these years the mayors of both Indianapolis and Gary were reputed to be members of the Klan, and a majority of the city councils of both cities had been elected with Klan support.

Klan influence may have played some part in the tightening of racial barriers in the 1920's, but it does not appear to have been the prime mover. Actually, the rapid influx of Negroes from the rural South into urban centers of a state where there had always been a tradition of racism seems to offer a sufficient explanation of the demand for segregation. The same attitudes among the people of Indiana which caused them to embrace the Klan caused them to favor separation of the races. Although Klan propaganda may have intensified race feeling, it is still conceivable that the segregation measures which were adopted in the 1920's might have been adopted if the Klan had not existed.

NOTES

1. In Indiana the Negro population increased from 60,320 in 1910 to 111,982 in 1930; in Illinois, from 104,049 to 328,972; in Ohio, from 111,452 to 309,304; in Michigan, from 17,115 to 169,453. United States Bureau of the Census, *Negroes in the United States, 1920–1932* (Washington, 1935), 9, 12, 15.

2. *Ibid.*, 34–36, 44, 49, 53, 55; John Foster Potts, "A History of the Growth of the Negro Population in Gary, Indiana" (M.A. thesis, Cornell University, 1937), 6, 9, 18, 27; Powell A. Moore, *The Calumet Region: Indiana's Last Frontier* (Indianapolis, 1959), 252.
3. See Emma Lou Thornbrough, *The Negro in Indiana before 1900* (Indianapolis, 1957), *passim,* especially 68–70, 120–27, 162–66, 233, 249. The Indiana constitution of 1851 absolutely prohibited Negroes from coming into the state to reside. Before 1866 Negroes were not allowed to testify in court in a case in which a white man was a party. Until 1869 Negro children were not admitted to the public schools.
4. *Ibid.*, 266–70, 329.
5. For example, one county history published in 1916 contains the statement: "Washington County has for several decades boasted that no colored man or woman lived within her borders." Quoted, *ibid.*, 225.
6. *The Freeman* (Indianapolis), April 22, 1916. When there were signs of opposition to the use of the public parks by Negroes, the *Freeman* warned that it was wiser not to go to the parks in large numbers. It asserted: "What we wish is our right of enjoyment rather than to be in the parks at all times. If we are careful in not overdoing the matter . . . the right to go where we wish will not be opposed." *Ibid.*, August 12, 1916.
7. Indianapolis *World,* May 6, 1921.
8. The group was said to aim at securing the dismissal of Negroes from positions in the federal civil service and from employment by local government. *Freeman,* July 26, 1924. The president of the White Supremacy League wrote a long letter to the Ku Klux Klan publication, *The Fiery Cross,* justifying white supremacy. She insisted that she had no animosity toward Negroes but had a "marked respect for the negro who keeps his own kind, who does not display an anomalous desire for 'social equality' and who respects the white authority of the United States." *The Fiery Cross* (Indianapolis), January 19, 1923.
9. *Freeman,* March 1, 1924.
10. *Journal of the Common Council of the City of Indianapolis, Indiana, from January 1, 1926, to December 1, 1926* (Indianapolis, 1927), 54. Persons who owned property before the adoption of the ordinance were permitted to reside in it and also to sell it, but if a Negro sold property to a white, or a white sold property to a Negro, the purchaser was not allowed to take up residence without obtaining the written consent of a majority of persons of the opposite race in the neighborhood. The term "community" as used in the ordinance was defined as every residence within 300 feet of the property involved.
11. The vote was five to one in favor of adoption. Three members of the council, two Republicans and one Democrat, were not present. *Ibid.*, 77–78; Indianapolis *News,* March 16, 1926; Indianapolis *Star,* March 16, 1926.
12. *Journal of the Common Council, 1926,* p. 82. The mayor was John L. Duvall, a Republican, who was elected with the backing of the Ku Klux Klan and subsequently sent to jail for violation of the Corrupt Practices Act.
13. *Tyler v. Harmon,* 158 La. 439 (1925). On a second hearing the Louisiana Supreme Court refused to reserve its decision. *Tyler v. Harmon,* 1960 La. 943 (1926). In the Louisville case, *Buchanan v. Warley,* 245 U.S. 60 (1917), the Supreme Court ruled that the ordinance violated the Fourteenth Amendment because it interfered with property rights without due process of law. The decision did not rest on the equal protection clause.

14. National Association for the Advancement of Colored People, *Seventeenth Annual Report* (1927), 10. The case was Edward S. Gaillard versus Dr. Guy L. Grant, decided in the Marion County Superior Court, November 23, 1926. Indianapolis *News,* November 24, 1926.

15. *Harmon v. Tyler,* 273 U.S. 668 (1927). In a per curiam decision the Louisiana court was reversed on the authority of *Buchanan v. Warley.* After the invalidation of the racial zoning ordinance, white property owners turned increasingly to the use of racially restrictive covenants, which continued to be enforceable in the courts until the decision of the United States Supreme Court in *Shelley v. Kraemer* (334 U.S. 1) in 1948.

16. Thornbrough, *Negro in Indiana,* 332–34, 341; Indianapolis *News,* May 13, 1919.

17. Indianapolis Board of School Commissioners (Office of the Board, Indianapolis), Minutes, Book W, 227.

18. *Ibid.,* 226–27.

19. *Ibid.,* Book Y, 22, 85, 159, 185, 304–305. See also Indianapolis *Times,* January 14, 1957, for a later survey of these problems.

20. Indianapolis Board of School Commissioners, Minutes, Book FF, 293.

21. *Ibid.,* Book W, 396. The Mapleton Civic Association also worked for a separate high school. A statement of its accomplishments said: "Through our efforts the School Board has promised to provide separate schools for the colored pupils of the city, especially a high school, this season, and we believe this will be of assistance in segregating these people." *Freeman,* March 1, 1924.

22. Indianapolis Board of School Commissioners, Minutes, Book X, 29, 50, 51.

23. *Ibid.,* 64.

24. Report of the Women's Department Club, *ibid.,* Book Y, 321; *Freeman,* March 21, 1924.

25. Indianapolis Board of School Commissioners, Minutes, Book Y, 319.

26. The *Freeman,* June 28, 1924, objected to the location chosen for the Negro school on the grounds that it was in a depressed residential area, near a glue factory and the city dump. Such a location, it declared, would have a depressing effect upon pupils "already humiliated by the fact that they are being forced from rooms of Shortridge, Manual and Arsenal Tech solely because of color."

27. *Greathouse v. Board of School Commissioners of City of Indianapolis,* 198 Ind. 95–107 (1926).

28. Indianapolis Board of School Commissioners, Minutes, Book CC, 166. Negro groups protested when the Board of School Commissioners announced that the new school would be known as Jefferson High School. As a result the name was changed to Crispus Attucks, a name suggested by some Negroes. *Ibid.,* Book BB, 113.

29. In 1910 the superintendent of schools, William A. Wirt, was quoted as saying: "We believe that it is only justice to the Negro children that they be segregated. There is naturally a feeling between the Negroes and the whites in the lower grades and we believe that the Negroes will be better cared for in their own schools. Besides they will take pride in their work and will accomplish better results." Moore, *Calumet Region,* 392.

30. Gary *Post Tribune,* September 27, 1927.

31. *Ibid.,* September 26, 27, 28, 29, 1927.

32. *Ibid.,* October 4, 1927.
33. National Association for the Advancement of Colored People, *Nineteenth Annual Report* (1928), 17.
34. *State ex rel. Cheeks v. Wirt,* 203 Ind. 121 (1932). The court pointed out that the Virginia Street school was but one of six elementary school buildings in Gary in which courses equivalent to the first two years of high school work were offered and that pupils were transferred from these schools to the four-year high schools to finish their work. This was held to meet the requirements of the state law.
35. *Ibid.,* 134; Federal Writers Project, Works Progress Administration, *The Calumet Region Historical Guide* (Gary, 1939), 54; Indianapolis *Times,* April 4, 1947.
36. Robin M. Williams, Jr., and Margaret W. Ryan (eds.), *Schools in Transition: Community Experiences in Desegregation* (Chapel Hill, 1954), 68–69, 118. In the cities with segregated school systems there were opportunities for employment for Negro teachers. South Bend, on the other hand, did not employ a single Negro teacher until 1950.
37. Indianapolis *Star,* June 8, 1929. Residence halls at Indiana University were opened to Negro men in 1948 and to Negro women in 1950. Indianapolis *News,* April 23, 1959.
38. Indianapolis *World,* July 18, 1921; *Freeman,* August 9, 1924; Moore, *Calumet Region,* 391.
39. Norman F. Weaver, "The Knights of the Ku Klux Klan in Wisconsin, Indiana, Ohio, and Michigan" (Ph.D. dissertation, University of Wisconsin, 1954), *passim,* especially 11–31.
40. Deposition of Hugh F. Emmons, p. 377, in Papers Relating to the Ku Klux Klan and D. C. Stephenson (Archives Division, Indiana State Library); *Fiery Cross,* February 16, September 28, 1923. In a typical piece of Klan oratory, defending the fact that the Klan was open to white members only, one speaker declared: "We are not anti anything. We are just white. We are not only white, but you just bet your life we are going to stay white. Whenever a man goes to mixing God's colors he gets into trouble, and he is not only doomed but he is damned and they [*sic*] ought to be." *Ibid.,* December 6, 1922.
41. *Fiery Cross,* July 6, August 31, 1923.
42. This incident occurred near Culver, Indiana. *Ibid.,* May 25, 1923. In another instance it was claimed that Klan members protected a Negro minister in Hammond who was threatened by Catholics and foreigners when he sought to have a Negro church built near a Catholic church. *Ibid.,* December 5, 1924.
43. *Freeman,* March 29, May 17, 1924; Indianapolis *News,* May 6, 1924.
44. *Freeman,* May 17, 1924.
45. *Ibid.,* February 14, 1924; Weaver, "The Knights of the Ku Klux Klan," 206.
46. *Freeman,* July 12, September 27, 1924.
47. *Ibid.,* September 20, October 4, October 25, 1924.
48. *Ibid.,* May 17, September 20, October 25, 1924.
49. This theme was used repeatedly by the Democrats. See, for example, Indianapolis *News,* October 17, 1924.
50 *Ibid.,* October 16, 1924.

51. *Freeman, September* 20, 1924; Mimeographed bulletin, October 25, 1924, in Papers Relating to the Ku Klux Klan.
52. *Fiery Cross,* October 24, 1924.
53. Indianapolis *News,* November 5, 1924; Indianapolis *Star,* November 4, 1925.
54. A bulletin issued from the office of the Grand Dragon of the Realm of Indiana, October 20, 1924, said that enemies of the Klan were importing Negro speakers, who were advising Negro voters that a Klan victory would mean that Negroes would be segregated or forced to return to the South. See Papers Relating to the Ku Klux Klan. The only measure mentioning race introduced in the 1925 session was a senate bill sponsored by William E. English, Republican of Marion County, which would have provided a training school in domestic arts for Negro girls. The bill passed the senate but not the house. Indiana Senate, *Journal,* 74th Session (1925), 132, 792; Indiana House of Representatives, *Journal,* 74th Session (1925), 751.
55. Indianapolis *News,* October 21, October 26, November 2, 1925.
56. *Ibid.,* November 2, November 4, 1925; Indianapolis *Star,* November 4, 1925; Moore, *Calumet Region,* 556.
57. Williams and Ryan (eds.), *Schools in Transition,* 50; statement of Dr. Hermann Shibler in Indianapolis *Times,* January 14, 1957.
58. See, for example, Indianapolis *News,* May 13, 1919.
59. Indianapolis *Times,* November 2, 1929.

VI ~ Manners and Morality: The Jazz Age

19 ~ The Revolution in Manners and Morals*

[Author's Note] *In his thoroughly enjoyable social history of the 1920's,* Only Yesterday, *Frederick Lewis Allen, the late* Harper's *Journalist, links the "revolution" in manners and morals to diverse influences—the post-war disillusion, the new status of women, the Freudian "gospel," the automobile, Prohibition, and the sex and confession magazines. "Each of them," states Allen, "was played upon by all the others; none of them could alone have changed to any great degree the folkways of America; together their force was irresistible." In* Only Yesterday, *the author set a lasting pattern for writing American social history. The amazing thing about the book is that it was written almost contemporaneously, yet it did not suffer from a lack of historical perspective.*

A first-class revolt against the accepted American order was certainly taking place during those early years of the Post-war Decade, but it was one with which Nikolai Lenin had nothing whatever to do. The shock troops of the rebellion were not alien agitators, but the sons and daughters of well-to-do American families, who knew little about Bolshevism and cared distinctly less, and their defiance was expressed not in obscure radical publications or in soap-box speeches, but right across the family breakfast table into the horrified ears of conservative fathers and mothers. Men and women were still shivering at the Red Menace when they awoke to the no less alarming Problem of the Younger Generation, and realized that if the Constitution were not in danger, the moral code of the country certainly was.

* Abridgement of "The Revolution in Manners and Morals," (Pages 88–122). *Only Yesterday* by Frederick Lewis Allen.

This code, as it currently concerned young people, might have been roughly summarized as follows: Women were the guardians of morality; they were made of finer stuff than men and were expected to act accordingly. Young girls must look forward in innocence (tempered perhaps with a modicum of physiological instruction) to a romantic love match which would lead them to the altar and to living-happily-ever-after; and until the "right man" came along they must allow no male to kiss them. . . .

The war had not long been over when cries of alarm from parents, teachers, and moral preceptors began to rend the air. For the boys and girls just growing out of adolescence were making mincemeat of this code.

The dresses that the girls—and for that matter most of the older women—were wearing seemed alarming enough. In July, 1920, a fashion-writer reported in the *New York Times* that "the American woman . . . has lifted her skirts far beyond any modest limitation," which was another way of saying that the hem was now all of nine inches above the ground. It was freely predicted that skirts would come down again in the winter of 1920–21, but instead they climbed a few scandalous inches farther. The flappers wore thin dresses, short-sleeved and occasionally (in the evening) sleeveless; some of the wilder young things rolled their stockings below their knees, revealing to the shocked eyes of virtue a fleeting glance of shin-bones and knee-cap; and many of them were visibly using cosmetics. "The intoxication of rouge," earnestly explained Dorothy Speare in *Dancers in the Dark,* "is an insidious vintage known to more girls than mere man can ever believe." Useless for frantic parents to insist that no lady did such things; the answer was that the daughters of ladies were doing it, and even retouching their masterpieces in public. Some of them, furthermore, were abandoning their corsets. "The men won't dance with you if you wear a corset," they were quoted as saying. . . .

Supposedly "nice" girls were smoking cigarettes—openly and defiantly, if often rather awkwardly and self-consciously. They were drinking—somewhat less openly but often all too efficaciously. There were stories of daughters of the most exemplary parents getting drunk—"blotto," as their companions cheerfully put it—on the contents of the hip-flasks of the new prohibition régime, and going out joyriding with men at four in the morning. And worst of all, even at well-regulated dances they were said to retire where the eye of the most sharp-sighted chaperon could not follow, and in darkened rooms or in parked cars to engage in the unspeakable practice of petting and necking.

It was not until F. Scott Fitzgerald, who had hardly graduated from

Princeton and ought to know what his generation were doing, brought out *This Side of Paradise* in April, 1920, that fathers and mothers realized fully what was afoot and how long it had been going on. Apparently the "petting party" had been current as early as 1916, and was now widely established as an indoor sport. . . .

It was incredible. It was abominable. What did it all mean? Was every decent standard being thrown over? Mothers read the scarlet words and wondered if they themselves "had any idea how often their daughters were accustomed to be kissed." . . . But no, this must be an exaggerated account of the misconduct of some especially depraved group. Nice girls couldn't behave like that and talk openly about passion. But in due course other books appeared to substantiate the findings of Mr. Fitzgerald: *Dancers in the Dark, The Plastic Age, Flaming Youth.* Magazine articles and newspapers reiterated the scandal. To be sure, there were plenty of communities where nice girls did not, in actual fact, "behave like that"; and even in the more sophisticated urban centers there were plenty of girls who did not. Nevertheless, there was enough fire beneath the smoke of these sensational revelations to make the Problem of the Younger Generation a topic of anxious discussion from coast to coast.

The forces of morality rallied to the attack. Dr. Francis E. Clark, the founder and president of the Christian Endeavor Society, declared that the modern "indecent dance" was "an offense against womanly purity, the very fountainhead of our family and civil life." The new style of dancing was denounced in religious journals as "impure, polluting, corrupting, debasing, destroying spirituality, increasing carnality," and the mothers and sisters and church members of the land were called upon to admonish and instruct and raise the spiritual tone of these dreadful young people. President Murphy of the University of Florida cried out with true Southern warmth, "The low-cut gowns, the rolled hose and short skirts are born of the Devil and his angels, and are carrying the present and future generations to chaos and destruction." A group of Episcopal church-women in New York, speaking with the authority of wealth and social position (for they included Mrs. J. Pierpont Morgan, Mrs. Borden Harriman, Mrs. Henry Phipps, Mrs. James Roosevelt, and Mrs. E. H. Harriman), proposed an organization to discourage fashions involving an "excess of nudity" and "improper ways of dancing." The Y.W.C.A. conducted a national campaign against immodest dress among high-school girls, supplying newspapers with printed matter carrying headlines such as "Working Girls Responsive to Modesty Appeal" and "High Heels Losing Ground Even in

France." In Philadelphia a Dress Reform Committee of prominent citizens sent a questionnaire to over a thousand clergymen to ask them what would be their idea of a proper dress, and although the gentlemen of the cloth showed a distressing variety of opinion, the committee proceeded to design a "moral gown" which was endorsed by ministers of fifteen denominations. The distinguishing characteristics of this moral gown were that it was very loose-fitting, that the sleeves reached just below the elbows, and that the hem came within seven and a half inches of the floor. . . .

Meanwhile innumerable families were torn with dissension over cigarettes and gin and all-night automobile rides. Fathers and mothers lay awake asking themselves whether their children were not utterly lost; sons and daughters evaded questions, lied miserably and unhappily, or flared up to reply rudely that at least they were not dirty-minded hypocrites, that they saw no harm in what they were doing and proposed to go right on doing it. From those liberal clergymen and teachers who prided themselves on keeping step with all that was new, came a chorus of reassurance: these young people were at least franker and more honest than their elders had been; having experimented for themselves, would they not soon find out which standards were outworn and which represented the accumulated moral wisdom of the race? Hearing such hopeful words, many good people took heart again. Perhaps this flare-up of youthful passion was a flash in the pan, after all. Perhaps in another year or two the boys and girls would come to their senses and everything would be all right again.

They were wrong, however. For the revolt of the younger generation was only the beginning of a revolution in manners and morals that was already beginning to affect men and women of every age in every part of the country.

A number of forces were working together and interacting upon one another to make this revolution inevitable.

First of all was the state of mind brought about by the war and its conclusion. A whole generation had been infected by the eat-drink-and-be-merry-for-tomorrow-we-die spirit which accompanied the departure of the soldiers to the training camps and the fighting front. There had been an epidemic not only of abrupt war marriages, but of less conventional liaisons. In France, two million men had found themselves very close to filth and annihilation and very far from the American moral code and its defenders; prostitution had followed the flag and willing mademoiselles from Armentières had been plentiful; American girls sent over as nurses and war workers had come under the influence of continental manners and standards without being subject to the rigid protections thrown about their continental sisters of the respectable classes; and there had been a very widespread and very natural breakdown of traditional restraints and reticences and taboos. It was impossible for this generation to return unchanged when the ordeal was over. Some of them had acquired under the pressure of war-time conditions a new code which seemed to them quite defensible; millions of them had been provided with an emotional stimulant from which it was not easy to taper off. Their torn nerves craved the anodynes of speed, excitement, and passion. They found themselves expected to settle down into the humdrum routine of American life as if nothing had happened, to accept the moral dicta of elders who seemed to them still to be living in a Pollyanna land of rosy ideals which the war had killed for them. They couldn't do it, and they very disrespectfully said so. . . .

The same disillusion which had defeated Woodrow Wilson and had caused strikes and riots and the Big Red Scare furnished a culture in which the germs of the new freedom could grow and multiply.

The revolution was accelerated also by the growing independence of the American woman. She won the suffrage in 1920. She seemed, it is true, to be very little interested in it once she had it; she voted, but mostly as the unregenerate men about her did, despite the efforts of women's clubs and the League of Women Voters to awaken her to womanhood's civic opportunity; . . .

Even more marked was the effect of woman's growing independence of the drudgeries of housekeeping. Smaller houses were being built, and they were easier to look after. Families were moving into apartments, and these made even less claim upon the housekeeper's time and energy. Women were learning how to make lighter work of the preparation of meals. Sales of canned foods were growing, the number of delicatessen stores had increased three times as fast as the population during the decade 1910–20, the output of bakeries increased by 60 per cent during the decade 1914–24. Much of what had once been housework was now either moving out of the home entirely or being simplified by machinery. The use of commercial laundries, for instance, increased by 57 per cent between 1914 and 1924. Electric washing-machines and electric irons were coming to the aid of those who still did their washing at home; the manager of the local electric power company at "Middletown," a typical small American city, estimated in 1924 that nearly 90 per cent of the homes in the city already had electric irons. The housewife was learning to telephone her shopping orders, to get her clothes ready-made and spare herself the rigors of dress-making, to buy a vacuum cleaner and emulate the lovely carefree girls in the magazine advertisements who banished dust with such delicate fingers. Women were slowly becoming emancipated from routine to "live their own lives."

And what were these "own lives" of theirs to be like? Well, for one thing, they could take jobs. Up to this time girls of the middle classes who had wanted to "do something" had been largely restricted to school-teaching, social-service work, nursing, stenography, and clerical work in business houses. But now they poured out of the schools and colleges into all manner of new occupations. They besieged the offices of publishers and advertisers; they went into tea-room management until there threatened to be more purveyors than consumers of chicken patties and cinnamon toast; they sold antiques, sold real estate, opened smart little shops, and finally invaded the department stores. In 1920 the department store was in the mind of the average college girl a rather bourgeois institution which employed "poor shop girls"; by the end of the decade college girls were standing in line for openings in the misses' sports-wear department and even selling behind the counter in the hope that some day fortune might smile upon them and make them buyers or stylists. . . .

With the job—or at least the sense that the job was a possibility—came a feeling of comparative economic independence. With the feeling of economic independence came a slackening of husbandly and parental authority. Maiden aunts and unmarried daughters were leaving the shelter of the family roof to install themselves in kitchenette apartments of their own. For city-dwellers the home was steadily becoming less of a shrine, more of a dormitory—a place of casual shelter where one stopped over-night on the way from the restaurant and the movie theater to the office. Yet even the job did not provide the American woman with that complete satisfaction which the management of a mechanized home no longer furnished. She still had energies and emotions to burn; she was ready for the revolution.

Like all revolutions, this one was stimulated by foreign propaganda. It came, however, not from Moscow, but from Vienna. Sigmund Freud had published his first book on psychoanalysis at the end of the nineteenth century, and he and Jung had lectured to American psychologists as early as 1909, but it was not until after the war that the Freudian gospel began to circulate to a marked extent among the American lay public. The one great intellectual force which had not suffered disrepute as a result of the war was science; the more-or-less educated public was now absorbing a quantity of popularized information about biology and anthropology which gave a general impression that men and women were merely animals of a rather intricate variety, and that moral codes had no universal validity and were often based on curious superstitions. A fertile ground was ready for the seeds of Freudianism, and presently one began to hear even from the lips of flappers that "science taught" new and disturbing things about sex. Sex, it appeared, was the central and pervasive force which moved mankind. Almost every human motive was attributable to it: if you were patriotic or liked the violin, you were in the grip of sex—in a sublimated form. The first requirement of mental health was to have an uninhibited sex life. If you would be well and happy, you must obey your libido. Such was the Freudian gospel as it imbedded itself in the American mind after being filtered through the successive minds of interpreters and popularizers and guileless readers and people who had heard guileless readers talk about it. New words and phrases began to be bandied about the cocktail-tray and the Mah Jong table—inferiority complex, sadism, masochism, Œdipus complex. Intellectual ladies went to Europe to be analyzed; analysts plied their new trade in American cities, conscientiously transferring the affections of their fair patients to themselves; and clergymen who preached about the virtue of self-control were reminded by outspoken critics that self-control was out-of-date and really dangerous.

The principal remaining forces which accelerated the revolution in manners and morals were all 100 per cent American. They were prohibition, the automobile, the confession and sex magazines, and the movies.

When the Eighteenth Amendment was ratified, prohibition seemed, as we have already noted, to have an almost united country behind it. Evasion of the law began immediately, however, and strenuous and sincere opposition to it—especially in the large cities of the North and East —quickly gathered force. The results were the bootlegger, the speakeasy, and a spirit of deliberate revolt which in many communities made drinking "the thing to do." From these facts in turn flowed further results: the increased popularity of distilled as against fermented liquors, the use of the hip-flask, the cocktail party, and the general transformation of drinking from a masculine prerogative to one shared by both sexes together. The old-time saloon had been overwhelmingly masculine; the speakeasy usually catered to both men and women. . . .

Meanwhile a new sort of freedom was being made possible by the enormous increase in the use of the automobile, and particularly of the closed car. (In 1919 hardly more than 10 per cent of the cars produced in the United States were closed; by 1924 the percentage had jumped to 43, by 1927 it had reached 82.8.) The automobile offered an almost universally available means of escaping temporarily from the supervision of parents and chaperons, or from the influence of neighborhood opinion. Boys and girls now thought nothing, as the Lynds pointed out in *Middletown,* of jumping into a car and driving off at a moment's notice—without asking anybody's permission—to a dance in another town twenty miles away, where they were strangers and enjoyed a freedom impossible among their neighbors. The closed car, moreover, was in effect a room protected from the weather which could be occupied at any time of the day or night and could be moved at will into a darkened byway or a country lane. The Lynds quoted the judge of the juvenile court in "Middletown" as declaring that the automobile had become a "house of prostitution on wheels," and cited the fact that of thirty girls brought before his court in a year on charges of sex crimes, for whom the place where the offense had occurred was recorded, nineteen were listed as having committed it in an automobile.

Finally, as the revolution began, its influence fertilized a bumper crop of sex magazines, confession magazines, and lurid motion pictures, and these in turn had their effect on a class of readers and movie-goers who had never heard and never would hear of Freud and the libido. The publishers of the sex adventure magazines, offering stories with such titles as "What I Told My Daughter the Night Before Her Marriage," "Indolent Kisses," and "Watch Your Step-Ins," learned to a nicety the gentle art of arousing the reader without arousing the censor. The publishers of the confesssion magazines, while always instructing their authors to provide a moral ending and to utter pious sentiments, concentrated on the description of what they euphemistically called "missteps." Most of their fiction was faked to order by hack writers who could write one day "The Confessions of a Chorus Girl" and the next day recount, again in the first person, the temptations which made it easy for the taxidriver to go wrong. Both classes of magazines became astonishingly numerous and successful. Bernarr McFadden's *True-Story,* launched as late as 1919, had over

300,000 readers by 1923; 848,000 by 1924; over a million and a half by 1925; and almost two million by 1926—a record of rapid growth probably unparalleled in magazine publishing.

Crowding the news stands along with the sex and confession magazines were motion-picture magazines which depicted "seven movie kisses" with such captions as "Do you recognize your little friend, Mae Busch? She's had lots of kisses, but she never seems to grow *blasé*. At least you'll agree that she's giving a good imitation of a person enjoying this one." The movies themselves, drawing millions to their doors every day and every night, played incessantly upon the same lucrative theme. The producers of one picture advertised "brilliant men, beautiful jazz babies, champagne baths, midnight revels, petting parties in the purple dawn, all ending in one terrific smashing climax that makes you gasp"; the venders of another promised "neckers, petters, white kisses, red kisses, pleasure-mad daughters, sensation-craving mothers, . . . the truth—bold, naked, sensational." Seldom did the films offer as much as these advertisements promised, but there was enough in some of them to cause a sixteen-year-old girl (quoted by Alice Miller Mitchell) to testify, "Those pictures with hot love-making in them, they make girls and boys sitting together want to get up and walk out, go off somewhere, you know. Once I walked out with a boy before the picture was even over. We took a ride. But my friend, she all the time had to get up and go out with her boy friend." . . .

Each of these diverse influences—the post-war disillusion, the new status of women, the Freudian gospel, the automobile, prohibition, the sex and confession magazines, and the movies—had its part in bringing about the revolution. Each of them, as an influence, was played upon by all the others; none of them could alone have changed to any great degree the folkways of America; together their force was irresistible. . . .

Changes in fashion—the short skirt, the boyish form, the straight, long-waisted dresses, the frank use of paint—were signs of a real change in the American feminine ideal (as well, perhaps, as in men's idea of what was the feminine ideal). Women were bent on freedom—freedom to work and to play without the trammels that had bound them heretofore to lives of comparative inactivity. But what they sought was not the freedom from man and his desires which had put the suffragists of an earlier day into hard straw hats and mannish suits and low-heeled shoes. The woman of the nineteen-twenties wanted to be able to allure man even on the golf links and in the office; the little flapper who shingled her hair and wore a manageable little hat and put on knickerbockers for the weekends would not be parted from her silk stockings and her high-heeled shoes. Nor was the post-war feminine ideal one of fruitful maturity or ripened wisdom or practiced grace. On the contrary: the quest of slenderness, the flattening of the breasts, the vogue of short skirts (even when short skirts still suggested the appearance of a little girl), the juvenile effect of the long waist,—all were signs that, consciously or unconsciously, the women of this decade worshiped not merely youth, but unripened youth: they wanted to be—or thought men wanted them to be—men's casual and light-hearted companions; not broad-hipped mothers of the race, but irresponsible playmates. Youth was their pattern, but not youthful innocence: the adolescent whom they imitated was a hard-boiled adolescent, who thought not in terms of romantic love, but in terms of sex, and who made herself desirable not by that sly art which conceals art, but frankly and openly. In effect, the woman of the Post-war Decade said to man, "You are tired and disillusioned, you do not want the cares of a family or the companionship of mature wisdom, you want exciting play, you want the thrills of sex without their fruition, and I will give them to you." And to herself she added, "But I will be free."

One indication of the revolution in manners which her headlong pursuit of freedom brought about was her rapid acceptance of the cigarette. Within a very few years millions of American women of all ages followed the lead of the flappers of 1920 and took up smoking. Custom still generally frowned upon their doing it on the street or in the office, and in the evangelical hinterlands the old taboo died hard; but in restaurants, at dinner parties and dances, in theater lobbies, and in a hundred other places they made the air blue. Here again the trend in advertising measured the trend in public opinion. At the beginning of the decade advertisers realized that it would have been suicidal to portray a woman smoking; within a few years, however, they ventured pictures of pretty girls imploring men to blow some of the smoke their way; and by the end of the decade billboards boldly displayed a smart-looking woman cigarette in hand, and in some of the magazines, despite floods of protests from rural readers, tobacco manufacturers were announcing that "now women may enjoy a companionable smoke with their husbands and brothers." . . .

Of far greater social significance, however, was the fact that men and women were drinking together. Among well-to-do people the serving of cocktails before dinner became almost socially obligatory. Mixed parties swarmed up to the curtained grills of speakeasies and uttered the mystic password, and girls along with men stood at the speakeasy bar with one foot on the old brass rail. The late afternoon cocktail party became a new American institution. When dances were held in hotels, the curious and rather unsavory custom grew up of hiring hotel rooms where reliable drinks could be served in suitable privacy; guests of both sexes lounged on the beds and tossed off mixtures of high potency. As houses and apartments became smaller, the country club became the social center of the small city, the suburb, and the summer resort; and to its pretentious clubhouse, every Saturday night, drove men and women (after a round of cocktails at somebody's house) for the weekly dinner dance. Bottles of White Rock and of ginger ale decked the tables, out of capacious masculine hip pockets came flasks of gin (once the despised and rejected of bartenders, now the most popular of all liquors), and women who a few years before would have gasped at the thought that they would ever be "under the influence of alcohol" found themselves matching the men drink for drink and enjoying the uproarious release. . . .

It [alcohol] lubricated, too, a new outspokenness between men and women. Thanks to the spread of scientific skepticism and especially to Sigmund Freud, the dogmas of the conservative moralists were losing force and the dogma that salvation lay in facing the facts of sex was gaining. An upheaval in values was taking place. Modesty, reticence, and chivalry were going out of style; women no longer wanted to be "ladylike" or could appeal to their daughters to be "wholesome"; it was too widely suspected that the old-fashioned lady had been a sham and that the "wholesome" girl was merely inhibiting a nasty mind and would come to no good end. "Victorian" and "Puritan" were becoming terms of opprobrium: up-to-date people thought of Victorians as old ladies with bustles and inhibitions, and of Puritans as blue-nosed, ranting spoilsports. It was better to be modern,—everybody wanted to be modern,—and sophisticated, and smart, to smash the conventions and to be devastatingly frank. And with a cocktail glass in one's hand it was easy at least to be frank.

"Listen with a detached ear to a modern conversation," wrote Mary Agnes Hamilton in 1927, "and you will be struck, first, by the restriction of the vocabulary, and second, by the high proportion in that vocabulary of words such as, in the older jargon, 'no lady could use.'" With the taste for strong liquors went a taste for strong language. To one's lovely dinner partner, the inevitable antithesis for "grand" and "swell" had become "lousy." An unexpected "damn" or "hell" uttered on the New York stage was no longer a signal for the sudden sharp laughter of shocked surprise; such words were becoming the commonpalce of everyday talk. The barroom anecdote of the decade before now went the rounds of aristocratic bridge tables. Every one wanted to be unshockable; it was delightful to be considered a little shocking; and so the competition in boldness of talk went on until for a time, as Mrs. Hamilton put it, a conversation in polite circles was like a room decorated entirely in scarlet—the result was over-emphasis, stridency, and eventual boredom.

Along with the new frankness in conversation went a new frankness in books and the theater. Consider, for example, the themes of a handful of the best plays produced in New York during the decade: *What Price Glory,* which represented the amorous marines interlarding their talk with epithets new to the stage; *The Road to Rome,* the prime comic touch of which was the desire of a Roman matron to be despoiled by the Carthaginians; *Strange Interlude,* in which a wife who found there was insanity in her husband's family but wanted to give him a child decided to have the child by an attractive young doctor, instead of by her husband, and forthwith fell in love with the doctor; . . .

The same thing was true of the novels of the decade; one after another, from *Jurgen* and *Dark Laughter* through the tales of Michael Arlen to *An American Tragedy* and *The Sun Also Rises* and *The Well of Loneliness* and *Point Counter Point,* they dealt with sex with an openness or a cynicism or an unmoral objectivity new to the English-speaking world. Bitterly the defenders of the Puritan code tried to stem the tide, but it was too strong for them. They banned *Jurgen*—and made a best seller of it and a public reputation for its author. . . .

With the change in manners went an inevitable change in morals. Boys and girls were becoming sophisticated about sex at an earlier age; it was symptomatic that when the authors of *Middletown* asked 241 boys and 315 girls of high-school age to mark as true or false, according to their opinion, the extreme statement, "Nine out of every ten boys and girls of high-school age have petting parties," almost precisely half of them marked it as true. How much actual intercourse there was among such young people it is of course impossible to say; but the lurid stories told by Judge Lindsay—of girls who carried contraceptives in their vanity cases, and of "Caroline," who told the judge that fifty-eight girls of her acquaintance had had one or more sex experiences without a single pregnancy resulting—were matched by the gossip current in many a town. Whether prostitution increased or decreased during the decade is likewise uncertain; but certain it is that the prostitute was faced for the first time with an amateur competition of formidable proportions. . . .

The petting party, which in the first years of the decade had been limited to youngsters in their teens and twenties, soon made its appearance among older men and women: when the gin-flask was passed about the hotel bedroom during a dance, or the musicians stilled their saxophones during the Saturday-night party at the country club, men of affairs and women with half-grown children had their little taste of raw sex. One began to hear of young girls, intelligent and well born, who had spent weekends with men before marriage and had told their prospective husbands everything and had been not merely forgiven, but told that there was nothing to forgive; a little "experience," these men felt, was all to the good for any girl. Millions of people were moving toward acceptance of what a *bon-vivant* of earlier days had said was his idea of the proper state of morality—"A single standard, and that a low one." . . .

There was an unmistakable and rapid trend away from the old American code toward a philosophy of sex relations and of marriage wholly new to the country: toward a feeling that the virtues of chastity and fidelity had been rated too highly, that there was something to be said for what Mrs. Bertrand Russell defined as "the right, equally shared by men and women, to free participation in sex experience," that it was not necessary for girls to deny themselves this right before marriage or even for husbands and wives to do so after marriage. It was in acknowledgment of the spread of this feeling that Judge Lindsay proposed, in 1927, to establish "companionate marriage" on a legal basis. He wanted to legalize birth control (which although still outlawed, was by this time generally practiced or believed in by married couples in all but the most ignorant classes) and to permit legal marriage to be terminated at any time in divorce by mutual consent, provided there were no children. His suggestion created great consternation and was widely and vigorously denounced; but the mere fact that it was seriously debated showed how the code of an earlier day had been shaken. The revolution in morals was in full swing. . . .

Another result of the revolution was that manners became not merely different, but—for a few years—unmannerly. It was no mere coincidence that during this decade hostesses—even at small parties—found that their guests couldn't be bothered to speak to them on arrival or departure; that "gate-crashing" at dances became an accepted practice; that thousands of men and women made a point of not getting to dinners within half an hour of the appointed time lest they seem insufficiently *blasé;* that house parties of flappers and their wide-trousered swains left burning cigarettes on the mahogany tables, scattered ashes light-heartedly on the rugs, took the porch cushions out in the boats and left them there to be rained on, without apology; or that men and women who had had—as the old phrase went—"advantages" and considered themselves highly civilized, absorbed a few cocktails and straightway turned a dinner party into a boisterous rout, forgetting that a general roughhouse was not precisely the sign of a return to the Greek idea of the good life. The old bars were down, no new ones had been built, and meanwhile the pigs were in the pasture. Some day, perhaps, the ten years which followed the war may aptly be known as the Decade of Bad Manners. . . .

There were not, to be sure, many Brett Ashleys* in the United States during the Post-war Decade. Yet there were millions to whom in some degree came for a time the same disillusionment and with it the same unhappiness. They could not endure a life without values, and the only values they had been trained to understand were being undermined. Everything seemed meaningless and unimportant. Well, at least one could toss off a few drinks and get a kick out of physical passion and forget that the world was crumbling. . . . And so the saxophones wailed and the gin-flask went its rounds and the dancers made their treadmill circuit with half-closed eyes, and the outside world, so merciless and so insane, was shut away for a restless night. . . .

It takes time to build up a new code. Not until the decade was approaching its end did there appear signs that the revolutionists were once more learning to be at home in their world, to rid themselves of their obsession with sex, to adjust themselves emotionally to the change in conventions and standards, to live the freer and franker life of this new era gracefully, and to discover among the ruins of the old dispensation a new set of enduring satisfactions.

* Editor's Note: From Ernest Hemingway's *The Sun Also Rises* (1926).

20 ∽ The Rebellion of the Intellectuals, 1912–1917*

[Author's Note] *Most historians have followed Allen by looking to the twenties for the repudiation of the genteel tradition. Henry F. May, Margaret Byrne Professor at the University of California at Berkeley, concedes that the post-war reaction broke the back of American innocence but he isolates the five years between 1912 and 1917 as the true watershed separating Victorian thought from modernity. The innocent cultural rebellion against old-fashioned mores that was sparked in those years was admittedly just a crack in the surface, but May argues that it opened the chasm that became clearly visible in Coolidge's America. Thus, for May, the intellectual roots of the "lost generation" ran deeper than is ordinarily thought. It follows as a corollary that World War I alone did not produce the social and cultural upheaval that followed the 1918 armistice.*

As the nineteen-twenties move from memory into history, a standard picture of the decade emerges from reminiscence and research into the textbooks. This picture is a puzzling one. The decade is still, as it was in the thirties, the last island of normalcy and isolation between wars and crises. Yet it is also, clearly, a period of major cultural revolution. Both the "revolt of the highbrows" and the "rebellion of youth," first sketched by F. L. Allen, are a standard part of our semiofficial self-picture. In response to current historical fashions and perhaps also to their own changing

* By Henry F. May. Reprinted with permission from *American Quarterly* (published by the University of Pennsylvania), III, no. ii (Summer, 1956), pages 114–126.

worries about their country, historians are giving more attention to the revolutionary aspect of this conservative decade.

Having dealt with other revolutions, historians should be able to appreciate both the importance and complexity of this one. For instance, they should be able to avoid taking to task the rebellious intellectuals of the twenties in the manner of some critics of the forties. The spokesmen of a revolution are not, after all, its sole cause, and a healthy regime is seldom overthrown. Yet anybody, today, must recognize that revolutions are expensive. They may release, as this one certainly did, a burst of creative vigor; but they inevitably leave behind division, hatred, and shock. In the twenties, for instance, beliefs and customs that still commanded the deepest loyalties of one part of the population became to another group a dead and repressive Genteel Tradition, to be ceremonially flouted whenever possible. Suspicions dating from this cultural cleavage still poison the air. The historian must hope that analysis of the revolution and its causes can eventually help a little to clear away some of the resentment.

Starting backward, as historians must, we arrive immediately at the First World War, and there many have stopped. It is obvious that America's first major venture into world tragedy, with its rapid cycle of national exaltation, exhaustion, and revulsion played a very large part in the emotional life of the postwar rebels. By contrast with 1918 or 1919 or even 1925, hundreds of autobiographies paint the prewar period as a time of unity, moderation, progress, and sheltered childhood.

Yet we all know that postwar reminiscence, whether of the old plantation or the old literary culture, is a dubious guide for history. Those who have looked even briefly at the social and literary criticism of the prewar years know that the period 1912–1917[1] was itself, for some, a time of doubt and fragmentation, of upheaval in ideas, of the disintegration of tradition—in other words it was a pre-revolutionary or early revolutionary period. Nearly every phenomenon of the twenties from Freudianism to expatriation or the abandonment of politics was present before the war, on a smaller scale and with certain differences. If we can recapture any of the meaning or content of this prewar ferment, we may be able to understand better in what sense the revolution of the twenties was and was not postwar. In this way we may even get a few suggestions as to the perennially baffling problem of the relation between ideas and events.

In an essay published in 1913 George Santayana made an attempt to catch and pin down on paper "The Intellectual Temper of the Age." To do this for one's own time is one of the hardest tasks a writer can undertake, yet for anybody who has been for a while immersed in the records of that period it is astonishing how well this brilliant essay seems to order and illuminate the times. To Santayana it seemed that "the civilisation characteristic of Christendom has not disappeared, yet another civilisation has begun to take its place."[2] In the resulting age of confusion and transition, men were giving up the search for lasting values and firm intellectual conclusions. Instead of these, they were placing a premium on sheer vitality, on movement, change, and emotion. According to Santayana, who sometimes enjoyed but did not admire this taste, the result was that in thought and art, his generation was "in full career toward disintegration."[3]

Whether or not one shares Santayana's cool disapproval of the tendencies of his day, the vitalist spirit he describes stares out from the sources. One recognizes on all sides its gaiety, its irresponsibility, its love of change, and also its contempt for reason. And it does not take much knowledge of American intellectual history to know that this spirit meant trouble. For a century and a half the dominant ideas in the national faith had been a confidence in secure moral values and a belief in progress. These two commitments had often been in conflict and formed at best a somewhat unstable compound. Now both at once were brought under devastating attack.

If one starts, as Santayana does, with philosophy, the tendencies he describes emerge very clearly. The young intellectuals of America were still most widely influenced by pragmatism, by what Morton G. White has called the revolt against formalism. Experience and movement were reality; potentiality more important than actuality. Dewey's program for intelligence remaking both the world and itself probably attracted the largest number of conscious disciples, some of them, like Randolph Bourne, soon to break away in a more emotionally satisfying direction. But it may well be that the influence of James, with his catholic and dangerous acceptance of the irrational, personal, and mysterious went deeper in a generation nourished on idealism. Emerson, universally read though misunderstood and underrated, and Whitman, the sole American patron of some of the rebels, as well as the German idealists casually studied in college courses, must have prepared them for a philosophy of intuition. Whatever the reason, it was the destructive elements in pragmatism that were the most influential. The avant-garde of 1912–17, the aggressive young innovators, were perfectly willing to see all of life as an experiment. But their purpose in experimenting was rather to express themselves and experience emotion than to solve problems in a disciplined manner.

Those who were sensitive to Atlantic breezes felt most keenly the swelling winds of antirationalism, which had been gathering force for a long time. Nietzsche, for long known vaguely by the American public as an Anti-christ, was becoming a major prophet. The most vigorous, though not the most accurate, of his American interpreters was H. L. Mencken, who in a widely read and widely praised book published first in 1908 and again in 1913 used the German prophet to belabor religion, women, and, most roughly of all, democracy in his already familiar manner.[4] But the most fashionable of Europeans was the still living and lecturing Henri Bergson, who pushed the current tendency to an extreme, contending that reality, being in constant flux and change, is only distorted by efforts to think about it and must be apprehended through intuition. His was not the only, but it was probably the dominant direction in which philosophy was moving in 1913, and there is plenty of evidence that he was extraordinarily attractive to up-to-date American intellectuals. Irving Babbitt, already an alarmed defender of traditional values, saw the rise of Bergsonism as the culmination of a long, deplorable irrationalist trend, and found it in 1912 "allied with all that is violent and extreme in contemporary life from syndicalism to "futurist' painting."[5]

Psychology, as well as philosophy, was dealing heavy blows to dominant assumptions and beliefs. From the time of Freud's famous trip to Clark University in 1908, the Viennese theories cropped up in popular magazines and political treatises as well as learned journals. Whether or not, as his supporters claim, Freud is to be regarded as himself a brave and determined champion of reason, the first impact of his doctrines in the United States seemed to confirm and deepen the hedonism, emotionalism, and egocentricity that were beginning to spread so widely.[6] On the other hand, Behaviorism, a movement launched in its most dogmatic form by John B. Watson in 1912, had to wait for its vogue until after the war.[7] Its extreme practicalism, its rejection not only of reason but of consciousness, its suspicion of emotion, did not fit the tastes of the prewar rebels.

It does not need demonstrating that restless and vigorous innovation in the graphic arts got its American start before the war. Two major tendencies already dazzled the intellectuals and startled the public. One was apparently native, the harsh and sometimes violent Ash Can realism of Sloan, Bellows and the *Masses* cartoons. The other was imported from Paris, and consisted of a kaleidoscopic series of schools of experiment in form and technique. Commenting on "Current Impressionism," a term already well out of date but helpful as a catch-all, Louis Weinberg extended his observations from and beyond contemporary art:

> Impressionism as a technique is a means of recording the transitory nature of phenomena and the fluidity of motion. As a principle it is based on a philosophy of change. . . . But this is not alone a description of the art of our times. It is the very essence of our lives.[8]

Wherever the impressionist or vitalist tendency arose, it was expressed most frequently and characteristically not in painting or philosophy, but in politics and literature. These are the forms in which most American cultural change has been recorded, and it is to them that we must turn for a slightly closer look at prewar tendencies. Santayana's brilliant summary suggests that in politics alone the current drift toward fragmentation and chaos may have reversed itself in the constructive and integrating (though to Santayana most uncongenial) movement towards collectivism.[9] In this one opinion, regarding an area which concerned him little, I think Santayana missed the current drift and underrated the force of his own generalization. It is true that progressivism, optimistic, gradual, and in some forms mildly collectivist, was the officially dominant ideology; and that socialism was a swelling movement on the left that seemed to many sober Americans to possess the future. Yet both these political tendencies were in the early teens already under devastating attack, and from much the same irrationalist quarter.

Progressivism in all its varieties took for granted one or both of the two fundamental assumptions which had so far underlain the whole American political tradition. One of these was that we possess secure criteria by which we can judge our political achievement, the other that human beings are able consciously to remold their environment. Now both of these basic assumptions were being seriously shaken by new doctrines that had penetrated the house of progressivism itself.

Recent studies have shown that moral standards of a highly traditional sort motivated a great many of the prewar progressives. Truth and falsehood, good and evil, stand out in nearly all the speeches of Theodore Roosevelt and Wilson and good men threw out bad in most American cities. These venerable distinctions were the first to go; the younger progressive intellectuals, nourished on Dewey and H. G. Wells, were quite willing to throw out moral categories and rely on the shaping intelligence. On a popular level Lincoln Steffens spread the picture of the good boss and the honest crook. James Harvey Robinson, speaking for the main organ of the pragmatic progressives, lumped together as obsolete the ideals of "sound doctrine, consistency, fidelity to conscience, eternal verities, immutable human nature, and the imprescriptable rights of man."[10]

With these went the state and law, the traditional locus and method of American reform. Many of the ablest political theorists of various schools, led by the brilliant Harold Laski, were redefining the state almost out of existence. To some it was a congeries of associations, to others the tool of a class, to still others the expression of the wish of those at present in authority. Its acts were no more final and deserved no greater obedience than those of other human groups, and it was less likely than many to be rationally motivated. Similarly, law, to the followers of the French positivist Leon Duguit or the American Roscoe Pound was no longer either the embodiment of a principle nor the command of a sovereign, but the complex resultant of social forces, prevailing opinion, and judicial will.

There remained the conscious intelligence, remolding the goals of action together with its methods. This was a moving conception, and a sufficient loyalty for many in this generation. Yet this too was seriously menaced by ideas that were attractive to the youngest generation of progressives. From the new and flourishing disciplines of sociology, anthropology and social psychology came an increasingly fashionable emphasis on custom and group emotion. It was sometimes hard to see what function this newest tendency left for intelligence and purpose.[11]

Walter Lippmann's two prewar studies, *A Preface to Politics* (1913) and *Drift and Mastery* (1914) bring together the pragmatist attack on tradition and the implicit Freudian attack on pragmatism. Appealing for a radically instrumental state, he denounces the "routineers" who rely on political machinery, law, and conventional morality. His fellow progressives seem to draw most of his fire from their naïve adherence to literal numerical democracy and narrow utilitarian goals. What is needed in politics is passion and creative emotion, still of course somehow constructively channeled and used by the far-seeing for purposes which will transcend woman suffrage or the eight-hour day.

> . . . the goal of action is in its final analysis aesthetic and not moral—a quality of feeling instead of conformity to rule.[12]

This formulation seems to me far closer to the view of postwar literary intellectuals than to that of the progressive standard-bearers. And the sources are explicit. Lippmann's friend Graham Wallas, the British author of *Human Nature in Politics*[13] had opened the eyes of his Harvard seminar to political psychology. Steffens had helped to guide Lippmann and so, in a negative direction, had his brief experience with municipal socialism in Schenectady. But beyond these immediate guides one finds recurring references to James, Nietzsche and Bergson and frequent, specific acknowledgment of the work of Freud.[14]

All these new insights enriched the social sciences, and for many they doubtless furnished in practice new sources of power and freedom. Traditional progressivism, with its facile assumptions and sometimes shallow purposes needed—and for that matter still needs—rethinking. Yet much had been accomplished under the auspices of ideas that were beginning to seem stale and boring. And the new beliefs that buzzed and swarmed through the immediate postwar years were not easy to introduce into the progressive hive. To combine Lippmann or Laski with Wilson was, and soon proved to be, as difficult as to match Bergson and Nietzsche with Lyman Abbott.

It is tempting to wonder whether the actual practical difficulties of progressivism from about 1914 to 1917 were not related in part to confusion of purposes and motives. It is true at least that the Wilsonian impetus began to bog down in these years. Already one finds in the up-to-the-minute *New Republic* troubled editorials that ask the common postwar question: what has happened to the progressives?[15]

On the far left much the same process was taking place, whether one labels it fertilization or disintegration or both. Not the Marxian dialectic, but the Bergsonian and mystical syndicalism of Sorel or the anarchism of Max Stirner or Emma Goldman seemed most exciting to the younger radical intellectuals.[16] Not the earnest socialism of Milwaukee or Schenectady, wtih its respectability and its reliance on the discredited machinery of the state, but the romantic activism of the I.W.W. captured the emotions of the sympathizers. One of America's waves of labor violence, running through the Northwest, Colorado, West Virginia and other centers of direct action, reflecting the primitive brutality of employers' methods in the same areas, aroused the generous emotions and seemed to some to make political action irrelevant. The climax came in 1912 at Lawrence and in 1913 at Paterson, when the I.W.W. penetrated the East and the writers and artists went to its aid, when Bill Haywood was a Greenwich Village social lion and John Reed staged an immense pageant in Madison Square Garden with the letters I.W.W. flaming from the roof in red electric signs ten feet high. Even Lippmann, viewing radicalism from the outside, approved the I.W.W. rather than the Socialist Party as less formalist and more in possession of the kind of emotional force that needed only to be constructively channeled.[17]

Naturally, when Max Eastman, a young man of impeccable ministerial stock, joined the Socialist Party, he chose the left wing rather than the gradualists. Under Eastman's editorship the *Masses,* focus of so much later radical nostalgia, became perhaps even more clearly than the sober *New Republic* the organ of youth. Publishing the magnificent and not always political cartoons of Sloan and Bellows, an occasional Picasso drawing, stories by Sherwood Anderson, and reporting by Reed, it fought for the new literature and the new sexual morality as well as the social revolution. The *Masses* was rich in humor and human emotion—qualities often enough lacking on the far left—and practically negligible in social program. Smashing idols was, in these years as after the war, a flourishing business, while Socialism as a political movement was already losing momentum in 1914–16.[18]

More spectacularly than anywhere else, the new spirit of 1910 or 1912 to 1917 was reflected in a literary renaissance. The story of this sudden creative outburst has often been told, and only two points need making for our present purpose. One of these is that literary departures in the prewar years were closely related to contemporary movements in other fields of thought, the other that prewar writing contains in embryo nearly all the developments of the twenties.

Here too the stimulus came in large part from abroad. Young Americans, brought up on Matthew Arnold and Thackeray, were following before he gave it the advice of Yeats at the *Poetry* dinner in 1912 to forget London and look to Paris for all that was excellent.[19] In Kroch's bookstore in Chicago, in the translations issued by a series of daring new publishers, in the eager if undiscriminating reviews by the young critics, this generation of rebels was nourished on a whole series of movements extending over the last generation in Europe. All the writers that had for so long been belaboring the European bourgeoisie—French symbolists and decadents and naturalists, Scandinavian pessimists and social critics, Russian apostles of mysticism and emotion; even from England D. H. Lawrence as well as Shaw, suddenly began to penetrate the American barrier. What this series of reagents produced was a series of explosions, and what exploded was more than the genteel tradition in literature, more than conventional moral categories. With the conventions of literary form and language went the underlying assumptions about thought and communication. Randolph Bourne perhaps described this grand explosion better than he realized in June, 1917:

> What becomes more and more apparent to the readers of Dostoevsky, however, is his superb modern healthiness. He is healthy because he has no sense of any dividing line between the normal and the abnormal, or even between the sane and the insane.[20]

When Harriet Monroe, full of civic feeling as well as poetic zeal, founded *Poetry* in 1912 she seemed to tap immediately a rich underground gusher of poetic impulse. Soon the flood of experiment became too thick and varied even for *Poetry* to contain and overflowed into *Others* and the *Little Review*. As in the visual arts, a rapid series of schools succeeded each other, but perhaps the literary movement most characteristic of the period, and most obviously related to its philosophic tendencies was that of the Imagists, with its manifestoes in favor of complete freedom, concentration on the fleeting and immediate image for its own sake, and refusal to assign an image any "external" meaning or reference. Already before the war the revolution in the use of language was under way toward its ultimate destinations; Joyce was being published in the London *Egoist* and Gertrude Stein, settled in Paris, had developed her opinions and her characteristic style.

It would be misleading to divide this literary outpouring into precise categories, yet one can find suggestions of two emergent ways of thinking and feeling among writers. One group demanded freedom from European forms, confidence in emotion and spontaneity, and in general preached democratic optimism in the Whitman tradition. The other, more disciplined but also more deeply rebellious against American culture, called for concentration, rejection of irrelevant moral and political purposes, and the development of conscious intellectual aristocracy.

Obviously the former, democratic and optimist group is more distant than the other from postwar directions. This is the tendency one associates particularly with the sudden and brief Chicago Renaissance, with Sandburg and Lindsay and Miss Monroe, though it is found also in other areas, for instance in the organized and vigorous character of what Francis Hackett labeled and dated forever as Miss Amy Lowell's "Votes for Poetry movement."[21] Yet even the most exuberant of the Chicago poets were, like contemporary political radicals, destroying for the sake of redemption, like Sandburg's personified city "Shovelling, wrecking, planning, building, breaking, rebuilding."

And even in Chicago pessimistic and sceptical tendencies were also, and had long been, at work. Dreiser's not exactly rosy picture of American city life was finally finding its audience; and the small town, from E. A. Robinson's New England Tilbury town to Masters' Middlewestern Spoon River, was preparing the way for Winesburg and Gopher Prairie. In the bosom of *Poetry* magazine, at the official heart of the Chicago movement, Ezra Pound, the magazine's foreign editor, was chafing at its cover slogan, the statement of Whitman that "to have great poets there must be great audiences too." Pound preferred Dante's pronouncement that the wisest in the city is "He whom the fools hate worst" and denied that poets have any need for the rabble.

> It is true that the great artist has always a great audience, even in his lifetime; but it is not the *vulgo* but the spirits of irony and of destiny and of humor, sitting with him.[22]

In that sentence lies the germ of a dozen ponderous manifestoes of the postwar Young Intellectuals. Pound stayed on *Poetry* long enough to persuade Miss Monroe to publish Eliot's "Prufrock" in 1915 and then found a refuge from uplift and Whitmanism in the *Little Review.*

In the Eastern centers of the new literary movement the mixture of optimism and nihilism, of reform and rejection was somewhat different. Harvard, which was incubating an extraordinary number of important writers, seemed to produce a strange and special mixture of ideas.[23] The dominant note in its teaching of literature was aestheticism, worship of Europe, and contempt for the native production. Irving Babbitt's vigorous attack on democratic sentimentality was already a major influence. Yet Walter Lippmann, for one, managed to combine presidency of the Harvard Socialist Club with assisting Professor Santayana. A certain survival of Emersonian and Puritan responsibility seems to have been a part of the prevalent passionate concern for literature. America might be vulgar and materialistic and nearly hopeless; if so one's duty was to search the harder for seeds of literary springtime, and literary revival would bring social regeneration as well. Like so many writers after the war, Van Wyck Brooks went to Europe to look for these seeds. He found in London in 1913–14 Ezra Pound, T. S. Eliot, John Gould Fletcher, Conrad Aiken, Elinor Wylie, Robert Frost and Walter Lippmann.[24] Across the channel he could already have run into an equally significant group of fellow-countrymen. It was in London that Brooks began to struggle seriously with the typical problem of the expatriate of the next decade: the love of European tradition and the nostalgic turning toward American vitality. He solved this problem by writing, in London in 1914, the book that most influenced the writers of the next decade, an attack on the Genteel Tradition and an appeal for a literary renaissance that seemed then, as its title implies, to mark an arrival and not just a beginning: *America's Coming-of-Age.*

From here we can see, even more clearly than Santayana could in 1913, the unrest, the disintegration of old standards, the search for vitality and movement that already was under way at that time.[25] We know, too, that what was then unrest later became cultural revolution and angry intellectual civil war. This brings us to the compelling question, what started it all? Why did this search for novelty, this gay destruction of traditional standards, occur at just this moment in the midst of an apparently placid and contented period?

This is hardly a question that can be answered with certainty. All that we know for sure is that a movement so general and noticeable in the prewar years was not started by the war. Perhaps the most obvious forces at work in early twentieth-century civilization were technological change and urban growth, but these had been at work reshaping American culture for several generations and do not afford a direct and simple explanation for the sudden restlessness of 1912–17. Moreover, an increase of mechanistic materialism rather than a new vitalism would seem a more easily understandable product of machine civilization. It may be that the prewar rebellion was in part a protest against such a long-run tendency; in 1915 the *Nation* suggested that the rising "Bergsonian school . . . owes not a little of its popularity to its expression of revolt from the dreary materialistic determinism of the closing years of the last century."[26]

One is tempted to wonder whether the new physics was at work already disintegrating the comparatively simple universe of nineteenth-century science. It seems, however, that although the Einstein revolution was being discussed before the war by American scientists and reported in the serious periodical press, it did not directly affect as yet the literary and political intellectuals to any great extent, and it was not, as it became after the war, a newspaper sensation.[27]

In part the American intellectual rebellion may be considered merely a belated phase of an European antirationalist tendency. Yet it remains puzzling that Nietzsche and Dostoevsky and Baudelaire waited for their most telling American impact until they competed with Freud and Joyce. Part of the violence of the American literary and intellectual battles of the next decade arises from the fact that influences that had gradually permeated European thought presented themselves to many Americans all at once and in their extreme forms.

The time and special character of the prewar rebellion were, I believe, determined in part by the very surface placidity of the Progressive Era. Traditional American beliefs in moral certainty and inevitable progress had for some time been subjected to inner strain and external attack, yet in the prewar decade, for the last time, the official custodians of culture were able to maintain and defend a common front. Yet these almost hereditary leaders—Roosevelt and Royce and Howells in their several spheres—

were growing weaker. A new generation, full of confidence and provided with leisure and libraries, was fairly literally looking for trouble. What attracts us about the standard culture of America in the early years of the century is its confident consensus, its lack of passion and violence. Passion and violence were exactly the demand of the young intellectuals of 1913 and 1914, of Lippmann and Brooks and Bourne and Pound. This was what they wanted, and this was what they got.

The war, then, was not the cause of the cultural revolution of the twenties. It played, however, the immense part that the Civil War played in the economic and political revolution of the mid-nineteenth century, speeding, widening and altering in kind a movement already under way.

The experiences of 1917–19 darkened and soured the mood of the rebels. Even at its most iconoclastic and even in those spokesmen who adopted the most pessimistic doctrines, the prewar renaissance was always exuberant. Pound, amid his fierce negations, still found it possible to make his famous and somewhat rash prophecy that the coming American Risorgimento would "make the Italian Renaissance look like a tempest in a teapot!"[28] The rejection of easy rationalism, the spurning of dull politics were to make America better and brighter. In the war and its aftermath however the rebellious generation learned something of the price of destruction and experienced personally both tragedy and (in 1919) failure. Many who had been rebellious optimists became despairing nihilists and those who had already been preaching the futility of conscious effort preached it with different emotional corollaries.

The other effect of the war was that the disintegration of traditional ideas spread far more widely among the population. Most of the prewar rebellion was confined to a small and isolated, though articulate and potentially influential, group of intellectuals. As yet the overwheming bulk of the people took for granted the truth of the old political and moral slogans. As long as this was so rebels could be ignored or patronized; they did not have to be feared and fought. Without the political events of 1917–19 traditional beliefs might perhaps have been slowly adapted to new realities instead of, for the moment, either smashed or blindly defended. And without the currents of doubt and disintegration already abroad, these political events themselves might have lacked their willing and ready Cassandras.

In 1913 *Sons and Lovers, A Preface to Politics,* and *Winds of Doctrine* were published, but *Pollyanna* and *Laddie* were the best-sellers. In 1925 the best-seller list itself had to find place for *An American Tragedy.*

See Daniel Bell, "Marxian Socialism in the United States," in D. D. Egbert and Stow Persons, eds., *Socialism and American Life* (Princeton, N.J.: Princeton University Press, 1952), I, 289–90.

Walter Lippmann, *Preface to Politics,* pp. 277–78.

See David L. Shannon, *The Socialist Party of America, A History* (New York: The Macmillan Company, 1955). As Shannon and other historians of socialism have pointed out, the apparent revival of the Socialist Party in the big Debs vote of 1920 is misleading. It belongs in the category of protest rather than party success.

Harriet Monroe, *A Poet's Life* (New York: The Macmillan Company, 1938), p. 337.

Randolph Bourne, "The Immanence of Dostoevsky," *The Dial, LXIII* (1917), 25.

In the *New Republic,* November 10, 1917, p. 52.

Ezra Pound, "The Audience," *Poetry, A Magazine of Verse,* V (1914–15), 30.

See the following helpful autobiographies of Harvard graduates: Malcolm Cowley, *Exile's Return* (New York: W. W. Norton & Company, 1934); Harold E. Stearns, *The Street I Know* (New York: L. Furman, 1935); Van Wyck Brooks, *Scenes and Portraits* (New York: E. P. Dutton & Co., 1954).

Brooks, *op. cit.,* pp. 123–48, 210 ff.

The same traits that one finds in the ideas of the period characterize much of its ocial life. Ragtime and the dance craze, the furore over alleged white slave dislosures, in 1913 seem to prefigure the feverishness and the moral divisions of he postwar decade.

'rom a review of Croly's *Progressive Democracy,* which the *Nation* associates vith the Bergson influence (April 29, 1915), pp. 469–70.

'his impression comes from an examination of periodicals and is confirmed by nd intensive though brief examination of popular scientific literature by Robert . Sumpter.

ound to Harriet Monroe, 24 September, 1914, in D. D. Paige, ed., *The Letters f Ezra Pound 1907–1941* (New York: Harcourt, Brace and Co., 1950), p. 10.

NOTES

1. Through this essay I treat this period as one instead of di 1914. The outbreak of the war in Europe shocked Americar not immediately become their main preoccupation. Until 1916, radical and progressive politics, together with the ne sophical tendencies, get more space than the war in the periodicals.
2. George Santayana, *Winds of Doctrine* (London and New ner's Sons, 1913), p. 1.
3. *Ibid.*, p. 10.
4. Henry L. Mencken, *The Philosophy of Friedrich Nietzsc* Co., 1918).
5. Irving Babbitt, "Bergson and Rousseau," *Nation,* Novem One of the more influential of the considerable number appearing in these years was H. M. Kallen, *William Jan* (Chicago: University of Chicago Press, 1914). There is periodical discussion from 1911.
6. For a helpful review see Frederick J. Hoffman, *Freudi Mind* (Baton Rouge, La.: Louisiana State University P impact of Freud and many other foreign influences is works of Floyd Dell, one of Freud's important America most specifically with these influences in his retrospe *bondage* (New York: George H. Doran Co., 1926).
7. See Lucille C. Birnbaum, "Behaviorism in the 1920's," (1955), 15–30, esp. p. 20.
8. Louis Weinberg, "Current Impressionism," *New Repul* 124–25.
9. George Santayana, *Winds of Doctrine,* p. 10.
10. James H. Robinson, "A Journal of Opinion," *New Re* 9–10.
11. An account of all these tendencies in prewar thought, t ography, can be found in two helpful summaries. Thes *Pragmatic Revolt in Politics* (New York: The Macmil C. E. Merriam and H. E. Barnes, eds., *A History of Times* (New York: The Macmillan Company, 1924).
12. Walter Lippmann, *A Preface to Politics* (New Yorl p. 200.
13. London: A. Constable and Co., 1908.
14. *e.g.*, Walter Lippmann, *Drift and Mastery* (New Yo pp. 249, 274.
15. *e.g.*, January 16, 1915, pp. 6–8; November 6, 1915, 159–61; July 1, 1916, pp. 211–13.

VII ~ The 1920's: Summary and Suggestions

21 ∽ The Twenties: A New Historiographical Frontier*

[Author's Note] *In the following pages, Burl Noggle of Louisiana State University explores the 1920's as a new frontier in American historiography. While he finds some areas of this arresting decade neglected, he predicts that scholarly revision now underway will upgrade the general image of the period.*

"The Twenties" is an entrenched concept in American historiography, but the precise beginning and end of this priod, and evaluations of it, vary from writer to writer. Rare, however, is the historian who fails to conceptualize American history, about 1919–1929, as a distinct unit, sharply set off from (and usually in unfavorable contrast to) the history which preceded and followed it.[1] Even before the end of the 1920s historians had begun to write the history of the decade and to offer characterizations that have lingered ever since. In 1926, John Spencer Bassett wrote of the nation's recent "weariness of reforms and reformers." The country craved rest,[2] for it was, he said, "exhausted by the emotions produced by the World War." No concept has endured longer or been more pervasive among historians than the one which views the 1920s as a time of reaction and isolationism induced by the emotional experience of World War I. Historians alone did not originate this concept; old prewar progressives themselves gave expression to it in the mid-1920s.[3] In fact, historians have more than once reaffirmed the analyses and findings made during the

* By Burl Noggle. Reprinted with permission from *The Journal of American History,* VIII (September, 1966), pages 299–314.

1920s by journalists and other students of the contemporary scene. And it was a "retrospective journalist," Frederick Lewis Allen, who in *Only Yesterday* first blocked out the 1919–1929 decennary as a unit of study, portraying it as a unique segment of American life with a style all its own.[4]

Almost as soon as the 1920s crashed on Black Thursday, Allen began writing *Only Yesterday.* Ever since its appearance in 1931, when it was a Book-of-the-Month Club choice, his book has been a popular success and has been frequently reprinted. Whatever its appeal or its qualities, Allen's account, published within a year of the end of the decade, has deeply shaped historical recall of the 1920s. Merely to list the titles and subheadings of *Only Yesterday* is to summarize an impression of the period that has long dominated history textbooks, not to mention television and movie screenplays.[5]

Roger Butterfield suggested in 1957 that none of the studies published since the appearance of *Only Yesterday* had "essentially changed the over-all picture that Allen gave us."[6] But for historians who read through the work done on the 1920s over the past fifteen years, it soon becomes evident that Allen has not been revised so much as he has been transcended. Historians are not finding Allen wrong (indeed, he was remarkably accurate and discerning). Rather, they are moving beyond him, asking questions that he never considered, finding issues and themes and patterns that he never explored or formulated.

Most of this new activity has developed since 1950. Little of it appeared in the two decades following the publication of Allen's book. Instead, the approach to the 1920s throughout the 1930s continued for the most part to be one of breezy surveys in the Allen tradition; at best, there was an occasional detailed analysis of some isolated subject that Allen had outlined in cursory fashion.[7] In the Great Depression—and probably because of it—the economy of the 1920s did capture much attention, but mostly from economists, not from historians.[8]

A study of dissertation listings indicates that graduate students in the 1930s produced more studies of the 1920s than did their mentors. Whether the latter would themselves have published more if not burdened with direction of these studies is a conjecture. Less conjectural is the predominance of economic topics relevant to the 1920s shown in the list of dissertations accepted in American colleges and universities during the 1930s. Perhaps economists, if not economic historians, tend to concentrate on the present or the recent past; it seems significant that the economy of the

1920s was the subject of proportionately more dissertations in the decade that followed than in the two succeeding ones and that subjects such as diplomacy or social history, which were minimized or neglected in the 1930s, became more and more popular in the 1940s and 1950s.[9] Apart from those specializing in economics, it is clear that few graduate students (or for that matter, established historians) in the 1930s had discovered, or at least chosen, the 1920s as a field for research.

The domestic political history of the 1920s was neglected in the 1930s and continued to be neglected until the late 1950s.[10] As Henry F. May has suggested, by the early 1930s historians were already making the 1920s "an unfortunate interregnum" between progressivism and the New Deal.[11] Malcolm Cowley once recalled that the 1920s had been "an easy, quick, adventurous age, good to be young in; and yet on coming out of it one felt a sense of relief, as on coming out of a room too full of talk and people into the sunlight of the winter streets."[12] Evidently political historians in the 1930s felt this same sense of relief (or perhaps release). The emphasis of political historiography in the 1930s was upon progressives, Populists, Jacksonians—men whose programs had, it seemed, been preludes to the New Deal.[13]

In the 1930s the domestic New Deal may have drawn historians away from domestic politics of the 1920s, but foreign policy issues of the 1930s, if they did anything, stirred up an increased interest in the diplomatic history of the preceding decade. Selig Adler has written of an "isolationist tornado" in the 1930s, during which Americans, including historians, sought safety from world conflict through economic nationalism, neutrality legislation, and other maneuvers usually labeled "isolationist."[14] Although a few revisionist histories of World War I (histories criticizing America's entry into the war) began to appear in the 1920s, not until the mid-1930s did many professional historians begin to produce such studies.[15] Whether this was due to the presumed "tornado" of the 1930s is a moot question; but however they felt about World War I in that third decade American historians simply did not then form a monolithic bloc of isolationists in their approach to foreign policy of the 1920s. Most of them did declare the existence of isolationism during this decade, but as often as not they deplored it and saw it as contributing to those war tensions of the 1930s they were trying to avoid.[16]

From any perspective and to whatever purpose, neither diplomatic studies nor what may be loosely termed "social history" of the 1920s flourished in the 1930s. Although Allen, and before him Preston Slosson, had shown the potential in such a subject, only tentative appraisals appeared before 1960.[17] In the wartime and postwar 1940s, historians brought little if any more depth or perception to the 1920s than they had brought during the depression years. Much of the historical work on the 1920s done during and immediately after World War II might have been produced in the 1930s for all it differed from the studies coming out of that depressed decade. The same superficial appraisals, the same pale imitations of *Only Yesterday,* continued to find a market.[18]

Yet, just as they had in the 1930s, more cautious scholars in the 1940s added a few notable volumes to the small shelf of worthwhile studies made of the 1920s. Economists and economic historians continued to build up imposing mounds of evidence, although they often touched upon the 1920s only indirectly or as part of a larger theme. The National Bureau of Economic Research, as it had during the 1930s, published several formidable volumes.[19] From such statistics and other quantitative material, George Soule was able to publish an economic history that showed, as he saw it, "the main currents of the economy of the 'New Era' more fully than at any previous period of American history."[20]

Among doctoral studies on the 1920s, economic themes outnumbered all the rest during the 1940s, although diplomatic history made a striking gain.[21] Here, no doubt, World War II had in effect aroused interest in international relations and suggested questions to pursue in the diplomacy of the 1920s. Not until the 1950s would the political historiography of the 1920s begin to thrive, but already in the 1940s some excellent dissertations had been written.[22] The intellectual, or at least literary, history of the 1920s also began to attract more attention.[23]

Meantime, at the annual meetings of the American Historical Association and the Mississippi Valley Historical Association, the professionals made several tentative approaches to the 1920s and presented a few pioneering essays. Infrequent though they were, these papers about the decade indicated a slowly growing interest that would soon quicken at mid-century.[24]

A few excellent essays on domestic and international politics appeared during the 1940s, as did biographies of politicians prominent in the 1920s. By the mid-1940s old political figures out of the decade were publishing their recollections, some of which were to be useful to the historian.[25] At the very end of the 1940s Samuel Eldersveld wrote an important analysis of the presidential elections of the period from 1920 through 1948, demonstrating the shift taking place in metropolitan areas away from the

Republican and into the Democratic party after 1920. Within a few years, this shift of urban areas into the Democratic column was given a brilliant analysis by Samuel Lubell, and by the late 1950s historians began to find more and more of value in a study of the urban-rural tensions and conflicts of the 1920s that lay behind, or resulted from, this shift in the voting pattern.[26]

Intellectual historians of the 1920s did such significant work in the 1940s as appraisals of Freud's impact upon American thought and literature, the life of the expatriate intellectual in Paris, the critique of American society by the American intellectual, the Sacco-Vanzetti case, and the response of American liberals to the Russian revolution.[27] These and other themes of the decade's intellectual history have still not received an authoritative synthesis, but studies done in the 1940s clarified some of the categories which that synthesis must include.

By 1950, then, some largely discursive pioneer probing had been made into the period of the 1920s. But among historians the image of the decade had changed little from the brilliant panorama offered by Allen in 1931. After mid-century a massive analysis got under way, one which continues to take on greater depth, complexity, and intensity. By comparison with what has appeared since the early 1950s, studies on the 1920s before then were negligible in scope, meager in detail, and artless in analysis.

Doctoral studies of the 1920s showed a spectacular increase after 1950 with diplomatic history in clear ascendancy, followed closely by studies of domestic politics.[28] At the annual meetings of the two major historical associations between 1950 and 1963, historians presented some thirty-five papers dealing with the 1920s.[29] Many of these papers, or versions of them, were subsequently published. And since 1950 books and articles have all but deluged the student of the 1920s who hopes to stay afloat in this new wave of scholarship.

The Ku Klux Klan, that perennial symbol of the decade's intolerance, is now receiving close and documented study. Historians are not merely describing the Klan's bigotry and violence but are studying its place in local and national politics; they are correlating it with prohibitionist, rural, and fundamentalist elements in the population and are viewing it as a symptom of the social tensions that permeated the 1920s.[30] This emphasis on tensions in the decade—brought on by a conflict between an older, rural, Anglo-Protestant America and a newer, urban, and cosmopolitan one—may well be the most revealing and comprehensive concept that historians of the 1920s have recently brought to the period. The Klan, the Scopes trial at Dayton, Tennessee, the National Origins Act of 1924, and the defeat of Alfred E. Smith in 1928 are among the subjects that have gained new meaning when viewed within a rural-urban context.[31]

Other standard themes of the 1920s have also either assumed new dimensions or have been viewed from new perspectives. Ideas and outlooks on and by the business community have begun to be charted, and as a result some old views about the businessman of the 1920s have been weakened and others strengthened; in both cases the intellectual history of the decade has been expanded. Morrell Heald, studying business leadership in the 1920s, has found that even the most ardent defenders of profit-making stressed that "management must think more than ever before of the social implications of its policies." "Far from being completely immobilized in adulation of the status quo," in the 1920s business leaders recognized that drastic changes were occurring in American society and they had begun to explore "new solutions for new, or recently recognized problems." On the other hand, Otis Pease, who analyzed "the extent to which concepts of public responsibility existed in the national advertising industry [between 1920 and 1940]," writes with irony and an implied distaste for the work of the advertising men who talked the cant of "responsibility" while perfecting new ways of appealing to the American consumer.[32]

James W. Prothro's *Dollar Decade* is also unflattering to the businessmen of the 1920s. Prothro found six recurrent themes expressed by business leaders in the decade: "elitism, materialism, economic pre-eminence, stability, antipopulism, individualism." Men with such an outlook had so much concern for "the immediate and narrow interests of the economic elite" that they were "blind to the most urgent needs of the public at large." But John P. Gleason, while not denying the self-interest that business displayed in the 1920s, has found that debate and publicity on the McNary-Haugen plan among businessmen was "decidedly beneficial" to the American farmer. Although most businessmen opposed the plan, they did begin to realize that something must be done about the farm problem. The McNary-Haugen campaign "helped to prepare the business community for [New Deal farm] legislation of the 1930s."[33]

The literary life of the 1920s continues to provoke quality work. The American intellectual's encounter with Paris in the 1920s shows no signs of losing favor as a subject for study. This is evidenced by the continued appearance of memoirs by those who lived in Paris at the time and by the steady publication of works by intellectual historians. In a recent memoir Matthew Josephson, one of the more famous expatriates of the 1920s, has challenged the "fallacy of the Lost Generation." While Josephson grants that the impact upon Americans of World War I was immense, he nonetheless writes, "it is nonsense to hold that a generation of American youth were 'lost' or driven to despair as a result of that brief war."[34] But however they may be described, a swarm of Americans moved into or through Paris in the 1920s, there to write, to live, and often to find a "second country." Appraising the lure of Paris, Warren Susman has demonstrated why it was Paris, and Paris in the 1920s, that attracted the American expatriate.[35] And Louise Cowan's study of the Fugitive poets at Nashville in the 1920s has served as a reminder that literary colonies of the period were not limited to those of New York and Paris.[36]

Politics in the 1920s, all but neglected before mid-century, has now become a favored field for research. The three presidential elections of the decade have been faithfully measured and weighed, enough to confirm some old notions and to refute others. The legend of the "smoke-filled room" of 1920 has been scotched. The nomination of Harding was not due to a conspiracy by vested oil interests; neither was it due to Senate "bosses" dictating to the convention. A small group of Republican senators did dominate the convention, and they did work for Harding's nomination, but only as a solution to a deadlock and in a more or less open convention. Furthermore, Harding's election did not register a repudiation of the League of Nations.[37]

The intricacies of the 1924 election have begun to be spelled out. Historians have indicated the varied factions in the Democratic party at the time, the significance of the rural-urban split in the party, and the suicidal brawl that the Democrats made of their Madison Square Garden nominating conventions.[38] The Teapot Dome affair (traditionally seen chiefly as a morality play) has been viewed from several angles, including an appraisal of its effect in the 1924 campaign. The scandal rose out of the struggle over the conservation of natural resources, but once it had developed as a great party liability in the winter of 1923–1924, it provoked some high political drama and some ingenious maneuverings within and between the two major parties.[39] For the 1928 campaign, the strife over liquor and religion has retained its significance, but recent studies have deepened the analysis, revealed certain ambiguities in the subject, and —perhaps most importantly—examined the election on the state and local level.[40]

These studies of politics have begun to provide, for the first time, depth and complexity for the political history of the 1920s. The structure of the two major parties, the motives that drove certain men into, and others out of, politics, and the relationships of religion to nativism and of prohibition to elections have all been appraised. As a result, politics in the 1920s stands revealed as infinitely more varied and subtle than is suggested by the conventional references to "normalcy," the Ohio Gang, and "Keep Cool with Coolidge."[41]

An intriguing but most debatable theme that political historians lately have enlarged upon is that of reform in the 1920s. Studies have begun to reveal survivals of Progressivism and preludes to the New Deal in the decade. Clarke Chambers has found a strong social welfare movement at work in the period, one concerned with child labor, slums, poor housing, and other problems that Progressives before the 1920s and New Dealers afterward also sought to alleviate. Preston J. Hubbard has studied the Muscle Shoals controversy of the 1920s and has demonstrated the essential role that Progressives in the decade played in laying the basis for the New Deal's TVA system. Donald C. Swain has shown that much of the conservation program of the New Deal originated in the 1920s. Howard Zinn has shown that Fiorello La Guardia, as congressman from New York in the 1920s, provided a "vital link between the Progressive and New Deal eras. La Guardia entered Congress as the Bull Moose uproar was quieting and left with the arrival of the New Deal; in the intervening years no man in national office waged the Progressive battle so long." La Guardia in the 1920s was "the herald of a new kind of progressivism, borne into American politics by the urban-immigrant sections of the population." Not only his background and his ideology, but also his specific legislative program, writes Zinn, were "an astonishingly accurate preview of the New Deal."[42]

Recognition of a surviving Progressivism in the 1920s leading into the New Deal may be an example of the "consensus and continuity" themes that John Higham and others have detected and criticized in recent historiography.[43] On the other hand, historians do continue to find "conflict" and reaction in the 1920s, as they delineate the decade's radicalism, nativism, and provincialism. Yet even here, a certain "continuity" is demonstrated by the fact that much of this behavior was hardly unique with the 1920s. Higham's comprehensive study shows that "the nativisms that came to the fore in 1920 essentially continued prewar trends. They consisted largely of hatreds . . . that had gathered strength in the late Progressive era." But the postwar depression, a fresh wave of immigration, the prohibition experiment, and its aggravation of lawlessness did give a special flavor to the wave of nativism that arose in the 1920s. In addition,

Paul Murphy has shown how the intolerance traditionally associated with the 1920s was, indeed, virulent, pervasive, and distinct in form during the decade.[44]

Finally, in diplomatic history one truth has become clearer than ever before: the "retreat to isolationism," however it be defined, is a dubious characterization of American foreign policy in the 1920s. Herbert Hoover, Charles Evans Hughes, Frank B. Kellogg, Henry L. Stimson, William E. Borah, Dwight W. Morrow, and others who formulated or criticized policy in the decade were men deeply concerned with the place of the United States in world affairs. Diplomacy in the decade may not always have served the best interests of the United States; nevertheless, policymakers and their critics often showed considerable energy and ambition in their response to the sweep of change that the Russian Revolution, the rise of anticolonialism in Latin America and the Far East, and the economic and psychological scars of World War I were generating in the world of the 1920s.

Hoover tried to develop American trade and investments abroad in a brand of neo-mercantilism designed to preserve (and profit) a democratic America and to forestall the growth of left-wing unrest in those areas reached by American goods and services. Hughes, for essentially the same reasons, worked to preserve an Open Door not only in the Far East but elsewhere as well. Stimson tried to control a revolutionary element in Nicaragua, but farther north, Morrow, recognizing the Mexican Revolution as a genuine social upheaval, tried with considerable success to come to terms with it while at the same time furthering American interests in Mexico. Kellogg, accepting the legitimacy of the Chinese Revolution, sought to work with the new revolutionary elements in that country. Borah, censurer of many official policies in the decade, called persistently for recognition of the Soviet Union.[45]

It is clear that, as Arthur S. Link has put it, "the period of the 1920s is the exciting new frontier of American historical research."[46] Some areas of the decade's history are still neglected. But others have recently been scrutinized with care, and the findings bear only partial resemblance to numerous portraits offered over the past thirty-five years.[47] The historian of the 1920s is now studying the decade from the sources, pushing aside the veil of memory and oral tradition that obscured the view for so long. The 1920s as a working concept of time and place is durably established, but the revision and amplification of the decade's history presently underway is a single accomplishment of American historiography for this generation.

NOTES

1. Henry F. May, "Shifting Perspectives on the 1920's," *Mississippi Valley Historical Review,* XLIII (Dec. 1956), 405–27, is a carefully structured survey of "the shifting and changing picture of the decade" held from the mid-1920s to to the mid-1950s. Although May analyzes the work of historians, he also appraises views of the period held by businessmen, sociologists, economists, literary critics, and other students. My own remarks concentrate more on historians, and particularly on those whose work has appeared within the past fifteen years.
2. John Spencer Bassett, *Expansion and Reform, 1889–1926* (New York, 1926), v, 293, 303–09. Two of the earliest attempts at a comprehensive view of the 1920s were James C. Malin, *The United States After the World War* (New York, 1930), and Preston William Slosson, *The Great Crusade and After, 1914–1928* (New York, 1930). Few historians of the 1920s have presented so much basic data in one volume as Malin did; nevertheless, most of his book is limited to economic history and does not include many of the subjects now standard for the period. In contrast, Slosson touched on almost all the things Malin had omitted and severely minimized those Malin had stressed. Slosson's and Malin's volumes, published at the end of the 1920s, exemplify the mass of material—often still lacking focus or patterns, but abundant in variety and potentiality, and already beginning to display certain enduring themes—that awaited the historical synthesizer. Slosson's volume contains an excellent bibliographical essay on material published during the period, 1914–1928, and pertinent to these years.
3. See a collection of observations about the end of reform in "Where Are the pre-War Radicals, A Symposium," *The Survey,* LV (Feb. 1926), 556–66.
4. *Only Yesterday: An Informal History of the Nineteen-Twenties* (New York, 1931). Allen himself chose the term "retrospective journalist." See "F. L. A. (1890–1954)," *Harper's Magazine,* CCVIII (April 1954), 74–75.
5. Some of the chapter titles are "Back to Normalcy," "The Big Red Scare," "The Revolution in Manners and Morals," "Harding and the Scandals," "Coolidge Prosperity," "The Ballyhoo Years," "The Revolt of the Highbrows," "Alcohol and Al Capone," and "The Big Bull Market." Even more evocative are subheadings in the 1931 edition, such as "The reign of intolerance," "the Sacco-Vanzetti Case," "The Younger Generation runs wild," "Freud," "The parked sedan, the confession magazines, the movies," "Valentino's funeral," and "Gang warfare in Chicago." The Frederick Lewis Allen Papers (Manuscript Division, Library of Congress) contain considerable information about *Only Yesterday,* such as publicity releases, the script of a 1931 radio broadcast entitled "Only Yesterday" that Allen made and other commentary and correspondence on the book. See especially Boxes 1 and 9.
6. *Only Yesterday,* ix.
7. Examples of the former include Mark Sullivan, *Our Times: The United States 1900–1925* (6 vols., New York, 1926–1935), Vol. VI, *The Twenties;* Samuel Hopkins Adams, *Incredible Era: The Life and Times of Warren Gamaliel Harding* (New York, 1939); and Laurence Greene, *The Era of Wonderful Nonsense*

(Indianapolis, 1939). Among more specialized studies, Malcolm Cowley's *Exile's Return: A Narrative of Ideas* (New York, 1956) and Caroline F. Ware's *Greenwich Village, 1920–1930* (Boston, 1935) were notable titles of the 1930s.

8. Significant titles include Adolph A. Berle, Jr. and Gardiner G. Means, *The Modern Corporation and Private Property* (New York, 1932; Harry W. Laidler, *Concentration of Control in American Industry* (New York, 1931); Maurice Leven, Harold G. Moulton, and Clark Warburton, *America's Capacity to Consume* (Washington, 1934); Edwin G. Nourse and others, *America's Capacity to Produce* (Washington, 1934); Harry Jerome, *Mechanization in Industry* (New York, 1934); Ralph Epstein, *Industrial Profits in the United States* (New York, 1934); David J. Saposs, "The American Labor Movement Since the War," *Quarterly Journal of Economics,* XLIX (Feb. 1935), 236–54; and Lyle W. Cooper, "The American Labor Movement in Prosperity and Depression," *American Economic Review,* XXII (Dec. 1932), 641–59.

9. The annual *Doctoral Dissertations Accepted by American Universities* lists some sixteen dissertation titles on economic themes done during the 1930s. There were some eight dissertations listed in all other areas of study. None of the figures on Ph.D. dissertations—here, and later in this essay—are necessarily comprehensive. Some titles are never published in the annual listings; some are not distinguishable by their titles as studies of the 1920s; still others encompassed the 1920s but (again, from their titles) did not seem to be directly focused on the decade. I have examined some of these studies but by no means all of them. All titles were taken from the annual *Doctoral Dissertations Accepted by American Universities* (New York, 1934–1956); and *Dissertation Abstracts: A Guide to Dissertations and Monographs Available in Microfilm* (Ann Arbor, 1952–).

10. One gauge of political histories during the 1930s was Gaston B. Means' ludicrous tale, *The Strange Death of President Harding* . . . as told to May Dixon Thacker (New York, 1930). The book revealed little, if anything, about politics in the 1920s and merely illustrated the sensationalism that has so often marked recall of politics and politicians in the decade.

11. May, "Shifting Perspectives," 412.

12. Cowley, *Exile's Return,* 309.

13. Arthur Mann, "The Progressive Tradition," John Higham, ed., *The Reconstruction of American History* (New York, 1962), 166; C. Vann Woodward, *The Burden of Southern History* (Baton Rouge, 1960), 141–43; Charles Grier Sellers, Jr., "Andrew Jackson versus the Historians," *Mississippi Valley Historical Review,* XLIV (March 1958), 615–34.

14. Selig Adler, *The Isolationist Impulse: Its Twentieth-century Reaction* (New York, 1961), 219 ff.

15. Selig Adler, "The War-Guilt Question and American Disillusionment, 1918–1928," *Journal of Modern History,* XXIII (March 1951), 1–28; Richard W. Leopold, "The Problem of American Intervention, 1917: An Historical Retrospect," *World Politics,* II (April 1950), 405–25.

16. Frank H. Simonds, *American Foreign Policy in the Post-War Years* (Baltimore, 1935), noted the considerable economic involvement in the world by the United States in the 1920s but found alongside this an American urge for peace and disarmament and traditional ideas of isolationism coming into conflict with the reality of world markets and world rivalries. Denna Frank Fleming's *The United States and World Organization, 1920–33* (New York, 1938) was a sprawling

study of world politics centered around the League of Nations and the United States that late in the 1930s pleaded for international harmony; on every page Fleming implicitly deplored American rejection of the League and American parochialism in the period of study, 1920–1933. Perhaps the clearest example of an "isolationist" approach to the 1920s was a 1935 article in which Samuel Flagg Bemis declared that America's expansion after 1898 and its entry into World War I in 1917 had been "deplorable blunders." Fortunately, beginning in the 1920s a turn "back to the policies of the Fathers" had been made. "A Clarifying Foreign Policy," *Yale Review,* XXV (Dec. 1935), 221–40. Bemis originally presented this essay as a paper before the American Historical Association at its 1935 meeting at Chattanooga, Tennessee, where it provoked vigorous discussion and dissent. See *American Historical Review,* XLI (April 1936), 443–44.

17. Charles Merz, *The Dry Decade* (Garden City, 1931), was one of the earliest attempts to study the "noble experiment" during its trial decade. Grace Adams, "The Rise and Fall of Psychology," *Atlantic Monthly,* CLIII (Jan. 1934), 82–92, bore out the author's suggestion that the decade of the Dollar "might also be appropriately recalled as the Period of the Psyche." Emerson Loucks' *The Ku Klux Klan in Pennsylvania* (Harrisburg, 1936) was not only one of the first historical studies of the Klan but remains one of the few studies yet made for a single state.
18. Stewart H. Holbrook, *Lost Men of American History* (New York, 1946), 320–48, contains a mocking essay on Harding; Peter R. Levin, *Seven by Chance: The Accidental President* (New York, 1948), 231–62, has a chapter on Coolidge, "an American primitive"; Karl Schriftgiesser, *This Was Normalcy: An Account of Party Politics During Twelve Republican Years, 1920–1932* (Boston, 1948), is a breezy tale done from a self-proclaimed bias; Henry Morton Robinson's *Fantastic Interim: A Hindsight History of American Manners, Morals, and Mistakes between Versailles and Pearl Harbor* (New York, 1943) is as wordy and free-wheeling as the title suggests.
19. Harold Barger, *Outlay and Income in the United States, 1921–1938* (New York, 1942); Harold Barger and Hans H. Landsberg, *American Agriculture, 1899–1939: A Study of Output, Employment and Productivity* (New York, 1942); Solomon Fabricant, *The Output of Manufacturing Industries, 1899–1937* (New York, 1940); Fabricant, *Employment in Manufacturing, 1899–1939: An Analysis of Its Relation to the Volume of Production* (New York, 1942); Simon Kuznets, *National Income and Its Composition, 1919–1938* (2 vols., New York, 1941); Jacob Martin Gould, *Output and Productivity in the Electric and Gas Utilities, 1899–1942* (New York, 1946); Kuznets, *National Products Since 1869* (New York, 1946).
20. George Soule, *Prosperity Decade: From War to Depression, 1917–1929* (New York, 1947. See also Keith Sward's brilliant study, *The Legend of Henry Ford* (New York, 1948); an incisive essay by Joseph Schumpeter, "The American Economy in the Interwar Period: The Decade of the Twenties," *American Economic Review: Papers and Proceedings,* XXXVI (May 1946), 1–10; and a great work, the *Yearbook of Agriculture, 1940* (Washington, 1940), that includes a brief appraisal of farm problems and farm legislation in the 1920s.
21. There were 16 titles in economic history; 15 in diplomatic history and international relations, including, for example, Dorothy Borg, "American Policy and the Chinese Revolution, 1925–1928" (doctoral dissertation, Columbia Univer-

sity, 1947), and George L. Grassmuck, "Congressional Politics in Foreign Affairs, 1921–1941" (doctoral dissertation, Johns Hopkins University, 1949). The first of these was published in New York under the same title in 1947; the second appeared as *Sectional Biases in Congress on Foreign Policy* (Baltimore, 1950).

22. There were eight titles in history or political science, among them Kenneth C. Mac Kay, "The Progressive Movement of 1924" (doctoral dissertation, Columbia University, 1945); James H. Shideler, "The Neo-Progressives: Reform Politics in the United States, 1920–1925" (doctoral dissertation, University of California, 1945); and Samuel J. Eldersveld, "A Study of Urban Electoral Trends in Michigan, 1920–1940" (doctoral dissertation, University of Michigan, 1947). Mac Kay's study was published as *The Progressive Movement in 1924* (New York, 1947). Shideler and Eldersveld published articles—see references elsewhere in this essay.

23. There were 16 titles in social and intellectual history, including John W. Higham, "European Immigration in American Patriotic Thought, 1885–1925" (doctoral dissertation, University of Wisconsin, 1949); and John M. Bradbury, "The Fugitive Critics: A Critical History" (doctoral dissertation, University of Iowa, 1949). Higham's study later appeared as *Strangers in the Land: Patterns of American Nativism, 1860–1925* (New Brunswick, 1955); Bradbury's as *The Fugitives: A Critical Account* (Chapel Hill, 1958).

24. For references to sessions and papers, see *American Historical Review,* XLIX (April 1944), 566; L (April 1945), 642; LV (April 1950), 753; *Annual Report of the American Historical Association for the Year 1944* (Washington, 1944), I, 11 ff; *Annual Report . . . 1946* (Washington, 1946), I, 10; *Mississippi Valley Historical Review,* XXX (Sept. 1943), 221–22; XXXV (Sept. 1948), 247; XXXVI (Sept. 1949), 287.

25. Randolph C. Downes, "A Crusade for Indian Reform, 1922–1934," *Mississippi Valley Historical Review,* XXXII (Dec. 1945), 331–54; Cyril Clemens and Athern P. Daggett, "Coolidge's 'I Do Not Choose to Run': Granite or Putty?" *New England Quarterly,* XVIII (June 1945), 147–63; David Fellman, "The Liberalism of Senator Norris," *American Political Science Review,* XL (Feb. 1946), 27–51; Joseph Schafer, "Thomas James Walsh: A Wisconsin Gift to Montana," *Wisconsin Magazine of History,* XXIII (June 1940), 448–73; James M. Cox, *Journey Through My Years* (New York, 1946); Cordell Hull, *The Memoirs of Cordell Hull* (2 vols., New York, 1948); George W. Norris, *Fighting Liberal . . .* (New York, 1945); Daniel C. Roper with Frank H. Lovette, *Fifty Years of Public Life* (Durham, 1941).

Diplomatic history titles include (besides the study by Dorothy Borg, cited in note 21) George T. Davis, *A Navy Second to None: The Development of Modern Naval Policy* (New York, 1940); Harold and Margaret Sprout, *Toward a New Order of Sea Power: American Naval Power and the World Scene, 1918–1922* (Princeton, 1940), in particular a chapter on the Washington Conference; Graham H. Stuart, *The Department of State: A History of Its Organization, Procedure, and Personnel* (New York, 1949), which contains chapters on the secretaries of state during the 1920s; John E. Stoner, *S. O. Levinson and the Pact of Paris: A Study in the Techniques of Influence* (Chicago, 1943); C. Leonard Hoag, *Preface to Preparedness: The Washington Disarmament Conference and Public Opinion* (Washington, 1941); and Denna Frank Fleming, *The United States and the World Court* (New York, 1945).

26. Samuel Eldersveld, "Influence of Metropolitan Party Pluralities in Presidential Elections since 1920," *American Political Science Review;* XLIII (Dec. 1949), 1189–1206; Samuel Lubell, *The Future of American Politics* (New York, 1952).

27. Frederick J. Hoffman, *Freudianism and the Literary Mind* (Baton Rouge, 1945); Hoffman, "Philistine and Puritan in the 1920's," *American Quarterly,* I (Fall 1949), 242–63; Celia Burns Stendler, "New Ideas for Old: How Freudism Was Received in the United States from 1900 to 1925," *Journal of Educational Psychology,* XXXVIII (April 1947), 193–206; R. P. Blackmur, "The American Literary Expatriate," in David F. Bowers, ed., *Foreign Influences in American Life: Essays and Critical Bibliographies* (Princeton, 1944), 126–45; Samuel Putnam, *Paris Was Our Mistress: Memoirs of a Lost & Found Generation* (New York, 1947); Robert E. Spiller and others, eds., *Literary History of the United States* (3 vols., New York, 1947–1948), 1135–56, 1222–50, 1296–1308; G. Louis Joughin and Edmund M. Morgan, *The Legacy of Sacco and Vanzetti* (New York, 1948); Dimitri S. von Mohrenschildt, "The Early American Observers of the Russian Revolution, 1917–1921," *Russian Review,* III (Autumn 1943), 64–74; Mohrenschildt, "The American Intelligentsia and Russia of the N. E. P.," *ibid.,* VI (Spring 1947), 59–66.

28. At least sixty titles on diplomatic topics of the 1920s are listed in *Doctoral Dissertations . . .* and in *Dissertation Abstracts . . .* for the years since 1950. The political history list is only slightly smaller and there are at least 100 more titles that may be classified as intellectual, social, economic, and literary history.

29. *American Historical Review,* LVI (April 1951), 716–17; LVII (April 1952), 806–07, 818; LXI (April 1956), 770, 784–85; LXII (April 1957), 766; LXIII (April 1958), 809; LXVI (April 1961), 882; LXVII (April 1962), 869–71; *Annual Report of the American Historical Association . . . 1962* (Washington, 1963), I, 18; *Mississippi Valley Historical Review,* XXXVIII (Sept. 1951), 274; XL (Sept. 1953), 313; XLI (Sept. 1954), 299–300, 305, 307–08; XLII (Sept. 1955), 305; XLIII (Sept. 1956), 288; XLIV (Sept. 1957), 329, 331; XLVI (Sept. 1959), 280; XLVIII (Sept. 1961), 274, 281–82, 286–87; L (Sept. 1963), 277.

30. Charles C. Alexander, *The Ku Klux Klan in the Southwest* (Lexington, 1965); David Chalmers, "The Ku Klux Klan in the Sunshine State: The 1920's," *Florida Historical Quarterly,* XLII (Jan. 1964), 209–15; Robert Moats Miller, "A Note on the Relationship between the Protestant Churches and the Revived Ku Klux Klan," *Journal of Southern History,* XXII (Aug. 1956), 355–68; Arnold S. Rice, *The Ku Klux Klan In American Politics* (Washington, 1962); Emma Lou Thornbrough, "Segregation in Indiana during the Klan Era of the 1920's," *Mississippi Valley Historical Review,* XLVII (March 1961), 594–618; Eckard V. Toy, Jr., "The Ku Klux Klan in Tillamook, Oregon," *Pacific Northwest Quarterly,* LIII (April 1962), 60–64.

In this and subsequent footnotes, I have made no attempt to offer a complete list of titles. Omission or inclusion of any title does not imply a judgment of quality. The purpose of citations here is to suggest the depth of the range of research now being done on the 1920s.

31. The rural-urban conflict, the social gospel, fundamentalism, and other themes of religious history in the 1920s are studied in Kenneth K. Bailey, *Southern White Protestantism in the Twentieth Century* (New York, 1964); Paul A. Carter, *The Decline and Revival of the Social Gospel: Social and Political Liberalism in American Protestant Churches, 1920–1940* (Ithaca, 1956); Norman F. Furniss,

The Fundamentalist Controversy, 1918–1931 (New Haven, 1954); Ray Ginger, *Six Days or Forever? Tennessee v. John Thomas Scopes* (Boston, 1958); Robert T. Handy, "The American Religious Depression 1925–1935," *Church History,* XXIX (March 1960), 3–16; Frederick J. Hoffman, "The Temper of the Twenties," *Minnesota Review,* I (Fall 1960), 36–45; William G. McLoughlin, *Billy Sunday Was His Real Name* (Chicago, 1955); Donald B. Meyer, *The Protestant Search for Political Realism, 1919–1941* (Berkeley, 1960); Robert Moats Miller, "The Protestant Churches and Lynching, 1919–1939," *Journal of Negro History,* XLIII (April 1957), 118–31; Miller, *American Protestantism and Social Issues, 1919–1939* (Chapel Hill, 1958).

32. Morrell Heald, "Business Thought in the Twenties: Social Responsibility," *American Quarterly,* XIII (Summer (1961), 126–39; Otis Pease, *The Responsibilities of American Advertising: Private Control and Public Influence, 1920–1940* (New Haven, 1958).

33. James W. Prothro, *Dollar Decade: Business Ideas in the 1920's* (Baton Rouge, 1954); John Philip Gleason, "The Attitude of the Business Community toward Agriculture during the McNary-Haugen Period," *Agricultural History,* XXXII (April 1958), 127–38. For studies of other business themes, see William T. Doherty, "The Impact of Business on Protestantism, 1900–29," *Business History Review,* XXVIII (June 1954), 141–53; William B. Kelly, Jr., "Antecedents of Commercial Policy, 1922–1934," Kelly, ed., *Studies in United States Commercial Policy* (Chapel Hill, 1963), 3–68; Richard S. Kirkendall, "A. A. Berle, Jr.: Student of the Corporation, 1917–1932," *Business History Review,* XXXV (Spring 1961), 43–58; and Giulio Pontecorvo, "Investment Banking and Security Speculation in the Late 1920's," *ibid.,* XXXII (Summer, 1958), 166–91.

34. Matthew Josephson, *Life Among the Surrealists . . .* (New York, 1962), 6–7.

35. Warren I. Susman, "A Second Country: The Expatriate Image," University of Texas *Studies in Literature and Language,* III (Summer 1961), 171–83. See also Susman, "Pilgrimage to Paris: The Backgrounds of American Expatriation, 1920–1934," (doctoral dissertation, University of Wisconsin, 1958); Susman, "The Useless Past: American Intellectuals and the Frontier Thesis, 1910–1930," *Bucknell Review,* XI (March 1963), 1–20; Arthur Mizener, "The 'Lost Generation'," Robert E. Spiller, ed., *A Time of Harvest: American Literature, 1910–1960* (New York, 1962), 73–82; Cushing Strout, *The American Image of the Old World* (New York, 1963); and Harold Loeb, *The way it was* (New York, 1959).

36. Louise Cowan, *The Fugitive Group: A Literary History* (Baton Rouge, 1959). See also Allen Tate, "Random Thoughts on the 1920's," *Minnesota Review,* I (Fall 1960), 46–56; Donald Davidson, *Southern Writers in the Modern World* (Athens, 1958). Frederick J. Hoffman, *The Twenties: American Writing in the Postwar Decade* (Baton Rouge, 1955), is a wide-ranging literary history that is frequently intellectual history as well. Daniel Aaron, *Writers on the Left: Episodes in American Literary Communism* (New York, 1961), is a richly detailed study of the idea of Communism among American writers from about 1912 to about 1940. See esp. 86–190 on the Twenties.

37. Wesley M. Bagby, "The 'Smoke Filled Room' and the Nomination of Warren G. Harding," *Mississippi Valley Historical Review,* XLI (March 1955), 657–74; Bagby, "Woodrow Wilson, a Third Term, and the Solemn Referendum," *American Historical Review,* LX (April 1955), 567–75; Bagby, "William Gibbs

McAdoo and the 1920 Democratic Presidential Nomination," *East Tennessee Historical Society Publications,* No. 31 (1959), 43–58; Bagby, *The Road to Normalcy* (Baltimore, 1962); and Herbert F. Margulies, "The Election of 1920 in Wisconsin: The Return to 'Normalcy' Reappraised," *Wisconsin Magazine of History,* XXXVIII (Autumn 1957), 15–22.

38. Lee N. Allen, "The Democratic Presidential Primary Election of 1924 in Texas," *Southwestern Historical Quarterly,* LXI (April 1958), 474–93; Allen, "The Underwood Presidential Movement of 1924," *Alabama Review,* XV (April 1962), 83–99; Allen, "The McAdoo Campaign for the Presidential Nomination in 1924," *Journal of Southern History,* XXIX (May 1963), 211–28; David B. Burner, "The Democratic Party in the Election of 1924," *Mid-America,* XLVI (April 1964), 92–113.

39. J. Leonard Bates, "The Teapot Dome Scandal and the Election of 1924," *American Historical Review,* LX (Jan. 1955), 303–22; Burl Noggle, "The Origins of the Teapot Dome Investigation," *Mississippi Valley Historical Review,* XLIV (Sept. 1957), 237–66; Noggle, *Teapot Dome: Oil and Politics in the 1920's* (Baton Rouge, 1962); David H. Stratton, "Behind Teapot Dome: Some Personal Insights," *Business History Review,* XXXI (Winter 1957), 385–402; Stratton, "Splattered with Oil: William G. McAdoo and the 1924 Democratic Presidential Nomination," *Southwestern Social Science Quarterly,* XLIV (June 1963), 62–75; Robert A. Waller, "Business and the Initiation of the Teapot Dome Investigation," *Business History Review,* XXXVI (Autumn 1962), 334–53.

40. Vaughn Davis Bornet, "The Communist Party in the Presidential Election of 1928," *Western Political Quarterly,* XI (Sept. 1958), 514–38; Paul A. Carter, "The Campaign of 1928 Re-Examined: A Study in Political Folklore," *Wisconsin Magazine of History,* XLVI (Summer 1963), 263–72; Carter, "The Other Catholic Candidate: The 1928 Presidential Bid of Thomas J. Walsh," *Pacific Northwest Quarterly,* LV (Jan. 1964), 1–8; Gilbert C. Fite, "The Agricultural Issue in the Presidential Campaign of 1928," *Mississippi Valley Historical Review,* XXXVII (March 1951), 653–72; Robert Moats Miller, "A Footnote to the Role of the Protestant Churches in the Election of 1928," *Church History,* XXV (June 1956), 145–59; Edmund A. Moore, *A Catholic Runs for President: The Campaign of 1928* (New York, 1956); Nevin E. Neal, "The Smith-Robinson Arkansas Campaign of 1928," *Arkansas Historical Quarterly,* XIX (Spring 1960), 3–11; Ruth C. Silva, *Rum, Religion, and Votes: 1928 Re-examined* (University Park, Pa., 1962); Richard L. Watson, Jr., "A Political Leader Bolts—F. M. Simmons in the Presidential Election of 1928," *North Carolina Historical Review,* XXXVII (Oct. 1960), 516–43.

41. Besides the titles in the above footnote, see Frank Freidel, *Franklin D. Roosevelt: The Ordeal* (Boston, 1954); Freidel, *Franklin D. Roosevelt: The Triumph* (Boston, 1956); Claude M. Fuess, "Calvin Coolidge—Twenty Years After," *Proceedings of the American Antiquarian Society,* LXIII (Oct. 1953), Pt. 2, pp. 351–69; Robert E. Hennings, "California Democratic Politics in the Period of Republican Ascendancy," *Pacific Historical Review,* XXXI (Aug. 1962), 267–80; J. Joseph Huthmacher, *Massachusetts People and Politics, 1919–1933* (Cambridge, 1959); William T. Hutchinson, *Lowden of Illinois: The Life of Frank O. Lowden* (2 vols., Chicago, 1957); Arthur M. Schlesinger, Jr., *The Crisis of the Old Order, 1919–1933* (Boston, 1957); and Richard L. Watson, Jr., "The Defeat of Judge Parker: A Study in Pressure Groups and Politics," *Mississippi Valley Historical Review,* L (Sept. 1963), 213–34.

42. Clarke A. Chambers, *Seedtime of Reform: American Social Service and Social Action, 1918–1933* (Minneapolis, 1963); Preston J. Hubbard, *Origins of the TVA: The Muscle Shoals Controversy, 1920–1932* (Nashville, 1961); Donald C. Swain, *Federal Conservation Policy, 1921–1933* (Berkeley, 1963); Howard Zinn, *La Guardia in Congress* (Ithaca, 1958). See also D. Joy Humes, *Oswald Garrison Villard, Liberal of the 1920's* (Syracuse, 1960); Arthur S. Link, "What Happened to the Progressive Movement in the 1920's " *American Historical Review*, LXIV (July 1959), 833–51; Robert L. Morlan, *Political Prairie Fire: The Nonpartisan League, 1915–1922* (Minneapolis, 1955); Anne Firor Scott, "After Suffrage: Southern Women in the Twenties," *The Journal of Southern History*, XXX (Aug. 1964), 298–318; George B. Tindall, "Business Progressivism: Southern Politics in the Twenties," *South Atlantic Quarterly*, LXII (Winter 1963), 92–106. Two studies of Progressivism's failures are James H. Shideler, "The La Follette Progressive Party Campaign of 1924," *Wisconsin Magazine of History*, XXXIII (June 1950), 444–57; and Shideler, "The Disintegration of the Progressive Party Movement of 1924," *The Historian*, XIII (Spring 1951), 189–201.
43. John Higham, "The Cult of the 'American Consensus': Homogenizing Our History," *Commentary*, XXVII (Feb. 1959), 93–100; Higham, "Beyond Consensus: The Historian as Moral Critic," *American Historical Review*, LXVII (April 1962); 609–25; J. Rogers Hollingsworth, "Consensus and Continuity in Recent American Historical Writing," *South Atlantic Quarterly*, LXI (Winter 1962), 40–50; Burl Noggle, "Variety and Ambiguity: The Recent Approach to Southern History," *Mississippi Quarterly*, XVII (Winter 1963–64), 21–35.
44. Higham, *Strangers in the Land;* Paul L. Murphy, "Sources and Nature of Intolerance in the 1920s," *Journal of American History*, LI (June 1964), 60–76. See also Paul S. Boyer, "Boston Book Censorship in the Twenties," *American Quarterly*, XV (Spring 1963), 3–24; Stanley Coben, *A. Mitchell Palmer: Politician* (New York, 1963); Coben, "A Study in Nativism: The American Red Scare of 1919–20," *Political Science Quarterly*, LXXIX (March 1964), 52–75; Theodore Draper, *The Roots of American Communism* (New York, 1957); Fdwin Layton, "The Better America Federation: A Case Study of Superpatriotism," *Pacific Historical Review*, XXX (May 1961), 137–47; Paul L. Murphy, "Normalcy, Intolerance, and the American Character," *Virginia Quarterly Review*, XL (Summer 1964), 445–59; Robert K. Murray, "Communism and the Great Steel Strike of 1919," *Mississippi Valley Historical Review*, XXXVIII (Dec. 1951), 445–66; Murray, *Red Scare: A Study in National Hysteria, 1919–1920* (Minneapolis, 1955); Kenneth B. O'Brien, Jr., "Education, Americanization and the Supreme Court: The 1920's," *American Quarterly*, XIII (Summer 1961), 161–71; William Preston, Jr., *Aliens and Dissenters: Federal Suppression of Radicals, 1903–1933* (Cambridge, Mass., 1963); and Nelson Van Valen, "The Bolsheviki and the Orange Growers," *Pacific Historical Review*, XXII (Feb. 1953), 39–50.
45. Joseph Brandes, *Herbert Hoover and Economic Diplomacy, Department of Commerce Policy, 1921–28* (Pittsburgh, 1962); Robert P. Browder, *The Origins of Soviet-American Diplomacy* (Princeton, 1953); David D. Burks, "The United States and the Geneva Protocol of 1924: 'A New Holy Alliance?' " *American Historical Review*, LXIV (July 1959), 891–905; Waldo Chamberlin, "Origins of the Kellogg-Briand Pact," *Historian*, XV (Autumn 1952), 77–92; L. Ethan Ellis, *Frank B. Kellogg and American Foreign Relations, 1925–29* (New Brunswick, 1961); Ellis, "Dwight Morrow and the Church-State Con-

troversy in Mexico," *Hispanic American Historical Review,* XXXVIII (Nov. 1958), 482–505; Herbert Feis, *The Diplomacy of the Dollar: First Era, 1919–1932* (Baltimore, 1950); Robert H. Ferrell, *Peace in Their Time: The Origins of the Kellogg-Briand Pact* (New Haven, 1952); Ferrell, "Frank B. Kellogg," Ferrell and Samuel Flagg Bemis, eds., *The American Secretaries of State and Their Diplomacy* (15 vols., New York, 1927–1965), XI, 1–135; Russell H. Fifield, "Secretary Hughes and the Shantung Question," *Pacific Historical Review,* XXIII (Nov. 1954), 373–85; Raymond G. O'Connor, "The 'Yardstick' and Naval Disarmament in the 1920's," *Mississippi Valley Historical Review,* XLV (Dec. 1958), 441–62; Stanley Robert Ross, "Dwight Morrow and the Mexican Revolution," *Hispanic American Historical Review,* XXXVIII (Nov. 1958), 506–28; J. Chal. Vinson, "The Annulment of the Lansing-Ishii Agreement," *Pacific Historical Review,* XXVII (Feb. 1958), 57–69; John Chalmers Vinson, *William E. Borah and the Outlawry of War* (Athens, 1957); Vinson, *The Parchment Peace: The United States Senate and the Washington Conference, 1921–1922* (Athens, 1955); Gerald E. Wheeler, "Republican Philippine Policy, 1921–1933," *Pacific Historical Review,* XXVIII (Nov. 1959), 377–90; Wheeler, *Prelude to Pearl Harbor: The United States Navy and the Far East, 1921–1931* (Columbia, Mo., 1963); Wheeler, "The United States Navy and the Japanese 'Enemy': 1919–1931," *Military Affairs,* XXI (Summer 1957), 61–74; William Appleman Williams, "China and Japan: A Challenge and a Choice of the Nineteen Twenties," *Pacific Historical Review,* XXVI (Aug. 1957), 259–80; Williams, "Latin America: Laboratory of Latin American Foreign Policy in the Nineteen-twenties," *Inter-American Economic Affairs,* XI (Autumn 1957), 3–31; Williams, "The Legend of Isolationism in the 1920's," *Science and Society,* XVIII (Winter 1954), 1–20.

46. Link, "What Happened to the Progressive Movement in the 1920's?" 834.

47. William E. Leuchtenburg's *The Perils of Prosperity, 1914–32* (Chicago, 1958) is a lucid history that incorporates many of the recent findings and interpretations by historians of the Twenties. John D. Hicks, *Republican Ascendancy, 1921–1933* (New York, 1960), is the work of a distinguished scholar who presents a more traditional view of the decade. For additional bibliography or for comment on the historiography of the Twenties, see Dewey W. Grantham, Jr., "Recent American History and the Great Depression," *Texas Quarterly,* VI (Winter 1963), 12–28; John D. Hicks, "Research Opportunities in the 1920's," *Historian,* XXV (Nov. 1962), 1–13; Richard Lowitt, "The Prosperity Decade, 1917–1928," William H. Cartwright and Richard L. Watson, Jr., eds., *Interpreting and Teaching American History* (Washington, 1961), 231–63; Herbert F. Margulies, "Recent Opinion on the Decline of the Progressive Movement," *Mid-America,* XLV (Oct. 1963), 250–68.

Suggestions for Further Reading

This bibliography is a highly selective one designed only as a guide to the more important works on the 1920's. Generally speaking, the following types of sources are not included: primary sources (for example, contemporary journals, newspapers, governmental reports, reminiscences), very specialized studies (for example, those dealing with a highly technical aspect of farm policy), textbooks, biographies (except those of the Presidents), monographs dealing only in part with the 1920's, and most secondary periodical articles. Omitted also are many of the books and articles from which the readings in the present volume are taken.

There are several works which deal with the entire period of the 1920's. Frederick L. Allen's *Only Yesterday, An Informal History of the Nineteen Twenties* (1931) is a lively, sound, and thoroughly enjoyable social history by a "retrospective journalist." Its entertaining tone unfortunately has tended to arouse some criticism of this pioneering work. John D. Hicks' *Republican Ascendancy, 1921–1933* (1960) is reliable, solid, and covers the ground adequately. Very perceptive and written in a sprightly style is William E. Leuchtenburg's *The Perils of Prosperity, 1914–1932* (1958). H. U. Faulkner's *From Versailles to the New Deal* (1950) is brief but enlightening. Arthur M. Schlesinger's first volume in his *Age of Roosevelt, The Crisis of the Old Order, 1919–1933* (1957) is excellent, but overly political in its emphasis, and unabashedly partisan. Preston W. Slosson, *The Great Crusade and After, 1914–1928* (1930), is valuable for its full bibliography. A recent treatment of mixed value is Elizabeth Stevenson, *Babbitts and Bohemians: The American 1920's* (1967). Richard W. Lowitt's chapter ("The Prosperity Decade, 1917–1928") in William H. Cartwright and Richard L. Watson, Jr., Eds., *Interpreting and Teaching American History* (1961) should be consulted for its historiographical contributions. See also Frederick J. Hoffman, "The Temper of the Twenties," *Minnesota Review,* I (Fall, 1960), 36–45. *American Heritage* (August, 1965) is devoted entirely to the '20's.

In the area of biography the following should be consulted: Samuel H. Adams, *Incredible Era: The Life and Times of Warren Gamaliel Harding* (1939), a scathing and sensationalist but extremely colorful treatment; Andrew Sinclair, *The Available Man: The Life Behind the Masks of Warren Gamaliel Harding* (1965), a readable, provocative, partial rehabilitation of Harding; Claude M. Fuess' *Calvin Coolidge; The Man from Vermont* (1940) is a favorable, even defensive treatment (See also his "Calvin Coolidge—Twenty Years After," *Proceedings of the American Antiquarian Society,* LXIII, Pt. 2 [1954], 351–369); William A. White, *A Puritan in Babylon: The Story of Calvin Coolidge* (1938) is admittedly a fine political biography of Coolidge, but it portrays him as misunderstanding the times; on Coolidge, consult, too, Edward C. Latham, *Meet Calvin Coolidge* (1960); Howard H. Quint and Robert H. Ferrell, Eds. *The Talkative President; The Off-the-Record Press Conferences of Calvin Coolidge* (1964); and Donald R. McCoy, *Calvin Coolidge: The Quiet President* (1967). Each of these works portrays Coolidge in a sympathetic vein. On the election of 1928, see the older work, H. F. Pringle, *Alfred E. Smith* (1927) and Oscar Handlin, *Al Smith and His America* (1958), a short but adequate treatment. Edmund A. Moore, *A Catholic Runs for President: The Campaign of 1928* (1956) is a full treatment which places the religious issue in a proper perspective, and Gilbert C. Fite, "The Agricultural Issue in the Presidential Campaign of 1928," *Mississippi Valley Historical Review* (hereafter *MVHR,*) XXXVII (March, 1951), 653–672, is also valuable.

The following works, dealing essentially with political events or issues, impart the flavor of the 1920's. Karl Schriftgeisser's *This Was 'Normalcy': An Account of Party Politics During Twelve Republican Years, 1920–1932* (1948) is a breezy pro-Democratic treatment. Wesley M. Bagby's "The 'Smoke Filled Room' and the Nomination of Warren G. Harding," *MVHR,* XLI (March, 1955), 657–674, and his full-length study, *The Road to Normalcy* (1962), are able treatments of the Election of 1920. Quite perceptive is Herbert F. Margulies, "The Election of 1920 in Wisconsin: The Return to Normalcy Reappraised," *Wisconsin Magazine of History,* XXXVIII (Autumn, 1957), 15–22. On Teapot Dome, see J. Leonard Bates, "The Teapot Dome Scandal and the Election of 1924," *American Historical Review* (Hereafter *AHR*), LX (January,

1955), 303–322 (a study which shows the bi-partisan effects of the oil scandal) and Burl Noggle, *Teapot Dome, Oil and Politics in the 1920's* (1962). The Progressive Movement in the 1920's is explored in Arthur S. Link, "What happened to the Progressive Movement in the 1920's?" *AHR,* LXIV (July, 1959), 833–851, an often cited revisionist defense of Progressivism's continuity; James H. Shideler, "The Disintegration of the Progressive Party Movement of 1924," *The Historian,* XIII (Spring, 1951), 189–201, and Kenneth C. MacKay, *The Progressive Movement of 1924* (1947), the standard viewpoint.

In the field of diplomatic history, see two articles by Selig Adler, "The War-Guilt Question and American Disillusionment," *Journal of Modern History,* XIII, (March, 1951), 1–28 and "Isolationism Since 1914," *American Scholar,* XXI (Summer, 1952), 335–344. Frank H. Simonds, a foe of collective security, makes some shrewd statements on America's world-wide economic involvement in *American Foreign Policy in the Post-War Years* (1935). Herbert Feis, *The Diplomacy of the Dollar: First Era, 1919–1932* (1950), is an excellent and penetrating study of our international financial problems. On the Washington Disarmament Conference, see John C. Vinson, *The Parchment Peace: The United States Senate and the Washington Conference, 1921–1922* (1955), a critical and full treatment, and C. Leonard Hoag, *Preface to Preparedness: The Washington Disarmament Conference and Public Opinion* (1941). See also Raymond G. O'Connor, "The Yardstick and Naval Disarmament in the 1920's," *MVHR,* XLV (December, 1958), 441–462, and Gerald E. Wheeler, *Prelude to Pearl Harbor: The United States Navy and the Far East, 1921–1931* (1963). Denna F. Fleming's works, *The United States and the League of Nations, 1918–1920* (1932) and *The United States and World Organization, 1920–1933* (1938) are fine studies written from a pro-League slant. On Secretary of State Hughes, see Merlo J. Pusey, *Charles Evans Hughes,* 2 Vols. (2nd ed., 1963), detailed, but not too critical, and Dexter Perkins, *Charles Evans Hughes and American Democratic Statesmanship* (1956), an interpretative, penetrating analysis. Two standard works on Secretary of State Frank B. Kellogg are L. Ethan Ellis, *Frank B. Kellogg and American Foreign Relations, 1925–1929* (1961), a valuable contribution, and Robert H. Ferrell's excellent and meticulous study of the Pact of Paris, *Peace in Their Time: The Origins of the Kellogg-Briand Pact* (1952). Brief but valuable is Allan Nevins, *The United States in a Chaotic World: A Chronicle of International Affairs, 1918–1933* (1950).

In economic affairs, a period such as the 1920's is especially rich in monographic material. Among the more helpful sources are George Soule, *Prosperity Decade: From War to Depression, 1917–1929* (1947), probably the best economic history of the period; Irving Bernstein, *The Lean Years: A History of the American Worker, 1920–1933* (1960); James W. Prothro, *Dollar Decade: Business Ideas in the 1920's* (1954); Gilbert C. Fite, *George N. Peek and the Fight for Farm Parity* (1954); and Otis Pease, *The Responsibilities of American Advertising: Private Control and Public Influence, 1920–1940* (1958). On farm problems, see James H. Shideler, *Farm Crisis 1919–1923* (1957). Consult, too, Preston J. Hubbard's excellent *Origins of the TVA, The Muscle Shoals Controversy, 1920–1932* (1961); Donald C. Swain, *Federal Conservation Policy, 1921–1933* (1963); Clarke A. Chambers, *Seedtime of Reform: American Social Service and Social Action, 1918–1933* (1963). Allan Nevins and Frank E. Hill, *Ford,* Vol. II (*Expansion and Challenge: 1915–1932*) (1957) is a treatment of the decade's leading entrepreneur. See also Keith Sward, *The Legend of Henry Ford* (1948). John K. Galbraith's *The Great Crash, 1929* (1955) proves that economics and economic history do not have to be dry. Several articles are also helpful: G. Cullom Davis, "The Transformation of the Federal Trade Commission, 1914–1929," *MVHR,* XLIX (December, 1962), 437–455; Joseph Schumpeter, "The American Economy in the Interwar Period: The Decade of the Twenties," *American Economic Review,* XXXVI (May, 1946), 1–10; John P. Gleason, "The Attitude of the Business Community toward Agriculture during the McNary-Haugen Period," *Agricultural History,* XXXII (April, 1958), 127–138.

On the social-cultural scene, a number of fascinating works make for excellent reading on the lighter side: Laurence Greene, *The Era of Wonderful Nonsense* (1939); Lewis Jacobs, *The Rise of the American Film* (1939); Arthur Mayer, *Merely Colossal* (on the movies) (1953); Charles Merz, *The Great American Band Wagon* (1928); Lloyd R. Morris, *Postscript to Yesterday* (1947); Morris, *Not so Long Ago* (on the automobile, movies, radio) (1949); Joe Alex Morris, *What A Year!* (on 1929) (1956); Henry M. Robinson, *Fantastic Interim* (1943); Paul Sann, *The Lawless Decade* (1957), a pictorial; and Paul Schubert, *The Electric Word; The Rise of the Radio* (1928). Robert S. and Helen M. Lynd, *Middletown* (1929) is a classic analysis of the social mores of the period. See also Allen's *Only Yesterday* and Mark Sullivan's sixth volume in his *Our Times, 1900–1925* (6 vols., 1926–1935) collection, "The Twenties."

Leading biographies of two of the age's arbiters are Charles Angoff,

H. L. Mencken (1956) and Arthur Mizener, *The Far Side of Paradise* (Fitzgerald) (1959). The "Lost Generation" is treated in Malcolm Cowley, *Exile's Return: A Literary Odyssey of the 1920's* (1934). Cowley feels that the post-war literary rebellion was a culmination of passions that were long in brewing. See also Warren I. Susman, "A Second Country: The Expatriate Image," University of Texas *Studies in Literature and Language,* III (Summer, 1961), 171–183. In the realm of literary criticism, the following should be consulted: John W. Aldridge, *After the Lost Generation* (1951), perceives the post-war years as a sharp but not laudatory break with past literary traditions. Bernard De Voto argued that the literary way of thinking about American civilization in the 1920's was bankrupt and labeled the literature as "trivial" (*The Literary Fallacy* [1944]). Van Wyck Brooks, *On Literature Today* (1941), found the literature of the 1920's aberrant and adolescent. More positive views of the literary 1920's are taken by Howard M. Jones, *The Bright Medusa* (1959), Cowley (already cited above), and Frederick J. Hoffman, *The Twenties: American Writing in the Post War Decade* (1955). See also Frederick H. Hoffman, *Freudianism and the Literary Mind* (1945) and George H. Knowles, *The Jazz Age Revisited, British Criticism of American Civilization during the 1920's* (1955).

On the Ku Klux Klan, see Charles C. Alexander, *The Ku Klux Klan in the Southwest* (1965); Arnold S. Rice, *The Ku Klux Klan in American Politics* (1962); David M. Chalmers, *Hooded Americanism: The First Century of the Ku Klux Klan* (1965); and Kenneth T. Jackson, *The Ku Klux Klan in the City, 1915–1930* (1967). Prohibition is ably treated in Herbert Asbury, *The Great Illusion, an Informal History of Prohibition* (1950); Charles Merz's standard treatment, *The Dry Decade* (1931); and Andrew Sinclair, *Prohibition, the Era of Excess* (1962). For Radicalism and the reaction to it, consult: John Blum, "Nativism, Anti-Radicalism, and the Foreign Scare, 1917–1920," *Midwest Journal,* III (Winter, 1950–51), 46–53; G. Louis Joughin and E. M. Morgan, *The Legacy of Sacco and Vanzetti* (1948); James Grossman, "The Sacco-Vanzetti Case Reconsidered," *Commentary,* XXXIII (January, 1962), 31–44; Paul S. Boyer, "Boston Book Censorship in the Twenties," *American Quarterly,* XV (Spring, 1963), 3–24; Paul L. Murphy, "Normalcy, Intolerance, and the American Character," *Virginia Quarterly Review,* XL (Summer, 1964), 445–459; and Stanley Coben, "A Study in Nativism: The American Red Scare of 1919–20," *Political Science Quarterly,* LXXIX (March, 1964), 52–75. Fundamentalist battles are described in Ray Ginger, *Six Days or Forever? Tennessee v. John Thomas Scopes* (1958) and Robert M. Miller, *American Protestantism and Social Issues, 1919–1939* (1958). Unfortunately, there is no adequate historical study of the so-called "revolution" among youth. The Lynds' *Middletown* and Allen's *Only Yesterday* volumes are helpful as are a number of sociological sources.

Several selections afford not only an excellent summary of the twenties but also provide incisive suggestions for future research and discussions of scholarly interpretations: Henry R. May, "Shifting Perspectives on the 1920's," *MVHR,* XLIII (December, 1956), 405–427; John D. Hicks, "Research Opportunities in the 1920's," *Historian,* XXV (November, 1962), 1–13, and Don S. Kirschner, "Conflicts and Politics in the 1920's; Historiography and Prospects," *Mid-America,* XLVIII (October, 1966), 219–233.